THE DIALOGUES OF PLATO

VOLUME 1

PLATO

EUTHYPHRO · APOLOGY · CRITO · MENO · GORGIAS · MENEXENUS

Translated with Comment by
R. E. ALLEN

Yale University Press
New Haven and London

Published with assistance from the foundation
established in memory of Henry Weldon Barnes
of the Class of 1882, Yale College

Designed by Sally Harris
and set in Baskerville type by
Brevis Press, Bethany, Connecticut.
Printed in the United States of America

Plato.
The dialogues of Plato.
Includes index.
Contents: v. 1. Euthyphro; Apology; Crito; Meno;
Gorgias; Menexenus—
1. Philosophy—Collected works. I. Allen, Reginald
E., 1931– . II. Title.
B358.A44   1984   184   84-17349
ISBN 0-300-03226-9 (v. 1: cloth)
ISBN-13 978-0-300-04488-1 (pbk.)

The paper in this book meets the guidelines for
permanence and durability of the Committee on
Production Guidelines for Book Longevity
of the Council on Library Resources.

To
Harold Frederick Cherniss
Platonist

CONTENTS

vii

PREFACE

This volume is the initial volume in a translation, with analysis, of all of Plato's works, the first by a single hand since Jowett's in the nineteenth century. The aim is to make Plato accessible in clear modern English to those who cannot read Greek, and also to provide comment in some sense Socratic, in that its primary purpose is not to set forth doctrine, but to help clear away obstacles which interfere with understanding the text.

Translation is a minor art but nonetheless an art, and like other arts it requires the persuasion by reason of necessity, the tactful adjustment of competing demands which cannot each fully be satisfied. Put another way, all translation, at least in philosophy and literature, involves compromise. This is true even between such modern languages as French and English. It is much truer between modern English and ancient Greek. We translate *chemin de fer* as railroad, and are fairly clear about what we mean. We are less clear when we translate *kratēr* as bowl, for our bowls are neither red- nor black-figured; and though the meaning of *bema* is clear—a raised place where a man may speak to a multitude— no English word, not stage or platform, pulpit, dock, or dais, will translate it. If problems arise even in translating words for familiar daily objects, they grow more serious when dealing with religious and moral terms, vocabulary which touches issues of central concern in Plato's dialogues.

It is sometimes said that a translation ideally should produce the same effect on its readers that the original was meant to produce on the audience for which it was intended. Such a translation would be completely faithful. But in translating Plato, fidelity is one ideal which is sometimes the better for being unrealized. Of course speeches should sound like the kind of speeches they are, conversations like conversations, and poetry like poetry. But claims of fidelity presuppose that the underlying Greek text is fully understood, that is, interpreted, and that translation can be done in terms of this interpretation. Interpretive translations, like newspaper editorials, have their value; but they decide in advance issues on which students may reasonably differ, and on which the English reader may be invited to make up his or her own mind. Some degree of interpretation, no doubt, is unavoidable, and a wholly neutral translation which preserved every ambiguity and all the overtones of connotation would require constant reference to the Greek in order to make sense of the English. Yet neutrality, no less than fidelity, remains an important value in translation. Let no man tell you what is in the text of Plato if you have means of finding out for yourself.

If fidelity and neutrality are values which do not always lie easily together, then literalness—congruence between Greek sentences and English—introduces further complexity. Literalness is not the simple substitution of English vocabulary into Greek syntax which produces the various dialects of Translatorese. It marks a translation which lets the original text show through clearly enough so that a fair estimate of the syntax and vocabulary of the underlying Greek language can be formed. Literalness, it may be observed, cannot be obtained by mechanical substitution: *chemin de fer* does not mean road of iron, but railroad, and *didonai diken* does not mean to give justice, but to be punished. Nor is literalness obtained by translating a Greek word by the same English word on every occasion; this is merely a variant of simple substitution, and it tends to produce English which is as unintelligible as it is execrable, and which is false to the meaning of the text. But the claim that a translation is false to the meaning of the text implies a claim about what the text means. So literalness requires interpretation after all. We are thus led from faithfulness toward neutrality, from neutrality toward literalness, and from literalness back toward faithfulness. Accuracy of translation involves all three elements, which sometimes strain against each other and cause forced choices.

The translation of great literature should itself be literature, or at least literate; so far as possible it should preserve the distinction and nuance of style, the rhythms and music, the dramatic elegance of the original. Plato, as a writer, stands with Shakespeare, but his translators do not, so this task is all but impossible. On the other hand, an attempt must be made. Gilbert Murray, reflecting on translation, remarked that "Hamlet, I am thy father's spirit" comes out in Afrikaans as "Omlet, eek bin dein papa's Spook." There are translations of Plato which sound a bit like this. Great prose is an art form, and Plato is the greatest and most varied of all prose writers; to translate him is necessarily to attempt some level of literary distinction, with stylistic variations which cannot match but may at least suggest something of the richness of his language.

The spirit of the translation is at least as important as the music. Paul Shorey, one of the most distinguished Platonists of this century, translated Polus's objection to Socrates (*Gorgias* 461c) thus: "No one but a hayseed and a fundamentalist would be so tactless as to drag his moral sentiments into the conversation in this way." And in a well-known passage of the *Republic* comparing the Good to the Sun and intelligence to vision, Shorey tried to catch a bit of wordplay by having Socrates contrast the eyeball with the skyball. The reader may perhaps be content with a rendering somewhat more subdued. In matters of translation and interpretation, the spirit killeth and the letter giveth life.

I have attempted to mitigate the stylistic strain which the letter sometimes imposes by paying close attention to sentence rhythm, one of the glories of the English tongue. Much can be said clearly and intelligibly, and yet quite literally, if, as the French say, it marches. But literalness itself is sacrificed if the reader is left with the sense that he is wading a vast and muddy field in heavy boots. Put otherwise, the spirit of the thing is sometimes best captured in music.

The comment offered here is not meant to be summary. Paul Shorey's *What Plato Said* and A. E. Taylor's *Plato: The Man and His Work* have already fulfilled this function admirably. In addition, W. K. C. Guthrie's discussion of Socrates and Plato in *A History of Greek Philosophy* provides valuable comment on individual dialogues and a barometer by which the current climate of opinion in Platonic studies can be gauged. I have been primarily concerned with removing obscurities in order that the reader can come to see things for himself; but the reader must understand that I have tried to see with my own eyes, too, so that this modest Socratic aim is not uncontroversial.

The text translated is the Oxford Classical Text, edited by John Burnet. I have occasionally departed from it, but have not thought it necessary to indicate variants except where they lead to important differences in translation. I am much indebted to Burnet's edition of the *Euthyphro, Apology,* and *Crito* and to R. S. Bluck on the *Meno* and E. R. Dodds on the *Gorgias*. My relatively frequent disagreements with Dodds will not, I hope, obscure how deep my debt to him on the *Gorgias* actually is.

If the dialogues collected in this book have a common theme, it is that what men believe ultimately determines not only what they do but what they are. Power does not come from the point of a sword or the barrel of a gun, but from what men understand about those things which are most specifically human. In order to obtain understanding, men must begin by searching themselves, begin by beginning from within. In the last decades of the twentieth century, standing in the shadows of irrationalism, it is useful to return to sources, as a means of letting in the light.

INTRODUCTION

Plato's Life

The sources for our knowledge of Plato's life are exiguous. The *Seventh Letter,* an open letter dealing with the tangled affairs of Sicily and Plato's role in them, sheds considerable light; whether it is Plato's own work, it is a contemporary or near-contemporary document which is probably trustworthy in the main outline of its account.[1] There are late biographies of relatively minor worth by Apuleius in the mid-second century A.D., Diogenes Laertius in the late second or early third century, and Olympiodorus in the sixth. Of these, that of Diogenes Laertius, though uneven in quality, is by far the most helpful. Further testimony dealing with Plato and his relation to the affairs of Syracuse can be found in Diodorus Siculus (first century B.C.) and in Plutarch's life of Dion (first century A.D.). These sources are Hellenistic, and they must be used with caution.[2] Biographical material by Speusippus, Plato's nephew, and Hermodorus, a contemporary member of the Academy, has been lost. This is the more unfortunate because the testimony which has survived is

1. See John Burnet, *Greek Philosophy: Thales to Plato,* London, 1950, pp. 205–06. Gilbert Ryle (*Plato's Progress,* Cambridge, 1966, pp. 55–57) argued, roughly on grounds of meteorology, that the *Seventh Letter* cannot be trusted because its chronology of Plato's second trip to Syracuse is mistaken. Ryle based his case on evidence drawn from Diodorus Siculus, and his use of that evidence is inconsistent. Also, his claim that *Seventh Letter* 347c and *Laws* 952e show that there was no winter sailing between Athens and Syracuse is not supported by the passages he cites.

2. For a collection of ancient sources for Plato's life, see *Rheinishes Museum für Philologie* XLIX, pp. 72 *ff.* For a general survey, with editions, see Paul Shorey, *What Plato Said,* Chicago, 1933, p. 447.

immensely fuller on the Syracusan affair than on any other event in Plato's life, and this imbalance inevitably affects interpretation. Sicily was undoubtedly important to Plato, and its story should not be neglected. But philosophy was a good deal more important to him, as was the work of the Academy.

Plato was probably born in Athens in the spring of 428 B.C., on the seventh day of Thargelion, roughly corresponding to the month of May.[3] His family was distinguished. His father, Ariston, traced his lineage to Codrus, who was, according to legend, the last of the kings of Athens. His mother, Perictione, belonged to the family of Solon, the great Athenian law-giver and reformer of the early sixth century. Little is known of Plato's elder brothers, Glaucon and Adeimantus, beyond his portrait of them in the *Republic*. He also had a sister, Potone, whose son Speusippus succeeded Plato in the leadership of the Academy. There was also a half-brother, Antiphon, his mother's son by her marriage to Pyrilampes, after Ariston's death.

Plato was born in the third year of the Peloponnesian War, and his childhood, youth, and early manhood were spent in the shadow of that war. Its prolonged effects on the social and political climate of Athens helped shape his own philosophy of government and, after Socrates' death, the aim and direction of his life. It is no accident that the central theme of Plato's political thought is unity, the wise and harmonious combination of various interests in the state so that the state will no longer be divided against itself. Nor is it an accident that Plato, as the follower of Socrates, was moved to found the Academy, a school whose aims included both scientific inquiry and the practical training of statesmen.

The lessons of the war were reinforced by its aftermath. The war ended in 404 B.C., after the battle of Aegospotami between Athens and Sparta in the summer of 405. Athens was defeated and drained, her power broken forever. An oligarchical revolution followed against the radical democratic leaders whose folly had helped precipitate the defeat. Plato's uncle, Charmides, and his mother's cousin, Critias, took part, becoming members of the Thirty Tyrants who usurped power. The extraordinary excesses of the Thirty provoked a reaction in turn, and in 403 democracy was restored. Though the new democratic government avoided anything resembling a proscription, it put Socrates to death in

---

3. For a fuller discussion of Plato's life, see: R. S. Bluck, *Plato's Life and Thought*, London, 1949, chaps. 1–4; John Burnet, *Greek Philosophy: Thales to Plato*, chap. 12; G. C. Field, *Plato and His Contemporaries*, London, 1948, chaps. 1–3; Shorey, *What Plato Said*, chap. 1; F. M. Cornford's discussion of the relation of Plato's political views to the events of his own earlier life (*Plato's Republic*, Oxford, 1950, pp. xv–xxix), though brief, is indispensable.

399, ostensibly for corrupting the youth and introducing strange gods, but actually because he had turned his habitual questioning on democratic pieties. In the uneasy political climate that prevailed, his questioning had not been welcomed, but feared.

We do not know when Plato first met Socrates. The dialogues are silent on the point, and later testimony is untrustworthy. Presumably it happened during Plato's childhood, because many members of his family—his brothers Glaucon and Adeimantus, as well as Charmides and Critias—were loosely connected with the Socratic circle. Plato must have been a member of that circle from early manhood. He offered surety for Socrates at his trial,[4] and he found it wise to withdraw for a time to Megara after Socrates' death due to the strength of feeling in Athens against Socrates' friends.[5] There are stories, not unreasonable, although late, that he also visited Egypt at this time.[6]

The *Seventh Letter* suggests that it was Socrates' death, rather than his life, which turned Plato against a practical career in politics, leading him rather to literature and education (the alternative to politics was the pen). The early dialogues, such as the *Apology,* the *Euthyphro,* the *Charmides,* and the *Laches,* presumably were written in the decade between the death of Socrates in 399 and Plato's first visit to Italy and Sicily in 388–87. In part, their purpose was apologetic—to portray Socrates as he had been and to defend his memory against his detractors.[7] But their main purpose was to carry on the Socratic mission to Athens, and more generally to Greece. Socrates had begun a moral revolution, had placed before men the ideal of moral knowledge founded on the nature of things as a guide to conduct. Plato determined to continue that revolution, and to apply it, as Socrates had not, to politics, and to provide a foundation for it in metaphysics.

Plato first visited Italy and Syracuse at the age of forty. His purpose in visiting Italy was almost certainly intellectual: the Greek city of Tarentum in Magna Graecia was a chief center of Pythagoreanism, and Plato was received by Archytas of Tarentum, a statesman who was also one of the foremost mathematicians and philosophers of his day. The result was an enduring friendship. Plato's reasons for visiting Sicily, and specifically Syracuse, are less clear. Diogenes Laertius suggests that he went as a

---

4. *Apology* 34a. See *Phaedo* 59b, where his absence at the death scene is explained by illness.

5. Diogenes Laertius III.6, following Hermodorus.

6. Diogenes Laertius III.6, cf. Strabo XVII.i.29.

7. Who continued their work after Socrates' death. The sophist Polycrates wrote as a set speech an accusation of Socrates before 390 B.C. See Isocrates, *Busiris* (xi.4).

tourist, to see the island and the craters of Aetna (III.18). Plutarch makes
him explain that he went to look for a virtuous man (*Dion* V.2)—a fore-
runner of the Cynic Diogenes and his lantern. Diodorus Siculus (XV.7)
probably preserves the real reason: Plato went because he was invited by
Dionysius I, the cruel, able, and unscrupulous despot of Syracuse, who
had a weakness for poetry (especially, it seems, his own) and enjoyed
entertaining the leading literary figures of his day (see Diod. Sic. XV.6).
Plato's reaction to Syracuse was approximately what it might have been
to Sodom and Gomorrah. Diogenes Laertius (III.19), Plutarch (*Dion* V.2–
3), and Diodorus Siculus (XV.6) all record, with variations, that
Dionysius I was so offended by Plato's frank opinions on the general
subject of virtues and vices that he attempted to sell him into slavery;
but this spectacular story may, after all, rest on little more than late
conjecture.

In any case, Plato returned from Syracuse to Athens, and there, perhaps in 385 B.C., he founded the Academy—the first university of Europe—in a park sacred to the hero Hecademus on the outskirts of
Athens. The Academy appears to have remained in continual existence
for nearly a thousand years, until it was closed by Justinian in 529 A.D.
Plato's aim of providing training for political service succeeded admirably; young men came from all over Greece to be his pupils and returned to take active roles in the life of their cities. The Academy became
a main source of authority in Greece on questions of jurisprudence, on
the giving of laws and the founding of constitutions.[8] The primary concern of the Academy, however, was not just education, but also research,
especially in mathematics and astronomy. One member, Theaetetus, advanced the study of incommensurability and performed the construction
of the five regular solids and their inscription in the sphere, laying the
foundations of solid geometry. Eudoxus of Cnidos, who moved his own
school of mathematics from Cyzicus to Athens to join the Academy perhaps around 368 B.C., formulated the generalized theory of proportion
found in Euclid V that is applicable to both commensurable and incommensurable magnitudes; developed the Method of Exhaustion, which
anticipates the calculus; and formulated—in response to a challenge by
Plato according to tradition—the famous astronomical hypothesis bearing his name which explains irregular motions of the heavens by a geo-
centric universe framed with twenty-seven concentric spheres.[9]

8. John Burnet suggested (*Platonism*, Berkeley, 1928, pp. 87–89) that Academic jurisprudence directly affected the development not only of Hellenistic but of Roman law.

9. See C. B. Boyer, *The Concepts of the Calculus*, New York, 1949, pp. 33–37; T. L. Heath,
Aristarchus of Samos, Oxford, 1913, pp. 195–96. The definitive treatment is now
O. Neugebauer, *A History of Ancient Mathematical Astronomy*, vol. I, New York, 1975.

The Academy, then, combined the functions of teaching and research. The teaching contained, if Plato's educational recommendations in *Republic* VII are an index to the curriculum of his school, a heavy emphasis on mathematics and on the developed form of philosophical inquiry which he came to call Dialectic. Isocrates, the scholarch of a rival school in Athens founded perhaps in 392 B.C. and devoted to the teaching of rhetoric, criticized dialectical education in the *Antidosis* (261–71); and Epicrates, a comic poet, satirized the associated methods of Collection and Division by having students in the Academy solemnly attempt by those means to define the essence of Pumpkinhood (Fr.11, Edmonds).

In the years following his return from Sicily, Plato probably wrote the *Meno, Gorgias, Phaedo, Symposium, Republic, Phaedrus, Parmenides,* and *Theaetetus.* The *Cratylus,* whether early or late, belongs somewhere in this group. In 368–67, twenty years after his first visit, Plato returned to Syracuse.

He went this time with a political motive. Dionysius I had died, leaving the government of Syracuse in the hands of his son, Dionysius II; but effective power was wielded by Dion, a close friend of Plato and perhaps for a time a member of the Academy. Dion had asked Plato to instruct the younger Dionysius in philosophy. It is easy to conjecture that Plato went, not believing but hoping that he might rear, in the lush and exuberant soil of a Sicilian court, a philosopher-king. He could not have been blind to the difficulties which stood in the way.

Plato was received with acclamation. For a short time, Dionysius went to school to him and gave his court an unwonted occupation: "There was something like a general rush for letters and philosophy, and the palace was filled with dust, as they say, owing to the multitude of geometricians there."[10] But the dust soon settled. Dionysius sent Dion into exile a few months after Plato arrived, accusing him of conspiring against the throne. Plato's support of Dion, far from helping, had made Dionysius jealous of their friendship. Plato himself was interned—in comfort, but against his will—for some months afterward. He was at length allowed to return to Athens, after promising Dionysius he would return if Dion was restored.

He did return, in the spring of 361. Dion had not been restored but had urged the visit in order to help heal the breach. Plato took some small measure of hope from the report that Dionysius was again pursuing his studies in mathematics and philosophy.

10. Plutarch, *Dion* XIII.5., trans. Perrin.

It is unnecessary to follow the story in more detail. Arete, Dion's wife
and Dionysius' sister, was compelled to divorce Dion and marry another
man. "From this time on Dion turned his thoughts to war."[11] He invaded
Sicily in 357 with a crew of mercenaries and the support of many friends
in the Academy. He won Syracuse, expelled Dionysius, attempted to im-
pose unpopular reforms, high-handedly executed a popular leader who
opposed him, and was compelled to maintain his continued presence by
force of arms. He was murdered in 353 and two of the men in the
conspiracy were certainly Athenians, and may well have been fellow-
members of the Academy. The attempt to found a philosophical kingdom
in Sicily was finished.

Plato lived some six years after this, perhaps with the taste of dust and
ashes in his mouth. He died in 348 as he had lived, writing to the last.

There is an epitaph for Plato, attributed to Speusippus, in the *Greek
Anthology*. It is the epitaph not of those clouded last years, but of the life
itself:

> Here Earth in her womb holds the body of Plato.
> His soul holds a place, blessed, with the immortal gods.

Plato's Writings

The *Euthyphro, Apology,* and *Crito* are early dialogues. The *Phaedo* is a
middle dialogue, as are the *Symposium* and *Parmenides*. The *Sophist* is late.
Behind this classification lies a complex issue of scholarship.

We are fortunate in possessing every dialogue that Plato wrote, and
we possess them very nearly as he wrote them, for our best manuscripts
are remarkably free of corruption. But apart from Aristotle's remark in
the *Politics* (II 1264b26) that the *Laws* is later than the *Republic*, there is
little in the way of ancient evidence for their order of composition. The
dialogues have come down to us ranked in tetralogies, groups of four,
and arranged loosely according to subject matter. This order is due to
Thrasyllus, an editor of the first century A.D. (Diogenes Laertius III.61.
Hereafter D.L.). It sheds no light on relative chronology. Neither does
the report of an earlier edition by Aristophanes of Byzantium in the late
second century B.C. (D.L.III.62), an edition arranged in trilogies, perhaps on the analogy of Attic drama.

Yet the question of chronology is one of some importance. Plato, as
E. R. Dodds once remarked, was a man, not a self-generating system of

11. Plutarch, *Dion* XXII.1.

metaphysics. His active literary career probably spanned fifty years, from shortly after Socrates' death in 399 B.C. to his own in 348–47; we should expect, if not change, then at least development of doctrine over so long a period.[12] The relative order of the dialogues may therefore be important to their interpretation. This order, if it is to be determined at all, can be determined only by evidence internal to the dialogues themselves. The labor and ingenuity of scholars, particularly in the latter part of the nineteenth century, has provided much of the evidence required, and their success, though incomplete, is a triumph of modern scholarship.

The Evidence of Content

It is possible to date the *Theaetetus* with some precision. The dialogue refers in its introduction to an Athenian siege of Corinth which took place in 369 B.C., where Theaetetus fell ill of the dysentery which was to kill him. Theaetetus was a member of the Academy and a brilliant mathematician, and the dialogue named for him reads like a memorial to an honored friend. It was probably written soon after his death, and before 367 B.C., when Plato left Athens for his second visit to Syracuse.

The *Theaetetus* helps date other dialogues. It ends with an appointment (210d) kept in the *Sophist* (216a). The *Statesman* is a direct continuation of the *Sophist* and refers to the *Theaetetus* (257a–258b). All three dialogues are later than the *Parmenides*, since both the *Theaetetus* (183e) and the *Sophist* (217c) refer to it. We can thus establish the relative order as *Parmenides, Theaetetus, Sophist,* and *Statesman;* the *Parmenides* and *Theaetetus* were probably written before 367 B.C.

The *Theaetetus* provides other information as well. It begins as a narrated dialogue, but the narrator, Euclid of Megara, complains of the tediousness of indirect discourse (143c), and the body of the dialogue is cast in straightforward dramatic form. As it happens, all dialogues known on independent grounds to be later than the *Theaetetus*—the *Sophist* and *Statesman,* for example, and the *Laws*—are cast in dramatic form. This suggests that such narrated dialogues as the *Phaedo, Symposium,* and *Parmenides,* as well as the *Republic, Lysis, Protagoras, Euthydemus,* and *Charmides,* may be earlier than the *Theaetetus* and written before 367 B.C.

It is also possible to date the *Laws.* Diogenes Laertius[13] preserves a tradition that it was the last of Plato's works; that it was still "in the wax"

---

12. But see H. F. Cherniss, *Lustrum* IV (1959), pp. 249–59 and 260. This bibliography contains a comprehensive survey of the literature on Plato from 1950 to 1957, annotated and conveniently arranged by topic; it mentions the main contributions to Platonism in this century to its date of publication.

13. III.37; see also Proclus (Olympiodorus), *Prolegomena* 25.5–7 (Westerink).

at the time of his death; and that it was transcribed and published post-humously by Philip of Opus, a member of the Academy. The testimony of Diogenes is not, by itself, dispositive; he was a popularizer, writing perhaps five hundred years after the fact and often at third hand, and he got things wrong. But in this case internal evidence bears him out. The text of the *Laws* shows signs of incomplete revision—for example, slight errors in grammar which do not spring from textual corruption. The Athenian Stranger who leads the dialogue—it is a dramatic, not a narrated, dialogue—is an old man, if not Plato himself then surely a surrogate for him. Furthermore, the first book of the *Laws* refers to a conquest of the Locrians by Syracuse which probably took place in 352 B.C., only a few years before Plato's death. Ancient testimony and internal evidence unite to suggest that the *Laws* is the last of Plato's works, though this does not, of course, imply that every part of it is later than every other work. The *Epinomis*, if it is genuine, is simply the thirteenth book of the *Laws*.

Reference to contemporary events in the dialogues is unusual. Although they were written in the fourth century, their dramatic dates are generally in the fifth, before the death of Socrates. But the speech of Aristophanes in the *Symposium* refers to a dispersion of the Arcadians by the Spartans, and such an event occurred in 418, and 385; the reference may therefore be double-edged. Because the dramatic date of the dialogue is 416, the year Agathon won the prize in tragic competition which the banquet celebrates, this would suggest a kind of anachronism. Anachronism in the dialogues is rare, but it does occur.[14] In the *Menexenus*, in a speech narrated by Socrates, who died in 399, Aspasia, mistress of Pericles, refers to events which must be dated to the time of the King's Peace in 387–86.

In addition to the foregoing kinds of evidence, drawn from dates and cross-references, there is the evidence of exposition and doctrinal development. The *Phaedrus* and *Timaeus*, for example, assume a tripartite account of the soul which is explained in the *Republic*. It is therefore reasonable to suppose that the *Republic* is the earliest of the three, a conjecture supported by the fact that the *Phaedrus* (245c) offers a proof of immortality from self-moving motion to which Plato continued to adhere in the *Laws* (X.896a). But the evidence of doctrinal development must be used with care lest it degenerate into arguments over what is "mature" and "immature" in Plato's thought. Estimates of philosophical

14. There is considerable, apparently intentional blurring of dates in the *Gorgias*, but no reference to events which occurred after the death of Socrates, though there is a prediction of the manner of his death.

maturity tend rather to reflect the interpreter's own philosophical pre-dilections than to constitute hard evidence. Speculative guesswork has been a main motive for attempting to determine the order of the dialogues on other grounds. In matters of scholarship, the patience of philology precedes philosophy.

The skeletal arguments here presented may appear to be simple inferences from given facts; it is difficult, in a brief summary, to present them otherwise. But facts are often not given, and given facts are often not facts. Beneath the surface simplicity of these arguments lies a complex structure of congruences which grounds their premises. And if this is true of the evidence of content, it is also true of the evidence of style.

The Evidence of Style

Molière's M. Jourdain was agreeably surprised to learn that he had been talking prose all his life without knowing it. But not Platonic prose. Plato's prose is something more than non-verse: it is an art form in its own right, and it changed under his hands as he grew older. The language of the *Laws* differs from that of the *Euthyphro* in much the same way that the prose of Milton differs from that of Addison or Swift. Plato's early style is light and graceful, the word order natural, the cadences akin to the rhythms of conversation, and the diction that of cultivated men speaking Attic Greek. But the style of the *Laws* is another matter. It is a periodic style, elaborate, highly mannered, magniloquent, grand; its word order is often inverted and unnatural; its cadences are repetitive and removed from the rhythm of ordinary speech; its diction is often archaic, poetical, or technical; Ionic rather than Attic dialect forms are often used. On the whole, it has about it the flavor of that *onkos* which Longinus ascribed to Aeschylus: *onkos*, like our "mass," means bulk or weight, but as a medical term tumor or tumidity.

The difference between the *Laws* and most of Plato's other writings can be detected by anyone with an ear for language, and if it were possible to classify dialogues by their style, we might shed further light on the question of their chronology. But some ears are tin, and no ear is an argument. Linguistic classification of the dialogues, the substitution of analysis for intuition, came with the development of stylometry, the statistical investigation of style.

The story begins in 1867, when Lewis Campbell, Professor of Greek at St. Andrews, published his edition of the *Sophist* and the *Politicus* (or *Statesman*). The authenticity of both dialogues had been challenged, and Campbell was concerned to defend their genuineness and to date them. To this end, he undertook a close analysis of their style.

He found, among other things, a variety of peculiar deviations from standard Attic, especially in diction; for example, there was a high incidence of archaic or poetic words chiefly of tragic origin, and a number of neologisms, mostly late derivatives and novel compound adjectives and verbs.[15] Campbell collected these peculiarities and compared other dialogues. He found that the *Timaeus, Critias,* and *Laws* shared them as well.[16] He also discovered that the *Sophist, Politicus, Timaeus, Critias,* and *Laws* shared a large number of words and idioms common to themselves but absent from or rare in other dialogues.[17] Because of the presence of the *Laws* in this group, he counted these dialogues among the latest of Plato's works.

The *Phaedrus* and the *Philebus* raised special problems. Campbell's investigation led him to suggest that the ornateness, novelty, and copiousness of diction in the *Phaedrus* anticipated the peculiarities which became fixed in the later dialogues, but that it was not a member of the late group. Further inquiry associated the *Phaedrus* with the *Republic, Parmenides,* and *Theaetetus.*[18] The *Philebus,* on the other hand, is less copious than other late dialogues, but when its features are examined not by number but by kind, its diction exhibits the special characteristics which mark the *Timaeus, Critias,* and *Laws.* Campbell supported the evidence of diction with consilient evidence drawn from syntax and sentence structure.

15. Notice that Campbell's emphasis was not strictly on vocabulary, which varies with subject matter, but on *kinds* of vocabulary, a less variable feature of language, though one influenced by the stylistic level at which the author aims. It should perhaps be noted that in the latter part of the nineteenth century stylistic analysis was also used in ordering Shakespeare's plays and determining issues of genuineness. As is natural with poetry, the emphasis lay more on prosody—end stopped lines, feminine endings, and so on—than on diction. See A. C. Bradley, *Shakespearean Tragedy,* Appendix B.B. More recently, stylometric methods have been used to determine which of certain disputed papers in the *Federalist* were written by Madison and which by Hamilton, as well as to determine the authorship of the Junius letters and certain other letters which appeared in the *New Orleans Daily Crescent* in 1861. These last were signed by one Quintus Curtius Snodgrass, and it was cautiously suggested that this might be a pseudonym. The author was Mark Twain.

16. For example, the *Sophist* and *Politicus* share 146 tragic words which are peculiar to them; of 81 words peculiar to the *Laws* and *Timaeus/Critias,* 40 are tragic; of 348 words peculiar to the *Timaeus* and *Critias,* over one-third are tragic. Campbell's statistics, it should be noted, relied on Ast's *Lexicon Platonicum* (1835), which is incomplete in that it does not cite every occurrence of a word nor every dialogue in which the word occurs—a fact which Ast himself pointed out. But Campbell's source was accurate enough. Further investigation, intensively pursued on independent lines of inquiry, served only to confirm his results.

17. Comparing the *Sophist* and *Politicus* with the *Laws, Timaeus,* and *Critias,* Campbell found that the incidence of common and peculiar words was: *Sophist/Laws,* 54; *Sophist/ Timaeus* and *Critias,* 36; *Politicus/Laws,* 72; *Politicus/Timaeus* and *Critias,* 42.

18. For further discussion, see Jowett and Campbell, *Plato's Republic,* vol. II, "On Plato's Use of Language."

Campbell's investigations, then, established two main groups of dialogues, stylistically distinct from each other and from the rest: a late group containing the *Sophist, Statesman, Philebus, Timaeus, Critias,* and *Laws,* though not necessarily in that order, and a middle group, the *Republic, Phaedrus, Parmenides* and *Theaetetus,* which anticipate the style of the late group but do not share it. These conclusions are consistent and consilient with the evidence of content.

Campbell's work suffered a peculiar fate: it was ignored for thirty years. The center of Platonic studies in the nineteenth century was Germany, and the Germans used Campbell's text of the *Sophist* and *Politicus* but ignored his introduction. The significance of the study was not recognized until the last decade of the century, when Wincenty Lutoslawski, an exiled Polish scholar living in Spain, drew attention to Campbell's work by traveling from one German university to another with the book in his hand. Lutoslawski, in his enthusiasm, made extreme claims for the study of style. In his own book, published in 1897 and dedicated to Campbell,[19] he undertook to develop a linguistic calculus by means of which all questions of chronology could be settled precisely and in detail. This cannot, in fact, be done. But at times even falsehood contributes to truth, and the controversy provoked by Lutoslawski's work did much to advance knowledge. Whether modern attempts to feed the text of Plato into a computer will prove more successful remains to be seen; the worth of the results will be determined by the worth of the program which produces them. Certainly Brandwood's *Word Index to Plato* (Leeds, 1976) is wonderful first fruit.

While Campbell's work lay dormant, Germany had not been idle. In the last decades of the nineteenth century another stylometric method developed which analyzed the relative frequency of conjunctions, particles, adverbs, and formulae of affirmation and response. These are formal items, items least likely to be affected by the subject matter or stylistic level of a dialogue. The results of this inquiry were summarized by Constantin Ritter just before and after the First World War.[20] Ritter, drawing on much previous work, showed that the *Sophist, Statesman, Philebus, Timaeus, Critias,* and *Laws* exhibit stylistic peculiarities which set them off from all other dialogues. For example, they and they alone use

19. *The Origin and Growth of Plato's Logic with an Account of Plato's Style and of the Chronology of His Writings,* London, 1897.

20. *Platon, Sein Leben, Seine Schriften, Seine Lehre,* Munich, vol. I, 1910, vol. II, 1920. Earlier, in response to a challenge by Eduard Zeller, Ritter had tested the method on a modern author whose dates of publication were known, namely Goethe, whose literary career spanned an even longer period than Plato's. The test was highly successful: the linguistic results corresponded to established chronology.

mechriper for *heos(per)* and they show a markedly higher frequency of *kathaper* for *hōsper*, of *ontōs* for *tōi onti*, and of *delon hōs* for *delon hoti* and a remarkably low incidence (which they share with the *Parmenides* and *Phaedrus*) of answers involving the use of a personal pronoun, such as "I agree" or "I don't think so."[21] Ritter's examination also established that there is a second group, stylistically akin to the later dialogues but significantly different from them in many respects, comprising the *Republic*, *Phaedrus*, *Theaetetus*, and *Parmenides*; the *Phaedo* and *Symposium* also show affinities to this group. All of this agreed neatly with Campbell's conclusions, though reached by a quite different line of analysis.[22]

Further evidence came from Plato's strenuous avoidance of hiatus in the later dialogues. Hiatus is the immediate succession of two vowels between separate words;[23] it is difficult to avoid in Greek, because the language includes not only its full share of words which begin with vowels, but many of its inflections end in vowels as well. The attempt to avoid hiatus accounts for much of the inverted word order which Campbell noticed in the later dialogues. The incidence of "illegitimate"—that is, avoidable—hiatus in the *Timaeus* averages 1.17 occurrences per single page of text; in the *Critias*, .80; in the *Politicus*, .44; in the *Sophist*, .61; in the *Philebus*, 3.68. The *Laws* as a whole averages less than 6.0. All other dialogues average between 30 and 45 occurrences per page, except for the *Phaedrus* and *Menexenus*, which imitate the rhetoric of orators who regarded the avoidance of hiatus as a grace of style but still average between 20 and 30 occurrences per page.[24] Once again, an independent test groups *Sophist*, *Statesman*, *Timaeus*, *Critias*, *Philebus*, and *Laws* together.

Then there is the evidence of sentence rhythm. Greek rhythm, unlike English, scans primarily by quantity rather than stress, and the later dialogues show an increased preference for rhythms with a succession of short syllables. The *Laws* averages 50.33 occurrences per page of more than two successive short syllables; the *Timaeus*, 46.14; the *Critias*, 53.59; the *Philebus*, 41.14; the *Politicus*, 47.30. The *Sophist* averages somewhat

21. 1% for the *Politicus* and *Philebus*, the highest of the late group, as against 5.5% for the *Republic* as a whole, 1.5% for the *Parmenides*, 2% for the *Phaedrus*, and 19% for the *Euthyphro*. For a summary of these and other statistics, see Ritter's table in *Platon*, vol. I, pp. 236–37.

22. John Burnet wrote, some fifty years ago, "As I have said, Campbell had analysed the vocabulary of the later dialogues, while Ritter confined himself mainly to adverbs and particles. It was sufficiently striking that these two methods should lead to precisely the same results. This is a remarkable fact, and I do not think it has been sufficiently appreciated even yet." *Platonism*, pp. 10–11.

23. We sometimes avoid hiatus in English by use of a movable consonant; for example, we say "an apple" rather than "a apple." Greek also uses this device.

24. *Phaedrus*, 23.9; *Menexenus*, 28.19. Ritter's statistics.

lower, 36.37. No other dialogue ranks so high, and most are much lower indeed. The *Phaedrus,* for example, averages only 19.81.²⁵ Again, there are the clausulae, end rhythms of sentences. In the later dialogues there is a marked increase in the use of the fourth paean, the V rhythm of three shorts and a long, which begins Beethoven's Fifth Symphony and which Aristotle in the *Rhetoric* singled out as a special excellence of prose style. Similar differences obtain for a variety of other end rhythms, though in several instances the *Timaeus* and *Critias* prove exceptional, a fact to be explained by special features of their style.²⁶

Lutoslawski's dream of ordering every dialogue by means of a linguistic calculus remains unrealized, and it is doubtful that it will ever be realized. Stylometry can establish certain broad groupings; it can do little to order dialogues within groups. But the patience and labor of scholars, the sheer blank drudgery of counting rhythms and particles or searching for neologisms—to which intelligent men in the service of knowledge have devoted years of their lives—has not been wasted. It has shed a flood of light on what once was dark, and that light, if it does not quite reach every corner, remains indispensable still.

The Order of the Dialogues

Plato's dialogues can be divided into three main groups: early, middle, and late.

The early dialogues probably include the *Apology, Crito, Laches, Ion, Hippias Major* and *Minor, Charmides, Alcibiades Major, Lysis, Euthyphro, Euthydemus,* and *Protagoras.* It is difficult to assign even a probable order to them: stylistic considerations will not serve, and there is little else in the way of direct evidence. But the *Protagoras,* which is by far the longest and most artistically complex, should be put late in the period; and the *Euthydemus,* by reason of content and similar dramatic form, belongs with it.²⁷ There is also some probability that the *Lysis, Alcibiades Major,* and *Charmides* belong late rather than early in the group. Because it is unlikely that Plato wrote Socratic dialogues before the death of Socrates, the terminus a quo of this group is 399 B.C.

The members of this group are stylistically similar to many of the

25. See the table given by F. Vogel, *Hermes* XLVIII (1923), pp. 101–02. The low figure for the *Phaedrus* is probably explained by its imitation of the Attic orators, who tended to avoid successions of short syllables.

26. Kaluscha's statistics, converted into percentages from his tables in *Wiener Studien* XXVI (1904), pp. 196, 198. See also DeGroot, *Antique Prose Rhythm,* Groningen, 1918, pp. 60–61.

27. Both the *Protagoras* and *Euthydemus* have dramatic introductions, with the body of the dialogue narrated—an experiment Plato was to repeat, flawlessly, in the *Phaedo.*

middle dialogues, but they also differ in a variety of important ways. With the single exception of the *Protagoras,* they are quite brief. They are critical and exploratory, rather than dogmatic, and they make no use of myth.[28] The *Meno* is closely connected with the *Protagoras* in theme, but seems transitional; this may also be true of the *Gorgias,* which reads like a comment in the *Apology* and the *Crito.* There is no good reason for putting the *Apology* at the beginning or even near the beginning of this group; the *Crito* may indeed be the earlier, as might be the *Euthyphro.* The terminus ad quem of this group is usually fixed, arbitrarily, at 387, the time of Plato's first visit to Italy and Syracuse. The early dialogues, then, are works of Plato's thirties and early forties.

The middle dialogues include the *Meno, Gorgias, Cratylus, Menexenus, Symposium, Phaedo, Republic,* and *Phaedrus.* They belong after 387 and before 367, when Plato undertook his second expedition to Syracuse. The *Phaedo* and *Symposium* were probably written very close together, and perhaps planned together in advance. The *Phaedo* refers to a proof of recollection given in the *Meno*; and it displays similarities to Plato's later style, similarities which became more marked in the *Republic* and *Phaedrus.* The *Phaedrus,* again, is later than the *Republic*; therefore, the order *Meno, Symposium, Phaedo, Republic, Phaedrus* must be approximately correct. The *Gorgias* and thus the *Menexenus* belong early in this group, though it is difficult to determine whether before or after the *Meno.* The *Cratylus,* which contains a great deal of satire on contemporary views of language, perhaps belongs early too, though some students have put it late on grounds of content.

The latest group contains the *Sophist, Politicus, Timaeus, Critias, Philebus,* and *Laws,* probably in that order. It is convenient to place the *Parmenides* and *Theaetetus* at the head of this group. Though stylistically they belong to the middle period, they belong at the end of it; and Plato meant them to be read in conjunction with the *Sophist* and *Politicus,* whose interests they share. The *Theaetetus,* as we have seen, cannot have been written earlier than 369, and probably was not finished later than 367. Since the dialogue differs markedly in style from the *Sophist* and all the later dialogues, it is reasonable to suppose that the change coincided with some prolonged interruption of work.[29] The *Sophist* and *Politicus,* then, pre-

28. There is a myth in the *Protagoras,* but it is offered by Protagoras, not Socrates; and it occurs in a passage meant to imitate the style of the historical Protagoras.

29. It has been claimed that Plato's style toward the end of the *Theaetetus* shifts toward his later manner; if that were true, it would provide good reason to think that the dialogue was not finished until after his return to Athens in 366. But it is not true. The touchstone of the later style is avoidance of hiatus; the man who wrote *oute ara aisthesis, o Theaitete, oute doxa alethes* on the last page of the dialogue (210a 9) was not attempting to avoid hiatus.

sumably were written after Plato's return to Athens in 366, and before his third and final visit to Syracuse in 361. He was then in his middle sixties. The *Timaeus* and the *Critias* probably also belong to this period.[30] The *Philebus*, *Laws*, and *Epinomis*, along with two open letters bearing on the situation in Sicily, the *Seventh* and *Eighth Letters*, were written after Plato's return to Athens in 360 and before his death in 348–47—an extraordinary achievement for a man in his seventies, whose mind was undimmed but whose energies must surely have been failing.[31]

The results of this discussion can be summarized thus:

428–27 B.C.	Birth of Plato		*Menexenus*
399 B.C.	Execution of Socrates		*Cratylus*
			Symposium
	Apology		*Phaedo*
	Crito		*Republic*
	Laches		*Phaedrus*
	Ion		*Parmenides*
	Hippias Major		*Theaetetus*
	Hippias Minor		
	Charmides	367 B.C.	Second Visit to Syracuse
	Alcibiades Major		*Sophist*
	Lysis		*Politicus*
	Euthyphro		*Timaeus*
	Euthydemus		*Critias*
	Protagoras		
		361 B.C.	Third Visit to Syracuse
388–87 B.C.	First Visit to Italy and Syracuse		*Philebus*
	Meno		*Laws*
	Gorgias		
		348–47 B.C.	Death of Plato

This represents a series of probabilities ranging from near certainty

30. They share with the *Sophist* and *Politicus* a more rigorous avoidance of hiatus than is found in the *Laws* or *Philebus*, and there are other stylistic similarities as well, though not decisive ones. The *Critias* breaks off in mid-sentence, and the projected trilogy was left incomplete; it is reasonable to suppose that the interruption of 361–60 explains this. It may also explain why, having written the *Sophist* and *Politicus*, Plato did not go on, as he had surely planned, to write the *Philosopher*.

31. Taylor (*Commentary on Plato's Timaeus*, Oxford, 1935, p. 6) suggests a date after 360 for the *Sophist* and every dialogue which followed it, on the ground that between 367 and 360, "what with his connexion with the troublesome politics of Syracuse and his work as a head of a great school of science and jurisprudence, Plato can have had little leisure to write books." But is it seriously to be believed that Plato wrote all of the later dialogues in his seventies, dialogues which account for nearly two-fifths of the whole of his production? That he should have managed the *Laws* and *Philebus* is astounding enough.

to something approaching sheer conjecture. In history, as in cosmology, we must sometimes rest content with "a likely story."[32]

Spurious and Doubtful Works

If we have every dialogue Plato wrote, we have also a number of dialogues he did not write. The canon of Thrasyllus accepted thirty-six works as genuine and appended several others recognized in antiquity as spurious—*On Justice, On Virtue,* the *Demodocus, Sisyphus, Eryxias,* and *Axiochus.*

The Higher Criticism of the nineteenth century added appreciably to the list. In its hands, the *Laws, Parmenides, Sophist, Politicus,* and many lesser dialogues were solemnly rejected; at one time the accepted canon shrank to nine. The texts of Plato seemed about to go the way of Holy Scripture, as Cornford recalled many years later:[33] "The critics of the Pauline Epistles, having condemned them all, one after another, were left with no means of knowing what a genuine Pauline Epistle would be like. If the game was to go on, it was necessary to restore at least one to serve as a criterion for rejecting the remainder; and when that had been done, most of the others crept back again one by one into the canon." It is not quite clear who those critics were, but that is unimportant; scholarship, after all, has its own legends and folk heroes. It is enough to know that these critics existed, as paradigms if not examples.

Of the dialogues accepted by Thrasyllus, serious doubts now obtain only for seven, the *Hipparchus, Amatores, Theages, Clitophon, Minos, Epinomis,* and *Alcibiades Minor.*[34] With the possible exception of the *Alcibiades Minor,* a brief treatment of prayer which has been thought to show Stoic influence, these dialogues appear to have been written in the fourth century B.C., if not by Plato himself, then presumably by his students in the Academy. They are imitations, not forgeries. The *Alcibiades Major* exhibits a power of thought and expression which is characteristically Platonic, and it should be accepted as genuine, as Proclus and the Neo-Platonists saw. The *Epinomis* should perhaps be ascribed to Plato's literary executor, Philip of Opus.

The *Definitions* are a collection of nearly two hundred philosophical definitions. Though they are not Plato's, they probably represent, in good part at least, the work of the Academy in or shortly after his time.[35]

32. For alternate lists and further discussion, see W. D. Ross, *Plato's Theory of Ideas,* Oxford, 1951, pp. 2–10.

33. *The Unwritten Philosophy,* p. 95.

34. For analysis and review of objections, see Taylor, *Plato: The Man and His Work,* New York, 1950, appendix, and W. H. Heidel, *Pseudo-Platonica,* Baltimore, 1896.

35. Cf. Taylor, ibid., pp. 544–45.

Then there are the *Letters*. Thrasyllus accepted thirteen of them, and so apparently did Cicero and Plutarch, though the *Twelfth Letter* became suspect in late antiquity. Ficino, during the Renaissance, rejected *Thirteen*, as did Cudworth at the end of the seventeenth century. Bentley, something of an authority on ancient epistles, defended *Thirteen* against Cudworth, and appears to have regarded all thirteen as genuine; but his own demonstration that the *Letters of Phalaris* were forgeries had the effect, in the eighteenth century, of calling many sets of ancient letters into question, Plato's among them. And at the hands of the Higher Criticism, the *Letters* went the way of all texts. Jowett, in the latter part of the nineteenth century, took their spuriousness for granted and left them untranslated.

This situation has changed, though the issue remains unsettled. It is now widely supposed[36] that the *Seventh* and *Eighth Letters*, at least, are genuine, for reasons given by Glenn Morrow:[37]

> The literary tradition of antiquity ascribed them to Plato, they conform in thought, style, and diction to the known works of Plato written at the time these letters are supposed to have been written; and furthermore, their relevancy to the situation they presuppose, their accuracy in referring to events and persons, the naturalness of the feelings they express, the appropriateness of their contents to the purpose of the letter in each case, and their conformity to the character of Plato as we know it from other sources, all point to their genuineness.

The matter of style is here, as always, of peculiar importance. It would be nearly impossible for a forger to undertake so long a work as the *Seventh Letter*, which runs to twenty Didot and twenty-nine Stephanus pages, without at some point betraying himself. Yet by all of the main tests—vocabulary, avoidance of hiatus, and end rhythms—the style of *Seven* and *Eight* which, if genuine, must have been written during the last six years of Plato's life, is identical with that of the *Laws*.

If *Seven* and *Eight* are genuine, others, notably *Three* and *Six*, are likely to be genuine too. Taylor, indeed, rejected only *One*, regarded *Twelve* as questionable, and remarked, "No grounds have ever been produced for

36. Specifically, by Hackforth, Harward, L. A. Post, Morrow, Ritter (who rejected, however, the "Philosophical Digression" in *Seven*), Wilamowitz, R. G. Bury, and Souilhé. Of recent major philological critics only Shorey and Cherniss, to my knowledge, have rejected *Seven*, and Shorey, at least, recognized that its claims were high. L. Edelstein, in *Plato's Seventh Letter*, Leiden, 1966, has also argued in favor of rejection.

37. *Studies in Plato's Epistles*, Illinois, 1935, p. 21.

questioning the authority of any of the rest which will bear examination."[38] This may well be extreme; scholarly opinion, at least, remains divided. But it is perhaps worth remarking in Taylor's support that in dealing with documents as brief as many of the *Letters* are, the testimony of the best ancient traditions must count for a good deal. This is not to say that we should accept, as Grote did, the whole Thrasyllean canon as genuine. It is to say that we should accept those which we do not have clear and powerful grounds for rejecting.

Socrates

The figure of Socrates dominates Plato's dialogues. Only in the *Laws*, Plato's last work, is he wholly absent; although he does not lead discussion in certain other late dialogues, he continues to play a role.

The historical Socrates, son of Sophroniscus, of the Athenian deme Alopece, was seventy or a little more when he was executed in 399 B.C. He must therefore have been born about 469 B.C., roughly a decade after Athens turned back the second and last great Persian invasion at Salamis, and two decades after Marathon. His youth and manhood were lived in the Golden Age; his contemporaries included Aeschylus, Sophocles, and Euripides in tragedy; Herodotus and Thucydides in history; and Parmenides, Zeno, Empedocles, and Anaxagoras in philosophy. In an age of towering literature, Socrates himself wrote nothing.

We know something of the externals of Socrates' life, and even something about how he looked. He was married to Xanthippe, whom Xenophon portrayed as a shrew and Plato did not. He had three children, the youngest still in arms at his death. There is a tradition, not well attested, that he was trained as a sculptor or stonecutter in youth. He saw military service in the early years of the Peloponnesian War, serving with distinction at the battles of Potidaea (432), Delium (424), and Amphipolis (422). He took little part in the political affairs of his city—an oddity for an Athenian. He was poor in his last years, though he had not always been so—his army service was as a hoplite, a heavy-armored infantryman, which indicates that at one time he had a competence. He was regarded by many people as an *eiron*, a word from which our "irony" derives but which had the connotation of slyness verging on dishonesty. A peculiar voice, a "divine thing," came to him; according to Plato it only turned him back from what he was about to do, whereas according to Xenophon it also urged him forward and even offered free advice to

38. Taylor, *Plato: The Man and His Work*, p. 16.

friends. He was wall-eyed, snubnosed, and had a peculiar rolling walk which reminded Aristophanes of a waterfowl. The face, with its directness of gaze, reminded Plato of a bull.

Put briefly, Socrates was poor, ugly, unpolitical, and of common birth, and he lived in a society which placed highest value on wealth, nobility of family, political power, and physical beauty. It was as if he summed up in his own person the moral revolution—from outer to inner, from goods of the body to goods of the soul—which he had won through to proclaim in later life.

There are three contemporary portraits of Socrates, by Aristophanes, Xenophon, and Plato, along with remains of a fourth in the fragments of Aeschines of Sphettos,[39] who appears to agree most closely with Xenophon. Aristophanes pictures Socrates in the *Clouds* as part sophist and part natural philosopher, and Socrates cited the *Clouds* at his trial as one of the main sources of prejudice against him. The play, produced in 423, shows only that Socrates in middle life was well enough known to be satirized, and that he was associated in the popular mind with "the wise," the Sophists.

The pictures drawn by Plato and Xenophon often conflict, not only in detail but also in their portrayals of the man's character, and students have been divided for centuries over their relative merits. The conflict need not be surprising. Xenophon was a retired soldier with a literary bent who had known Socrates in youth. Plato was both a dramatist and a philosopher of genius. It is important to remember that ancient literary conventions in matters of biography were a good deal more flexible than our own. Even Thucydides, most "scientific" of historians, remarks that he will often represent men as saying in their speeches what he considers it appropriate that they should have said on the occasion. Still, it is clear that Xenophon in the *Memorabilia* and in two shorter works, the *Apology* and the *Symposium,* undertook to give an accurate account of Socrates and to defend him against misunderstandings and false charges. It seems equally clear that this must also have been, in part at least, Plato's purpose in the early dialogues.

Xenophon's Socrates is a man of quick wit and prosy common sense, great strength of character and quite usual moral attitudes and doctrines. He is abstemious in matters of the intellect: he dismisses as "useless" the physical speculation of his day and much of geometry, astronomy, and number theory. Xenophon begins the *Memorabilia* by saying that he is at

39. For translation, see Field, *Plato and His Contemporaries,* pp. 146–57; for text, see H. Dittmar, *Aischines von Sphettos,* Berlin, 1912.

a loss to understand how the Athenians could ever have condemned such a man, and the reader of the *Memorabilia* will find himself, in the end, at a loss to understand it too. As John Burnet once remarked, Xenophon's memoir, written as a defense of Socrates, fails because it is too successful. Nor could a man of the sort Xenophon portrays have altered, as Socrates did, the form and intention of future thought.

Plato's portrait is different. The Platonic Socrates of the early dialogues is complex and many-faceted; it is not difficult to understand how such a person could have been both immensely loved and immensely hated, or why his ruthless criticism of received beliefs should have led him to his death. From Plato's portrait we can understand why Aristophanes treated Socrates as a sophist, why Aristippus took from him the view that the good is pleasure, why Antisthenes was persuaded that the good is to live according to nature. Most important, we can understand how this Socrates could have quickened the mind of a Plato and turned him to philosophy. Plato's portrait of Socrates is instinct with life; it also conveys something of that power of mind and personality which so indelibly marked the generations of philosophers which followed.

Aristotle's Testimony

Aristotle came to the Academy from Macedon in 368–67 as a youth of seventeen. He remained for twenty years, until Plato's death in 348–47. He was a Platonist during this period: his earliest publications were dialogues, which Cicero praised for their golden style, and in certain of those dialogues he appears to have argued for the immortality of the soul, the reality of Forms, and the theory that learning is recollection.[40] His testimony—there is much of it—as to Plato's ultimate meaning and intention would seem to be of unexampled authority, for he had the character of an excellent witness: intelligence, transparent honesty, ample opportunity to learn, and early intellectual sympathy.

If his testimony is reliable, it is important. He ascribes to Plato several metaphysical doctrines, including a theory of Idea Numbers, which do not appear in the dialogues. His source was presumably lectures and discussions in the Academy, direct oral communication with Plato.

This led Léon Robin to undertake the reconstruction of Plato's ultimate philosophy from the testimony of Aristotle alone, without recourse

---

40. So Werner Jaeger, *Aristotle*, Oxford, 1948, chaps. 2–4.

to the evidence of the dialogues.[41] It led A. E. Taylor to say:[42] "We have to discover Plato's ultimate metaphysical positions indirectly from references to them in Aristotle, supplemented by occasional brief excerpts, preserved by later Aristotelian commentators, from the statements of Academic contemporaries of Aristotle, like Xenocrates and Hermodorus." This rests on a doctrine of privileged access; it assumes that Aristotle had resources for understanding Plato's ultimate views on metaphysics which are denied to those who must rely for their information on the evidence of the dialogues alone. But the crucial difficulty with the doctrine of privileged access is the quality of the testimony Aristotle provides.

Aristotle on Plato resembles one of Hesiod's Muses: he knows how to tell the truth, and some things which are not the truth. For example, in a single chapter of *Metaphysics* A,[43] he ranges from the obvious to the absurd. He testifies that Plato "separated" changing sensible objects from the unchanging Forms in which they partake; and the dialogues provide ample evidence for his claim. He claims that Plato posited a class of "intermediates" between Forms and sensibles—the objects of mathematics—and if this is not supported by the dialogues, there are at least scattered passages which suggest it. He testifies to the existence of Idea Numbers, derived from "the One" and "the Great and Small" or "the Dyad"; and this cannot directly be confirmed or disconfirmed by the dialogues, unless it is an interpretation of the Deductions in the *Parmenides*. Finally, he testifies that Plato used only formal and material causes in explanation, and by implication he denies that efficient and final causality have any role in Plato's philosophy.[44] That is, Aristotle claims in effect that the man who in the *Phaedrus* and *Laws* defined soul as self-moving motion, and held it to be the source of all other motion in the universe, had no place in his philosophy for an efficient cause. He claims that the man who in the *Phaedo* said that sensible objects strive to be like Forms, and in the *Republic* defined the Good as the first principle of existence and intelligibility, and in the *Timaeus* proclaimed the world a

41. L. Robin, *La Théorie Platonicienne des Idées et des Nombres d'après Aristote*, Paris, 1908.
42. Taylor, *Plato: The Man and His Work*, p. 503.
43. A. vi., which contains Aristotle's first survey of Plato's doctrines in the *Metaphysics*. For further discussion of the chapter, see H. F. Cherniss, *Riddle of the Early Academy*, Berkeley, 1945, pp. 6–8, and *Aristotle's Criticisms of Plato and the Academy*, vol. I, Baltimore, 1944, pp. 177–84; and Ross, *Aristotle's Metaphysics*, vol. I, Oxford, 1924, pp. 157–77.
44. Cf. A. ix., 992a29*ff.*, and Ross, *Plato's Theory of Ideas*, pp. 233–39.

work of rational design, had no place in his philosophy for a final cause. This testimony suffers from a cardinal defect: it is incredible.[45]

Aristotle's testimony is sometimes inaccurate on the most fundamental aspects of Plato's thought. How then are we to use that testimony to verify issues on which the dialogues are silent? The answer, surely, is that when Aristotle's testimony cannot be measured against an independent control, it is insufficient warrant for Plato's views. If Plato proclaimed "unwritten doctrines" in the Academy, we cannot now determine what those doctrines were except insofar as they are reflected in such texts as the *Parmenides,* texts already in our possession.

It will be argued in reply that Aristotle's testimony remains vitally important. Plato surely taught in the Academy, and Aristotle surely heard him. And Aristotle's testimony to what he heard, with all its faults, is all we have.

The force of this turns largely on what we conceive teaching in the Academy to have been. Most pictures agree in representing Plato as a professor, attired in cap and gown, lecturing to a class of students, their styluses scribbling furiously on wax.

And lecture he did—at least once. Aristoxenus, a younger contemporary of Aristotle, relates of the audience that attended Plato's lecture on the Good that[46]

> they came, every one of them, in the conviction that they would get
> from the lecture[s] some one or other of the things that the world
> calls good; riches or health, or strength—in fine, some extraordinary
> gift of fortune. But when they found that Plato's reasonings were of
> mathematics—numbers, geometry, and astronomy—and, to crown
> all, to the effect that there is one Good, methinks their disenchant-
> ment was complete. The result was that some of them sneered at
> the thing, while others vilified it.

The lecture(s) referred to must have been public; students in the Acad-

---

45. There are ways, of course, to make the incredible palatable: for example, one may jettison the text of Plato. Perhaps the "exoteric" Plato published dialogues, more or less misleading as to his true views, for a popular audience, while the "esoteric" Plato reserved his more intimate and advanced theories, the so-called "unwritten doctrines," for his students in the Academy. We may then suppose, relying on Aristotle, that the exoteric Plato proclaimed a Divine Maker in the *Timaeus* because the esoteric Plato thought it good for the troops. This approach has at least one sterling advantage: consistently applied, no appeal to the text of Plato can refute it.

46. Aristoxenus, *Harm. El.* ii. 30–31, cited and translated in Ross, *Plato's Theory of Ideas,* pp. 147–48. Brackets added.

emy would have been prepared for what they got. And given the popular reaction, it would be surprising indeed if Plato gave many of them.[47] But there is a certain irony, which has its own delight, in the picture of Plato lecturing on mathematics and metaphysics to an audience who came to improve their health, strengthen their muscles, and get rich quick.

It has often been claimed that Aristotle got his knowledge of the theory of Idea Numbers from this lecture or series of lectures. This is unlikely. Plato surely would not have revealed his deepest thoughts on metaphysics to a popular audience, largely untrained in mathematics and philosophy, if he did not reveal those thoughts in the *Parmenides* and later dialogues, which were far too technical and difficult for general publication and which were written with members of his own Academy in view. The "unwritten doctrines" traced to this lecture are not of the sort that any sensible man would broadcast to an ignorant multitude. But this means that there is no evidence whatever that Plato expounded his ultimate metaphysical views by means of lectures. For Aristoxenus provides the only direct evidence for a lecture that we have.

This is not to deny that Plato taught. It would be strange indeed for a man who so elevated the spoken word over the written,[48] and who believed so passionately in education, not to have taught. But the dialogues suggest that his teaching was of a peculiar sort. They suggest that Plato taught through conversation: the conversation which the dialogues themselves portray, which is dialectic. To construe philosophy as dialectic is to view it primarily as an activity, not a product, as a discovering of truth rather than a set of truths discovered. The dialectician is unlikely to be a man with an official doctrine, oral or otherwise. The whole spirit of Plato's teaching, insofar as his writing reflects the man who wrote, lies not in promulgation of doctrine, not in expounding, as Aristotle and others have sought to expound, a necessary system demonstratively derived from self-evident truths, but in leading men to see things for themselves. The aim, if you will, is education, not instruction. At the end of

47. Ross (ibid., p. 148) is convinced that we have here a report of a series, or even a course, of lectures. Given the reception and corroborative evidence of the *Seventh Letter* (341e–342a), this is improbable. Ross argues from the fact that Simplicius, Philoponus, and Aesclepius, three commentators on Aristotle writing some eight hundred years after the event, sometimes use the plurals *logoi* and *sunousiai* in referring to it. This, if it is not contradicted, is surely not supported by the text of Aristoxenus; for *akroasin*, the word Ross translates as "lectures," is singular. Ross holds that the singular may mean a course or a single lecture, as in *phusike akronsis*; but he gives no examples to show that this is true in the absence of the modifying adjective, expressed or understood.

48. *Phaedrus* 275c–277b: the written word serves only as a reminder of the truth, an image of the living *logos* put forward by the man who knows through dialectic. Cf. *Seventh Letter* 341b–d.

his life as at the beginning, Plato remained faithful in this to the spirit of Socrates, and perhaps no less ironic.

There is truth in the doctrine of privileged access: Plato surely taught. But there is nothing to suggest that Plato's teaching in the Academy was different in kind, or markedly different in content, from that teaching of which the dialogues are a *mimesis,* and the very existence of the *Parmenides* is massive evidence to the contrary. Our evidence for what Plato thought is what Plato wrote.

This last point perhaps should be put more precisely. A pervasive element in the use of Aristotle as a primary witness for Plato's thought has been the apparently ineradicable psychologism which infects the study of the history of philosophy, and specifically of Plato. It is supposed that the student of Plato has as his object the discovery of Plato's thoughts—that is, his beliefs—and that the student is to use Plato's writings merely as evidence for those beliefs. Now, there is another source of evidence which is independent of what Plato wrote—so at least it is supposed—namely, Aristotle's testimony. What Plato wrote sometimes conflicts with what Aristotle says Plato believed, so it is the task of the historian somehow to adjudicate the dispute, weighing these two classes of partially inconsistent evidence in order to strike a balance purportedly representing historical fact—that is, what Plato *really* believed. We are then well on our way to belief in esoteric doctrines.

It is preferable to choose another way of proceeding: to view Plato's text, not as evidence for something else, but as the primary object of historical understanding. The aim of inquiry is to interpret a set of literary documents, not to fathom the beliefs of their author. It is reasonable, of course, to assume that the documents are a reliable index to the beliefs; but the question of whether Plato held beliefs he did not express, or beliefs contrary to what he did express, may be left to those with skill in the arts of divination. The historian may limit himself to the study of texts and their meaning. If inquiry is construed in this way, it is self-referentially inconsistent to prefer the testimony of Aristotle to the evidence of Plato's texts in the interpretation of Plato.

As it happens, there is good reason to suppose that Aristotle faced the same kind of interpretive problems that we face. This follows from more than the conjecture that Plato's teaching in the Academy was dialectical; for the main source of the criticisms Aristotle directs against Plato's theory of Ideas lies in the perplexities raised about Ideas in the *Parmenides.* Aristotle, who assumed the independent reality of sensibles, did not think the intellectual knots involved in those perplexities could be untied. Again, his testimony about the One and the Indefinite Dyad, or the Great

and Small, turns out to be an interpretation of substrate doctrines offered about Unity in the concluding hypotheses of the *Parmenides*. Given
that he assumed Plato was committed to those doctrines, the denial of
final and efficient causality necessarily follows. It is very likely, indeed,
that the single reference in Aristotle to "the so-called unwritten doctrines" of Plato (*Physics* 209b.14–15) in fact refers to the *Parmenides*, in
contrast to the *Timaeus*;[49] the doctrines are called "unwritten" because
aporetic. If this is so, then Aristotle's criticisms are based on a Platonic
text which we possess, and which we must therefore interpret if we are
to interpret the criticisms. What as a matter of method had been self-
referentially inconsistent becomes factually *husteron-proteron*—the cart before the horse.

49. For further discussion, see R. E. Allen, *Plato's Parmenides*, Minnesota, 1983, pp. 269–
72.

I: THE EUTHYPHRO

COMMENT

Socrates has come to the Porch of the King Archon to answer an indictment which will lead to his conviction and death. Euthyphro, an Athenian *mantis,* or seer, has come to prosecute his aged father for murder,
lodging his prosecution in behalf of a man who was himself a murderer.
It is, he thinks, the pious or holy thing to do, and the gods demand it.

In Athens, homicide differed from impiety in that it was not a crime
against the City, and therefore not prosecuted under a *graphe,* or public
indictment; it was treated as a private wrong actionable by *dike,* or civil
suit. Yet murder was unusual, in that suit was initiated before the King,
a religious magistrate, because murder implied the contagion of pollution and was therefore affected with a public interest.

The story of Euthyphro's prosecution may well have a basis in fact, on
the ground, often excellent in history, that it is too good not to be true.
Plato tells the story with a delicate irony all his own, but he uses it to
point a philosophical moral. Euthyphro is prosecuting his father because
he is convinced that it is right to do so, and piety or holiness requires it.
But Euthyphro's father, his relatives, and most ordinary Athenians would
have regarded such a prosecution, although lodged in the name of piety,
as monstrously impious. In this conflict of moral opinion, with each side
holding to incompatible views with lofty confidence, where can there be
found a sufficient basis for decision?

Plato's introduction to the *Euthyphro* is meant to exhibit a need which
will later be explicitly stated: the need to find a standard by which to
determine what things are holy and what are not.

Socrates begins the dialectic with a request. Euthyphro, in undertaking
the prosecution, must surely know divine law and matters of holiness

29

and unholiness. So Socrates would like to become his pupil; after all, he has himself an indictment for impiety to meet. Just what is holiness?

The question is a highly ambiguous one. Socrates might have been asking for a synonym of holiness, an example of holiness, or a distinguishing mark by which to set off holy things from other things. But he is in fact asking for a definition of the essential nature of holiness, and he works to make his meaning clear (5c–d).

Euthyphro, however, misses the point of the question. He replies with an example: holiness, he thinks, is doing just what he is doing now, prosecuting murderers and temple thieves; and not prosecuting them is unholy. In the same way, Laches, a soldier, thinks that courage is sticking to your post and not running away in the face of the enemy (*Laches* 190e). Charmides, a sought-after youth, thinks that temperance is keeping quiet and being modest (*Charmides* 159b), Cephalus, an elderly businessman, will say that justice is telling the truth and paying your debts (*Republic* I. 331c). And Hippias, a sophist with other intersts, thinks that the beautiful is a beautiful maiden, though he later hazards the guess that it is gold (*Hippias Major* 287e, 289e).

Socrates repeats his question. Other things are holy besides prosecuting murderers and temple thieves, and what he wants is an account of the character of all holy things (6d–e). The words *eidos* and *idea*, derived from the same root, are here translated neutrally as "characteristic" and "character." They have a range of ordinary meanings: sort or kind, figure, including the human figure, the nature of a thing, or the look of a thing, *species* or outward appearance. But the words are here used in a special way. The *eidos* or *idea* of holiness is a universal, the same in all its instances, and something all its instances have; it appears to be a condition for the existence of holy things, that *by which* (the dative is instrumental) holy things are holy; and it is a standard or paradigm for determining what things are holy and what are not. In short, the words *eidos* and *idea* here carry freight they do not ordinarily bear; for that reason, commentators have often translated them as "Idea" or "Form." "Form," while it has Aristotelian overtones, escapes the subjective and psychological connotations that hover around the word "idea" in English.

Socrates will not accept an example in reply to his question "What is holiness?" for many things are holy, and Socrates wishes to know what is the same in every holy action—what is the nature of the Form all holy actions share.

This pattern of argument is found in other dialogues. In the *Laches* (191e–192b), when courage is defined by the example of courage in battle, Socrates argues that this is not enough. Courage is found, not only in war, but in perils at sea, in disease, poverty, and politics; Socrates wishes to be told what is the same in all these instances. In the *Hippias Major* (300a–b), Socrates claims that if two different things are beautiful, they must have something identical which makes them beautiful, and that this common thing must be present in them. When Meno, in an early middle dialogue, undertakes to define virtue with a list of examples, Socrates corrects him with an analogy. Suppose you are asked what a bee is. There are many different kinds of bees, but it does no good to name them; the question demands some account of the character all bees share. So it is with virtue: "However diverse and multitudinous the virtues may be, they have all a common characteristic through which they are virtues, and it is on this that anyone who would say what virtue is must fix his gaze" (*Meno* 72c).

The claim that the *eidos* or *idea* of holiness is the same in all holy things, and that it is something they all have (5d), can be abbreviated as the claim that Forms are universals. As universals, they play a regulative role in dialectic. As the implied antecedents of "it" in Socrates' question "What is it?" they restrict the range of answers which may sensibly be given. Because holiness is a universal, Euthyphro cannot answer the question "What is holiness?" by offering examples of things which are holy.

Socrates wishes to be told the nature of holiness so he can use it as a standard by which to determine what things are holy and what are not (6e, cf. *Lysis* 223b, *Hippias Major* 286c–d). This demand for a standard is of the essence of Socratic dialectic, which is directed not merely toward abstract understanding, but toward the right ordering of life. The aim is to grasp the principles of that order, and to be able to identify them in concrete cases. The *Republic* (I 344d–e) claims that it is important to know what is holy and what is just and what is virtuous, because on that knowledge depends the conduct of a life. In the *Charmides* (175e), the young Charmides is said to be most temperate; but without knowing what temperance is, he will have no advantage from its presence in his life—this to a man who later became one of the Thirty Tyrants. If the aim of dialectic is to define a Form, the practical aim is the discernment of form in things. Forms are to moral matters what scales are to weight and yardsticks to length—a basis for sufficient decision (7b–d).

As with the assumption that Forms are universals, the assumption that they are standards plays a regulative role in dialectic, ruling out all answers to the "What is it?" question which imply that the Form is in some way qualified by its opposite (6e–8b). This is where Euthyphro's next attempt at definition goes wrong. The formula, "holiness is what is loved by the gods," escapes a principal defect of his first attempt: it provides, not an example, but a distinguishing mark, setting off, at least in intention, all and only those things which are holy. The requirement of universality has now been met. But the definition still proceeds in a sense by example: it specifies a group of individuals—things, actions, persons (7a)—marked off from the rest by being loved by the gods. And it is the individuals, not their distinguishing mark, which are identified with holiness.

Euthyphro's theology is, so to speak, vulgarly Olympian. The gods quarrel among themselves, loving and hating the same things. So some holy things, by this account, are also unholy, and Socrates still has not found out what holiness is.

This refutation, at first glance, seems worthless. A definition of animal which applied to non-animals would clearly be too broad; no animal is a non-animal. Neither is any odd number even. But some tall things are also short—tall pygmies, for example—and Hippias's maiden, though beautiful, was ugly compared to a goddess. It is not self-evidently false that some holy things are also unholy, and if Euthyphro's theology is sound, his definition implies that it is true.

This neglects the peculiar character of Socrates' question. Euthyphro's definition specifies, not a universal, but a group of things set off from others by a distinguishing mark, that of being loved by the gods. But Socrates had requested, not an account of things which are holy, but an account of a Form of holiness, which might serve as a standard for judging what things are holy and what are not. A set of things which are examples of holiness, but also in some part examples of unholiness, is hardly fitted to serve as such a standard. We can scarcely identify a thing as holy by comparing it to things some of which are also unholy. The difficulty, indeed, lies even deeper. We cannot determine whether that to which we compare it is holy or unholy, without knowledge of holiness and unholiness in and of themselves.

This is directly connected with the self-identity of Forms. Socrates had suggested earlier on that holiness is the same in itself, and that its opposite, unholiness, is like itself (5d). This suggestion is expanded at 7a to mean that holiness is not identical with unholiness, but rather is its complete opposite. Socrates' refutation implies that Euthyphro's definition violates this principle (8a); he assumes that if holiness were in any way unholy, it would not be the opposite of unholiness. The intuitive principle underlying this inference is plain: that by which or in virtue of which things are holy cannot be itself in any way unholy. The self-identity of Forms implies the radical exclusion of their opposites, and that exclusion is directly connected with the use of the Form as a standard. One can never correctly answer the question "What is holiness?" by naming something which is in any way unholy. Likewise, holiness cannot be identified with a group of things which are holy, if some of those things are unholy too. But the difficulty underlying Euthyphro's definition is fully exposed by his attempt to amend it. He had offered a definition by distinguishing mark. The flaw in this shows up when he tries to avoid the problem of qualification by opposites by defining holiness as what is loved by *all* the gods.

Socrates begins by asking whether the group of things which are holy are loved because they are holy, or holy because they are loved. Euthyphro gives the common sense answer: they are loved because they are holy. He has already granted without question that the gods love what they believe noble, good, and right, and hate what they think is otherwise (7e); the goodness in things is, for him as for most plain men, a reason for loving and not a consequence of it. But this leads to the collapse of his definition. Socrates, by a beautiful and ingenious argument, demonstrates that if this is so, being loved by all the gods is not the nature and reality, or essence, of holiness, its *ousia*, but merely a property which happens to be connected with it, a *pathos* of it (10e–11a). For holiness is loved because it is holy, not holy because it is loved.

Just as with the assumption that Forms are universals and standards, so the assumption that an account of them must state essence plays a regulative role in dialectic. An answer to the question "What is holiness?" cannot merely provide a distinguishing mark which happens to characterize holy things; it must provide an analysis of the nature of holiness, that by which holy things are holy.

The request to know the essence of holiness, as opposed to a distinguishing mark of holy things, involves a peculiar priority. Just as one cannot know what things are holy without knowing what holiness is, so one must know what holiness is before one can know what properties— or distinguishing marks—happen to be connected with it. This point is not explicitly made in the *Euthyphro*. But in the *Laches* (190b–c), one cannot know how virtue can be acquired without knowing what it is; in the *Republic* (I 354b–c) one cannot know whether justice is profitable, or if it makes its possessors happy, without knowing what it is; in the *Protagoras* (359e–361d), Socrates and Protagoras cannot agree on whether virtue is teachable, or whether it is knowledge, because they do not know what it is. In the *Meno* (71b, cf. 86e), Socrates cannot say whether virtue is taught, acquired by practice, or present by nature, because he does not know what it is. Attempts to answer these questions without having

determined the essence of virtue lead to the failure of the dialectic at
100b.

The priority of the "What is it?" question is directly implicated with
the fact that Forms are standards. The connection between holiness and
other properties must lie either in the nature of holiness itself or in the
things which are holy; that holiness is teachable, for example, is a claim
either about the Form of holiness or about those things which partake
of the Form. In either case, one cannot estimate the truth of the claim
without knowing what holiness is, since one must know what holiness is
before one can determine what things are holy.

Aristotle defines essence as "what a thing is in itself, the account of
which is a definition." Socrates, having demanded of Euthyphro an account of what holiness is in itself, next proceeds to give him a lesson in
how to define (11e–12a). Euthyphro must begin by saying what holiness
is a part of—as reverence, for example, is a part of fear. He must then
say what part it is—as "even number" is that part of "number" divisible
by two. Euthyphro's remaining attempts at definition in the dialogue
conform to this plan. He next defines holiness as that part of justice
concerned with service to the gods, and then, when that is refuted, as
an art of (that is, that part of art concerned with) prayer and sacrifice.

It is not misrepresenting Socrates' plan to say that he is here after
definition *per genus et differentiam,* though it must be added that such
definition will involve, not division into simpler elements from which the
species may be constructed, but a kind of mapping within genera. For
present purposes, however, the important thing is that the definition is
real and not nominal. It is analysis of essence, rather than stipulation as
to how words shall be used or a report on how they are in fact used.
Mill claims that real definition is simply nominal definition plus an existence claim. Thus the real definition of triangularity would be: "'Triangle' means 'plane rectilinear figure with three angles,' and there are
triangles." This view is probably at least as old as Euclid, and in some
passages, it is Aristotle's own. Aristotle certainly thought that "what is
meant by a unit and the fact that a unit exists are different things"
(*Post.Anal.*I.72a24); and in Euclid's *Elements,* existence is not deduced
from definitions but demonstrated by construction. All of this may have
its roots in the *Phaedo,* where Socrates, after failing to grasp the nature
of things directly, recommends the use of a method of hypothesis (99d;
cf. 100a–b, 101c–d). And, of course, it is very similar to the account of
the connection between existence and analyticity offered in much modern logical theory.

But it is not what real definition involves in the *Euthyphro.* The dialectical procedure there cannot be described simply as an attempt to define the word "holy" coupled with an attempt to find out whether it applies to anything. In the first place, the requirements for answering the "What is it?" question are not those of nominal definition. Nominal definitions are definitions of words, not of standards or essences, and there is no good reason why they should be required always to be per genus et differentiam. In the second place, existential import is taken for granted, not demonstrated, in the early dialogues; Euthyphro and Socrates assume without question that there are holy things and ask only what their nature is. This assumption of existence is made in every early dialogue in which the "What is it?" question is initially answered by appeal to examples—that is, in every early dialogue in which it is asked. The reason is not difficult to discover. An essence is not a possibility or a hypostatized meaning; it is the nature of something which is. And real definition, in the early dialogues, is analysis of essence.

This seems to imply something which is properly called a theory of Forms or Ideas. That theory is, in the first place, a technical theory, a body of rules governing the practice of a useful art, that of dialectic. Thus, the question "What is holiness?" cannot be answered by examples, or by specifying a group of things some of which are unholy, or by providing a distinguishing mark. It must be answered by an analysis of the essence of holiness, because holiness is a Form.

So it is a technical theory—a logical theory, if you will, in one sense of that much used and abused term. But it is also a metaphysical theory. It assumes the existence of Forms, as universals, standards, and essences, and that assumption is stated or implied throughout the early dialogues.

One mark of being is power. As essences, Forms do not, so to speak, just sit there. They do honest work. They affect the career of the world, being that by which things are what they are. An argument in the *Hippias Major* makes this point explicitly. Socrates leads Hippias to agree that justice *is* something and that this is true of wisdom too, for "things which are just and wise and so on would not be such *by* them, if they were not something." Because beautiful things are beautiful by beauty, Hippias is compelled to agree that beauty *is* something too. Socrates then goes on to ask, "What is it?" (287c–d)

The argument is an excellent one. If beauty is that by which beautiful things are beautiful, and beautiful things exist, then beauty must also exist. Beauty is not merely a word, a thought, or a concept. It is an existing thing, for the things it makes beautiful are existing things, and they are not made beautiful by our words or thoughts or concepts.

This conflicts with the commonly held view that there is no commitment to the existence of Forms in the early dialogues, and that talk of them there is "merely a matter of language." That view confuses language with what it is used to affirm. The Muses may inspire a poet, made drunk by their presence, to compare the redness of a rare sunset to the redness of a rare beefsteak; they do not thereby inspire him with the belief that he has added redness along with sunsets and beefsteaks to his ontology. But if that same poet, in more sober mood, were to ask what redness is, explaining that he wished to be told the nature of a characteristic common not only to sunsets and beefsteaks, but to barns, fire engines, Russians, and all such similar things; and if he went on to add that when he learned what it is, he expected to use it as a standard for distinguishing what is really red from what isn't; and if he expected a proper account of it to state its nature and reality, and be formulated per genus et differentiam—if, in short, he laid down rules for real definition and followed them in his inquiry, we should begin to suspect that the inspiration the Muses had visited upon him was metaphysical, rather than poetical, and that he now came equipped with a view of the way the world is and what it contains which goes considerably beyond anything which ordinary language or common sense can show.

If this is true, if Socrates' question involves a metaphysical assumption about existence, how is it that his respondents are able to reply? Surely it is significant that a man like Euthyphro, who is no dialectician, should accept without demur the suggestion that there is an idea of holiness, or that Protagoras, whom Plato himself portrayed as a conventionalist in morals, agrees without hesitation that justice "is something." Protagoras can hardly have meant to embrace an ontology of abstract entities; his agreement is more likely to be prompted by the uses of language. All of us who are not cynics or otherwise disreputable believe, after all, that there is such a thing as justice.

Socrates, armed with a metaphysical theory, is able to apply it—indeed, take it for granted—in conversation with ordinary men. The reason is that though the Socratic theory of Forms is a metaphysical theory, it is also essentially continuous with common sense. It is, in one sense of that overworked word, a theory of meaning. "What do you say temperance is?" Socrates asks Charmides. "Since you know how to speak Greek, you no doubt can say what it seems to you to be" (*Charmides* 159a; cf. *Laches* 197e; *Protagoras* 329d; *Alcibiades* I 111c, 112a–d). When Critias charges Socrates with arguing only to refute him, Socrates replies (*Charmides* 166c–d): "How can you believe, if I try my best to refute you, that I do so from any other motive than to examine what my own words mean, for fear that it may at some point escape my notice that I think I know something I do not?" Plain men had talked of holiness long before Socrates came to ask them what it was exactly that they meant. His inquiry is distinguished by its precision. He does not want synonyms, examples, or distinguishing marks of holiness, but an analysis of the nature of it. His question is hardly one which common sense, left to its own devices, will ask. But it is a question to which common sense may certainly be led, and the dialectic of the *Euthyphro* is in fact a record of such leading, as Socrates works to make Euthyphro see the real nature of his question. The progress of dialectic involves passage from the naive existence claim that "there is such a thing as holiness" to the highly sophisticated existence claim that there is an essence of holiness, and that it can be defined. But if we are willing to admit this last, the passage is continuous; for the commitment to essence is then latent in the commonsense use of words. The essence of holiness is what we mean by the word "holiness"—when we finally understand our meaning.

Not all philosophers, of course, would admit this. It implies that questions of meaning are in the final analysis ontological questions, questions about the nature and structure of the world; they are not merely "second-order" questions, concerning the language in which we discuss the world. Since we understand the nature and structure of the world only imperfectly, the argument also implies that we often do not know what we mean by our words—witness Euthyphro. If meaning implies essence, it is simply not true of ordinary language that "Everything is in order as it is."

The solution, it may be, is to deny essences. In the *Philosophical Investigations,* Wittgenstein remarks, "One thinks that one is tracing the outline of the thing's nature over and over again, and one is merely tracing round the frame through which we look at it. A picture held us captive. And we could not get outside it, for it lay in our language and language seemed to repeat it to us inexorably. When philosophers use a word . . . and try to grasp the *essence* of the thing, one must ask oneself: is the word ever actually used this way in the language-game which is its original home?—What *we* do is to bring words back from their metaphysical to their everyday use" (paras. 114–16). If this view is true, the assumptions on which Socratic dialectic rests are false, as are the typical Socratic claims that virtue is knowledge, that courage is wisdom, and that holiness is just. These words are not used that way every day—no more in ordinary ancient Greek than in ordinary modern English. Socrates' identification, or connection, of things which are linguistically distinct is unintelligible without the notion of essence, unless we are to explain his claim about the unity of the virtues as mere tyrannical legislation over language.

There is a theory of Forms in the early dialogues, and it involves a metaphysical claim, but it is not *the* theory of Forms—that theory of the choir of heaven and the furniture of earth found in the *Phaedo*, *Republic*, and other middle dialogues. Burke once remarked, "Though no man can draw a stroke between the confines of night and day, yet light and darkness are upon the whole tolerably distinguishable." So it is with the early and the middle dialogues. The difference between the *Euthyphro* on one hand, and the *Phaedo* and *Republic* on the other, is perhaps not the difference of light and darkness, but it too is tolerably plain. The philosophy of the middle dialogues is a nest of coupled contrasts: Being and Becoming, Appearance and Reality, Permanence and Flux, Reason and Sense, Body and Soul, Flesh and Spirit. Those contrasts are rooted in an ontology of two Worlds separated by a gulf of deficiency. The World of Knowledge, whose contents are the eternal Forms, stands to the World of Opinion, whose contents are sensible and changing, as the more real stands to the less real, as originals stand to shadows and reflections. The visible world is an image, unknowable in its deficiency, of an intelligible world apprehended by reason alone.

This is "separation," and it is possible to fix with some precision the kind of separation it is. It assumes that sensible instances of Forms are deficient resemblances of Forms and less real than Forms. There is no trace of either of these claims in early dialogues such as the *Euthyphro*, nor of the characteristic doctrines of the middle dialogues with which those claims are implicated—Recollection, and the radical distinction between Knowledge and Opinion. The Theory of Forms in the middle dialogues is meant to answer questions, especially questions arising out of problems of knowledge, which the early dialogues have not yet raised.

W. A. Heidel remarked in his edition of the *Euthyphro* that "none of the briefer Platonic dialogues can be compared with it for the value of its suggestions towards philosophical theory." This is surely true. The philosophical interest of the dialogue does not lie in the product of its dialectic—no product is announced—but in the rules by which that dialectic proceeds. Those rules, and the assumptions on which they rest, constitute a (not *the*) theory of Forms. It is a theory which operates more at the level of assumption than of explicit statement; but a theory nonetheless, and one whose elements may be put with some precision.

Socrates' aim in the *Euthyphro* is to obtain an answer to the question "What is holiness?" In pursuing his inquiry, he assumes that there is an

Idea or Form of holiness, and that this Form is the same in all holy things. He further assumes that the Form of holiness can be used as a standard by which to judge what things are holy and what are not; that it is an essence, by which or in virtue of which holy things are holy; that it is capable of essential definition, and (apparently) that this definition will be per genus et differentiam. These assumptions constitute a theory of Forms.

The theory is both logical and metaphysical. Logically, Forms play a regulative role in dialectic: as antecedents of "it" in the question "What is it?" they determine the kinds of answer which are acceptable and, perhaps more important, unacceptable in Socrates' search for definition. Metaphysically, Forms exist and affect the career of the world; they are the real natures of things, and the world is what it is because they are what they are.

These two sides of Plato's theory, logical and metaphysical, meet in the notion of real definition. Dialectic is governed by rules and directed toward discovering the nature of things. Its rules are determined by its aim. To say that Forms exist is to say that real definition is possible; to say that real definition is possible is to say that Forms exist. The theory of Forms in the *Euthyphro* is not a superstructure gracelessly added on to dialectic; it is the foundation of dialectic. Without it, dialectic would not proceed by the rules it uses, or work toward the goal at which it aims. Socratic moral inquiry is inquiry about reality.

This is metaphysics, but not the metaphysics of the middle dialogues. The middle dialogues do not abandon the "What is it?" question, but they pursue it in the light of a new ontology. That ontology rests on two principles: the immortality and divinity of the rational soul, and the complete reality and eternity of the objects of knowledge. Those principles, in F. M. Cornford's phrase, are the pillars of Platonism; their architrave is the doctrine of Recollection, the doctrine that the truth of things is always in the soul. The foundation on which this lofty structure rests is a theory of Forms which implies the diminished reality and deficiency of resemblance of sensible objects. None of this is found in the early dialogues.

The theory of Forms in the middle dialogues, then, is neither the same theory as that of the early dialogues, nor a different one. Not different, because it contains the earlier theory as a part. Not the same, because it is directed toward issues which the early dialogues do not raise.

TRANSLATION

EUTHYPHRO / SOCRATES

Characters and Setting (2a–5c)

2a EUTH. What has happened, Socrates, to make you leave your accustomed pastimes in the Lyceum and spend your time here today at the King's Porch? You can hardly have a suit pending before the King, as I do.

SOC. In Athens, Euthyphro, it is not called a suit, but an indictment.

b EUTH. Really? Someone must have indicted you. For I will not suspect you of indicting someone else.

SOC. Certainly not.

EUTH. But someone you?

SOC. Yes.

EUTH. Who is he?

SOC. I do not know the man well, Euthyphro; it appears he is young and not prominent. His name, I think, is Meletus. He belongs to the deme of Pitthus, if you recall a Pitthean Meletus with lanky hair and not much beard, but a hooked nose.

c EUTH. I have not noticed him, Socrates. But what is the charge?

SOC. Charge? One that does him credit, I think. It is no small thing for him, young as he is, to be knowledgeable in so great a matter, for he says he knows how the youth are being corrupted and who is corrupting them. No doubt he is wise, and realizing that, in my ignorance, I corrupt his comrades, he comes to the City as to a mother to accuse me. He alone seems to me to have begun his

41

d   political career correctly, for the right way to begin is to look after
the young men of the City first so that they will be as good as
possible, just as a good farmer naturally looks after his young
plants first and the rest later. So too with Meletus. He will perhaps
3a   first weed out those of us who blight the young shoots, as he
claims, and afterwards he will obviously look after their elders
and become responsible for many great blessings to the City, the
natural result of so fine a beginning.

EUTH. I would hope so, Socrates, but I fear lest the opposite may
happen. He seems to me to have started by injuring the City at
its very hearth in undertaking to wrong you. But tell me, what
does he say you do to corrupt the youth?

b   SOC. It sounds a bit strange at first hearing, my friend. He says I
am a maker of gods, and because I make new ones and do not
worship the old ones, he indicted me on their account, he says.

EUTH. I see, Socrates. It is because you say the divine sign comes
to you from time to time. So he indicts you for making innova-
tions in religious matters and hales you into court to slander you,
knowing full well how easily such things are misrepresented to
c   the multitude. Why I, even me, when I speak about religious
matters in the Assembly and foretell the future, why, they laugh
at me as though I were mad. And yet nothing I ever predicted
has failed to come true. Still, they are jealous of people like us.
We must not worry about them, but face them boldly.

SOC. My dear Euthyphro, being laughed at is perhaps a thing of
little moment. The Athenians, it seems to me, do not much mind
if they think a man is clever as long as they do not suspect him
of teaching his cleverness to others; but if they think he makes
d   others like himself they become angry, whether out of jealousy
as you suggest, or for some other reason.

EUTH. On that point I am not very anxious to test their attitude
toward me.

SOC. Perhaps they think you give yourself sparingly, that you are
unwilling to teach your wisdom. But I fear my own generosity is
such that they think I am willing to pour myself out in speech to
any man—not only without pay, but glad to pay myself if only
someone will listen. So as I just said, if they laugh at me as you
e   say they do at you, it would not be unpleasant to pass the time
in court laughing and joking. But if they are in earnest, how it
will then turn out is unclear—except to you prophets.

EUTH. Perhaps it will not amount to much, Socrates. Perhaps you
will settle your case satisfactorily, as I think I will mine.

SOC. What about that, Euthyphro? Are you plaintiff or defendant?

EUTH. Plaintiff.

SOC. Against whom?

4a EUTH. Someone I am again thought mad to prosecute.

SOC. Really? Has he taken flight?

EUTH. He is far from flying. As a matter of fact, he is well along
in years.

SOC. Who is he?

EUTH. My father.

SOC. Your *father*, dear friend?

EUTH. Yes, indeed.

SOC. But what is the charge? What is the reason for the suit?

EUTH. Murder, Socrates.

SOC. Heracles! Surely, Euthyphro, the majority of people must be
ignorant of what is right. Not just anyone would undertake a
b thing like that. It must require someone quite far gone in wisdom.

EUTH. Very far indeed, Socrates.

SOC. Was the man your father killed a relative? But, of course, he
must have been—you would not be prosecuting him for murder
in behalf of a stranger.

EUTH. It is laughable, Socrates, your thinking it makes a difference
whether or not the man was a relative, and not this, and this
alone: whether his slayer was justified. If so, let him off. If not,
c prosecute him, even if he shares your hearth and table. For if
you knowingly associate with a man like that and do not cleanse
both yourself and him by bringing action at law, the pollution is
equal for you both. Now as a matter of fact, the dead man was a
day-laborer of mine, and when we were farming in Naxos he
worked for us for hire. Well, he got drunk and flew into a rage
with one of our slaves and cut his throat. So my father bound
him hand and foot, threw him in a ditch, and sent a man here
to Athens to consult the religious adviser as to what should be
d done. In the meantime, my father paid no attention to the man
he had bound; he neglected him because he was a murderer and
it made no difference if he died. Which is just what he did. Before
the messenger got back he died of hunger and cold and his bonds.
But even so, my father and the rest of my relatives are angry at
me for prosecuting my father for murder in behalf of a murderer.

He did not kill him, they claim, and even if he did, still, the fellow was a murderer, and it is wrong to be concerned in behalf of a man like that—and anyway, it is unholy for a son to prosecute

e his father for murder. They little know, Socrates, how things stand in religious matters regarding the holy and the unholy.

SOC. But in the name of Zeus, Euthyphro, do you think you yourself know so accurately how matters stand respecting divine law, and things holy and unholy, that with the facts as you declare you can prosecute your own father without fear that it is you, on the contrary, who are doing an unholy thing?

EUTH. I would not be much use, Socrates, nor would Euthyphro
5a differ in any way from the majority of men, if I did not know all such things as this with strict accuracy.

SOC. Well then, my gifted friend, I had best become your pupil. Before the action with Meletus begins I will challenge him on these very grounds. I will say that even in former times I was much concerned to learn about religious matters, but that now, in view of his claiming that I am guilty of loose speech and innovation in these things, I have become your pupil. "And if, Meletus," I shall say, "if you agree that Euthyphro is wise in such

b things, then assume that I worship correctly and drop the case. But if you do not agree, then obtain permission to indict my teacher here in my place for corrupting the old—me and his own father—by teaching me, and by chastising and punishing him." And if I can not persuade him to drop charges or to indict you in place of me, may I not then say the same thing in court that I said in my challenge?

EUTH. By Zeus, if he tried to indict me, I would find his weak spot,
c I think, and the discussion in court would concern him long before it concerned me.

The Request for a Definition (5c–6e)

SOC. I realize that, my friend. That is why I want to become your pupil. I know that this fellow Meletus and no doubt other people too pretend not even to notice you; but he saw through me so keenly and easily that he indicted me for impiety. So now in Zeus's name, tell me what you confidently claimed just now that you knew: what sort of thing do you say the pious and impious are,
d with respect to murder and other things as well? Or is not the holy, just by itself, the same in every action? And the unholy, in

turn, the opposite of all the holy—is it not like itself, and does not everything which is to be unholy have a certain single character with respect to unholiness?

EUTH. No doubt, Socrates.

SOC. Then tell me, what do you say the holy is? And what is the unholy?

EUTH. Well, I say that the holy is what I am doing now, prosecuting murder and temple theft and everything of the sort, whether

e father or mother or anyone else is guilty of it. And not prosecuting is unholy. Now, Socrates, examine the proof I give you that this is a dictate of divine law. I have offered it before to other people to show that it is established right not to let off someone guilty of impiety, no matter who he happens to be. For these same people worship Zeus as the best and most righteous of the gods. They agree that he put his own father in bonds for unjustly

6a swallowing his children; yes, and that that father had in his turn castrated his father for similar reasons. Yet me they are angry at for indicting my father for his injustice. So they contradict themselves: they say one thing about the gods and another about me.

SOC. I wonder if this is why I am being prosecuted, Euthyphro, because when anyone says such things about the gods, I somehow find it difficult to accept? Perhaps this is why people claim I transgress. But as it is, if even you who know such things so well

b accept them, people like me must apparently concede. What indeed are we to say, we who ourselves agree that we know nothing of them. But in the name of Zeus, the God of Friendship, tell me: do you truly believe that these things happened so?

EUTH. Yes, and things still more wonderful than these, Socrates, things the multitude does not know.

SOC. Do you believe there is really war among the gods, and terrible enmities and battles, and other sorts of things our poets tell, which embellish other things sacred to us through the work of

c our capable painters, but especially the robe covered with embroidery that is carried to the Acropolis at the Great Panathenaea? Are we, Euthyphro, to say those things are so?

EUTH. Not only those, Socrates. As I just said, I shall explain many other things about religion to you if you wish, and you may rest assured that what you hear will amaze you.

SOC. I should not be surprised. But explain them another time at

d your leisure; right now, try to answer more clearly the question I just asked. For, my friend, you did not sufficiently teach me

before, when I asked you what the holy is; you said that the thing
you are doing now is holy, prosecuting your father for murder.

EUTH. Yes, and I told the truth, Socrates.

SOC. Perhaps. But, Euthyphro, are there not many other things
you say are holy too?

EUTH. Of course there are.

SOC. Do you recall that I did not ask you to teach me about some
one or two of the many things which are holy, but about that
e   characteristic itself by which all holy things are holy? For you
agreed, I think, that it is by one character that unholy things are
unholy and holy things holy. Or do you not recall?

EUTH. I do.

SOC. Then teach me what this very character is, so that I may look
to it and use it as a standard by which, should those things which
you or someone else may do be of that sort, I may affirm them
to be holy, but should they not be of that sort, deny it.

EUTH. Well if you wish it so, Socrates, I shall tell you.

SOC. I do indeed wish it.

First Definition: The Holy,
What Is Loved by the Gods (6e–8b)

EUTH. Then what is dear to the gods is holy, and what is not dear
7a   to them is unholy.

SOC. Excellent, Euthyphro. You have now answered as I asked.
Whether correctly, I do not yet know—but clearly you will now
go on to teach me in addition that what you say is true.

EUTH. Of course.

SOC. Come then, let us examine what it is we are saying. The thing
and the person dear to the gods is holy; the thing and the person
hateful to the gods is unholy; and the holy is not the same as the
unholy, but its utter opposite. Is that what we are saying?

EUTH. It is.

SOC. Yes, and it appears to be well said?

b EUTH. I think so, Socrates.

SOC. Now, Euthyphro, we also said, did we not, that the gods quarrel and disagree with one another and that there is enmity among
them?

EUTH. We did.

SOC. But what is that disagreement which causes enmity and anger
about, my friend? Look at it this way: If you and I disagreed

about a question of number, about which of two sums is greater, would our disagreement cause us to become angry with each

c other and make us enemies? Or would we take to counting in a case like that, and quickly settle our dispute?

EUTH. Of course we would.

SOC. So too, if we disagreed about a question of the larger or smaller, we would take to measurement and put an end to our disagreement quickly?

EUTH. True.

SOC. And go to the balance, I imagine, to settle a dispute about heavier and lighter?

EUTH. Certainly.

SOC. But what sort of thing would make us enemies, angry at each other, if we disagree about it and are unable to arrive at a deci-

d sion? Perhaps you cannot say offhand, but I suggest you consider whether it would not be the just and unjust, beautiful and ugly, good and evil. Are not these the things, when we disagree about them and cannot reach a satisfactory decision, concerning which we on occasion become enemies—you, and I, and all other men?

EUTH. Yes, Socrates. This kind of disagreement has its source there.

SOC. What about the gods, Euthyphro? If they were to disagree, would they not disagree for the same reasons?

EUTH. Necessarily.

e SOC. Then by your account, my noble friend, different gods must believe that different things are just—and beautiful and ugly, good and evil. For surely they would not quarrel unless they disagreed on this. True?

EUTH. You are right.

SOC. Now, what each of them believes to be beautiful and good and just they also love, and the opposites of those things they hate?

EUTH. Of course.

SOC. Yes, but the same things, you say, are thought by some gods to be just and by others unjust. Those are the things concerning

8a which disagreement causes them to quarrel and make war on one another. True?

EUTH. Yes.

SOC. Then the same things, it seems, are both hated by the gods and loved by the gods, and would be both dear to the gods and hateful to the gods.

EUTH. It seems so.

soc. Then by this account, Euthyphro, the same things would be both holy and unholy.

EUTH. I suppose so.

soc. Then you have not answered my question, my friend. I did not ask you what same thing happens to be both holy and unholy; yet what is dear to the gods is hateful to the gods, it seems. And so, Euthyphro, it would not be surprising if what you are now b doing in punishing your father were dear to Zeus, but hateful to Cronos and Uranus, and loved by Hephaestus, but hateful to Hera, and if any of the other gods disagree about it, the same will be true of them too.

First Interlude (8b–9c)

EUTH. But Socrates, surely none of the gods disagree about this, that he who kills another man unjustly should answer for it.

soc. Really, Euthyphro? Have you ever heard it argued among *men* c that he who kills unjustly or does anything else unjustly should not answer for it?

EUTH. Why, people never stop arguing things like that, especially in the law courts. They do a host of wrongs and then say and do everything to get off.

soc. Yes, but do they admit the wrong, Euthyphro, and admitting it, nevertheless claim they should not answer for it?

EUTH. No, they certainly do not do that.

soc. Then they do not do and say everything: for they do not, I think, dare to contend or debate the point that if they in fact did d wrong they should not answer for it. Rather, I think, they deny they did wrong. Well?

EUTH. True.

soc. So they do not contend that those who do wrong should not answer for it, but rather, perhaps, about who it is that did the wrong, and what he did, and when.

EUTH. True.

soc. Now is it not also the same with the gods, if as your account has it, they quarrel about what is just and unjust, and some claim that others do wrong and some deny it? Presumably no one, god e or man, would dare to claim that he who does a wrong should not answer for it.

EUTH. Yes, on the whole what you say is true, Socrates.

soc. But I imagine that those who disagree—both men and gods, if indeed the gods do disagree—disagree about particular things which have been done. They differ over given actions, some claiming they were done justly and others unjustly. True?

EUTH. Certainly.

9a SOC. Come now, my friend, teach me and make me wiser. Where is your proof that all gods believe that a man has been unjustly killed who was hired as a laborer, became a murderer, was bound by the master of the dead slave, and died of his bonds before the man who bound him could learn from the religious advisers what to do? Where is your proof that it is right for a son to indict and prosecute his father for murder in behalf of a man like that? Come, try to show me clearly that all the gods genuinely believe

b this action right. If you succeed, I shall praise you for your wisdom and never stop.

EUTH. Well, I can certainly do it, Socrates, but it is perhaps not a small task.

SOC. I see. You think I am harder to teach than the judges, for you will certainly make it clear to them that actions such as your father's are wrong, and that all the gods hate them.

EUTH. Very clear indeed, Socrates, if they listen to what I say.

Second Definition: The Holy, What Is Loved by All the Gods (9c–11b)

c SOC. They will listen, if you seem to speak well. But here is something that occurred to me while you were talking. I asked myself, "If Euthyphro were to teach me beyond any question that all the gods believe a death of this sort wrong, what more have I learned from Euthyphro about what the holy and the unholy are? The death, it seems, would be hateful to the gods, but what is holy and what is unholy proved just now not to be marked off by this, for what was hateful to the gods proved dear to the gods as well." So I let you off on that point, Euthyphro: if you wish, let all the

d gods believe your father's action wrong and let all of them hate it. But is this the correction we are now to make in your account, that what *all* the gods hate is unholy, and what *all* the gods love is holy, but what some love and some hate is neither or both? Do you mean for us now to mark off the holy and the unholy in that way?

EUTH. What is to prevent it, Socrates?

SOC. Nothing, at least as far as I am concerned, Euthyphro. But, examine your account to see whether if you assume this, you will most easily teach me what you promised.

e EUTH. But I would certainly say that the holy is what all the gods love, and that the opposite, what all the gods hate, is unholy.

SOC. Well, Euthyphro, should we examine this in turn to see if it is true? Or should we let it go, accept it from ourselves or anyone else without more ado, and agree that a thing is so if only someone says it is? Or should we examine what a person means when he says something?

EUTH. Of course. I believe, though, that this time what I say is true.

10a SOC. Perhaps we shall learn better, my friend. For consider: is the holy loved by the gods because it is holy? Or is it holy because it is loved by the gods?

EUTH. I do not know what you mean, Socrates.

SOC. Then I will try to put it more clearly. We speak of carrying and being carried, of leading and being led, of seeing and being seen. And you understand in such cases, do you not, that they differ from each other, and how they differ?

EUTH. I think I do.

SOC. Now, is there such a thing as being loved, and is it different from loving?

EUTH. Of course.

b SOC. Then tell me: if a thing is being carried, is it being carried because of the carrying, or for some other reason?

EUTH. No, for that reason.

SOC. And if a thing is being led, it is being led because of the leading? And if being seen, being seen because of the seeing?

EUTH. Certainly.

SOC. Then it is not because a thing is being seen that the seeing exists; on the contrary, it is because of the seeing that it is being seen. Nor is it because a thing is being led that the leading exists; it is because of the leading that it is being led. Nor is it because a thing is being carried that the carrying exists; it is because of

c the carrying that it is being carried. Is what I mean quite clear, Euthyphro? I mean this: if something comes to be or something is affected, it is not because it is a thing which is coming to be that the process of coming to be exists, but, because of the process of coming to be, it is a thing which is coming to be; and it is not because it is affected that the affecting exists, but because of the affecting, the thing is affected. Do you agree?

EUTH. Yes.

soc. Now, what is being loved is either a thing coming to be something or a something affected by something.

EUTH. Of course.

soc. And so it is as true here as it was before: it is not because a
thing is being loved that there is loving by those who love it; it is
because of the loving that it is being loved.

EUTH. Necessarily.

d soc. Then what are we to say about the holy, Euthyphro? Is it loved
by all the gods, as your account has it?

EUTH. Yes.

soc. Because it is holy? Or for some other reason?

EUTH. No, for that reason.

soc. Then it is loved because it is holy, not holy because it is loved?

EUTH. It seems so.

soc. Moreover, what is loved and dear to the gods is loved because
of their loving.

EUTH. Of course.

soc. Then what is dear to the gods is not [the same as] holy, Euthyphro, nor is the holy [the same as] dear to the gods, as you
claim: the two are different.

e EUTH. But why, Socrates?

soc. Because we agreed that the holy is loved because it is holy,
not holy because it is loved.

EUTH. Yes.

soc. But what is dear to the gods is, because it is loved by the gods,
dear to the gods by reason of this same loving; it is not loved
because it is dear to the gods.

EUTH. True.

soc. But if in fact what is dear to the gods and the holy were the
same, my friend, then, if the holy were loved because it is holy,
11a   what is dear to the gods would be loved because it is dear to the
gods; but if what is dear to the gods were dear to the gods because
the gods love it, the holy would be holy because it is loved. But
as it is, you see, the opposite is true, and the two are completely
different. For the one (what is dear to the gods) is of the sort to
be loved *because* it is loved; the other (the holy), because it is of
the sort to be loved, *therefore* is loved. It would seem, Euthyphro,
that when you asked what the holy is, you did not mean to make
its nature and reality clear to me; you mentioned a mere affection
of it—the holy has been so affected as to be loved by all the gods.
b   But what it really is, you have not yet said. So if you please,

Euthyphro, do not conceal things from me: start again from the beginning and tell me what sort of thing the holy is. We will not quarrel over whether it is loved by the gods, or whether it is affected in other ways. Tell me in earnest: what is the holy and unholy?

Second Interlude: Socrates and Daedalus (11b–e)

EUTH. But, Socrates, I do not know how to tell you what I mean. Somehow everything I propose goes round in circles on us and will not stand still.

SOC. Your words are like the words of my ancestor, Daedalus. If I
c had offered them, if I had put them forward, you would perhaps have laughed at me because my kinship to him makes my words run away and refuse to stay put. But as things are, it is you who put them forward and we must find another joke. It is for you that they refuse to stand still, as you yourself agree.

EUTH. But, Socrates, the joke, I think, still tells. It is not me who makes them move around and not stay put. I think you are the
d Daedalus. If it had been up to me, they would have stayed where they were.

SOC. Then apparently, my friend, I am even more skillful than my venerated ancestor, inasmuch as he made only his own works move, whereas I, it seems, not only make my own move but other people's too. And certainly the most subtle feature of my art is that I am skilled against my will. For I really want arguments to stand still, to stand fixed and immovable. I want that more than
e the wealth of Tantalus and the skill of Daedalus combined. But enough of this. Since you seem to be lazy and soft, I will come to your aid and help you teach me about the holy. Don't give up; consider whether you do not think that all the holy is necessarily just.

EUTH. I do.

Requirements for Definition (11e–12e)

SOC. Then is all the just holy? Or is all the holy just, but not all the
12a just holy—part of it holy, part something else?

EUTH. I don't follow you, Socrates.

SOC. And yet you are as much wiser than I am as you are younger. As I said, you are lazy and soft because of your wealth of wisdom.

My friend, extend yourself: what I mean is not hard to understand. I mean exactly the opposite of what the poet meant when he said that he was "unwilling to insult Zeus, the Creator, who made all things; for where there is fear there is also reverence."

b I disagree with him. Shall I tell you why?

EUTH. Yes, certainly.

SOC. I do not think that "where there is fear there is also reverence." I think people fear disease and poverty and other such things—fear them, but have no reverence for what they fear. Do you agree?

EUTH. Yes, certainly.

SOC. Where there is reverence, however, there is also fear. For if anyone stands in reverence and awe of something, does he not

c at the same time fear and dread the imputation of wickedness?

EUTH. Yes, he does.

SOC. Then it is not true that "where there is fear there is also reverence," but rather where there is reverence there is also fear, even though reverence is not everywhere that fear is: fear is broader than reverence. Reverence is part of fear just as odd is part of number, so that it is not true that where there is number there is odd, but where there is odd there is number. Surely you follow me now?

EUTH. Yes, I do.

SOC. Well then, that is the sort of thing I had in mind when I asked

d if, where there is just, there is also holy. Or is it rather that where there is holy there is also just, but holy is not everywhere just is, since the holy is part of the just. Shall we say that, or do you think differently?

EUTH. No, I think you are right.

SOC. Then consider the next point. If the holy is part of the just, it would seem that we must find out what part of the just the holy is. Now, to take an example we used a moment ago, if you were to ask what part of number the even is, and what kind of number it is, I would say that it is number with equal rather than unequal sides. Do you agree?

EUTH. Yes, I do.

e SOC. Then try in the same way to teach me what part of the just is holy, so that I may tell Meletus to wrong me no longer and not to indict me for impiety, since I have already learned from you what things are pious and holy and what are not.

Third Definition: The Holy,
Ministry to the Gods (12e–14b)

EUTH. Well, Socrates, I think that part of the just which is pious
and holy is about ministering to the gods, and the remaining part
of the just is about ministering to men.

SOC. That appears excellently put, Euthyphro. But there is still one

13a   small point left; I do not yet understand what you mean by "ministering." You surely do not mean that ministering to the gods is
like ministering to other things, though I suppose we do talk that
way, as when we say that it is not everyone who knows how to
minister to horses, but only the horse-trainer. That is true, is it
not?

EUTH. Yes, certainly.

SOC. Because horse-training takes care of horses.

EUTH. Yes.

SOC. And it is not everyone who knows how to minister to dogs,
but only the huntsman.

EUTH. True.

SOC. Because huntsmanship takes care of dogs.

b EUTH. Yes.

SOC. And the same is true of herdsmanship and cattle?

EUTH. Yes, certainly.

SOC. And holiness and piety minister to the gods, Euthyphro? Is
that what you are saying?

EUTH. Yes, it is.

SOC. Now, is not all ministering meant to accomplish the same
thing? I mean this: to take care of a thing is to aim at some good,
some benefit, for the thing cared for, as you see horses benefited
and improved when ministered to by horse-training. Do you not
agree?

EUTH. Yes, I do.

SOC. And dogs are benefited by huntsmanship, and cattle by herds-

c   manship, and similarly with other things as well—or do you think
ministering can work harm to what is cared for?

EUTH. No, by Zeus, not I.

SOC. But rather is beneficial?

EUTH. Of course.

SOC. Now, does holiness, which is to be a kind of ministering, benefit the gods? Does it improve them? Would you really agree that
when you do something holy you are making some god better?

EUTH. No, by Zeus, not I.

soc. I did not think you meant that, Euthyphro. Far from it. That
d   is why I asked you what you meant by ministering to the gods: I
     did not believe you meant such a thing as that.

EUTH. Yes, and you were right, Socrates. I did not mean that.

soc. Very well. But what kind of ministering to the gods is holiness?

EUTH. The kind, Socrates, which slaves minister to their masters.

soc. I see. Holiness would, it seems, be a kind of service to gods.

EUTH. Quite so.

soc. Now, can you tell me what sort of product service to physicians
     would be likely to produce? Would it not be health?

EUTH. Yes.

e   soc. What about service to ship-builders? Is there not some prod-
     uct it produces?

EUTH. Clearly it produces a ship, Socrates.

soc. And service to house-builders produces a house?

EUTH. Yes.

soc. Then tell me, my friend: What sort of product would service
     to the gods produce? Clearly you know, for you say you know
     better than anyone else about religious matters.

EUTH. Yes; and I am telling the truth, Socrates.

soc. Then in the name of Zeus, tell me: What is that fine product
     which the gods produce, using us as servants?

EUTH. They produce many things, Socrates, excellent things.

14a soc. So do generals, my friend, but still their work can be summed
     up quite easily. Generals produce victory in war. Not so?

EUTH. Of course.

soc. And farmers too produce many excellent things, but still their
     work can be summed up as producing food from the earth.

EUTH. Of course.

soc. But what about the many excellent things the gods produce?
     How does one sum up their production?

EUTH. I told you a moment ago, Socrates, that it is difficult to learn
b   accurately how things stand in these matters. Speaking freely,
     however, I can tell you that if a man knows how to say and do
     things acceptable to the gods in prayer and sacrifice, those things
     are holy; and they preserve both families and cities and keep
     them safe. The opposite of what is acceptable to the gods is im-
     pious, and this overturns and destroys all things.

Fourth Definition: The Holy,
an Art of Prayer and Sacrifice (14b–15c)

soc. You could have summed up the answer to my question much

more briefly, Euthyphro, if you had wished. But you are not eager
to instruct me; I see that now. In fact, you just came right up to

c   the point and turned away, and if you had given me an answer,
I would by now have learned holiness from you. But as it is, the
questioner must follow the answerer wherever he leads: So what
do you say the holy and holiness is this time? Knowledge of how
to pray and sacrifice?

EUTH. Yes.

SOC. Now, to sacrifice is to give to the gods and to pray is to ask
something from them?

EUTH. Exactly, Socrates.

d   SOC. Then by this account, holiness is knowledge of how to ask
from and give to the gods.

EUTH. Excellent, Socrates. You have followed what I said.

SOC. Yes, my friend, for I am enamored of your wisdom and attend
to it closely, so naturally what you say does not fall to the ground
wasted. But tell me, what is the nature of this service we render
the gods? You say it is to ask from them and give to them?

EUTH. Yes, I do.

SOC. Now, to ask rightly is to ask for things we need from them?

EUTH. Certainly.

e   SOC. And again, to give rightly is to give in return what they happen to need from us? For surely there would be no skill involved
in giving things to someone that he did not need.

EUTH. You are right, Socrates.

SOC. So the art of holiness would be a kind of business transaction
between gods and men.

EUTH. Yes; if it pleases you to call it that.

SOC. Why, nothing pleases me unless it happens to be true. But tell
me, what benefit do the gods gain from the gifts they receive
from us? It is clear to everyone what they give, for we have noth-

15a   ing good they have not given. But how are they benefited by what
they get from us? Or do we claim the larger share in the transaction to such an extent that we get all good from them, and they
nothing from us?

EUTH. But, Socrates, do you think the gods benefit from the things
they receive from us?

SOC. Why, Euthyphro, whatever could these gifts of ours to the
gods then be?

EUTH. What do you suppose, other than praise and honor and as
I just said, things which are acceptable?

b soc. Then the holy is what is acceptable, Euthyphro, and not what is beneficial or loved by the gods?

EUTH. I certainly think it is loved by the gods, beyond all other things.

soc. Then, on the contrary, the holy is what is loved by the gods.

EUTH. Yes, that beyond anything.

soc. Will it surprise you if in saying this your words get up and walk? You call me a Daedalus. You say I make them walk. But I say that you are a good deal more skillful than Daedalus, for you make them walk in circles. Or are you not aware that our account

c has gone round and come back again to the same place? Surely you remember in what went before that the holy appeared to us not to be the same as what is loved by the gods: the two were different. Do you recall?

EUTH. Yes, I recall.

soc. Then do you not now realize that you are saying that what is loved by the gods is holy? But the holy in fact is something other than dear to the gods, is it not?

EUTH. Yes.

soc. Then either we were wrong a moment ago in agreeing to that, or, if we were right in assuming it then, we are wrong in what we are saying now.

EUTH. It seems so.

Conclusion (15c–16a)

soc. Let us begin again from the beginning, and ask what the holy is, for I shall not willingly give up until I learn. Please do not

d scorn me: bend every effort of your mind and now tell me the truth. You know it if any man does, and, like Proteus, you must not be let go before you speak.[1] For if you did not know the holy and unholy with certainty, you could not possibly undertake to prosecute your aged father for murder in behalf of a hired man. You would fear to risk the gods, lest your action be wrongful, and you would be ashamed before men. But as it is, I am confident that you think you know with certainty what is holy and

e what is not. So say it, friend Euthyphro. Do not conceal what it is you believe.

1. See *Od.* iv. 456–58.

EUTH. Some other time, Socrates. Right now I must hurry somewhere and I am already late.

SOC. What are you doing, my friend! You leave me and cast me
down from my high hope that I should learn from you what
things are holy and what are not, and escape the indictment of
Meletus by showing him that, due to Euthyphro, I am now wise
in religious matters, that I no longer ignorantly indulge in loose
speech and innovation, and most especially, that I shall live better
the rest of my life.

II: THE APOLOGY

COMMENT

In the year 399 B.C., in Athens, Socrates son of Sophroniscus, of the deme Alopece, aged seventy, was brought to trial on a writ of impiety, a *graphe asebeias*. He was found guilty and condemned to death. The exact indictment or, more accurately perhaps, sworn information has been preserved by Diogenes Laertius (II.40) on the authority of the scholar Favorinus, who found the information in the Athenian archives: "This indictment and affidavit is sworn by Meletus, the son of Meletus of Pitthus, against Socrates, the son of Sophroniscus of Alopece: Socrates is guilty of refusing to recognize the gods recognized by the state, and of introducing other new divinities. He is also guilty of corrupting the youth. The penalty demanded is death." There were, then, three counts: refusing to acknowledge the gods acknowledged by the City, introducing new (or strange, *kaina*) divinities, and corrupting the youth.

It was, of course, a celebrated case, and for years afterward controversy swirled around the verdict. Unlike most controversies, however, this one produced great literature, specifically Plato's *Apology*. The *Apology* is not a dialogue but a speech, a speech of such force and directness that at one level it cannot be misunderstood. Yet despite its surface simplicity, it is a complex document and contains several levels of irony in its depths. Irony, indeed, attaches to its very name. An apologia is a defense. But the *Apology* is something other than a defense, at least as that term is commonly understood.

The Silence of Socrates

There is a Hellenistic tradition that Socrates stood mute at his trial, or at least had as good as nothing to say in his own behalf. The tradition is late, and "the Silence of Socrates" might easily be dismissed—if it were not for the fact that it is supported by and almost certainly derived from Plato's *Gorgias*.

Callicles in the *Gorgias* attacks philosophy and condemns it as useless— it is, he says, a charming thing to pursue in moderation while young, but it becomes the ruin of a man if pursued too intensely or too long. His advice to Socrates issues in a prediction (486a–b): "If someone were to take you or anyone like you and drag you off to jail, accusing you of guilt when you had done no wrong, you know perfectly well that you wouldn't know what to do. You would gape with dizziness, and not have a word to say. Once brought to court, though your accuser was ever so contemptible a knave, you would die if he chose to demand death." Socrates himself later repeats the prediction. He claims at the conclusion of his discussion with Callicles that he is the only true statesman in Athens, and he foresees his own death. Put on trial, he will have nothing to say in his own defense: "I shall be like a doctor tried before a jury of children on charges brought by a pastry-cook." The doctor, whose healing ministrations consist in cutting, burning, and administering vile-tasting doses, would have nothing to say (522b).

> I know that if I am brought into court, it will be the same with me. . . . If someone accuses me of corrupting the youth by reducing them to perplexity, or of abusing their elders with sharp and pointed speech, in public or private, I won't be able to tell the truth, which is, "I say all these things justly, Gentlemen and Judges, and do so for your benefit." Nor will I be able to say anything else. The result, no doubt, will be that I'll take whatever comes.

This is a powerful variation on a theme which recurs in many dialogues: the helplessness of the philosopher in a court of law. He will appear ridiculous, even mad, to the multitude. So far, at least, Callicles is right.

In the *Apology*, of course, Socrates has a great deal to say, and he says it with high art. Yet the *Gorgias* passage, far from contradicting the *Apology*, is meant to comment on it. As Dodds remarks in *Gorgias*, "The pastry-cook's speech is a witty parody of the complaints brought against Socrates at his trial." The speech is followed by a passage which recapitulates the main theme of the *Apology*: the only genuine evil is the evil of wickedness; for the good man there is no evil in death, as there is none in life. The myth which concludes the *Gorgias* provides that theme with an eschatology.

Rhetoric in the Apology

Socrates cannot speak in his own defense. Yet the *Gorgias* is a comment on the *Apology*. This is incongruous, and the incongruity is repeated within the body of the *Apology* itself. The *Apology* falls into three main parts: Socrates' speech of defense (17a–35d); the speech of the counter-penalty, which follows Socrates' conviction (35e–38b); and an epilogue, addressed respectively to those who voted for and against condemnation (38c–42a). The first and longest of these, the speech of defense, is of primary importance here.

The problem with that speech, simply stated, is that it seems to bear the mark of falsehood. In the Introduction (17a–18a), Socrates denies that he has any skill in speaking, unless that means ability to speak the truth. He asks his judges to overlook the fact that he will make his defense with the same *logoi*—the word could mean "arguments" but in its context must have been taken by his audience to mean "words"—which he has been accustomed to use in the marketplace. He remarks on his advanced age, on the fact that he has not previously been brought to trial, and on his unfamiliarity with the ways of the lawcourts. All of this is parallel, point by point, to other speeches which have come down to us from Lysias, Isocrates, and Aeschines. The man who cannot make a speech is providing a textbook example of a forensic exordium.

The exordium is not only rhetorical. As Burnet points out, it is a rhetorical parody of rhetoric. The diction is far removed from the marketplace: it is periodic and marked by the neatly balanced antitheses characteristic of Greek rhetorical style. As with diction, so with structure. The speech, having begun with a proper Exordium, proceeds to a Prothesis, a statement of the case and plan of the plea (18a–19a); it then offers a Refutation (19a–28a), first directed against the Old Accusers who have stirred up prejudice against Socrates (19a–24b) and then against the actual charges brought by Meletus with the support of Anytus and Lycon (24a–28a). There follows a Digression (28a–34b), normally used to win the audience to the speaker's side, here used to describe Socrates' peculiar mission to Athens; the speech then closes with a well-marked Peroration (34b–35d). As Dyer and Seymour remark, "All the laws of oratorical art are here carefully observed, though the usual practices of oratory are sharply criticized. The five natural heads of the argument are unmistakable."

We happen to have a remarkable piece of contemporary evidence which shows how highly Socrates' speech was regarded. Isocrates, who was a young man at the time of the trial, later founded a school of rhetoric in Athens which competed with the Academy. At the end of his long life, he wrote a kind of *apologia pro sua vita*, the *Antidosis*. He there adopts the fiction of a capital charge brought against him by an informer and constructs a set-piece courtroom defense. At point after point, he implicitly compares himself to Socrates, and he studiously echoes the speech of the *Apology*. From a self-acknowledged master of rhetoric comes a tribute: the *Apology* was regarded in its own time as a paradigm of rhetorical art.

This, then, is the first level of irony in Socrates' speech of defense. Irony, pitched at its lowest, involves saying less than you think and sometimes the opposite of what you mean. It can look very much like dishonesty. This first level of irony in the *Apology* presents an apparent falsehood: Socrates disclaims ability to make a speech, then proceeds to make so able a speech that it is a masterpiece of rhetoric.

Rhetorical Incongruity

But the *Apology* is a highly peculiar masterpiece. Socrates constructs an engine of rhetoric according to a well-marked plan. But engines have a function, and the function of forensic rhetoric is to win conviction if prosecuting and acquittal if accused. The engine Socrates constructs does not work this way at all. Far from aiming at acquittal, the speech avowedly aims at telling the truth in accordance with justice even if the truth leads to conviction. Far from attempting to prove the charges in the indictment false, it does not even deny them. There is, then, gross incongruity between the form of the speech and its function: whereas in diction and structure it is a superb example of forensic rhetoric, in method and aim, at least in the ordinary sense, it is not rhetorical at all.

Socrates does not so much as deny the charges against him. He meets the charge of irreligion by cross-examining Meletus, his accuser, and trapping him in inconsistency. Meletus is incautious enough to assert that Socrates acknowledges no gods, that he is a complete atheist, although he had sworn in his indictment that Socrates had introduced new divinities. Socrates merely shows that since divinities are either gods or children of gods, acknowledgment of divinities implies acknowledgment of gods (26b–27e). He later denies atheism (35d); but he does not deny the charge of failing to acknowledge the gods the City acknowledges, presumably for the reason given in the *Euthyphro* (6a–b, cf. 5a–b)—namely, that he finds it difficult to accept the traditional stories of the gods' hatred and enmity toward each other. Nor does he anywhere deny the charge of introducing strange divinities; he explains the charge only by referring to his accustomed Sign, which he explicitly describes as godlike and divine. He nowhere denies corrupting the youth. He argues against Meletus that either he does not corrupt them or he corrupts them unintentionally (25d–26a)—but this is not to deny that he corrupts them, and mens rea was not a developed concept in Athenian law. He offers witnesses who will testify on the point in his behalf and suggests that Meletus call them (33d–34b). He denies that he corrupts by teaching, on the ground that he has never taught or taken money for teaching; but he admits that any man is free to hear what he has to say (33a–b). The closest he comes to denying the charge of corrupting the youth is to describe his peculiar mission to Athens: that of turning men to the pursuit of virtue at the behest of the god at Delphi. He adds, "If in saying these things I corrupt the youth, that would be terrible indeed." Finally, he nowhere denies the charge of impiety, though he describes a kind of defense, expected and unoffered, which would have made him guilty of it (35c–d).

This, then, is the second level of irony in the *Apology*. The man who cannot give a speech gives a speech. The speech he gives shows he cannot give a speech. On trial for his life, in a circumstance which calls for forensic rhetoric, he offers rhetoric which is not forensic.

Counter-Rhetoric

Socrates' speech might easily be construed as a kind of counter-rhetoric.

In diction and structure, the speech is rhetorical. The bulk of Socrates' Refutation is directed, not toward Meletus and the formal indictment, but toward the prejudice raised against him by the Old Accusers, especially Aristophanes, for the reason that, as Socrates himself says, he was confused in the popular mind with the Sophists. Aristophanes portrayed him in the *Clouds* as a man who inquired into things in the heavens and beneath the earth, and made the weaker argument stronger. Socrates remarks, "The men who spread that report are my dangerous accusers; for their hearers believe that those who inquire into such things acknowledge no gods" (18c). The charge of making the weaker argument stronger—Wrong Logic triumphs over Right Logic in the *Clouds*—was particularly damaging, because it carried the implication of pernicious skepticism, associated with sophistry.

The Sophists' stock in trade was rhetoric; Socrates was popularly identified with them, and this was a serious complaint against him. If his primary aim were to avoid conviction, true rhetoric would require that he abstain from anything that even hinted of rhetoric. Had he chosen to conduct his defense in the plain speech he seemed to promise, he would have done much to allay the prejudice against him; as it was, the vote was very close (36a). Instead, he disclaims ability to speak in the course of a masterful speech before an audience thoroughly familiar with the uses of political and forensic oratory. His hearers would not have found the apparent attempt at deception amusing. Irony, *eironeia*, was no virtue, but rather a defect of character, as Theophrastus' portrait of the Ironical Man in the *Characters* makes clear: it was an attribute typically associated with foxes—and with Socrates. Thus, though Socrates denies the truth of the portrait drawn of him in the *Clouds*, his use of rhetoric suggests sophistry, and the very skill of his use confirms the suggestion. His substantive claims, though true, are made to seem false by the manner in which they are issued. In circumstances which call for appearing as an ordinary, domesticated farmyard fowl, he has given himself the character of the fox.

As Aristotle remarks, one rule of rhetoric is to make your character look right. This Socrates does not do. Another rule is to put your audience in the right frame of mind, to make them feel, as Aristotle puts it, friendly and placable. Clearly, if you mean to persuade, it is best not to offend, and the advice becomes more urgent if you are pleading a cause before five hundred dicasts who function as both jurymen and judges, finding law as well as fact, and who will be moved, humanly, quite as much by their emotions as by their intellects.

Socrates does little enough to make his judges feel "friendly and placable." The manner in which he deals with the counter-penalty stands as a vivid symbol of the speech of defense itself. He has been found guilty. Meletus has proposed death. Socrates must suggest an alternate penalty, and between those two penalties the court by law must choose—no splitting the difference. At this of all points, Socrates suggests that if penalty is to be assessed according to desert, his penalty should be public subsistence in the Prytaneum in the manner of an Olympic victor. The same tone is a constant undercurrent in his speech of defense. He disclaims clever speaking before an audience quite familiar with its devices, and he uses clever speech. He uses rhetoric to deny sophistry. On trial for impiety, he politely explains that the conduct which brought him into court was prompted by obedience to the god. Before a jury holding power of life and death, he says that he will not give up his service to the god no matter what their decision; in the circumstances, this appears as something very close to outright defiance. After remarking that his habit of cross-questioning people—itself associated with sophistry and with making the weaker argument stronger—has been a source not only of prejudice but hatred, he gives a public specimen of it in his cross-examination of Meletus; the results are devastating, but in the circumstances, tell against Socrates himself. He attacks politicians, poets, and craftsmen for claiming knowledge of things of which they are ignorant; and he does this before a jury of five hundred men and a large and restless audience, most of whom had served in some political office, most of whom were craftsmen, and most of whom regarded poets as sources of moral and religious instruction. Socrates is here doing something more than suggesting to his judges that they are a group of ignorant men: he is prodding an exposed political nerve. He is telling a jury of democrats, who have vivid, sore recollections of oligarchical persecution under the Thirty Tyrants, and who fear for the stability of their constituted democracy, that they and their leadership are grossly and radically ignorant, if not morally bankrupt. He goes so far, indeed, as to suggest that it is impossible for a decent man to play an active part in political life and service (31e–32a). He is speaking to a large group of survivors.

Socrates, in short, challenges the basic piety on which government by the Many rested—and his habit of so doing was a principal reason for the charge that he corrupted the youth. It is beside the point that he would have challenged with equal vigor the pieties of government by the few.

Socrates' speech of defense is magnificent. But if rhetoric is, as Aristotle says, the faculty of observing in each case the available means of persuasion, the speech is not forensic rhetoric. Disclaiming clever speech, Socrates gives a speech which seems too clever by half but is not half clever enough. He offers rhetoric which seems very like the opposite of rhetoric.

Two Concepts of Rhetoric

The connection between the *Gorgias* and the *Apology* is intimate. To understand more fully how this is so, it is helpful to realize that the *Gorgias* puts forward not one but two concepts of rhetoric.

Rhetoric is usually defined as power of persuasion, indifferent to truth. Gorgias, after several false starts, is led to define it as "the ability to persuade with words—in law courts, in Council and Assembly, in civic gatherings of any kind" (452e). The persuasion primarily involves what is just and unjust (454b), but it is irrational in that it is based, not on knowledge derived from instruction, but on belief without knowledge. Rhetoric is, in fact, a kind of trick. The orator has no need to know the

actual truth of things, for his aim is a kind of persuasion which enables
him to appear to the ignorant to know more than those who have knowledge (459c).

This is why Socrates, in conversation with Polus, denies that rhetoric
is an art at all; for art implies knowledge, but rhetoric lacks knowledge
and cannot render an account: it is *alogon* as being without a *logos*. It is
a mere knack, the intellectual counterpart of pastry-cooking, a species
of *kolakeia*—"flattery," though the word has baser connotations—aimed
at gratification and pleasure and indifferent to truth. Though often mistaken for statesmanship, it is a mere image or counterfeit of statesmanship. Rhetoric stands to the art of the statesman as pastry-cooking stands
to medicine; far from being a noble thing, as Polus claimed, it is base.
The same point is made succinctly and forcefully by Socrates in the
Phaedrus (260c): "When a rhetorician who is ignorant of good and evil
tries to persuade a city similarly circumstanced, not by praising the
shadow of an ass as though it were a horse, but by praising evil as though
it were good, and having studied the beliefs of the multitude, persuades
them to do what is evil instead of good, what harvest do you think his
rhetoric will reap from the seeds he has sown?" This sort of rhetoric
Socrates condemns as a mere artless knack, or *atechnos tribe*. He says in
the *Gorgias*, "A real art of speaking which does not lay hold of truth does
not exist and never will."

This talk of rhetoric may seem pleasantly archaic to the contemporary
reader, and irrelevant to today's business. The antique veneer will vanish
if he reminds himself of the content of most political discourse, courtroom declamations, or advertisements he hears. He will then better understand what is meant by *kolakeia* and a knack without a *logos*.

But the *Gorgias*, like the *Phaedrus*, carries the issue of rhetoric further.
In argument with Callicles, Socrates envisages another sort of rhetoric:
a philosophical rhetoric aimed at truth and excellence of soul whether it
gives pleasure or pain to the hearers, an art of rhetoric based on knowledge, whose object is to produce justice and that order of soul associated
with lawfulness and law. The practitioner of this kind of rhetoric stands
to the soul as the physician stands to the body; he is not a shadow of a
statesman, but the statesman himself; he does not speak at random, but
like a craftsman he organizes his materials with a view to his single aim.
A primary example of this sort of rhetoric is the speech of the Laws of
Athens in the *Crito* (50a–54d), which can be compared to the random
rhetoric of Crito's plea to Socrates to escape (45a–46a).

There are, then, two concepts of rhetoric in the *Gorgias*. Base rhetoric
aims at gratification and pleasure and is indifferent to truth or the good

of the soul. The *Apology* is philosophical rhetoric, aimed at truth and indifferent to gratification and pleasure. The clarity of its rhetorical structure answers the requirements of the *Phaedrus* (264c): that every discourse should be organized like a living thing, possessed of a body of its own, so that it lacks neither head nor foot, but has a middle and extremities composed in due relation to each other and to the whole. Ordinary rhetoric—base rhetoric—is represented in the *Phaedrus* by the speech of Lysias, which is contemptuously dismissed as disorganized: like the epitaph of Midas the Phrygian, its parts may be taken in any order. The concern of philosophical rhetoric is with rational structure, as distinct from emotional appeal; this structure is an element in Socrates' overriding concern for truth in accordance with justice.

The association in the *Gorgias* between philosophical rhetoric and the art of the statesman, on the ground that both possess knowledge and are directed toward the good of the soul, becomes the basis for the claim, astonishing from a man who held public office only once in his life and apparently by sortition, that Socrates is the one true statesman in Athens. It is not surprising that when put to trial he was mistaken for something else. In the *Sophist*, a dialogue written many years after the *Gorgias* and *Apology*, an Eleatic Stranger, searching for the Sophist, stumbles across a class of men who purify the soul from deceit; they are not Sophists, though they have some resemblance to them. But then, as the Stranger remarks, "so has the dog to the wolf—the fiercest of animals to the tamest. But a cautious man should above all be on his guard against resemblances; they are a very slippery sort of thing." As the *Phaedrus* makes clear, you can deal with resemblances only if you understand the nature of things: dogs and wolves are easily mistaken at a distance. In the *Apology*, Socrates practices an art of persuasion directed toward truth; ignorance, not surprisingly, mistakes it for a form of base rhetoric— though a queer one. The philosopher is taken for the Sophist, the dog for the wolf.

Irony and Rhetoric

The two concepts of rhetoric in the *Gorgias* answer to the two levels of irony in the *Apology*. The rhetoric which Socrates offers in the *Apology* is directed not at flattery but at truth; to the degree that his speech required the kind of persuasion that only flattery could produce, to the degree that it required the tricks of forensic rhetoric, he gives no speech at all. Socrates is the doctor before a jury of children. He offers philosophical rhetoric where forensic rhetoric is expected, and he cannot meet the expectation because he is a philosopher and not a Sophist. Tried on a charge of impiety, he is prevented by concern for piety from putting forward the expected defense. Found guilty and condemned, he tells those who voted for his conviction that he has not been found guilty for lack of words to convince them, had he been willing to use them, but for lack of the shamelessness to say the things they would have found most pleasant to hear—"weeping and wailing, saying and doing a multitude of things which I hold to be unworthy, but of a sort you are accustomed to hear from others." Philosophical rhetoric can accomplish the aim of forensic rhetoric only *per accidens*, if at all; in Socrates' case it failed *per accidens* precisely because it did not fail of its own aim.

Big Talk

We can now answer an ancient question which puzzled Xenophon: Why did not Socrates defend himself to better effect? Xenophon began his own *Apology of Socrates* with an attempt at an answer:

> It seems to me fitting to hand down to memory, furthermore, how Socrates, on being indicted, deliberated on his defense and on his end. It is true that others have written about this, and that all of them have reproduced the loftiness of his words [*megalegoria*]—a fact which proves that his utterance really was of the character inti- mated—but they have not shown clearly that he had now come to the conclusion that for him death was more to be desired than life, and hence his lofty utterance appears rather ill considered.

Megalegoria means more than "loftiness of words": it also means "big talk," and it implies arrogance. If Socrates spoke as Plato represents him, Xenophon found his megalegoria unexplained.

Xenophon's explanation of the "loftiness" is that Socrates' Sign op- posed preparation of a defense, and that Socrates inferred from this that the god thought it better for him to die now and so be spared the evils of old age. This merely picks up a minor theme at the end of Plato's *Apology*: "What has now come did not come of its own initiative: it is clear that to die now and be released from my concerns is better. That is why the Sign did not turn me back" (41d). Xenophon himself is less than consistent in his account, since he goes on to have Socrates provide a point-by-point refutation of the charges, while yet maintaining that his "loftiness" is aimed at obtaining conviction. Socrates, far from attempting to gain acquittal, was actively courting condemnation: he was committing suicide by judicial process, one of the rarer forms of suicide by blunt instrument.

As we have seen, the true explanation lies elsewhere. Socrates' aim was neither acquittal nor conviction, but to tell the truth in accordance with justice, let the chips fall where they may. Acquittal could only have been obtained by a defense which would have amounted to abject pandering, or *kolakeia*—a defense which, because it corrupted the function of a judge, Socrates himself declares impious (35d).

The "Silence of Socrates" is not silence, but speech based on truth, and fatal in the circumstances. Socrates' character, in the *Apology*, is consistent with his character in the *Euthyphro* and other early dialogues. Because he knew himself ignorant in matters which appeared obvious to men who thought themselves wise, he seemed sly and dishonest: irony, sometimes, is in the eye of the beholder. But his ignorance was real, not feigned, and it issued in a form of inquiry which involved *elenchus*, or refutation. The merit of elenchus was to purge the false conceit of knowledge; if it thereby chastened some, it also stirred many to wrath, and their anger was kindled higher by the appearance of Wrong Logic and deceit. Socrates had no wish to be hated. His service to the god caused him to be hated, and he perceived the fact with grief and pain. But he still maintained the soldier's station in which the god had placed him. Brought into court and compelled to abandon his customary form of inquiry by question and answer, he aimed at truth, so far as he could tell it, about his own character and the nature of his mission to Athens. Because he was, after all, an ignorant man, and yet concerned to persuade his hearers of the truth so far as he could tell it, he used the rhetoric appropriate to a philosopher. The result appeared as astonishing arrogance. His was not the guarded truth of a defendant on trial for his life; it appeared, in fact, very like the truth of a prophet in calm wrath. But Socrates was carrying on philosophy by other means. If he was hated for telling the truth, it was not because he was indifferent to hate, but because he was not indifferent to the truth. His speech was an exhibition, not of arrogance, but of service to the god and his own mission, as well as of that courage, allied to wisdom, which consists in knowing when to be afraid and when not to be.

Socrates not only did not but could not answer the charges against him. Whatever else we may think of Meletus, Anytus, and Lycon, his accusers, they had seen deeply enough into the character of the man they pursued to draw up an indictment distinguished by lawyerly cunning, one which Socrates could no more have answered than a child. Socrates, wiser than other men only in knowing that he did not know,

could not with knowledge deny the charges against him. He was indicted
on a writ of impiety. But in order to know whether or not his conduct
had been impious, it was necessary first to know what piety is, its essential
idea or nature; he had sought to learn this in the *Euthyphro* in order to
prepare for his trial and had failed. Is it impious to urge men to pursue
virtue and human excellence, and to convict them of ignorance? That
question cannot be answered with knowledge—truth in accordance with
justice—by a man who knows himself ignorant of what piety is.

As with the writ, so with the counts. A man who does not know what
virtue is can deny that he intentionally corrupts the youth; but he cannot
deny that he corrupts them, since knowledge of vice implies knowledge
of its opposite, and he does not know what virtue is. He can deny that
he corrupts by teaching if in fact he has never taught but only questioned.
But he cannot deny that he corrupts by introducing strange divinities
and failing to acknowledge old ones if he is himself ignorant, not only
in matters of virtue, but of religion. Does one or does one not acknowledge the gods the City acknowledges, if one doubts that certain of the
terrible stories told about them and embroidered on the robe carried to
the Acropolis at the Greater Panathenaea are true? Does one corrupt
the youth by expressing those doubts? Can one or can one not deny the
introduction of strange divinities, given the presence of an accustomed
Sign believed to be divine? Does one corrupt the youth by mentioning
the Sign? To deny such charges on the basis of knowledge—on the basis
of truth in accordance with justice—one must first understand what they
mean; this understanding requires inquiry into just those things of which
Socrates knew himself to be ignorant—for example, the real nature of
virtue and of piety. The appropriate inquiry would take more time than
was offered by a lawcourt, in which one spoke against a waterclock. It is
not too much to say, indeed, that a lifetime had already proved too short.
The doctor, put on trial before a jury of children on charges brought by
a clever pastry-cook, has nothing to say.

So the two levels of irony in the *Apology* mesh. The man who cannot
give a speech gives a speech. The speech he gives proves that he cannot
give a speech. The two levels are so related as to turn apparent falsehood
into literal truth.

This is not to say that Socrates does not reply to Meletus. If Socrates
does not know what piety and impiety are, he knows at least that Meletus
does not know either. If he knows that he cannot answer the charges "in
truth according to justice," he also knows—and by his cross-examination
and refutation of Meletus proves—that his accusers could not "in truth
according to justice" bring those charges against him. He departs con-

victed by the Athenians of impiety and sentenced to death. They depart convicted by the Truth of villainy and injustice, and they will abide their penalty. This is not a defense against the charges; it is in the nature of a counter-claim.'

By his use of rhetoric without forensic content, Socrates does not state but shows the difference between base rhetoric and philosophical rhetoric and shows also that the difference is not merely a matter of form. The verdict of the Athenians indicates that, just as Meletus and those around him do not know what piety and impiety are, so the Athenians do not know what sophistry is, or what it really means for the stronger argument to be strong. Standing at a distance from reality, they cannot tell the dog from the wolf. What is shown is not said, and cannot be said except to those who have learned to see and need not hear it.

"The Silence of Socrates" indeed exists. It is found, not only in the *Apology,* but in every early dialogue in which he inquires by refutation. It testifies, perhaps, that only those who care most about words have fully learned both their seriousness and their ultimate uselessness and have learned too, like Prospero, on occasion to summon a solemn music, and deeper than did ever plummet sound, drown their book.

The Historical Background of the Charges

The author of the *Seventh Letter,* writing some forty years or more after the trial, described Socrates as the best and most righteous man of his time and dismissed the charge of impiety as one which he least of all men deserved. Whether or not those are Plato's own words, they most certainly represent Plato's views (see *Phaedo* 118a), as well as the opinions of many other Athenians. Yet Socrates died a condemned criminal.

Impiety was a serious matter in Athens, prosecuted by *graphe* or writ of public indictment, as technically even murder was not, because it directly affected the welfare and safety of the City as a whole. As Euthyphro puts it, "Piety preserves both families and cities and keeps them safe. The opposite of what is acceptable to the gods is impious, and impiety overturns and destroys all things" (14b). To leave impiety unpunished was to invite divine retribution. Still, impiety usually lay for a well-defined class of wrongs: for profanation of the Eleusinian Mysteries, for mutilation of sacred objects, and for blasphemy or sacrilege affecting the religion of the City. Socrates was guilty of none of these. Impiety did not in general lie for unorthodoxy in belief; Athens was singularly free of the unlovely habit of persecuting men for their opinions, and indeed, it would be difficult to say what religious orthodoxy in Athens consisted in. Athenian religion was not a matter of creed and dogma but of ritual observance, *dromena*, things done, rather than *legomena*, things said—and this was appropriate, given a polytheistic religion whose doctrinal content, to the degree it might be said to have any at all, consisted mainly in the myths of Homer and Hesiod. Impiety, in short, normally lay for definite kinds of acts.

The reach of the writ appears to have been extended perhaps some forty years earlier, when Anaxagoras, philosopher and friend of Pericles, was indicted for saying the Sun was stone and the Moon earth, and thus (by implication) neither was the god which tradition accepted it to be. But the prosecution of Anaxagoras was politically motivated, a means of striking at Pericles, and it seems that it took special legislation to bring the case within the writ.

Still, the bad precedent was remembered. Meletus actually confuses Anaxagoras with Socrates at one point (28d–e). But Socrates did not teach what Anaxagoras taught, and indeed, there is no evidence that he taught about religious matters at all, though there is clear evidence in the *Euthyphro* and elsewhere that he asked questions about theology which embarrassed Olympian fundamentalists. Still, Socrates had walked his peculiar way for years without attracting a charge, and this would not have been so if his conduct fell within any clearly defined standard of wrong.

The claim that Socrates did not acknowledge the gods the City acknowledged seems to have rested on little more than his reputation as a sophist. Certainly he questioned the tales of gore and immorality told in Homer and Hesiod about the gods, as the *Euthyphro* shows; but this was common among educated Athenians in the late fifth century. The charge that he introduced new or strange divinities rested solely on his peculiar Sign. None of this is enough to explain how he came to attract an indictment for impiety, let alone a finding of guilt.

In fact, the charges probably had a procedural rather than a substantive effect: they served to bring his conduct within the reach of a writ of impiety. The heart of the charge against him—and this is confirmed by the controversy over the verdict afterward—was that he was corrupting the youth. Fifty years after the trial, Aeschines suggested that Athens put Socrates to death because he had been a teacher of Critias, one of the Thirty Tyrants; Charmides, a member of the Socratic circle, was also among that unholy number. Still another associate of Socrates was the brilliant and unrestrained Alcibiades, who turned traitor to Athens during the Peloponnesian War. We know that the sophist Polycrates cited his example in the "Accusation of Socrates," a set speech written in or after 393 B.C. and roundly condemned as bad rhetoric by Isocrates in the *Busiris*.

We do not have Meletus's speech of accusation, or the speeches of the supporting witnesses, Anytus and Lycon. The names of Critias, Charmides, and Alcibiades may not even have been directly mentioned. But the charge of corrupting the youth would surely have been without effect had Meletus and those around him not been able to count on appropriate examples springing nimbly to mind. Socrates' conduct under the Thirty was heroic (32c–e) and widely known, but the fact remained that he was tied by association to leading members of the Thirty, and to Alcibiades, the brilliant traitor.

All this still does not explain why Socrates was brought to trial in 399. Aristophanes' *Clouds* was an important source of prejudice, but the *Clouds* was first produced in 423. Alcibiades was Socrates' associate, but that was before the Sicilian Expedition in 415. Critias and Charmides were also his associates, but the Thirty fell in 404–03. Politically speaking, four or five years is a long time, and the time lapse could not have been due merely to busy courts and crowded dockets. A general amnesty had been issued after the Thirty fell. Charges might have stuck due to past history, but they must have been prompted by present offense.

Plato exhibits the nature of that offense in the *Meno* (89e–95a), in a discussion between Socrates and Anytus, a leader of the restored democracy and one of the principal witnesses against Socrates. The dramatic date of the dialogue is probably the early months of 402. Anytus's belief that the citizens of Athens offer education in virtue, a traditional piece of democratic piety reaffirmed by Meletus in the *Apology* (24d–25a), is subjected to merciless criticism, which cuts the more deeply for its very lightness of touch: Men held up as virtuous cannot teach virtue to their own sons. How then can they teach others? Socrates chooses as examples the democratic worthies of Athens's Golden Age—Themistocles, Pericles, and so on—and Anytus, angered far out of proportion to anything which has been said, accuses Socrates of slander and issues a veiled threat (94e). The very intensity of Anytus's emotion, and its disproportionateness, is significant. So in the *Apology* (21c–22a) Socrates tells how he went to the politicians, and later the poets and craftsmen, and questioned them, and made them angry, and became hated.

Their unreasonable anger came from something more than wounded pride. It was a time when the fabric of shared loyalties and beliefs which serve to bind a people had been rent; and although for five years that fabric had been patched, it was very far from mended. A quiet, tightknit people can accept criticism of their ways with tolerance, even with a smile; but a people hammered apart on the anvil of history has known fear, and Socrates' criticism roused memories of past danger. He touched, even in his very speech of defense, the most powerful and terrible of political motives—fear, whose shadow is anger. He did not walk away alive.

The reasons for finding him guilty may be cast into a kind of syllogism: impiety threatens the safety of the City; Socrates threatens the safety of the City; therefore Socrates is impious. Popular emotion, the grudging slander of the Many, represented in all its unreasoning intensity by Anytus, is not halted in its course by logic. Socrates went to his death on the basis of an undistributed middle. The gadfly was swatted.

The Historicity of the Apology

Plato's *Apology* purports to represent a historical occurrence, namely, the speech which the historical Socrates made at his trial. It is a natural question, and one often asked, whether Plato's representation of that speech is historically accurate.

A kind of conventional wisdom has grown up as an answer. It claims that the *Apology* represents sheer idealization of the master's life, that it is a fiction. I believe that within such limits of proof as the subject matter admits, this answer is provably mistaken. As a matter of best evidence, the *Apology* should be accepted as essentially accurate to historical fact.

By saying that the *Apology* is essentially accurate, I do not mean that it is a word-for-word presentation of Socrates' speech. Textual evidence suggests it is not. In the *Crito* (45b), Crito claims that Socrates said at his trial that if he left, "he would not know what to do with himself." The expression is idiomatic; it has the ring of quotation; it fits the sense of *Apology* 37c–e; but it is not found there. Again, at *Crito* 52c, the Laws of Athens say that Socrates said at his trial that he preferred death to exile. This may be implied by *Apology* 37c–e, but it is nowhere explicitly stated. So there is good reason to suppose that the *Apology* is not a stenographic report, even though Plato takes pains to indicate that he was present and heard the speech (34a, 38b), something he does nowhere else in the dialogues. Thus, to say that the *Apology* is essentially accurate is not to say that it is word for word, but that it reproduces the general substance of what Socrates said and the way he said it.

Let us begin with a negative point. There is no good evidence that the *Apology* is inaccurate to the speech. I shall assume on the basis of what has gone before that this is true internally of the *Apology* itself and of its coherence with other early dialogues, and I shall deal with external evidence.

We may begin by setting aside the "Accusation of Socrates," written by the Sophist Polycrates sometime after 393 B.C., and criticized by Isocrates in the *Busiris*. Our knowledge of this speech is fragmentary, but it was a sophistical *epideixis*, a set speech, and it referred explicitly to Socrates' association with Alcibiades as a matter of reproach. This sort of reference should have been excluded in court, according to the terms of the amnesty issued by the restored democracy after the fall of the Thirty. Although it does not follow thereby that it was in fact excluded, it does suggest, as a matter of evidence, that the speech written by Polycrates probably had little relation to the original speeches of Socrates' accusers and still less to the original speech of Socrates himself.

Next, we may set aside the Hellenistic tradition that Socrates stood mute at his trial. This, as we have seen, was a mistaken interpretation of Plato's *Gorgias*. It is contradicted by all the direct contemporary evidence that we have, including Plato's *Apology*, Xenophon's *Apology*, and Isocrates' *Antidosis*.

We come now to Xenophon's *Apology*. This conflicts with Plato's *Apology* yet in a crucial respect confirms it. The fact which Xenophon sets out to explain is Socrates' use of megalegoria, loftiness of speech or big talk. That fact is amply attested in Plato's *Apology*. Xenophon, of course, is not an independent witness. He was not present at the trial, and he confesses in his first paragraph that he does not know what was said except insofar as it was written about. He can explain the megalegoria, which he finds universally attested, only in intellectually impoverished terms: it is aimed at suicide by judicial process. If this is a mere perversion of Plato's account, it is also indirect testimony to the accuracy of the most striking single feature of that account, namely, a tone which seems to verge on arrogance. So Xenophon's account, however far it may diverge from Plato in its explanation, confirms Plato's account in respect to the fact to be explained.

The strongest external evidence for the accuracy of Plato's account is Isocrates' *Antidosis*. Isocrates knew Socrates and admired him, as the *Antidosis* shows. There is an ancient tradition that he was deeply grieved at Socrates' death and put on mourning for him; in the circumstances, that would have been no light thing to do. There is no reason to suppose that Isocrates was not thoroughly familiar with the circumstances of the trial: born in 436 B.C., he was at the time of the trial a grown man. The *Antidosis* was written in or around 354 B.C., and it is surely no accident that Isocrates, in constructing a defense of his own life and career by imagining himself as a defendant on trial for corrupting the youth and making the worse argument better, should echo the *Apology* of Plato, and constantly so. But Isocrates surely meant to compare himself to Socrates, not to Plato's portrait of Socrates. It follows that Isocrates, who was in a position to know, must have supposed Plato's *Apology* essentially accurate to the speech which Socrates gave.

There is no good evidence that the *Apology* is inaccurate. There is good evidence that the *Apology* is accurate. Therefore, as a matter of best evidence, we must accept the *Apology* as accurate. This need hardly occasion surprise. Plato could have had no good reason for presenting an account of Socrates' defense which was at variance with the facts to an audience thoroughly familiar with what Socrates had actually said. This point, indeed, applies in general to the early dialogues. Given that Socrates cared deeply to know what piety and other virtues are, and knew that he did not know, his ignorance would have prevented him from denying the charges brought against him. It follows that Socrates could have made essentially the speech which Plato presents, and perhaps he could have made no other.

TRANSLATION

SOCRATES / MELETUS

The Speech of Defense (17a–35d)

Introduction (17a–18a)

17a soc. To what degree, Gentlemen of Athens, you have been affected by my accusers, I do not know. I, at any rate, was almost led to forget who I am—so convincingly did they speak. Yet hardly anything they have said is true. Among their many falsehoods, I was especially surprised by one: they said you must be on guard

b lest I deceive you, since I am a clever speaker. To have no shame at being directly refuted by facts when I show myself in no way clever with words—that, I think, is the very height of shamelessness. Unless, of course, they call a man a clever speaker if he speaks the truth. If that is what they mean, why, I would even admit to being an orator—though not after their fashion.

These men, I claim, have said little or nothing true. But from me, Gentlemen, you will hear the whole truth. To be sure, it will not be prettily tricked out in elegant speeches like theirs, words

c and phrases all nicely arranged. On the contrary, you will hear me speak naturally in the words which happen to occur to me. For I believe what I say to be just, and let no one of you expect otherwise. Besides, it would hardly be appropriate in a man of my age, Gentlemen, to come before you making up speeches like a boy.[1] So I must specifically ask one thing of you, Gentlemen. If

---

1. Meletus was quite young when he lodged his prosecution. See *Euthyphro* 2b.

you hear me make my defense in the same words I customarily
use at the tables in the Agora, and other places where many of
you have heard me, please do not be surprised or make a dis-
d   turbance because of it. For things stand thus: I am now come
into court for the first time; I am seventy years old; and I am an
utter stranger to this place. If I were a foreigner, you would
18a   unquestionably make allowances if I spoke in the dialect and
manner in which I was raised. In just the same way, I specifically
ask you now, and justly so, I think, to pay no attention to my
manner of speech—it may perhaps be poor, but perhaps an improvement—and look strictly to this one thing, whether or not I
speak justly. For that is the virtue of a judge, and the virtue of
an orator is to speak the truth.

Statement (18a–19a)

soc. First of all, Gentlemen, it is right for me to defend myself
against the first false accusations lodged against me, and my first
accusers; and next, against later accusations and later accusers.
b   For the fact is that many accusers have risen before you against
me; at this point they have been making accusations for many
years, and they have told no truth. Yet I fear them more than I
fear Anytus and those around him—though they too are clever.
Still, the others are more dangerous. They took hold of most of
you in childhood, persuading you of the truth of accusations
which were in fact quite false: "There is a certain Socrates . . .
wise man . . . thinker on things in the Heavens . . . inquirer into
things beneath Earth . . . making the weaker argument stronger."
c   Those men, Gentlemen of Athens, the ones who spread that report, are my dangerous accusers; for their hearers believe that
those who inquire into such things acknowledge no gods.

Again, there have been many such accusers, and they have now
been at work for a long time; they spoke to you at a time when
you were especially credulous—some of you children, some only
a little older—and they lodged their accusations quite by default,
no one appearing in defense. But the most absurd thing is that
d   one cannot even know or tell their names—unless perhaps in the
case of a comic poet.[2] But those who use malicious slander to
persuade you, and those who, themselves persuaded, persuade

2. A reference to Aristophanes, whose description of Socrates in the *Clouds* has
in effect just been quoted, and who will later (19c) be mentioned by name.

others—all these are most difficult to deal with. For it is impossible to bring any one of them forward as a witness and cross-examine him. I must rather, as it were, fight with shadows in making my defense, and question where no one answers.

Please grant, then, as I say, that two sets of accusers have risen against me: those who now lodge their accusations, and those
e who lodged accusations long since. And please accept the fact that I must defend myself against the latter first. For in fact you heard their accusations earlier, and with far greater effect than those which came later.

Very well then. A defense is to be made, Gentlemen of Athens.
19a I am to attempt to remove from you in this short time that prejudice which you have been so long in acquiring. I might wish that this should come to pass, if it were in some way better for you and for me—wish that I might succeed in my defense. But I think that difficult, and its nature hardly escapes me. Still, let that go as pleases the God; the law must be obeyed, and a defense conducted.

Refutation of the Old Accusers (19a–24b)

soc. Let us then take up from the beginning the charges which
b have given rise to the prejudice—the charges on which Meletus in fact relied in lodging his indictment. Very well, what do those who slander me say? It is necessary to read, as it were, their sworn indictment: "Socrates is guilty of needless curiosity and meddling interference, inquiring into things beneath Earth and in the Sky, making the weaker argument stronger, and teaching others to do
c the same." The charge is something like that. Indeed, you have seen it for yourselves in a comedy by Aristophanes—a certain Socrates being carried around on the stage, talking about walking on air and babbling a great deal of other nonsense, of which I understand neither much nor little. Mark you, I do not mean to disparage such knowledge, if anyone in fact has it—let me not be brought to trial by Meletus on such a charge as that! But Gentlemen, I have no share in it. Once again, I offer the majority
d of you as witnesses, and ask those of you who have heard me in conversation—there are many among you—inform each other, please, whether any of you ever heard anything of that sort. From that you will recognize the nature of the other things the multitude says about me.

The fact is that there is nothing in these accusations. And if

you have heard from anyone that I undertake to educate men,
e   and make money doing it, that is false too. Once again, I think
it would be a fine thing to be able to educate men, as Gorgias of
Leontini does, or Prodicus of Ceos, or Hippias of Elis. For each
of them, Gentlemen, can enter any given city and convince the
20a   youth—who might freely associate with any of their fellow citizens
they please—to drop those associations and associate rather with
them, to pay money for it, and give thanks in the bargain. As a
matter of fact, there is a man here right now, a Parian, and a
wise one, who, as I learn, has just come to town. For I happened
to meet a person who has spent more money on Sophists than
everyone else put together: Callias, son of Hipponicus. So I asked
him—for he has two sons—"Callias," I said, "if your two sons
were colts or calves, we could get an overseer for them and hire
b   him, and his business would be to make them excellent in their
appropriate virtue. He would be either a horse-trainer or a
farmer. But as it is, since the two of them are men, whom do you
intend to get as an overseer? Who has knowledge of that virtue
which belongs to a man and a citizen? Since you have sons, I'm
sure you have considered this. Is there such a person," I said,
"or not?"

"To be sure," he said.

"Who is he?" I said. "Where is he from, and how much does
he charge to teach?"

"Evenus, Socrates," he said. "A Parian. Five minae."[3]

And I counted Evenus fortunate indeed, if he really possesses
c   that art and teaches it so modestly. For my own part, at any rate,
I would be puffed up with vanity and pride if I had such knowledge. But I do not, Gentlemen.

Perhaps one of you will ask, "But Socrates, what is this all
about? Whence have these slanders against you arisen? You must
surely have been busying yourself with something out of the ordinary; so grave a report and rumor would not have arisen had
you not been doing something rather different from most folk.
Tell us what it is, so that we may not take action in your case
d   unadvisedly." That, I think, is a fair request, and I shall try to
indicate what it is that has given me the name I have. Hear me,
then. Perhaps some of you will think I joke; be well assured that
I shall tell you the whole truth.

3. Callias's answer is in the "short-answer" style of the Sophists. Cf. *Gorgias*
449b*ff.*, *Protagoras* 334e–335c.

Gentlemen of Athens, I got this name through nothing but a kind of wisdom. What kind? The kind which is perhaps peculiarly human, for it may be I am really wise in that. And perhaps the men I just mentioned are wise with a wisdom greater than human—either that, or I cannot say what. In any case, I have no knowledge of it, and whoever says I do is lying and speaks to my slander.

Please, Gentlemen of Athens. Do not make a disturbance, even if I seem to you to boast. For it will not be my own words I utter; I shall refer you to the speaker, as one worthy of credit. For as witness to you of my own wisdom—whether it is wisdom of a kind, and what kind of wisdom it is—I shall call the God at Delphi.

You surely knew Chaerephon. He was my friend from youth, and a friend of your democratic majority. He went into exile with you,[4] and with you he returned. And you know what kind of a man he was, how eager and impetuous in whatever he rushed into. Well, he once went to Delphi and boldly asked the oracle—as I say, Gentlemen, please do not make a disturbance—he asked whether anyone is wiser than I. Now, the Pythia[5] replied that no one is wiser. And to this his brother here will testify, since Chaerephon is dead.

Why do I mention this? I mention it because I intend to inform you whence the slander against me has arisen. For when I heard it, I reflected: "What does the God mean? What is the sense of this riddling utterance? I know that I am not wise at all; what then does the God mean by saying I am wisest? Surely he does not speak falsehood; it is not permitted to him." So I puzzled for a long time over what he meant, and then, with great reluctance, I turned to inquire into the matter in some such way as this.

I went to someone with a reputation for wisdom, in the belief that there if anywhere I might test the meaning of the utterance and declare to the oracle that "this man is wiser than I am, and you said I was wisest." So I examined him—there is no need to mention a name, but it was someone in political life who produced this effect on me in discussion, Gentlemen of Athens—and I concluded that though he seemed wise to many other men, and most especially to himself, he was not. I tried to show him

4. The leading democrats in Athens were forced into exile when the Thirty Tyrants came to power in 404 B.C.

5. The Priestess of Apollo, whose major shrine was Delphi.

this; and thence I became hated, by him and by many who were
d   present. But I left thinking to myself, "I am wiser than that man.
Probably neither of us knows anything worthwhile; but he thinks
he does and does not, and I do not and do not think I do. So it
seems at any rate that I am wiser in this one small respect: I do
not think I know what I do not." I then went to another man who
was reputed to be even wiser, and the same thing seemed true
e   again; there too I became hated, by him and by many others.

Nevertheless, I went on, perceiving with grief and fear that I
was becoming hated, but still, it seemed necessary to put the God
first—so I had to go on, examining what the oracle meant by
22a testing everyone with a reputation for knowledge. And by the
Dog,[6] Gentlemen—I must tell you the truth—I swear that I had
some such experience as this: it seemed to me, as I carried on
inquiry in behalf of the God, that those most highly esteemed
for wisdom fell little short of being most deficient, and that others
reputedly inferior were men of more discernment.

But really, I must tell you of my wanderings, the labors I
performed[7]—all to the end that I might not leave the oracle un-
tested. From the politicians I went to the poets—tragic, dithy-
b   rambic, and the rest—thinking that there I would discover myself
manifestly less wise by comparison. So I took up poems over
which I thought they had taken special pains, and asked them
what they meant, so as also at the same time to learn from them.
Now, I am ashamed to tell you the truth, Gentlemen, but still, it
must be told. There was hardly anyone present who could not
give a better account than they of what they had themselves pro-
c   duced. So presently I came to realize that poets too do not make
what they make by wisdom, but by a kind of native disposition
or divine inspiration, exactly like seers and prophets. For the
latter also utter many fine things, but know nothing of the things
they speak. That is how the poets also appeared to me, while at
the same time I realized that because of their poetry they thought
themselves the wisest of men in other matters—and were not.
Once again, I left thinking myself superior to them in just the
way I was to the politicians.

Finally I went to the craftsmen. I was aware that although I
d   knew scarcely anything, I would find that they knew many fine

6. A humorous oath. The Dog is the Egyptian dog-headed god, Anubis.
7. I.e., like Heracles.

things. In this I was not mistaken: they knew things that I did
not, and in that respect were wiser. But, Gentlemen of Athens, it
seemed to me that the poets and our capable public craftsmen
had exactly the same failing: because they practiced their own
arts well, each deemed himself wise in other things, things of
great importance. This mistake quite obscured their wisdom.

e   The result was that I asked myself on behalf of the oracle whether
I would accept being such as I am, neither wise with their wisdom
nor foolish with their folly, or whether I would accept then wisdom and folly together and become such as they are. I answered,
both for myself and the oracle, that it was better to be as I am.

     From this examination, Gentlemen of Athens, much enmity

23a   has risen against me, of a sort most harsh and heavy to endure,
so that many slanders have arisen, and the name is put abroad
that I am "wise." For on each occasion those present think I am
wise in the things in which I test others. But very likely, Gentlemen, it is really the God who is wise, and by his oracle he means
to say that "human nature is a thing of little worth, or none." It
appears that he does not mean this fellow Socrates, but uses my

b   name to offer an example, as if he were saying that "he among
you, Gentlemen, is wisest who, like Socrates, realizes that he is
truly worth nothing in respect to wisdom." That is why I still go
about even now on behalf of the God, searching and inquiring
among both citizens and strangers, should I think some one of
them is wise; and when it seems he is not, I help the God and
prove it. Due to this pursuit, I have no leisure worth mentioning

c   either for the affairs of the City or for my own estate; I dwell in
utter poverty because of my service to God.

     Then too the young men follow after me—especially the ones
with leisure, namely, the richest. They follow of their own initiative, rejoicing to hear men tested, and often they imitate me and
undertake to test others; and next, I think, they find an ungrudging plenty of people who know little or nothing but think they
have some knowledge. As a result, those whom they test become
angry at me, not at themselves, and say that "this fellow Socrates

d   is utterly polluted, and corrupts the youth." And when someone
asks them what it is this Socrates does, what it is he teaches, they
cannot say because they do not know; but so as not to seem at a
loss, they mutter the kind of things that lie ready to hand against
anyone who pursues wisdom: "things in the Heavens and beneath
the Earth," or "not acknowledging gods," or "making the weaker

argument stronger." The truth, I suppose, they would not wish
to state, namely, that it is become quite clear that they pretend

e   to knowledge and know nothing. And because they are concerned for their pride, I think, and zealous, and numerous, and
speak vehemently and persuasively about me, they have long
filled your ears with zealous slander. It was on the strength of
this that Meletus attacked me, along with Anytus and Lycon—
Meletus angered on behalf of the poets, Anytus on behalf of the
public craftsmen and the politicians, Lycon on behalf of the or-

24a   ators. So the result, as I said to begin with, is that I should be
most surprised were I able to remove from you in this short time
a slander which has grown so great. There, Gentlemen of Athens,
you have the truth, and I have concealed or misrepresented nothing in speaking it, great or small. Yet I know quite well that it is
just for this that I have become hated—which is in fact an indication of the truth of what I say—and that this is the basis of the

b   slander and charges against me. Whether you inquire into it now
or hereafter you will find it to be so.

Refutation of Meletus (24b–28a)

soc. Against the charges lodged by my first accusers, let this defense suffice. But for Meletus—the good man who loves his City,
so he says—and for my later accusers, I shall attempt a further
defense. Once more then, as before a different set of accusers,
let us take up their sworn indictment.[8] It runs something like
this: it says that Socrates is guilty of corrupting the youth, and
of not acknowledging the gods the City acknowledges, but other

c   new divinities. Such is the charge. Let us examine its particulars.
    It claims I am guilty of corrupting the youth. But I claim,
Gentlemen of Athens, that it is Meletus who is guilty—guilty of
jesting in earnest, guilty of lightly bringing men to trial, guilty of
pretending a zealous concern for things he never cared about at
all. I shall try to show you that this is true.
    Come here, Meletus. Now tell me. Do you count it of greatest

d   importance than the young should be as good as possible?
mel. I do.
soc. Then come and tell the jurors this: Who improves them?
Clearly you know, since it is a matter of concern to you. Having

---

8. The exact indictment is probably preserved in D.L. II.40; cf. Xenophon, *Memorabilia* I.i.1.

discovered, so you say, that I am the man who is corrupting them, you bring me before these judges to accuse me. But now come and say who makes them better. Inform the judges who he is.

You see, Meletus. You are silent. You cannot say. And yet, does this not seem shameful to you, and a sufficient indication of what I say, namely, that you never cared at all? Tell us, my friend. Who improves them?

MEL. The laws.

e SOC. But I did not ask you that, dear friend. I asked you what man improves them—whoever it is who in the first place knows just that very thing, the laws.

MEL. These men, Socrates. The judges.

SOC. Really, Meletus? These men here are able to educate the youth and improve them?

MEL. Especially they.

SOC. All of them? Or only some?

MEL. All.

SOC. By Hera, you bring good news. An ungrudging plenty of
25a benefactors! But what about the audience here. Do they improve them or not?

MEL. They too.

SOC. And members of the Council?

MEL. The Councilors too.

SOC. Well then, Meletus, do the members of the Assembly, the Ecclesiasts, corrupt the young? Or do they all improve them too?

MEL. They too.

SOC. So it seems that every Athenian makes them excellent except me, and I alone corrupt them. Is that what you are saying?

MEL. That is exactly what I am saying.

SOC. You condemn me to great misfortune. But tell me, do you
b think it is so with horses? Do all men improve them, while some one man corrupts them? Or quite to the contrary, is it some one man or a very few, namely horse-trainers, who are able to improve them, while the majority of people, if they deal with horses and use them, corrupt them? Is that not true, Meletus, both of horses and all other animals? Of course it is, whether you and Anytus affirm or deny it. It would be good fortune indeed for the youth if only one man corrupted them and the rest benefited.
c But the fact is, Meletus, that you sufficiently show that you never gave thought to the youth; you clearly indicate your own lack of

concern, indicate that you never cared at all about the matters in which you bring action against me.

But again, dear Meletus, tell us this: Is it better to dwell among fellow citizens who are good, or wicked? Do answer, dear friend; surely I ask nothing hard. Do not wicked men do evil things to those around them, and good men good things?

MEL. Of course.

d SOC. Now, is there anyone who wishes to be harmed rather than benefited by those with whom he associates? Answer me, dear friend, for the law requires you to answer. Is there anyone who wishes to be harmed?

MEL. Of course not.

SOC. Very well then, are you bringing action against me here because I corrupt the youth intentionally, or unintentionally?

MEL. Intentionally, I say.

SOC. How can that be, Meletus? Are you at your age so much wiser
e   than I at mine that you recognize that evil men always do evil things to those around them, and good men do good, while I have reached such a pitch of folly that I am unaware that if I do some evil to those with whom I associate, I shall very likely receive some evil at their hands, with the result that I do such great evil intentionally, as you claim? I do not believe you, Meletus, and I do not think anyone else does either. On the contrary: either I
26a do not corrupt the youth, or if I do, I do so unintentionally. In either case, you lie. And if I corrupt them unintentionally, it is not the law to bring action here for that sort of mistake, but rather to instruct and admonish in private; for clearly, if I once learn, I shall stop what I unintentionally do. You, however, were unwilling to associate with me and teach me; instead, you brought action here, where it is law to bring those in need of punishment rather than instruction.

Gentlemen of Athens, what I said is surely now clear: Meletus
b   was never concerned about these matters, much or little. Still, Meletus, tell us this: How do you say I corrupt the youth? Or is it clear from your indictment that I teach them not to acknowledge the gods the City acknowledges, but other new divinities? Is this what you mean by saying I corrupt by teaching?

MEL. Certainly. That is exactly what I mean.

SOC. Then in the name of these same gods we are now discussing, Meletus, please speak a little more plainly still, both for me and
c   for these gentlemen here. Do you mean that I teach the youth to

acknowledge that there are gods, and thus do not myself wholly
deny gods, and am not in that respect guilty—though the gods
are not those the City acknowledges, but different ones, and that
this is the cause of my indictment, that they are different? Or are
you claiming that I do not myself acknowledge any gods at all,
and that I teach this to others?

MEL. I mean that. You acknowledge no gods at all.

d SOC. Ah, my dear Meletus, why do you say such things? Do I not
at least acknowledge Sun and Moon as gods, as other men do?

MEL. No, no, Gentlemen and Judges, not when he says the Sun is
a stone and the Moon earth.

SOC. My dear Meletus! Do you think it is Anaxagoras you are accusing? Do you so despise these judges here and think them so
unlettered that they do not know it is the books of Anaxagoras
of Clazomenae which teem with such statements? Are young men
to learn these things specifically from me when they can buy them

e sometimes in the Orchestra for a drachma, if the price is high,
and laugh at Socrates if he pretends they are his own—especially
since they are so absurd? Well, dear friend, is that what you
think? I acknowledge no gods at all?

MEL. No, none whatever.

SOC. You cannot be believed, Meletus—even, I think, by yourself.
Gentlemen of Athens, I think this man who stands here before
you is insolent and unchastened, and has brought this suit precisely out of insolence and unchastened youth. He seems to be

27a conducting a test by propounding a riddle: "Will Socrates, the
wise man, realize how neatly I contradict myself, or will I deceive
him and the rest of the audience?" For certainly it seems clear
that he is contradicting himself in his indictment. It is as though
he were saying, "Socrates is guilty of not acknowledging gods,
and acknowledges gods." Yet surely this is to jest.

Please join me, Gentlemen, in examining why it appears to me
that this is what he is saying. And you answer us, Meletus. The

b rest of you will please remember what I asked you at the beginning, and make no disturbance if I fashion arguments in my
accustomed way.

Is there any man, Meletus, who acknowledges that there are
things pertaining to men, but does not acknowledge that there
are men? Let him answer for himself, Gentlemen—and let him
stop interrupting. Is there any man who does not acknowledge
that there are horses, but acknowledges things pertaining to

horsemanship? Or does not acknowledge that there are flutes, but acknowledges things pertaining to flute playing? There is not, my good friend. If you do not wish to answer, I'll answer for you and for the rest of these people here. But do please answer my question, at least: Is there any man who acknowledges that there

c   are things pertaining to divinities, but does not acknowledge that there are divinities?

MEL. There is not.

SOC. How obliging of you to answer—reluctantly, and under compulsion from these gentlemen here. Now, you say that I acknowledge and teach things pertaining to divinities—whether new or old, still at least I acknowledge them, by your account; indeed you swore to that in your indictment. But if I acknowledge that there are things pertaining to divinities, must I surely not also acknowledge that there are divinities? Isn't that so? Of course it

d   is—since you do not answer, I count you as agreeing. And divinities, we surely believe, are either gods or children of gods? Correct?

MEL. Of course.

SOC. So if I believe in divinities, as you say, and if divinities are a kind of god, there is the jesting riddle I attributed to you; you are saying that I do not believe in gods, and again that I do believe in gods because I believe in divinities. On the other hand, if divinities are children of gods, some born illegitimately of nymphs,[9] or others of whom this is also told,[10] who could possibly

e   believe that there are children of gods, but not gods? It would be as absurd as believing that there are children of horses and asses, namely, mules, without believing there are horses and asses. Meletus, you could not have brought this indictment except in an attempt to test us—or because you were at a loss for any true basis of prosecution. But as to how you are to convince anyone of even the slightest intelligence that one and the same man can believe that there are things pertaining to divinities and gods,

28a   and yet believe that there are neither divinities nor heroes—there is no way.

Digression: Socrates' Mission to Athens (28a–34b)

SOC. Gentlemen of Athens, I do not think further defense is needed

---

9. Aesclepius, for example, son of Apollo and the nymph Coronis. Note that nymphs are themselves goddesses.

10. For example, Achilles, son of the nymph Thetis and Peleus, a mortal father; or Heracles, son of Zeus and Alcmene, a mortal mother.

to show that, by the very terms of Meletus' indictment, I am not guilty; this, surely, is sufficient. But as I said before, a great deal of enmity has risen against me among many people, and you may rest assured this is true. And that is what will convict me, if I am convicted—not Meletus, not Anytus, but the grudging slander of

b the multitude. It has convicted many another good and decent man; I think it will convict me; nor is there any reason to fear that with me it will come to a stand.

Perhaps someone may say, "Are you not ashamed, Socrates, at having pursued such a course that you now stand in danger of being put to death?" To him I would make a just reply: You are wrong, Sir, if you think that a man worth anything at all should take thought for danger in living or dying. He should look when he acts to one thing: whether what he does is just or unjust, the work of a good man or a bad one. By your account, those demigods and heroes who laid down their lives at Troy would be of

c little worth—the rest of them, and the son of Thetis. Achilles so much despised danger instead of submitting to disgrace that when he was intent on killing Hector his goddess mother told him, as I recall, "My son, if you avenge the slaying of your comrade Patroclus with the death of Hector, you yourself shall die; for straightway with Hector is his fate prepared for you."[11] Achilles heard, and thought little of the death and danger. He was more afraid to live as a bad man, with friends left unavenged.

d "Straightway let me die," he said, "exacting right from him who did the wrong, that I may not remain here as a butt of mockery beside crook-beaked ships, a burden to the earth." Do you suppose that he gave thought to death and danger?

Gentlemen of Athens, truly it is so: Wherever a man stations himself in belief that it is best, wherever he is stationed by his commander, there he must I think remain and run the risks, giving thought to neither death nor any other thing except disgrace. When the commanders you chose stationed me at Potidaea

e and Amphipolis and Delium,[12] I there remained as others did, and ran the risk of death; but I should indeed have wrought a fearful thing, Gentlemen of Athens, if then, when the God stationed me, as I thought and believed, obliging me to live in the

11. This is not a wholly accurate quotation from the *Iliad*, but describes the scene at XVIII 94*ff.*

12. All battles in which Socrates fought with conspicuous bravery. See *Symposium* 220d–221b, *Laches* 181b.

29a　pursuit of wisdom, examining myself and others—if then, at that point through fear of death or any other thing, I left my post. That would have been dreadful indeed, and then in truth might I be justly brought to court for not acknowledging the existence of gods, for willful disobedience to the oracle, for fearing death, for thinking myself wise when I am not.

For to fear death, Gentlemen, is nothing but to think one is wise when one is not; for it is to think one knows what one does not know. No man knows death, nor whether it is not the greatest
b　of all goods; and yet men fear it as though they well knew it to be the worst of evils. Yet how is this not folly most to be reproached, the folly of believing one knows what one does not? I, at least, Gentlemen, am perhaps superior to most men here and just in this, and if I were to claim to be wiser than anyone else it would be in this: that as I have no satisfactory knowledge of things in the Place of the Dead, I do not think I do. I do know that to be guilty of disobedience to a superior, be he god or man, is shameful evil.

So as against evils I know to be evils, I shall never fear or flee from things which for aught I know may be good. Thus, even if
c　you now dismiss me, refusing to do as Anytus bids—Anytus, who said that either I should not have been brought to trial to begin with or, since brought, must be put to death, testifying before you that if I were once acquitted your sons would pursue what Socrates teaches and all be thoroughly corrupted—if with this in view you were to say to me, "Socrates, we shall not at this time be persuaded by Meletus, and we dismiss you. But on this condition: that you no longer pass time in that inquiry of yours, or pursue philosophy. And if you are again taken doing it, you die."
d　If, as I say, you were to dismiss me on that condition, I would reply that I hold you in friendship and regard, Gentlemen of Athens, but I shall obey the God rather than you, and while I have breath and am able I shall not cease to pursue wisdom or to exhort you, charging any of you I happen to meet in my accustomed manner: "You are the best of men, being an Athenian, citizen of a city honored for wisdom and power beyond all others. Are you then not ashamed to care for the getting of
e　money, and reputation, and public honor, while yet having no thought or concern for truth and understanding and the greatest possible excellence of your soul?" And if some one of you disputes this, and says he does care, I shall not immediately dismiss him and go away. I shall question him and examine him and test
30a　him, and if he does not seem to me to possess virtue, and yet

says he does, I shall rebuke him for counting of more importance things which by comparison are worthless. I shall do this to young and old, citizen and stranger, whomever I happen to meet, but I shall do it especially to citizens, in as much as they are more nearly related to me. For the God commands this, be well assured, and I believe that you have yet to gain in this City a greater good than my service to the God. I go about doing nothing but persuading you, young and old, to care not for body or money

b   in place of, or so much as, excellence of soul. I tell you that virtue does not come from money, but money and all other human goods both public and private from virtue. If in saying this I corrupt the youth, that would be harm indeed. But anyone who claims I say other than this speaks falsehood. In these matters,

c   Gentlemen of Athens, believe Anytus, or do not. Dismiss me, or do not. For I will not do otherwise, even if I am to die for it many times over.

Please do not make a disturbance, Gentlemen. Abide in my request and do not interrupt what I have to say, but listen. Indeed, I think you will benefit by listening. I am going to tell you certain things at which you may perhaps cry out; please do not do it. Be well assured that if you kill me, and if I am the sort of man I claim, you will harm me less than you harm yourselves. There is no harm a Meletus or Anytus can do me; it is not pos-

d   sible, for it does not, I think, accord with divine law that a better man should be harmed by a worse. Meletus perhaps can kill me, or exile me, or disenfranchise me; and perhaps he and others too think those things great evils. I do not. I think it a far greater evil to do what he is now doing, attempting to kill a man unjustly. And so, Gentlemen of Athens, I am far from making a defense for my own sake, as some might think; I make it for yours, lest

e   you mistake the gift the God has given you and cast your votes against me. If you kill me, you will not easily find such another man as I, a man who—if I may put it a bit absurdly—has been fastened as it were to the City by the God as, so to speak, to a large and well-bred horse, a horse grown sluggish because of its size and in need of being roused by a kind of gadfly. Just so, I think, the God has fastened me to the City. I rouse you. I per-

31a   suade you. I upbraid you. I never stop lighting on each one of you, everywhere, all day long. Such another will not easily come to you again, Gentlemen, and if you are persuaded by me, you will spare me. But perhaps you are angry, as men roused from

sleep are angry, and perhaps you will swat me, persuaded by
Meletus that you may lightly kill. Then will you continue to sleep
out your lives, unless the God sends someone else to look after
you.

That I am just that, a gift from the God to the City, you may
b   recognize from this: It scarcely seems a human matter merely,
that I should take no thought for anything of my own, endure
the neglect of my house and its affairs for these long years now
and ever attend to yours, going to each of you in private like a
father or elder brother, persuading you to care for virtue. If I
got something from it, if I took pay for this kind of exhortation,
that would explain it. But as things are, you can see for yourselves
that even my accusers, who have accused me so shamefully of
everything else, could not summon shamelessness enough to pro-
c   vide witnesses to testify that I ever took pay or asked for it. For
it is enough, I think, to provide my poverty as witness to the truth
of what I say.

Perhaps it may seem peculiar that I go about in private advising
men and busily inquiring, and yet do not enter your Assembly in
public to advise the City. The reason is a thing you have heard
me mention many times in many places, that something divine
d   and godlike comes to me—which Meletus, indeed, mocked in his
indictment.[13] I have had it from childhood. It comes as a kind of
voice, and when it comes, it always turns me away from what I
am about to do, but never toward it. That is what opposed my
entering political life, and I think it did well to oppose. For be
well assured, Gentlemen of Athens, that had I attempted to enter
political affairs, I should long since have been destroyed—to the
e   benefit of neither you nor myself.

Please do not be angry at me for telling the simple truth. It is
impossible for any man to be spared if he publicly opposes you
or any other democratic majority, and prevents many unjust and
32a   illegal things from occurring in his city. He who intends to fight
for what is just, if he is to be spared even for a little time, must
of necessity live a private rather than a public life.

I shall offer you a convincing indication of this—not words,
but what you respect, deeds. Hear, then, what befell me, so that
you may know that I will not through fear of death give way to

13. The suggestion is that Meletus lodged his accusation of acknowledging new
(or strange) gods because of the Sign. Cf. *Euthyphro* 3b.

any man contrary to what is right, even if I am destroyed for it. I shall tell you a thing which is tedious—it smacks of the law courts—but true. Gentlemen of Athens, I never held other office
b   in the City, but I was once a member of the Council. And it happened that our Tribe, Antiochis, held the Prytany when you decided to judge as a group the cases of the ten generals who had failed to gather up the bodies of the slain in the naval battle—illegally, as later it seemed to all of you. But at the time, I alone of the Prytanies opposed doing a thing contrary to law, and cast my vote against it. And when the orators were ready to imc   peach me and have me arrested—you urging them on with your shouts—I thought that with law and justice on my side I must run the risk, rather than concur with you in an unjust decision through fear of bonds or death. Those things happened while the City was still under the Democracy. But when the oligarchy came, the Thirty in turn summoned me along with four others to the Rotunda and ordered us to bring back Leon the Salamanian from Salamis so that he might be executed, just as they ordered many others to do such things, planning to implicate as
d   many people as possible in their own guilt. But I then showed again, not by words but deeds, that death, if I may be rather blunt, was of no concern whatever to me; to do nothing unjust or unholy—that was my concern. Strong as it was, that oligarchy did not so frighten me as to cause me to do a thing unjust, and when we departed the Rotunda, the other four went into Salamis and brought back Leon, and I left and went home. I might have been killed for that, if the oligarchy had not shortly afterward
e   been overthrown. And of these things you will have many witnesses.

Now, do you think I would have lived so many years if I had been in public life and acted in a manner worthy of a good man, defending what is just and counting it, as is necessary, of first importance? Far from it, Gentlemen of Athens. Not I, and not
33a any other man. But through my whole life I have shown myself to be that sort of man in public affairs, the few I've engaged in; and I have shown myself the same man in private. I never gave way to anyone contrary to what is just—not to others, and certainly not to those slanderously said to be my pupils. In fact, I have never been teacher to anyone. If, in speaking and tending to my own affairs, I found anyone, young or old, who wished to hear me, I never begrudged him; nor do I discuss for a fee and

b   not otherwise. To rich and poor alike I offer myself as a questioner, and if anyone wishes to answer, he may then hear what I have to say. And if any of them turned out to be useful men, or any did not, I cannot justly be held responsible. To none did I promise instruction, and none did I teach; if anyone says that he learned from me or heard in private what others did not, you may rest assured he is not telling the truth.

c   Why is it, then, that some people enjoy spending so much time with me? You have heard, Gentlemen of Athens; I told you the whole truth. It is because they enjoy hearing people tested who think they are wise and are not. After all, it is not unamusing. But for my own part, as I say, I have been ordered to do this by God—in oracles, in dreams, in every way in which other divine apportionment orders a man to do anything.

d   These things, Gentlemen of Athens, are both true and easily tested. For if I am corrupting some of the youth, and have corrupted others, it must surely be that some among them, grown older, if they realize that I counseled them toward evil while young, would now come forward to accuse me and exact a penalty. And if they were unwilling, then some of their relatives—fathers, brothers, other kinsmen—would now remember, and exact a penalty, if their own relatives had suffered evil at my hands. Certainly there are many such men I see present. Here is Crito,

e   first, of my own age and deme,[14] father of Critobulus; then there is Eysanias of Sphettos, father of Aeschines[15] here. Next there is Antiphon of Cephisus, father of Epigenes. Then there are others whose brothers engaged in this pastime. There is Nicostratus, son of Theozotides, brother of Theodotus—and Theodotus is dead, so he could not have swayed him—and Paralus here, son

34a   of Demococus, whose brother was Theages. And here is Adeimantus, son of Ariston, whose brother is Plato here; and Aeantodorus, whose brother is Apollodorus here. I could name many others, some of whom at least Meletus ought certainly have provided in his speech as witnesses. If he forgot it then, let him do it now—I yield the floor—and let him say whether he has any witnesses of the sort. You will find that quite to the contrary, Gentlemen, every one of these men is ready to help me, I, who corrupt their relatives, as Meletus and Anytus claim. Those who

14. Alopece. A deme was roughly the equivalent of a township.
15. Who, like Plato, went on to write Socratic dialogues.

b are themselves corrupted might perhaps have reason to help me; but their relatives are older men who have not been corrupted. What reason could they have for supporting me except that it is right and just, because they know Meletus is lying and I am telling the truth?

Peroration (34b–35d)

soc. Very well, then, Gentlemen. This, and perhaps a few other things like it, is what I have to say in my defense. Perhaps some

c of you will remember your own conduct and be offended, if when brought to trial on a lesser charge than this, you begged your judges with tearful supplication and caused your children along with other relatives and a host of friends, to come forward so that you might be the more pitied, whereas I shall do none of these things, even though I am, as it would seem at least, in the extremity of danger. Perhaps someone with this in mind may become hardened against me; angered by it, he may cast his vote

d in anger. If this is true of any of you—not that I expect it, but if it is—I think it might be appropriate to say, "I too have relatives, my friend; for as Homer puts it, I am not 'of oak and rock,' but born of man, so I have relatives—yes, and sons too, Gentlemen of Athens, three of them, one already a lad and two of them children. Yet not one of them have I caused to come forward here, and I shall not beg you to acquit me." Why not? Not out of stubbornness, Gentlemen of Athens, nor disrespect for you.

e Whether or not I am confident in the face of death is another story; but I think that my own honor, and yours, and that of the whole City would suffer, if I were to behave in this way, I being of the age I am and having the name I have—truly or falsely it

35a being thought that Socrates is in some way superior to most men. If those of you reputed to be superior in wisdom or courage or any other virtue whatever were men of this sort, it would be disgraceful; I have often seen such people behave surprisingly when put on trial, even though they had a reputation to uphold, because they were persuaded that they would suffer a terrible thing if they were put to death—as though they would be immortal if you did not kill them. I think they cloak the City in shame, so that a stranger might think that those men among the Athenians who are superior in virtue, and whom the Athenians

b themselves judge worthy of office and other honors, are not better than women. These are things, Gentlemen of Athens, which those of you who have a reputation to uphold ought not to do; nor if we defendants do them, ought you permit it. You ought rather make it clear that you would far rather cast your vote against a man who stages these pitiful scenes, and makes the City a butt of mockery, than against a man who shows quiet restraint.

But apart from the matter of reputation, Gentlemen, it does
c   not seem to me just to beg a judge, or to be acquitted by begging; it is rather just to teach and persuade. The judge does not sit to grant justice as a favor, but to render judgment; he has sworn no oath to gratify those whom he sees fit, but to judge according to law. We ought not accustom you, nor ought you become accustomed, to forswear yourselves; it is pious in neither of us. So do not consider it right, Gentlemen of Athens, that I do such things in your presence as I believe to be neither honorable nor just nor
d   holy, especially since, by Zeus, it is for impiety that I am being prosecuted by this fellow Meletus here. For clearly, if I were to persuade and compel you by supplication, you being sworn as judges, I would teach you then indeed not to believe that there are gods, and in making my defense I would in effect accuse myself of not acknowledging them. But that is far from so; I do acknowledge them, Gentlemen of Athens, as none of my accusers does, and to you and to the God I now commit my case, to judge in whatever way will be best for me and also for you.

The Counterpenalty (35e–38b)

e   I am not distressed, Gentlemen of Athens, at what has happened,
36a   nor angered that you have cast your votes against me. Many things contribute to this, among them the fact that I expected it. I am much more surprised at the number of votes either way; I did not think the censure would be by so little, but by more. As it is, it seems, if only thirty votes had fallen otherwise, I would have been acquitted.[16] And so far as Meletus at least is concerned, it seems to me, I am already acquitted—and more than acquitted, since it is clear that if Anytus and Lycon had not come forward to accuse me, Meletus would have been fined a thousand drach-
b   mas for not obtaining a fifth part of the vote.

The man demands death for me. Very well. Then what coun-

16. Granting that there were 500 judges, the vote must have been 280 to 220.

terpenalty shall I propose to you, Gentlemen of Athens?[17] Clearly something I deserve, but what? What do I deserve to pay or suffer because I did not through life keep quiet, and yet did not concern myself, as the multitude do, with money or property or military and public honors and other office, or the secret societies and

c political clubs which keep cropping up in the City, believing that I was really too reasonable and temperate a man to enter upon these things and survive? I did not go where I could benefit neither you nor myself; instead, I went to each of you in private, where I might perform the greatest service. I undertook to persuade each of you not to care for anything which belongs to you before first caring for yourselves, so as to be as good and wise as possible, nor to care for anything which belongs to the City before caring for the City itself, and so too with everything else in the

d same way. Now, what do I deserve to suffer for being this sort of man? Some good thing, Gentlemen of Athens, if penalty is really to be assessed according to desert. What then is fitting for a poor man who has served his City well, and needs leisure to exhort you? Why, Gentlemen of Athens, nothing is more fitting for such a man than to be fed in the Prytaneum,[18] at the common table of the City—yes, and far more fitting than for one of you who has been an Olympic victor in the single-horse or two- or four-horse chariot races. For he makes you seem happy, whereas I make you happy in truth; and he does not need subsistence, and

e I do. If then I must propose a penalty I justly deserve, I propose

37a that, public subsistence in the Prytaneum.

Perhaps some of you will think that in saying this I speak much as I spoke of tears and pleading, out of stubborn pride. That is not so, Gentlemen of Athens, though something of this sort is: I am persuaded that I have not intentionally wronged any man, but I cannot persuade you of it; we have talked so short a time.

b Now, I believe if you had a law, as other men do, that cases involving death shall not be decided in a single day, that you would be persuaded; but as things are, it is not easy in so short a time to do away with slanders grown so great. Being persuaded,

17. Under Athenian law, the prosecutor proposed a penalty, and the convicted defendant a counterpenalty; the jury was required to choose between them without alteration. The usual practice was for a convicted person to propose a penalty as heavy as he could bear short of that which the prosecutor demanded, in hope that the jury might accept it.

18. Public subsistence in the Prytaneum was a great honor, traditionally given to Olympic victors in major events.

however, that I have wronged no one, I am quite unwilling to wrong myself, or to claim that I deserve some evil and propose any penalty of the kind. What is there to fear? That I may suffer the penalty Meletus proposes, when as I say, I do not know whether it is good or evil? Shall I choose instead a penalty I know very well to be evil? Imprisonment, perhaps? But why should I live in prison, a slave to men who happen to occupy office as the

c   Eleven? A fine, then, and prison till I pay it? But that comes to the same thing, since I have no money to pay it. Shall I then propose exile? Perhaps you would accept that. But I must indeed love life and cling to it dearly, Gentlemen, if I were so foolish as

d   to think that although you, my own fellow-citizens, cannot bear my pursuits and discussions, which have become so burdensome and hateful that you now seek to be rid of them, others will bear them lightly. No, Gentlemen. My life would be fine indeed, if at my age I went to live in exile, always moving from city to city, always driven out. For be well assured that wherever I go, the young men will listen to what I say as they do here; if I turn them away, their fathers and relations will drive me out in their

e   behalf.

Perhaps someone may say, "Would it not be possible for you to live in exile, Socrates, if you silently kept quiet?" But this is the hardest thing of all to make some of you believe. If I say that

38a   to do so would be to disobey the God, and therefore I cannot do it, you will not believe me because you will think that I am being sly and dishonest.[19] If on the other hand I say that the greatest good for man is to fashion arguments each day about virtue and the other things you hear me discussing when I examine myself and others, and that the unexamined life is not for man worth living, you will believe what I say still less. I claim these things are so, Gentlemen; but it is not easy to convince you. At the same time, I am not accustomed to think myself deserving of any evil.

b   If I had money, I would propose a fine as great as I could pay—for there would be no harm in that. But as things stand, I have no money, unless the amount I can pay is the amount you are willing to exact of me. I might perhaps be able to pay a mina of

19. That is, an *eiron*. "Irony" was regarded as a defect of character, not a virtue, as Theophrastus's portrait in the *Characters* of the ironical man makes clear.

silver.[20] So I propose a penalty in that amount. But Plato here, Gentlemen of Athens, and Crito and Critobulus and Apollodorus bid me propose thirty minae, and they will stand surety. So I propose that amount. You have guarantors sufficient for the sum.

Epilogue (38c–42a)

c   For the sake of only a little time, Gentlemen of Athens, you are to be accused by those who wish to revile the City of having killed Socrates, a wise man—for those who wish to reproach you will say I am wise even if I am not. And if you had only waited a little, the thing would have come of its own initiative. You see my age. You see how far spent my life already is, how near I am to death.

d   I say this, not to all of you, but to those of you who voted to condemn me. To them I also say this: Perhaps you think, Gentlemen of Athens, that I have been convicted for lack of words to persuade you, had I thought it right to do and say anything to be acquitted. Not so. It is true I have been convicted for a lack; not a lack of words, but lack of bold shamelessness, unwillingness to say the things you would find it pleasant to hear—weeping and wailing, saying and doing many things I claim to be unworthy of

e   me, but things of the sort you are accustomed to hear from others. I did not then think it necessary to do anything unworthy of a free man because of danger; I do not now regret so having conducted my defense; and I would far rather die with that defense than live with the other. Neither in court of law nor in war ought I or any man contrive to escape death by any means pos-

39a   sible. Often in battle it becomes clear that a man may escape death by throwing down his arms and turning in supplication to his pursuers; and there are many other devices for each of war's dangers, so that one can avoid dying if he is bold enough to say and do anything whatever. It is not difficult to escape death, Gentlemen; it is more difficult to escape wickedness, for wicked-

b   ness runs faster than death. And now I am old and slow, and I have been caught by the slower runner. But my accusers are

20. It is useless to try to give modern money equivalents, but the ultimate fine proposed is substantial: Aristotle gives one mina as the conventional ransom for a prisoner of war (*Nicomachean Ethics* V 1134b21). Why did Socrates propose a fine at all, or accept his friends' offer of suretyship? See 29d–30b, 30d–e.

clever and quick, and they have been caught by the faster runner, namely Evil. I now take my leave, sentenced by you to death; they depart, convicted by Truth for injustice and wickedness. I abide in my penalty, and they in theirs. That is no doubt as it should be, and I think it is fit.

c   I desire next to prophesy to you who condemned me. For I have now reached that point where men are especially prophetic—when they are about to die. I say to you who have decreed my death that to you there will come hard on my dying a punishment far more difficult to bear than the death you have visited upon me. You have done this thing in the belief that you would be released from submitting to examination of your lives. I say that it will turn out quite otherwise. Those who come to examine
d   you will be more numerous, and I have up to now restrained them, though you perceived it not. They will be more harsh inasmuch as they are younger, and you shall be the more troubled. If you think by killing to hold back the reproach due you for not living rightly, you are profoundly mistaken. That release is neither possible nor honorable. The release which is both most honorable and most easy is not to cut down others, but to take proper care that you will be as good as possible. This I utter as prophecy to you who voted for my condemnation, and take my leave.

e   But with you who voted for my acquittal, I should be glad to discuss the nature of what has happened, now, while the authorities are busy and I am not yet gone where, going, I must die. Abide with me, Gentlemen, this space of time; for nothing pre-
40a   vents our talking with each other while we still can. To you, as my friends, I wish to display the meaning of what has now fallen to my lot. A remarkable thing has occurred, Gentlemen and Judges—and I correctly call you Judges. My accustomed oracle, which is divine, always came quite frequently before in everything, opposing me even in trivial matters if I was about to err. And now a thing has fallen to my lot which you also see, a thing which some might think, and do in fact believe, to be ultimate among evils. But the Sign of the God did not oppose me early
b   this morning when I left my house, or when I came up here to the courtroom, or at any point in my argument in anything I was about to say. And yet frequently in other arguments, it has checked me right in the middle of speaking; but today it has not opposed me in any way, in none of my deeds, in none of my words. What do I take to be the reason? I will tell you. Very likely

c   what has fallen to me is good, and those among us who think
       that death is an evil are wrong. There has been convincing in-
       dication of this. For the accustomed Sign would surely have op-
       posed me, if I were not in some way acting for good.

       Let us also consider a further reason for high hope that death
       is good. Death is one of two things. Either to be dead is not to
       exist, to have no awareness at all, or it is, as the stories tell, a kind
       of alteration, a change of abode for the soul from this place to
       another. And if it is to have no awareness, like a sleep when the
d   sleeper sees no dream, death would be a wonderful gain; for I
       suppose if someone had to pick out that night in which he slept
       and saw no dream, and put the other days and nights of his life
       beside it, and had to say after inspecting them how many days
       and nights he had lived in his life which were better and sweeter,
       I think that not only any ordinary person but even the Great
       King[21] himself would find them easily numbered in relation to
e   other days, and other nights. If death is that, I say it is gain; for
       the whole of time then turns out to last no longer than a single
       night. But if on the contrary death is like taking a journey, pass-
       ing from here to another place, and the stories told are true, and
       all who have died are there—what greater good might there be,
41a   my Judges? For if a man once goes to the place of the dead, and
       takes leave of those who claim to be judges here, he will find the
       true judges who are said to sit in judgment there—Minos, Rhad-
       amanthus, Aeacus, Triptolemus, and the other demigods and he-
       roes who lived just lives. Would that journey be worthless? And
       again, to meet Orpheus and Musaeus, Hesiod and Homer—how
       much would any of you give? I at least would be willing to die
b   many times over, if these things are true. I would find a wonderful
       pursuit there, when I met Palamedes, and Ajax, son of Telemon,
       and any others among the ancients done to death by unjust ver-
       dicts, and compared my experiences with theirs. It would not, I
       think, be unamusing. But the greatest thing, surely, would be to
       test and question there as I did here: Who among them is wise?
       Who thinks he is and is not? How much might one give, my
c   Judges, to examine the man who led the great army against Troy,
       or Odysseus, or Sisyphus, or a thousand other men and women
       one might mention—to converse with them, to associate with
       them, to examine them—why, it would be inconceivable happi-

21. Of Persia, a proverbial symbol of wealth and power.

ness. Especially since they surely do not kill you for it there. They are happier there than men are here in other ways, and they are already immortal for the rest of time, if the stories told are true.

d But you too, my Judges, must be of good hope concerning death. You must recognize that this one thing is true: there is not evil for a good man either in living or in dying, and the gods do not neglect his affairs. What has now come to me did not occur of its own initiative. It is clear to me that to die now and be released from my affairs is better for me. That is why the Sign did not turn me back, and I bear no anger whatever toward those who voted to condemn me, or toward my accusers. And yet, it was not with this in mind that they accused and convicted me.

e They thought to do harm, and for that they deserve blame. But this much would I ask of them: When my sons are grown, Gentlemen, exact a penalty of them; give pain to them exactly as I gave pain to you, if it seems to you that they care more for wealth or anything else than they care for virtue. And if they seem to be something and are nothing, rebuke them as I rebuked you, because they do not care for what they ought, because they think

42a themselves something and are worth nothing. And should you do that, both I and my sons will have been justly dealt with at your hands.

But it is now the hour of parting—I to die and you to live. Which of us goes to the better is unclear to all but the God.

III: THE CRITO

COMMENT

The central issue of the *Crito* is briefly stated. Socrates, lying in prison awaiting execution, is presented with an opportunity to escape. He chooses instead to go to his death, because the law requires his execution and it would be unjust to break the law. As a complicating factor in his decision, it is suggested that the particular application of the law which requires his death is unjust, because he is not guilty of the charge of impiety under which he lies condemned.

By any standards, this is a hard case. It raises a simple question: Can it conceivably be true that a man ought to abide by his own death sentence, given that the sentence was rendered according to law and that he is not guilty?

Few documents in history have pitched the obligations of citizenship so high, and, perhaps for this reason, the *Crito* has often been treated not as philosophical argument, but as a document in the biography of Socrates, an exhibition of his strength of character in the face of death. The *Crito* itself tells a different story. Socrates went to his death on the basis of *logos*, an argument. He chose to die because he was convinced by reasoning that it was wrong to escape. That reasoning is brought to conclusion in a speech by the personified Laws of Athens.

The speech of the Laws is rhetoric of such force that when it is finished Socrates turns and says, "Crito, my dear and faithful friend, I think I hear these things as the Corybants think they hear the pipes, and the droning murmur of their words sounds within me and makes me incapable of hearing aught else." And Crito too is silenced. But, we may ask, if rhetoric, how philosophy? In a famous passage of the *Gorgias*, Socrates denies that rhetoric is an art, for it is based on no knowledge and unable

107

to render an account. It is a mere knack of persuasion, aimed at gratification and indifferent to truth.

Yet the speech of the Laws is hardly flattery: it leads Socrates to his
death. And the *Gorgias* also envisages a philosophical rhetoric aimed at
excellence of soul, indifferent to whether it gives pleasure or pain to the
hearers, and directed toward producing that order of soul associated
with lawfulness and law. This kind of rhetorician is to the soul as the
physician is to the body: he is a statesman, possessed of knowledge, and
when he speaks he does not speak at random, but like a craftsman organizes his materials with a view to his single aim, that of the moral good
of his hearers.

The *Crito* presents not one but two specimens of rhetoric: the speech
of the Laws, and Crito's plea to escape. Crito's plea begins with and twice
repeats the injunction "Be thou persuaded by me," but the persuasion
offered is, as the *Gorgias* puts it, "at random." Crito offers, not a sequen-
tial argument organized around a single principle, but a cluster of considerations that might have been offered in any order, like the epitaph
of Midas the Phrygian. Escape is possible, easy, inexpensive. There is no
real danger to Socrates' friends. There is a place for him in Thessaly,
where he will be protected. If he does not escape, he will leave his children orphans at a time when they need him. His friends will be disgraced
for not having saved him; and he for not saving himself. His enemies
will triumph. He himself will be "bad" and "unmanly."

Crito's plea begins, ends, and is mainly based on "how things will look."
The pivot of his reasoning, to the degree that it has a pivot, turns on
the connected concepts of shame and success. Shame is an external standard of judgment in which a man's estimate of himself and his actions
is a function of the estimate of other people, or of the community at
large. Success is external as well. The good man succeeds and helps his
friends. Thus Meno and Polemarchus think that the excellence of a man
consists in helping friends and harming enemies. The bad man fails, and
in his failure he becomes disgraced; he has fallen short of the standard
of performance that he must attain to be considered a man—a failure
which may be involuntary and yet eventuates in blame. To be convicted
of a crime is to fail conspicuously and be disgraced; to go to execution
when one might escape is to compound on that failure, and in the Athens
of Socrates' time, as in the Athens of St. Paul, such death was not regarded as a likely prelude to transfiguration.

Crito stands as an advocate, pleading a cause to his friend in behalf
of his friend, using, as a pleader will, such terms as he can muster to
persuade. The randomness of his persuasion answers to an underlying

incoherence in his plea. If shame and success were the only elements operative in his moral universe, he would be unable to understand, let alone accept, the appeal that Socrates makes to justice and the excellence of the soul. Further, there is implicit inconsistency in the plea. Shame and success may seem to go hand in hand—one must succeed or be disgraced. But they do not present a coherent basis of judgment, because the man best able to satisfy the standard of success is precisely the tyrant, who can rule without shame. Thus it is that Callicles, who dares to say what many believe but are ashamed to say, rejects as fit only for slaves the morality of ordinary social convention and the praise and blame that attend on it, and he criticizes philosophy on the ground that it unfits a man to defend himself. It is a law of nature—*nomos* of *phusis*—that the strong should rule with the high hand and oppress the weak. Success, become power, conquers shame. Callicles, it may be observed, is no sophist, but a well-educated young Athenian gentleman; it is presumably no accident that his words echo those of the Athenian emissaries in the Melian Dialogue. Crito is a good and decent man, and he speaks the language of popular morals; but popular morality was many things, not one, and in its incoherence combined surface decency with sinister depths.

Socrates' reply to Crito epitomizes what F. M. Cornford once called, without apology to Copernicus or Kant, the Socratic Revolution. The reply represents a transformation from outer to inner: shame becomes reverence for truth, success attainment of justice. As Callicles remarks in the *Gorgias*, "Socrates, if you are serious and if what you say is really true, our human life would be turned upside down; we are doing exactly the opposite of what we should." Whether Socrates should escape has nothing to do with what people think or with their ignorant praise and blame; it is a question to be settled by *logoi*—arguments, accounts, reasoned conclusions. The issue rests with "he who understands things just and unjust"—the Truth itself. If shame we are to feel, it is before truth as discovered in reasoning that Shame should be felt.

If Socrates alters the terms of shame, he also alters the meaning of success. We have a possession that is benefited by justice and harmed by injustice and is of higher worth than the body. It is not living, but living well, which is of more importance, and to live well is to live justly. The question of whether to escape reduces to the question of whether it is just or unjust to do so.

There is a faint suggestion of paradox in a standard of success which may require voluntary acceptance of execution as the duty of the successful man. The paradox is founded directly on the Socratic Proportion, that justice is to the soul as health is to the body, with its corollary that, as we look to the arts of the physician and trainer in matters of health, so we must look to the wise man—the statesman and true rhetorician of the *Gorgias*—in matters of justice and virtue. The Laws in the *Crito* speak as physicians of soul. Their speech is not "at random": it is a unified and organic whole with head, trunk, and limbs, organized around a single self-consistent principle, the primacy of justice. Their speech is rhetoric, and appeals, as rhetoric should, to powerful emotions: religious feeling, love of country, gratitude for the gift of life and education, the moral sentiments that attach to promises. The speech also meets, point by point, the prudential considerations that Crito urged in favor of escape. But though the speech appeals to emotion, it does not rest on emotional appeal; though it deals with prudential considerations, it does not turn on them. It is both rhetoric and dialectic—dialectical rhetoric—even though only intermittently cast in dialogue form. Socrates had earlier said that he would be persuaded only by that logos which on reflection proved best to him. The speech of the Laws presents that logos at its very head: escape is unjust because it involves the doing of injury. This logos rests on two premises which Socrates and Crito have already agreed to in their conversation, and the Laws, as they continue, elicit by questioning further agreement at every major step of the way.

The two premises on which the argument of the Laws turns are that it is wrong to do injury or return it, and that it is right to abide by agreements, given that they are just. The qualification "given that they are just" is important. Socrates does not suppose that the obligation to abide by agreements is "strict" or "perfect," that once agreement has been entered, nothing can justify its breach. Compare the example given to Polemarchus in the *Republic* (it may be glossed from the *Memorabilia*) of not returning weapons held in keeping for a friend who has gone mad, or always telling him the truth. In the concrete situation envisaged in the *Crito*, there is something eccentric—not to say repugnant—in the notion that the abstract duties of promise keeping may obligate a man to accept an unjust sentence of death. The source of the eccentricity is the assumption that the existence of an agreement is the sole ground for the justice of abiding by it, whereas in fact the justice of abiding by it is a condition for honoring the agreement.

An agreement, then, does not serve as an independent ground for refusing to escape: it is rather an essential link in a concatenated argument which rests on the primacy of justice. That one ought never do injury or return it is treated as a direct implication of the proposition that one is never to do injustice or return injustice for injustice—two wrongs don't make a right. It is also treated as a paradox the Many will never accept. Socrates' point here is essentially the same as that made in the cross-examination of Meletus in the *Apology*: to injure or harm something, or to corrupt it, is to make it worse with respect to its proper excellence. It cannot be a function of justice to do injustice, of excellence to diminish excellence in others, or of goodness to do harm.

It is against this background that the Laws present the head of their argument, which consists of an astonishing charge: that Socrates, if he escapes, will thereby attempt so far as in him lies to destroy the City and the Laws. For no city can exist and not be overturned in which legal judgments are without force, but may be rendered unauthoritative and corrupted by private citizens. To escape is to destroy the law which enjoins that judgments judicially rendered are authoritative; the fact that the City did not decide the case correctly is irrelevant, for Socrates has entered into agreement with the Laws to abide by such decisions as the City may render.

It will be observed that this argument is not primarily contractual, but delictual: its gist lies, not in breach of agreement, but in claim of injury. The brunt of the charge against Socrates is not that he will break a promise if he escapes, but that he will to the degree he is able attempt to destroy the Laws and the City. This charge matches precisely the structure of the premises Socrates and Crito have already agreed upon.

Socrates, by voluntarily assuming the status of citizenship, has entered into a tacit agreement—an intendment attaching to the status—to abide by the law that judgments rendered judicially are authoritative. If he escapes, he will act in breach of that law and thereby attempt the destruction of law itself. We may well ask in what that destruction consists. Breaking jail is not like sacking or attempting to sack Troy, or like causing or attempting to cause a revolution. Destruction aside, where is there harm? In plain utilitarian terms, Socrates' escape would probably have benefited Athens by relieving her of the odium attached to the execution of a distinguished and widely honored man. It would have salved the consciences of many of his judges and prevented the grief of wife, family, and friends. There are, in short, multiple utilitarian grounds for escape, and no ordinary grounds for claiming that escape implies an attempt at destruction. Why then is that proposition to be maintained?

The key presumably lies in the nature of judicial authority. To escape is to act in breach of the sentence of execution. That sentence was rendered according to law, and *as legal*, owes its authority precisely to the court empowered to render it. To deny the authority of a given sentence so rendered is to deny authority to any sentence so rendered; this denies authority to law itself, because it denies authority to its application. Since the application of law is essential to the existence of law, to act in breach of any given application by a court of law is—by so much—destructive of law. Because law without application is not law, and a city without law is not a city, the Laws of Athens claim that Socrates, if he escapes, will attempt to destroy the City and its laws. As Aristotle remarked in the *Politics,* with the *Crito* presumably in mind, "Judicial decisions are useless if they take no effect; if society cannot exist without them, neither can it exist without their execution."

This is essentially a universalization argument, and explains why escape implies injury. But breach of legal authority does not imply immortality without the additional premises, not supplied by a universalization argument, that it is wrong to do injury or return it and right to abide by agreements, given that they are just. Universalization is offered not as an independent test of right and wrong, but as a principle attaching to legality. There is a certain trick of perspective in the *Crito*; for its primary concern is not with legal authority, but with the question of why the law stating that judgments judicially rendered are authoritative is itself authoritative.

The *Crito* does not attempt a definition of law, and its discussion of legal obligation is directed to one particular and practical decision: whether to escape or die. But the principles by which that decision is reached are, because they are principles, more general than their application, and if the *Crito* does not say what law is, it implies much about what it is not.

Hobbes once remarked that in government, when nothing else is turned up, clubs are trumps. But in real life, clubs are no longer trumps when one is facing spades. If law consisted, as H. L. A. Hart's excellent phrase has it, in orders backed by threats, if from the point of view of the citizen the authority of law were derived only from coercion, the issue discussed in the *Crito* would not arise. The *Crito* supposes that law retains its binding claim on conduct even when the force that backs it has in effect been exhausted through application; and the very application of that force has itself a binding claim, not because it is force, but because it is force of law. Legal sanctions, though they may provide a motive for obedience to law, are not an element in the analysis of legal obligation. The obligation that law imposes is moral: it rests on agreement and the wrongfulness of injury, and it obtains even though given verdicts may be incorrect and though given laws may differ from what is by nature just. The citizen is under obligation to obey all laws unless he can alter them by persuasion rather than force; his obligation, it will be observed, is not to law as coinciding with a given moral content, but to positive law as positive, to rules and principles, laws which are in fact laid down in a legal system, whether or not they coincide with a given moral content.

This leads to a difficulty. The *Crito* appears to maintain the following propositions: (i) positive law imposes a moral obligation on citizens to obedience; (ii) positive law—rule, verdict, and presumably, therefore, edict or decree—may require what is unjust. It seems a direct inference from (i) or (ii) that (iii) a citizen may be morally obligated to do what he is morally obligated not to do. In short, if you claim that there is a moral obligation to obey the law and claim also that given laws or their application may run contrary to what is by nature just, then you appear committed to the proposition that, on occasion, you ought to do what you ought not to do.

But the premises of the *Crito*, far from implying this absurdity, preclude it. If one ought never do injustice, one ought not do injustice when the laws enjoin it. If one ought to abide by agreements when it is just to do so, and one ought never do injustice, a binding agreement cannot require the doing of injustice. There is more to legal authority than validity: there is also the issue of scope. Although citizenship implies agreement, the doing of injustice at the behest of law is not a part of the terms of that agreement, so a law or decree that requires injustice is in a strict sense *ultra vires*. Because injury to law arises only from breach of authority and authority extends only so far as agreement binds, disobeying a law or decree that commands the doing of injustice does not injure the law. The *Crito*'s claim that positive law imposes a moral obligation to obedience, in short, is true only under the restriction inherent in the premises by which the argument proceeds.

This restriction applies to the doing of injustice. It does not thereby apply to the suffering of it. Thus in the *Apology* Socrates states flatly that he will not give up his inquiry even if the court should require it; he will obey the God rather than Athens, avoiding the specific form of injustice which is impiety. In the *Crito*, he holds himself under obligation to accept a sentence of death for that refusal. Law and sanction are separable. One may be obligated to accept legal punishment for not doing what one was obligated not to do—a paradox most men will never accept.

If this account of the *Crito* is true, it may be contrasted with a more usual one, neatly summed up by Hume at the conclusion of his essay "Of the Original Contract": "The only passage I meet with in antiquity, where the obligation of obedience to government is ascribed to a promise, is in Plato's *Crito*; where Socrates refused to escape from prison, because

he had tacitly promised to obey the laws. Thus he builds a *Tory* consequence of passive obedience on a *Whig* foundation of the original contract." But the *Crito*, though it establishes no right of revolution where
citizenship is the result of voluntary agreement, hardly recommends passive obedience. Nor does the obligation of obedience to law rest simply
on a promise. Socrates goes to his death because he has, by agreeing to
live as a citizen, brought himself within the scope of legal authority, and
because action in breach of that authority constitutes an injury to law. It
is a curiosity of intellectual history that this structure of argument should
match with considerable precision the medieval writ of Assumpsit at
common law, the basis of the modern law of contract.

The argument of the *Crito* rests on a revolution in morals and implies
paradox. We are sometimes told that this new morality, if it is to be viable,
must satisfy the claims of popular morality. If it did, it would be inconsistent, but not paradoxical. Anytus and Meletus, acting by the standards
of popular morality, condemned Socrates to death for impiety; another
man, Crito, acting by the same standards, urged him to escape. At the
level of principle, popular morality was many things, not one. At the
level of rules, it was at best a container requiring further content. Do
not steal. Do not murder. Do not commit adultery. But theft is wrongful
taking, murder wrongful killing, adultery wrongful intercourse—in what
does wrongfulness consist? One way of answering that question is by
appeal to law, *nomos*—prescriptive as well as stone-chiseled rules. Unless
justice requires otherwise, the citizen owes obedience to *nomos,* and since
there are many who will never discover for themselves what justice requires, it is all the more important that the laws be good. It is no accident
that the Socratic legacy issues in a school of jurisprudence. But the criterion of wrongfulness lies ultimately not in any set of rules, however
skillfully framed, but in a single self-consistent standard of justice, fixed
in the nature of things, by which the worth of rules and all else is to be
judged, and whose use is essential to genuine virtue, which is based on
knowledge and allied to art.

Socrates never claimed to have attained certain knowledge of that standard. The man who in the *Apology* knew only that he did not know does
not in the *Crito* lay claim to full knowledge of justice and virtue. The
Crito presents not demonstration, but dialectic, with the provisional quality that dialectic entails. But when dialectic has been carried as far as
possible and when such degree of clarity has been attained as human
limitation permits, one must act on the conclusions that appear true and
good. This conception of human rationality, lofty in its aim, is tentative
and modest in its estimate of attainment; but in its insistence on the

sovereignty of reason, it is immodest in its rejection of the contrary view that reason is, and of a right ought to be, only the slave of the passions. That is the doctrine of Callicles, and it is the unstated underlying assumption of popular rhetoric, the image of statesmanship. In the depths of that image lie disintegration, both personal and social. The *Gorgias* is an account of the descent into hell.

TRANSLATION

SOCRATES / CRITO

Introductory Conversation (43a–44b)

43a SOC. Why have you come at this hour, Crito? Isn't it still early?

CRI. Very early.

SOC. What time, exactly?

CRI. Depth of dawn, before first light.

SOC. I'm surprised the guard was willing to admit you.

CRI. He's used to me by now, Socrates, because I come here so often. Besides, I've done him a kindness.

SOC. Did you come just now, or a while ago?

CRI. Quite a while ago.

b SOC. Then why didn't you wake me right away, instead of sitting there in silence?

CRI. No, Socrates. I might wish I weren't in such wakeful pain myself, and I've been marveling for some time at how sweetly you sleep. I didn't wake you on purpose, so that you could spend the time as pleasantly as possible. Often before, through the whole of our lives, I've thought you happy in your ways, but never more than now in the present misfortune—so cheerfully and lightly do you bear it.

SOC. But surely, Crito, it would scarcely be appropriate in a man of my age to be distressed that he now has to die.

c CRI. Other men as old have been taken in similar misfortune, Socrates, and age did not relieve their distress at what faced them.

117

soc. True. But why are you here so early?

CRI. I bring grievous news, Socrates. Not grievous to you, it appears, but grievous to me and to all your companions, and heaviest to bear, I think, for me.

d soc. What is it? Has the ship come from Delos, on whose arrival I'm to die?

CRI. Not yet. But I think it will come today, to judge from the report of some people who've arrived from Sunium and left it there. From what they say, it will clearly come today, and then tomorrow, Socrates, your life must end.[1]

soc. Well, Crito, let it be for the best. If so it pleases the Gods, let it be so. Still, I do not think it will come today.

44a CRI. From what do you infer that?

soc. I'll tell you. I am to die, I think, the day after the ship arrives.

CRI. Yes—so the authorities say, at any rate.

soc. Then I think it will come tomorrow, not today. I infer that from a dream I saw a little while ago tonight. Perhaps you chose a good time not to wake me.

CRI. What was the dream?

soc. A woman appeared to me. She came, fair and beautiful of

b   form, clothed in white, and she called to me and said, "Socrates, on the third day shalt thou go to fertile Phthia."

CRI. A strange dream, Socrates.

soc. But Crito, I think a clear one.

CRI. Yes, too clear, it seems.

Crito's Exhortation to Escape (44b–46a)

CRI. But, please, Socrates, my beloved friend, please let me persuade you even at this point. Save yourself. As for me, if you should die it will be a multiple misfortune. Quite apart from the loss of such friendship as I shall not find again, people who don't

c   really know us will think I didn't care, because I could have saved you if only I'd been willing to spend the money. Yet what could seem more shameful than the appearance of putting money before friends? People won't believe that you refused to escape even though we were eager to help.

soc. But Crito, why should we be so concerned about what people

1. See *Phaedo* 58a–c.

will think? Reasonable men, who are the ones worth considering, will believe that things happened as they did.

d CRI. Surely at this point, Socrates, you see how necessary it really is to care about what people think. The very things now happening show that they can accomplish, not the least of evils, but very nearly the greatest, if a man has been slandered among them.

SOC. If only they could work the greatest evils, Crito, so that they might also work the greatest goods, it would truly be well. But as it is, they can do neither; they cannot make a man wise or foolish. They only act at random.

e CRI. Very well, let that be so. But tell me this, Socrates. Are you worried about me and the rest of your friends? Are you afraid that, if you escape, the sycophants will make trouble for us for helping you, so that we may be compelled to forfeit our estates or a great deal of money, or suffer more besides? If you're afraid

45a of something of that sort, dismiss it. It is right for us to run that risk to save you, and still greater risk if need be. Please, let me persuade you to do as I say.

SOC. Of course I'm worried about those things, Crito, and many other things too.

CRI. Then don't be afraid. In fact, it's not a large sum which certain people are willing to take to manage your escape, and as for the sycophants, you see how cheaply they can be bought; it wouldn't

b take much money for them. You have mine at your disposal, and it is, I think, enough, but if you're at all worried about me and think you shouldn't spend mine, your friends from abroad are ready. One of them, Simmias of Thebes, has brought enough money, just for this purpose, and Cebes and quite a few others are ready, too. So as I say, you mustn't hesitate because of that. Nor should you be troubled about what you said in court, how if you went into exile you wouldn't know what to do with yourself.

c There are many places for you to go where they'd welcome you warmly, but if you want to go to Thessaly, I have friends there who will honor and protect you, so that no one will cause you distress.

Furthermore, Socrates, I think the thing you're doing is wrong. You betray yourself when you could be saved. You hasten a thing for yourself of a kind your very enemies might hasten for you— and have hastened, wishing you destroyed. In addition, I think

d you're betraying your sons. You desert them when you could raise and educate them; so far as you're concerned, they're to take what comes, and what is likely to come is just what usually comes to orphans in the poverty of their orphanhood. No. Either a man shouldn't have children, or he should accept the burden of raising and educating them; the choice you're making is one of the most heedless indifference. Your choice should be that of a good and courageous man—especially since you say you've had a lifelong concern for virtue. I'm ashamed, Socrates, ashamed both for you

e   and for your friends, because it's going to seem that the whole business was done through a kind of cowardice in us. The case was brought to court when it needn't have been. Then there was the conduct of the trial. And now, as the final absurdity of the whole affair, it will look as if we let slip this final opportunity because of our own badness and cowardice, whereas we could have saved you or you could have saved yourself if we were worth

46a   anything at all. These things are bad, and shameful both to you and to us. Decide. Or rather, at this hour, it isn't time to decide but to have decided. This is the last chance, because everything must be done this coming night, and if we wait it will not be possible any longer. Please, Socrates, be persuaded by me and do as I ask.

Socrates' Reply to Crito (46b–49a)

b SOC. My dear Crito, your eagerness is worth much, if rightly directed. But if not, then the greater it is, the worse. We must consider carefully whether this thing is to be done, for I am now and always have been the sort of man who is persuaded only by the argument which on reflection proves best to me, and I cannot

c   throw over arguments I formerly accepted merely because of what has come; they still seem much the same to me, and I honor them as I did before. If we can't find better ones, be assured that I will not give way to you, not even if the power of the multitude were far greater than it now is to frighten us like children with its threats of confiscation, bonds, and death.

Now, how might we most fairly consider the matter? Perhaps we should first take up this argument of yours about beliefs. We

d   often used to say that some beliefs are worth paying attention to and others not. Was that wrong? Or was it right before I had to die, whereas it is now obviously idle nonsense put for the sake of arguing? I'd like to join with you in common inquiry, Crito. Does

that appear in any way changed now that I'm here? Let us dismiss
it or be persuaded by it. We often used to say, I think—and we
e   used to think it made sense—that among the beliefs men entertain, some are to be regarded as important and others are not.
Before the Gods, Crito, were we wrong? At least insofar as it lies
47a   in human agency, you aren't about to die tomorrow, and the
present situation won't distort your judgment. So consider the
matter. Don't you think it's satisfactory to say that one shouldn't
value the beliefs of every man, but rather of some men and not
others, and that one shouldn't value every belief of men, but some
beliefs and not others? Isn't that right?

CRI. It is.

SOC. Now, it's useful beliefs which should be valued, not harmful
or bad ones?

CRI. Yes.

SOC. Useful ones being those of the wise, bad ones those of the
foolish?

CRI. Of course.

SOC. To continue, what did we use to say about things like this?
b   Suppose a man goes in for athletics. Does he pay attention to the
opinions, the praise and blame, of everybody, or only the one
man who is his physician or trainer?

CRI. Only the one.

SOC. Then he ought to welcome the praise and fear the blame of
that one man, not of the multitude.

CRI. Clearly.

SOC. So he is to train and exercise, eat and drink, in a way that
seems good to a supervisor who knows and understands, rather
than anyone else.

CRI. True.

c SOC. Very well. But if he disobeys that supervisor, scorns his judgment and praises, values those of the multitude who are without
understanding, won't he suffer an evil?

CRI. Of course.

SOC. What is that evil? Whither does it tend, and into what possession of the man who disobeys?

CRI. Into the body, clearly, for it ruins that.

SOC. Right. And isn't this also true in other matters, Crito? We
don't need to run through them all, but isn't it especially true of
what is just and unjust, honorable and shameful, good and evil—
just the things our decision is now concerned with? Are we to

d   fear and follow the multitude in such matters? Or is it rather the
opinion of one man, if he but have knowledge, which we must
reverence and fear beyond all the rest? Since, if we do not follow
it, we will permanently damage and corrupt something that we
used to say becomes better by justice and is harmed by injustice.
Or is there no such thing?

CRI. I certainly think there is, Socrates.

SOC. Very well then, suppose that, by disobeying the opinion of
those who understand, we were to ruin what becomes better by
e   health and is damaged by disease. Would life be worth living for
us once it has been damaged? That is the body, of course?

CRI. Yes.

SOC. Well, would life be worth living with a wretched, damaged
body?

CRI. Surely not.

SOC. Then is it worth living when there is damage to what the just
benefits and the unjust corrupts? Or do we think that this—
48a whatever it is of ours to which justice and injustice pertain—is of
less worth than the body?

CRI. Surely not.

SOC. Of more worth?

CRI. Far more.

SOC. Then perhaps we shouldn't give much thought to what the
multitude tells us, my friend. Perhaps we should rather think of
what he will say who understands things just and unjust—he
being but one man, and the very Truth itself. So your first claim,
that we ought to pay attention to what the multitude thinks about
what is just and honorable and good, is mistaken. "But then,"
someone might say, "the multitude can kill us."

b CRI. Yes, Socrates, it is very clear someone might say that.

SOC. And yet, my friend, the conclusion we've reached still seems
much as it did before. Then too, consider whether this agreement
also still abides: that it is not living which is of most importance,
but living well.

CRI. It does.

SOC. But "well" is the same as honorably and justly—does that abide
too?

CRI. Yes.

SOC. Then in light of these arguments, we must consider whether
or not it would be right for me to try to escape without permission
c   of the Athenians. If it proves right, let us try; if not, let us dismiss

the matter. But as for these other considerations you raise about loss of money and raising children and what people think—Crito, those are really fit topics for people who lightly kill and would raise to life again without a thought if they could—the multitude. As for us, the argument has chosen; there is nothing to be considered but the things we've already mentioned—whether it is

d right to give money with our thanks to those who are going to manage my escape, whether in actual fact we shall do injustice by doing any of these things. If it proves to be unjust, then perhaps we should give thought neither to death nor to anything else except the doing of injustice.

CRI. You are right, Socrates. Look to what we should do.

soc. Let's examine the matter together, my friend, and if you can somehow refute what I'm going to say, do so, and I'll be per-

e suaded. But if not, then please, my dear friend, please stop returning over and over again to the same argument about how I ought to escape from here without permission from the Athenians. For I count it important that I act with your agreement, not against your will. So look to the starting point of the inquiry.

49a See whether it is satisfactorily stated, and try to answer what I ask as you think proper.

CRI. I'll certainly try.

Two Premises (49a–50a)

soc. Do we say that there are any circumstances in which injustice ought willingly or wittingly be done? Or is injustice to be done in some circumstances but not others? Is the doing of injustice in no way honorable or good, as we often in the past agreed, or have those former agreements been cast aside these last few days?

b Has it long escaped our notice, Crito, that as old men in serious discussion with each other we were really no better than children, or is it rather precisely as we used to claim: that whether the multitude agrees or not, whether we must suffer things still worse than this or things more easy to bear, still, the doing of injustice is in every circumstance shameful and evil for him who does it. Do we affirm that, or not?

CRI. We do.

soc. Then one must never do injustice.

CRI. Of course not.

soc. Nor, as most people think, return injustice for injustice, since one must never do injustice.

c CRI. That follows.

soc. Then does this? Ought one work injury, Crito?

CRI. No, surely not, Socrates.

soc. Then is it just to work injury in return for having suffered it, as the multitude affirms?

CRI. Not at all.

soc. No, for surely there is no difference between doing ill to men and doing injustice.

CRI. True.

soc. Then one ought not return injustice for injustice or do ill to any man, no matter what one may suffer at their hands. Look to
d   this, Crito. Do not agree against your real opinion, for I know that few men think or will ever think it true. Between those who accept it and those who do not, there is no common basis for decision; when they view each others' counsels, they must necessarily hold each other in contempt. So consider very carefully whether you unite with me in agreeing that it can never be right to do injustice or return it, or to ward off the suffering of evil by doing it in return, or whether you recoil from this starting
e   point. I have long thought it true and do still. If you think otherwise, speak and instruct me. But if you abide by our former agreements, hear what follows.

CRI. I do abide. Please go on.

soc. I say next, or rather, I ask, whether one is to do things he agreed with someone to do, given that they are just, or is one to deceive?

CRI. One is to do them.

soc. Then observe what follows. If I escape from here without
50a persuading the City, am I not injuring someone, and someone I least ought? And am I not failing to abide by agreements that are just?

CRI. Socrates, I can't answer what you ask, for I don't understand.

The Speech of the Laws of Athens (50a–54d)

soc. Look at it this way. Suppose I was about to run off from here, or whatever the thing should be called. And suppose the Laws, the common constitution of the City, came and stood before me
b   and said, "Tell us, Socrates, what you intend to do. Do you mean

by this to destroy us? To destroy, as far as in you lies, the Laws and the City as a whole? Or do you think that a city can continue to exist and not be overturned, in which legal judgments once rendered are without force, but may be rendered unauthoritative by private citizens and so corrupted?"

How are we to answer that, Crito, and questions like it? A good deal might be said, especially by an orator, in behalf of that law, now to be broken, which requires that judgments judicially ren-
c dered be authoritative. Or are we to reply that the City did us an injustice and didn't decide the case correctly. Is that what we're to say?

CRI. Most emphatically, Socrates.

SOC. Then what if the Laws were to reply, "Socrates, was that really our agreement? Or was it rather to abide by such judgments as the City might render?" And if I were surprised at the question, they might go on, "There's no reason for surprise, Socrates. An-swer the question, especially since you're so used to questions
d and answers. Come then, what charge do you lay against us and the City, that you should undertake to destroy us? We gave you birth. It was through us that your father took your mother to wife and begot you. Tell us, then, those of us who are the Laws of Marriage, do you find some fault in us for being incorrect?"

"No fault," I would say.

"Then what about the Laws governing the rearing of children once born, and their education—the Laws under which you your-self were educated. Did we who are the Laws established for that
e purpose prescribe incorrectly when we directed your father to educate you in music and gymnastic?"

"Correctly," I'd say.

"Very well, then. We bore you, reared you, educated you. Can you then say, first of all, that you are not our offspring and our slave—you, and your fathers before you? And if that's true, do you think that justice is on a level between you and us—that it is right for you to do in return what we may undertake to do to you? Was there such an equality relative to your father, or your master if you had one, so that you might return whatever was
51a done to you—strike back when struck, speak ill when spoken ill to, things like that? Does such a possibility then exist toward your Country and its Laws, so that if we should undertake to destroy you, believing it just, you in return will undertake so far as you are able to destroy us, your Country and its Laws? Will you claim

that this is right—you, who are so profoundly concerned about virtue? Or are you so wise that you have let it escape your notice that Country is to be honored beyond mother and father or any
b forebears; that it is more holy, more to be revered, of greater apportionment among both gods and men of understanding; that an angered Country must be reverenced and obeyed and given way to even more than an angered father; that you must either persuade it to the contrary or do what it bids and suffer quietly what it prescribes, whether blows or bonds, whether you are led to war for wounds or death, still, these things are to be done. The just lies here: never to give way, never to desert, never to leave your post, but in war or court of law or any other place to
c do what City and Country command—that, or to persuade it of what is by nature just. It is not holy to use force against a mother or father; and it is far more unholy to use force against your Country."

What are we to say to that, Crito? Do the Laws speak the truth?
CRI. Yes, I think they do.
SOC. "Then consider this, Socrates," the Laws might say. "If we speak the truth, aren't you attempting to wrong us in what you
d now undertake? We gave you birth. We nurtured you. We educated you. We gave to you and to every other citizen a share of every good thing we could. Nonetheless, we continue to proclaim, by giving leave to any Athenian who wishes, that when he had been admitted to the rights of manhood and sees things in the City and its Laws which do not please him, he may take what is his and go either to one of our colonies or a foreign land. No law among us stands in the way or forbids it. You may take what is yours and go where you like, if we and the City do not please
e you. But whoever among you stays, recognizing the way we render judgment and govern the other affairs of the City, to him at that point we say that by his action he has entered agreement with us to do as we bid. And if he does not obey, we say that he commits injustice in three ways: because he disobeys us, and we gave him birth; because he disobeys us, and we nurtured him; because he agreed to obey us and neither obeys nor persuades
52a us that we are doing something incorrect—even though we did not rudely command him to do as we bid, but rather set before him the alternatives of doing it or persuading us to the contrary. Those are the charges, Socrates, which we say will be imputable

to you if you do what you're planning. To you, and to you not least, but more than any other Athenian."

And if I were to ask, "Why is that?" they might justly assail me with the claim that, as it happened, I more than most Athenians

b   had ratified this agreement. They might say, "Socrates, we have ample indication that we and the City pleased you. You would not have stayed home in it to a degree surpassing all other Athenians, unless it pleased you in surpassing degree. You never left to go on a festival, except once to the Isthmian Games. You never went anywhere else except on military service. You never journeyed abroad as other men do, nor had you any desire to gain knowledge of other cities and their laws—we and this our City

c   sufficed for you. So eagerly did you choose us, so eagerly did you agree to live as a citizen under us, that you even founded a family here. So much did the City please you. Even at your very trial, you could have proposed exile as a penalty, and done with the City's knowledge and permission what you're now attempting to do against her will. But at the time, you made a fine pretense of not being distressed at having to die. You'd choose death before exile—so you said. But now you feel no shame at those words,

d   nor any concern for us, who are the Laws. You attempt to destroy us by trying to run off like the meanest of slaves, contrary to the compacts and agreements you entered with us to live as a citizen. First of all, then, tell us this: do we or do we not speak the truth when we say that by your actions, if not by your words, you have agreed to live as a citizen under us?"

What am I to say to that, Crito? Must I not agree?

CRI. Necessarily, Socrates.

SOC. "Very well then," they might say. "Aren't you trespassing

e   against your compacts and agreements with us? You didn't agree under constraint, you weren't misled or deceived, nor were you forced to decide in too little time. You had seventy years, during which time you could have gone abroad if we did not please you, or if your agreement came to seem to you unjust. But you preferred neither Sparta nor Crete, which you often used to say were

53a well governed, or any other city, Greek or barbarian. Quite the contrary; you traveled abroad less often than the halt, the lame, and the blind. So the City pleased you, to a degree surpassing all other Athenians. Therefore, we pleased you, too, for to whom would a city be pleasing without laws? Are you, then, now not to abide by your agreements? If you are persuaded by us, Socrates, you will. You will not make yourself a butt of mockery by escaping.

"Consider too what good you will accomplish for yourself or your friends if you transgress or offend in this way. That your friends risk prosecution themselves, with deprivation of city and confiscation of estate, could hardly be more clear. But you first. If you were to go to any of the cities nearest Athens—Thebes, say, or Megara, for both are well governed—you would go as an enemy to their polity. Those concerned for their own cities would eye you with suspicion, believing you to be a corrupter of laws. Again, you would confirm the opinion of your judges and lead them to think they rendered judgment justly, for a corrupter of laws may surely also be thought, and emphatically, a corrupter of young and ignorant men. Will you then shun well-governed cities, and men of the more estimable sort? Or will you associate with them and without sense of shame discuss—What will you discuss, Socrates? What arguments? The ones you used to offer here, about how virtue and justice are of highest worth for men, along with prescriptive custom and the Laws? "The affair of Socrates"—don't you think it will look indecent? Surely you must. Then will you keep clear of such places and go to Thessaly among Crito's friends? There is plenty of license and unchastened disorder in Thessaly, and no doubt they'd delight in hearing you tell your absurd story about how you ran off from prison dressed up in disguise—a peasant's leather coat, perhaps? Disguised like a runaway slave, just to change your looks! That you are an old man with probably only a little time to live, and yet you cling boldly to life with such greedy desire that you will transgress the highest laws—will there be no one to say it? Perhaps not, if you give no offense. But otherwise, Socrates, you will hear many a contemptuous thing said of you. Will you then live like a slave, fawning on every man you meet? And what will you do in Thessaly when you get there, besides eat, as if you'd exiled yourself for a banquet. But as for those arguments of yours about justice and the other virtues—what will they mean to us then?

"Still, you want to live for your children's sake, so you can raise and educate them. Really? Will you take them to Thessaly and raise and educate them there, and make foreigners out of them so they can enjoy that advantage too? If you don't, will they be better reared for your being alive but not with them? Your

friends will look after them. Will they look after them if you go
b   to Thessaly, but not if you go to the Place of the Dead? If those
who call themselves your friends are really worth anything, you
cannot believe that.

"Socrates, be persuaded by us, for we nurtured you. Put not
life nor children nor anything else ahead of what is just, so that
when you come to the Place of the Dead you may have all this to
say in your defense to those who rule there. It will not appear
better here, more virtuous, more just, or more holy, for you or
any of those around you to do this kind of thing here. And it
c   will not be better for you on your arrival there. You now depart,
if you depart, the victim of injustice at the hands of men, not at
the hands of us who are the Laws. But if you escape, if you thus
shamefully return injustice for injustice and injury for injury, if
you trespass against your compacts and agreements with us, and
work evil on those you least ought—yourself, your friends, your
Country and its Laws—we shall be angered at you while you live,
and those our brothers who are the Laws in the Place of the Dead
will not receive you kindly, knowing that you undertook so far as
in you lay to destroy us. Do not be persuaded to do what Crito
d   bids. Be persuaded by us."

Crito, my dear and faithful friend, I think I hear these things
as the Corybants think they hear the pipes, and the droning
murmur of the words sounds within me and makes me incapable
of hearing aught else. Be assured that if you speak against the
things I now think true, you will speak in vain. Still, if you suppose you can accomplish anything, please speak.

CRI. Socrates, I cannot speak.

e SOC. Very well, Crito. Let us so act, since so the God leads.

IV: THE MENO

IV. THE MENO

COMMENT

In the *Euthyphro*, Socrates distinguished between the *ousia*, the nature and reality, of holiness, and a *pathos*, something which happens to be true of it. He showed that if holiness is loved because it is holy, Euthyphro's suggestion that holiness is what is loved by the gods states pathos, not ousia—accident, not essence—and therefore fails to achieve definition. Euthyphro's account is implicitly circular: he must first know what holiness is if he is to know that it is loved by the gods, since he has agreed that what is loved by the gods is loved because it is holy, not holy because it is loved. One cannot identify instances of holiness without knowing what holiness is; in the same way, one must know what holiness is before knowing what attributes happen to be connected with it.

Put another way, there is an epistemic priority of the "What is it?" question to other questions about "it," and this implies a distinction of modality, a distinction between necessary and contingent connections of attributes. It is of the essence of even number, and therefore necessary, that it is divisible by two. But if true, it is contingent that holiness is loved by the gods, although contingency might be turned into necessity, if we understood what holiness is. In the *Meno*, the issues of epistemic priority, necessity and contingency, are dramatized, and the result is a new theory of knowledge.

Introduction (70a–71d)

The *Meno* begins abruptly with the question "Is virtue taught?" (or "teachable": the Greek first verbal adjective *didakton* bears both meanings). The question divided the Sophistic movement of the fifth century:

133

Protagoras claimed that virtue can be taught and Gorgias denied it. The question is pursued through the rest of the *Meno,* and in the end it remains unanswered. Meno and Socrates cannot determine whether virtue is taught because they do not know what virtue is.

The opening is so abrupt that there is no setting of scene, though we may perhaps imagine that the dialogue takes place in the Lyceum, where Socrates often met his friends and where there was ample sand for geometrical demonstrations. The dramatic date is after the fall of the Thirty Tyrants in 403 B.C., when the democracy was restored, and before 401, when Meno, like Xenophon, left Greece for military service in Persia. Meno was about eighteen years old, a Thessalian noble visiting Athens as a guest-friend of the democratic politician Anytus, who was to become one of the chief accusers at Socrates' trial.

When little more than twenty, Meno became a commander of Greek mercenaries in the service of Cyrus of Persia. A small portion of his band lived to take part in the Anabasis, the march to the sea, but Meno did not. Xenophon, who ran afoul of him in army politics, loved him little, and described the outstanding features of his character as greed and faithlessness. Plato's portrait is far more generous. Meno is young, good-looking, impulsive and somewhat spoiled; but he is polite to Socrates throughout the conversation, even when the argument turns against him, and he has enough intellectual interest to be a follower of Gorgias. He believes that silver, gold, honor, and high office in the state are the main goods of life, but is quick to agree also that those goods must be acquired justly. He seems, in short, a decent and intelligent youth who values the things natural to persons in his circumstances; there is nothing in this portrait to suggest the travesty of a man which Xenophon drew. But whether or not Meno was so grievously affected as Xenophon claimed, most grievously did he suffer. Suspected of treachery by fellow officers, he was betrayed after the death of Cyrus, sent to the Persian court at Babylon, imprisoned for a year, and finally put to death in the Persian manner: he was impaled.

No shadow of this future darkens Plato's portrait of the past. In the *Meno,* a boy and an elderly man meet in the twilight years of the fifth century, and discuss whether virtue can be taught. Behind the play of personality and the thrust of argument and the reader's awareness of the decrees of fate, there is great proportion and immense calm. The *Meno* is Attic marble brought to prose.

Socrates, asked whether virtue is taught or how it comes to be present, disclaims ability to answer. He cannot say what sort of thing virtue is or what characteristics belong to it, because he does not know what it is.

The question "What is virtue?" must be answered first if other questions about virtue are to be settled with certainty. The *Meno* begins, then, with a direct statement of the claim of epistemic priority implied in the *Euthyphro*. Socrates' insistence on the distinction between the essence of a thing and its characteristics, his insistence on the priority of the "What is it?" question over others, is the major theme of the *Meno* and the key to its interpretation.

The distinction is mentioned three times in course of the discussion, at beginning (71b), middle (87b), and end (100b), and as it happens, these coincide with the three main parts of the dialogue. In the first, Meno undertakes to say what virtue is, and fails; as in the *Euthyphro*, his attempt to say what is true of virtue without first defining it issues in (repeated) circularity. In the second part, Meno challenges the very possibility of inquiry, and Socrates answers with the theory of Recollection. But Meno still evades the question of what virtue is and forces Socrates to return to the question of how it is acquired, and so, in the concluding part, Socrates lets Meno have his way and asks whether virtue is taught. To help inquiry along, he borrows a method of hypothesis from the geometers, but unfortunately even that method will not work: contradictory results are obtained, which reveal a perplexing distinction between knowledge and opinion. The dialogue ends with Socrates once more stressing the priority of determining what virtue is before attempting to say whether it is taught. The question of whether virtue is taught is left unanswered.

The Request for a Definition (71d–73c)

When Socrates asks Meno to say what virtue is, Meno replies with a list of various kinds of virtues. In the same way, Socrates asks what holiness is in the *Euthyphro*, what temperance is in the *Charmides*, what courage is in the *Laches*, what justice is in *Republic* I. In each case, his respondents initially answer with examples.

But if the pattern of the *Meno* is in this respect similar to that of the early dialogues, it is also subtly and importantly different. In the first place, Socrates' "What is it?" question in the *Meno* is asked about the genus of which given virtues are species. The *Euthyphro* had envisaged definition as per genus et differentiam. But it cannot be assumed in advance that virtue, the genus of which justice, temperance, wisdom, courage and holiness are species, is not itself a summum genus, an ultimate genus which cannot be subsumed under any further genus. In that case, definition might involve mapping, a collection apt for division, but no statement of difference within the genus.

As Socrates' question is more general, so is Meno's initial answer. In earlier dialogues, the first answer to the "What is it?" question is an example. Euthyphro thinks holiness is just what he is doing, prosecuting his father for murder; Laches thinks courage is sticking to your post in battle; Charmides thinks temperance is keeping quiet and being modest. Meno, on the other hand, offers not specific examples but an ordered list: virtue in a man is managing the affairs of his city so as to harm his enemies and help his friends; virtue in a woman is managing the affairs of her household and obeying her husband; and there are other virtues for children and old men, free men and slaves. The list is compiled from a formula Meno got from Gorgias: "Each of us has his virtue according to his particular actions and time of life, and in relation to the particular functions he performs" (72a). Meno's answer to the "What is it?" question, then, differs from those found in the early dialogues: it is not a naive appeal to examples, but a self-conscious account. He anticipates F. H. Bradley's account of ethics in terms of "My Station and Its Duties."

Socrates replies with an analogy. Suppose Meno were asked to state the ousia, the nature and reality, the "What is it?" of a bee. It would not do to reply that there are many different kinds of bees, and to name them; bees do not differ as bees, and the question demands an account of that in which all bees are the same. So too with virtue.

Socrates assumes that there is an eidos, an Idea or Form, of virtue, the same in all instances of virtue and through which those instances are what they are. One must look to this Form or essence in attempting to say what virtue is. This parallels the *Euthyphro*, where Socrates assumed that there is an eidos of holiness, the same in all holy actions, that by which holy things are holy. In the *Euthyphro*, Socrates wanted to know the nature of holiness in order to use it as a standard or criterion for determining whether given actions, such as Euthyphro's prosecution of his father for murder, are holy or unholy. Knowledge of Ideas was sought in order to provide a basis for moral judgment of particular actions. In the *Meno*, on the other hand, Socrates' motive in requesting a definition is not to identify given things as virtuous, but to determine how virtue is connected with the attribute of being teachable or taught.

Meno's answer differs from Euthyphro's too. Where Euthyphro gave only an example, Meno offers a formula. His view—a perfectly reasonable one—is that "virtue" is a blanket word, covering particular kinds of virtue, all of which belong to particular kinds of things. The virtue of a man is therefore different from the virtue of a woman, because the conditions which imply that a man is virtuous are different from those which imply that a woman is virtuous. If this is true, then an enumeration of different kinds of virtue appropriate, for example, to men as distinct from women, is a legitimate answer to the "What is it?" question. Penelope, no doubt, was a virtuous woman; but Odysseus would not have seemed admirable in Greek eyes if he had stayed at home, defended his chastity, and spun.

But Socrates supposes that virtues do not differ in respect of being virtues, that there is a single eidos in question whether the virtue is that of a man, a woman, or a child, just as a single eidos is shared by different kinds of bees. His argument is by analogy. As we speak of the virtue of a man and the virtue of a woman, so we speak of the health of a man and the health of a woman, and Meno is quick to agree that health is the same characteristic in both. Meno also agrees that the same is true of tallness and strength: whether found in man or woman, strength does not differ in being strength. Following analogy, virtue should be the same wherever found. In other words, "virtue" is not a blanket word but designates a single characteristic. But to this suggestion, Meno demurs.

How much weight does this argument have? The answer is: as demonstration, very little, but as dialectic, a great deal. It is weak as demonstration not only because it is an argument from analogy, which does not strictly demonstrate, but also because Meno might have treated words like "strength" as blanket words too—"strong for an old man," for example. On the other hand, Meno clearly has not answered Socrates' question, because Socrates is asking for what is common in all kinds of human excellence. If Meno's answer were to be satisfactory, he would first have to show that nothing is common to the various kinds of virtue— that Socrates' question is in a strict sense unanswerable. Yet it is surely odd to claim that in discussing virtue, or just and temperate conduct, one is not discussing characteristics in which all human beings are the same. Behind Socrates' logical point lies a substantive issue in moral philosophy. Because universality attaches to virtue, virtue cannot be identified with social role: the claims of morality extend beyond and are not exhausted in "my station and its duties." What is primarily at issue in the *Meno*, however, is not ethics, but the structure of response to a request for definition.

Virtue as Ability to Rule (73c–74b)

Meno now defines virtue as ability to rule. The definition is at once too broad and too narrow. Too broad, because Meno forgets that ruling, if it is to qualify as a human excellence, must be just. Too narrow, because the definition does not apply, for example, to children and slaves. But the most serious defect in the definition is that it is implicitly circular: virtue is ability to rule, but Meno agrees that this implies just rule, because justice is virtue. Socrates' initial response is to introduce the distinction between virtue and *a* virtue, between genus and species, and Meno is puzzled. Socrates offers an analogy: Roundness is a kind of figure, but it is not identical with figure, because there are other figures as well. In the same way, justice is a kind of virtue, but Meno admits there are other virtues too, for example, courage, temperance, and wisdom. Yet Meno cannot grasp anything common to justice, temperance, wisdom, and the other virtues, and Socrates, to help the discussion forward, returns to the example of figure.

Requirements for Definition (74b–77b)

One of Meno's reasons for thinking that virtue is not a single characteristic is that some virtues are opposite to others: the virtue of a freeman, for example, is to rule, whereas the virtue of a slave is to obey. Socrates counters with the example of figure: round is the opposite of straight, but each is as much a figure as the other, and therefore they must have something in common. Socrates offers a specimen definition: figure is what always follows color.

It has been objected that this formula merely states what *sort* of thing figure is, not *what* it is: at best, it provides a convertible property, not an account of essence. This is true, but it mistakes the function of the formula in its context. In the first place, the definition *is* a formula, and therefore it serves as an example of the kind of answer Socrates wants; for Meno, having begun by defining virtue as ability to rule—also a formula—has found his definition unsatisfactory and abandoned it for a mere list of virtues. In the second place, Socrates' formula corrects by example several defects in Meno's account. It is not too broad or too narrow, nor is it circular. It shows that round and straight admit a common character because they fit a common formula, even though, when compared to each other, they are contrary and opposite. Socrates, then, is right to suggest that he would be happy to see Meno define virtue "even that way" (75b). He is suggesting, not that his definition of figure is final or formally adequate, but that it is a relevant improvement on Meno's pattern of definition—exactly as he promised.

That figure always follows color implies that anything which has a color has a shape. Meno's objection that it is foolish to accept the formula until color has first been defined is itself foolish. Applied in all cases, it would imply infinite regress in any attempt at definition; and in the case of color we are dealing with a thing which, definable or not, is hardly obscure.

But Socrates offers a different, friendlier, more "dialectical" reply, a second definition of figure which eschews reference to color and rests instead on geometry: figure is the limit of a solid.

This definition differs in an interesting way from Euclid, *Elements* I, Definition 14, which states, "A figure is that which is contained by any boundary or boundaries." This definition implies that figure is always a contained magnitude, and that a straight line or angle cannot be a figure. By Socrates' definition in the *Meno*, figure is not a limited magnitude but the limit itself, not that which has a boundary but the boundary itself, whether line or surface. This treatment of figure, which is in fact more abstract than Euclid's, is clearly the product of considerable precision of thought. At least in structure, the definition is per genus et differentiam. Clearly, however, not all genera can be defined this way, on pain of an infinite regress in which nothing is definable.

Having twice defined figure, Socrates next proceeds, at Meno's request, to define color in the manner of Gorgias and Empedocles: color is an effluence of figures, commensurable with sight and therefore perceptible. The definition has multiple defects. It is inconsistent with the definition of figure just given, since it treats figure not as boundary but as bounded magnitude; and it is absurdly broad, since as Socrates points out (76d–e), it will not only define mutatis mutandis sound, smell, and the rest (smell is an effluence of figures, commensurable with sniffing, therefore perceptible), but also blood, sweat, and tears. But it is "a stately style of answer," and Meno enthusiastically, even extravagantly, approves of it.

He seems unaware of the circle in which he has landed. Offered a definition of figure in terms of color, he objected that color was undefined. So Socrates defined figure without reference to color, and then at Meno's request defined color in terms of figure—though in terms, not of the limit of a solid, but of the solid which is limited. Meno has in fact accepted a definition of color in terms of figure which leaves the notion of figure undefined, unless it be defined as what always follows color. This explains Socrates' ambiguous comment that his other answer about figure was better (76e), for both of his other answers were better. Meno has been led to agree that there is something common to the various figures, but he still lacks insight into what it is. His enthusiasm for Socrates' definition of color does not bespeak prosperity in the dialectical future. And so it will prove. His attempts to define virtue will be dogged by circularity, an adequate indication that he has failed to state essence.

Virtue as Desire for Good Things and Ability to Attain Them (77b–78c)

Meno now offers his third and final definition of virtue. Unable to defend Gorgias' view, he quotes an unnamed poet to produce a high-sounding definition not unlike Socrates' definition of color: virtue is desire for beautiful things and ability to attain them.

Socrates first elicits Meno's agreement that by beautiful things Meno means good things, and then he undertakes to show that desire for good things is common to everyone and therefore cannot be part of the definition of virtue: it is surplusage. But Meno rejects the claim that everyone desires good things: some people desire evil things believing them good, and some people desire evil things believing them evil.

Socrates quickly performs a reduction: those who desire evil things believing them good in fact desire good things. So there is a single proposition left to be examined: that it is possible to desire evil things believing them to be evil.

Socrates' refutation is indirect. To desire evil is to desire what is, when possessed, not beneficial but harmful: for if evils were beneficial, they would be desired as good. Now, insofar as anyone is harmed, he is made wretched; to be wretched is to be unhappy; no one wishes to be unhappy; therefore no one desires evils as evil, and all desire is for good. Because the wish for happiness is a constant, a given of our human nature, it is impossible to desire evils as evils, since that would be to desire one's own harm.

Meno finds it impossible to say that anyone can wish his own unhappiness, and he is therefore led to admit that the first conjunct of his definition, that virtue is desire for good things, is superfluous. Desire always aims at the good of the agent, however confused the agent may be about where his real good lies. So the only way to distinguish good men from bad men is on the basis of their ability to obtain what everyone by nature seeks: their own good.

Virtue as Ability to Attain Good Things (78c–80d)

By logical simplification, virtue has become ability to attain good things. But an ability or power, by itself, is morally neutral, and Meno is forced to modify his definition: virtue is ability to acquire good things, provided this is done in a just and pious way. And this is again circular, since justice and piety are parts of virtue.

At this point, Meno compares Socrates to the stingray, which numbs whatever it touches. Socrates admits the comparison, provided that Meno will admit that the stingray numbs itself. The reader of the *Apology* will remember that Socrates is wise only in knowing that he does not know. The reader of the *Euthyphro* will remember that circularity is a mark of epistemic contingency, of failure to achieve that insight into essence necessary for definition.

Inquiry and Recollection (80d–81e)

At the beginning of the dialogue (71a), Socrates maintained that he did not know what virtue is, and after talking with Socrates, Meno makes the same claim (80b). Having failed to answer the "What is it?" question, Meno now suggests that there may be no point in asking it. As Socrates sums up his argument, it is impossible for a man to inquire either into what he knows or what he does not know; he cannot inquire into what he knows, because he already knows it, so there is no need of inquiry; he cannot inquire into what he does not know, for he does not know what it is he is to inquire into.

This paradox bears some resemblance to the foolish paradoxes about learning introduced in the *Euthydemus* (275d–278c, 295e–296d), and Socrates calls it eristic (80e). But it is a mistake to dismiss it as a sophism, for in order to solve it, Socrates does not undertake to correct its logic, as in the *Euthydemus,* but introduces the theory of Recollection, which states that the truth of things is always in the soul, and that to learn is to recollect what is already known. It is said that this doctrine was held by ancient priests and priestesses, and Pindar and other poets, but it is not in its central claim mythical: it is a serious answer to a serious question, and Plato maintained it long after the *Meno* (cf. *Phaedo* 72eff., *Phaedrus* 249e–250c).

Meno's paradox has little to do with contingent matters of fact—inquiry, say, into the exact date of the battle of Marathon. Socrates maintains that the soul is through all time in a state of having learned (86a, cf. 81d). Recollection does not, therefore, involve truths about states of affairs in this or any other life. It is knowledge a priori.

Is there good reason for accepting the existence of a priori knowledge? In the context of a philosophy which demands a search for essence, surely there is. Consider the request for definition. Does Meno know what virtue is? Then inquiry is pointless, since if he knows, he can say, and dialectic will end without beginning. Perhaps then Meno is ignorant of what virtue is. But in that case, why ask him to define it? Being ignorant, he will have no ground for supposing that one answer to the Socratic question is any more appropriate than another, no criterion by which to determine when he has hit the right answer or offered a wrong one.

The pressure of Meno's paradox is increased rather than diminished by the assumption in earlier dialogues, such as the *Euthyphro,* that Forms are standards for determining what things possess them. One cannot gain knowledge of holiness by inspecting holy things, since one cannot determine what things are holy without knowledge of holiness. The "What is it?" question is removed from common opinion, ordinary language, and empirical fact: it is a question about Forms or essences, about characteristics as they exist in themselves. If that question can be answered, the mind cannot be a mere tabula rasa, and empiricist theories of mind, with their doctrine that nothing is in the intellect which is not first in the senses, are radically false.

Socrates solves the paradox of inquiry by slipping between the horns. The paradox assumes an exclusive and exhaustive disjunction between explicit knowledge—the ability to render an account—and sheer ignorance. But if learning and inquiry are recollection, then to inquire is to bring to explicit awareness what is already implicitly known. If this is true, the primary function of education and teaching is not to impart information, but to rid the soul of false beliefs which cloud vision and cause blindness; if the doctrine of Recollection is true, education in some primary sense is a process of refutation, and inherently Socratic.

The doctrine of Recollection is put forth, not as an ordinary part of dialectic, not as a further attempt to say what virtue is, but as an attempt to explain how dialectic is possible—to explain how the question "What is virtue?" may be asked and answered. Meno's paradox, by challenging this possibility, raises an obvious metaphysical issue. The inquiry has aimed at real definition, the definition of an eidos, a Form or characteristic of virtue. If knowledge of that characteristic is presupposed by ability to say what attributes are connected with it, the doctrine of Recollection explains how this epistemic priority is possible. It provides a basis for apprehension of essence as exhibited in definition, and thereby of necessary connection of attributes *de re*.

A Proof of Recollection (81e–86c)

Socrates next undertakes to show by example that learning is Recollection. A slave boy ignorant of geometry is led to recognize the truth of a complex and deductively fertile theorem: that the square on the diagonal of a square is double the square of the side. The *Meno* thus offers a dramatic demonstration of the validity of the first argument for Recollection, later put in the *Phaedo* (73a): "When people are questioned, if you put the questions well, they state the truth about everything by themselves; and yet, if there were not knowledge and right account in them, they could not do this. That this is so is shown most clearly if one takes them to mathematical diagrams or anything else of that sort."

It is often objected that Socrates' questions to the slave are leading questions, and thus his example in no way indicates that learning is recollection. But this objection is confused. A leading question is one which suggests its own answer, and so defined, many of Socrates' questions are clearly leading. But it is relevant to observe that, in matters mathematical, the mind of the boy is capable of being led. In the law of evidence, which deals with empirical fact, leading questions are open to objection on the ground that they may cause a witness to acquiesce in a false suggestion. But this is clearly irrelevant when questions deal with a complex geometrical proof. No false suggestions have been planted; the evidentiary problem does not arise. The boy is assisted by questions as he is assisted by the figures inscribed in the sand at his feet, and he several times makes intellectual leaps which correspond to no question because he suddenly sees the point. Socrates tells the boy always to answer exactly what he thinks (83d, cf. 85b), and the slave does so. This is inference, based neither on empirical fact nor on analytic deduction from an axiom set.

The fourth-century reader trained in geometry would have realized that, if the boy came to know as well as anyone at last, he would have been brought by reflecting on this theorem to the very frontiers of Greek mathematical inquiry. It is an easy next step for the boy to prove that the square on the hypotenuse of an isosceles right triangle is equal to the sum of the squares on the sides, which leads to the discovery, original to Greek mathematics and unanticipated in Babylonia or Egypt, of the incommensurability of the diagonal, and the general problems of irrationality and infinite divisibility. The problem of doubling the square leads straight to the problems which lay at the frontiers of mathematics at the dramatic date of the *Meno*. Socrates' example is nicely chosen to indicate not only the truth of Recollection, but its reach.

It also indicates something of what is meant by Socrates' claim that all nature is *suggenes*—"akin," or interconnected—so that by learning one single thing, we can recover all the rest (81d). The theory of Recollection is not only a theory of inquiry but also one of inference. A single bit of genuine knowledge can serve as the terminal link in a golden chain by which we can, Zeus-like, draw to ourselves the whole of intelligible reality. The objects recollected must have among them Forms or characteristics (including mathematical Forms)—the realities whose nature is sought in the "What is it?" question; and those objects must stand in intimate and necessary connection with each other if to recover one link is to gain means to recover them all. The epistemic priority of the "What is it?" question implies intensional implication among Ideas; the modality implied by the contrast between pathos and ousia is based on intensional necessity, whose foundations are exhibited in definition.

The paradox Meno urged has now been answered. The point of claiming that learning is recollection is precisely to insist that in addition to explicit knowledge—that is, ability to render an account, *logon didonai*—there is also implicit knowledge, which is possessed but not articulated. The boy so far has only true opinions, stirred up in him as in a dream, rather than knowledge (85c). But when roused by questioning, those true opinions may become knowledge by "reflection on the reason" (98a).

The Method of Hypothesis (86c–87c)

Having removed an obstruction which blocks inquiry, namely, the denial that inquiry is possible, Socrates again asks, "What is virtue?" Meno, still unwilling to face that question, asks again whether virtue is taught. Reluctantly, Socrates agrees to inquire into Meno's question rather than his own, using a method of hypothesis borrowed from the geometers. They will discuss whether virtue can be taught without knowing what it is.

The geometrical problem Socrates uses to illustrate inquiry by hypothesis is generally taken to be that of inscribing a rectilinear figure in a circle. This is a reading which the Greek does not require, and which we cannot be confident that it admits: Euclid's word for inscription is *eggraphein*, "to write in," whereas we are here given *enteinein*, "to stretch out." Nor does inscription fit the needs of the passage. Meno is a young Thessalian noble, literate in geometry but hardly expert in it; the problem is alluded to in such a way as to imply that it is one whose conditions for solution Meno will immediately recognize from a brief reference. So the problem must be both well-known and simple. We may perhaps also expect the problem to throw light on the dialectic of the *Meno*: Plato is an economical writer.

Now, if the problem is one of inscription, it is neither famous nor simple nor tightly connected with the dialectic of the *Meno*. Blass knew thirty different interpretations of the passage in 1861. Bluck discusses six interpretations and offers a seventh of his own. All of them involve complex constructions and are irrelevant to the dialectic of the dialogue; none are such as Meno might be expected to recognize immediately.

The problem is in fact that of determining whether it is possible for a given circle to be equal in area to a given triangle. Since the area of any triangle is equal to that of some square, the problem is equivalent to that of squaring the circle, quadrature. This was a famous crux in the mathematics of the fifth century; the problem was so well known that Aristophanes refers to it in the *Birds,* so Meno may be expected to be familiar with it. He may also be expected to be familiar with the technique of application of areas which Socrates employs: it was a well-established part of the geometry of his time, and it was the foundation of Greek geometrical algebra (Euclid, *Elements* I.44).

Given that the problem is whether it is possible to transform a given triangular area into a given circle, the statement of conditions necessary for solution is direct. Apply the area to a line given for it. Then if the area falls short by an amount which is the same or similar to that which has already been applied (i.e., the area of the circle), the transformation is possible; if not, then not.

On what does the impossibility rest? It rests on denial that the two areas are same or similar, where by "similar" we must understand "commensurable." The transformation of commensurable areas into each other is in principle possible; the transformation of incommensurable areas into each other is in principle impossible. The issue of incommensurability, it will be recalled, lay in the depths of the slave boy's problem of doubling the square.

There is a peculiarity in all this which Meno does not remark. No one, at the end of the fifth century B.C., knew how to apply a circle to a line, using straightedge and compass alone. Archimedes would later prove that the area of a circle is equal to that of the right triangle whose height is the radius of the circle and whose base is the circumference; but he could not perform the construction. The ratio of circumference to radius is, of course, pi, and it was not until the eighteenth century that pi was proved to be a transcendental number, and quadrature was shown to be impossible. So we deal here with a question which mathematics at the end of the fifth century B.C. was powerless to solve.

We also address (if one may say so without punning) a circular argument. In order to compare areas to determine if they are commensurable, the circle must already be applied to the line. It can be applied, however, only as a rectilinear figure. In short, boundary conditions for quadrature may be defined in terms of application of areas, but only by assuming the very thing to be proved, namely, that the circle can be applied as a rectilinear figure—that quadrature is possible. The question of whether this triangular figure is equal in area to that circle can be dealt with by a hypothesis involving application of areas only by assuming the possibility of quadrature, itself unproven.

The method of hypothesis, which was meant to relieve the necessity of answering the "What is it?" question, is in this case implicitly prey to the same sort of circularity Meno's attempts at defining virtue evinced. The method of hypothesis states boundary conditions but yields no conclusion. In the same way, the dialectical development of the *Meno* will leave the question of whether virtue can be taught unresolved.

What is the hypothesis which the mathematical example is meant to clarify? The ambiguity of the text is itself instructive of Meno's state of mind. The hypothesis might be that Virtue is Knowledge. It might even be that Virtue is Taught, or that Virtue is Good (87d). But if the hypothesis in moral philosophy is to parallel the mathematical example, it must be this: if Virtue is Knowledge, then Virtue is Taught; and if not, then not. That is, the hypothesis is the implication of knowledge and teachability, at least in the special case of virtue (87c).

That Virtue Is Knowledge (87c–89a)

Socrates begins by affirming the antecedent of the hypothesis, *modus ponens*. If virtue is good, then it is necessarily always beneficial (87d–e, 88c, cf. 78c–80d). Therefore, virtue cannot be identified with something which is beneficial in one case but harmful in another. Now, if there is some good apart from knowledge, then virtue may not be knowledge; but if there is no good apart from knowledge, then virtue is knowledge, in whole or in part. It is agreed that of everything the soul undertakes or endures, knowledge is the only thing from which it never fails to benefit. Therefore, virtue is knowledge, and since knowledge is the only thing which is taught, virtue is taught. This argument, it will be observed, is not tightly reasoned.

That Virtue Is Not Taught (89a–e)

Having affirmed the antecedent of the hypothesis, Socrates proceeds to deny the consequent, *modus tollens*. If virtue is taught, we may expect that there are teachers of it; but neither Meno nor Socrates can say who

those teachers are. It follows that virtue is not taught, whence it follows
ex hypothesi that virtue is not knowledge.

It has been often suggested that this argument is fallacious, playing
on the ambiguity of *didakton*: it does not follow formally from the fact
that no one teaches it that virtue cannot be taught. But there is a distinction between formal proof and reasonable inference, and it is surely
a reasonable inference that if virtue could be taught, then, since it is a
great good, someone would teach it. And if we assume, with F. M. Cornford, that knowledge is not taught but recollected, the way is then open
to conclude that virtue is knowledge. But we do not know that virtue is
knowledge because we do not know what virtue is or what knowledge is.
The very claim that virtue is good is described as a hypothesis (87d).
The *Meno* neither asserts nor denies that virtue is knowledge: it merely
examines a hypothesis.

The Interview with Anytus (89e–96d)

The dialogue is now interrupted by the arrival of Meno's host, Anytus.
Socrates' praise of Anytus's character would have seemed ironic to the
audience for whom the *Meno* was originally intended. Aristotle records
that, as a general, he was brought to trial for failing to hold Pylos in
409 B.C. and got off by bribing the jury. Anytus, along with Meletus and
Lycon, brought the capital charge of impiety against Socrates. He is here
portrayed as a man with a closed mind and short temper, and his concluding remark to Socrates is a threat.

Anytus is provoked by Socrates' suggestion (91b) that the sophists
teach virtue, and suggests instead that it can be learned from the gentlemen of Athens (92e, cf. *Apology* 24d–25a). Socrates delicately replies that
if this were so, we should expect men who excel in virtue to teach it to
their sons, but a brief induction shows that the greatest statesmen of
Athens were unable to pass on their virtue to anyone else. So virtue is
not taught.

This conclusion flies in the face of the conclusion of 87c–89a. One
may here recall the *Protagoras*, which begins with Socrates arguing that
virtue is not taught (320b), and Protagoras arguing that it is; by the end
of the dialogue (361a–c), they have switched positions. The reason for
this curious result is offered in the *Meno*. Until the respondents determine what virtue is, they encounter hopeless tangles in trying to decide
whether it is taught (*Protagoras* 360e–361c). The lesson, again, is the
priority of the "What is it?" question.

Knowledge and Right Opinion (96d–98b)

Is it then true that knowledge is the only thing which allows men to conduct their affairs rightly? For practical purposes, Socrates suggests, right opinion is as good a guide to action as knowledge. A person who knows the road to Larisa can take you there; but so can a person with a right opinion about the way, even if he doesn't know it. But right opinion is like the statues of Daedalus, which run away unless they are tied down. It can be bound by "reflection on the reason," and so transformed into knowledge. The slave boy, questioned repeatedly, will ultimately come to know as well as anyone.

A helpful comment on the distinction between knowledge and opinion in the *Meno* is offered by Aristotle as part of his own account in the *Posterior Analytics* (I.89a17–24, trans. Mure):

> If a man grasps truths that cannot be other than they are, in the way he grasps the definitions through which demonstrations take place, he will have not opinion but knowledge: if on the other hand he apprehends these attributes as inhering in their subjects, but not in virtue of the subjects' substance and essential nature, he possesses opinion and not genuine knowledge; and his opinion, if obtained through immediate premises, will be both of the fact and of the reasoned fact; if not so obtained, of the fact alone. The object of opinion and knowledge is not quite identical; it is only in a sense identical, just as the object of true and false opinion is in a sense identical. . . . There are really many senses of "identical," and in one sense the object of true and false opinion can be the same, in another it cannot. Thus, to have a true opinion that the diagonal is commensurate with the side would be absurd: but because the diagonal with which they are both concerned is the same, the two opinions have objects so far the same: on the other hand, as regards their essential definable nature these objects differ. The identity of the objects of knowledge and opinion is similar.

The boy has apprehended the fact, and even to a certain extent the reasoned fact, but not that the fact could not be otherwise: knowledge has not yet come. It can come perhaps only through apprehension of the essential natures of the things with which he deals, of squareness and triangularity. Knowledge requires the further step that its objects, mathematical and moral, are the Ideas, and that sensibles are but deficient imitations of Ideas. Contingency and changeability of opinion are then identified with the domain of the sensible, and Ideas with the world of knowledge. This is the doctrine of Two Worlds in *Republic* V. But opinion, in the sense in which it is used in the *Meno,* and as Aristotle understood it, is contingent precisely in its apprehension of essences or Ideas, insofar as relations among Ideas, which are necessary, are apprehended by opinion only as contingent. The distinction between knowledge and opinion in the *Meno,* therefore, works differently than does the distinction in the *Republic.*

Conclusion (98b–100c)

The final section of the *Meno* begins with an ironic summary of results obtained since the method of hypothesis was introduced. Virtue implies right guidance; right guidance comes about as the result of either knowledge or true opinion; virtue is not knowledge, since knowledge is taught and virtue is not taught; therefore, virtue must be true opinion. Socrates continues his criticism of Athenian politicians by suggesting that they do not manage the affairs of the city by knowledge, but by right opinion— this a few years after the loss of the Peloponnesian War. The politicians do not differ in this respect from oracles or priests, who say many valuable things but have no knowledge of what they are saying (cf. *Apology* 21c–22c, *Phaedrus* 244b).

Return then to the question with which the *Meno* began: Is virtue taught? Socrates now suggests that virtue comes to be present "by divine apportionment, without intelligence." Preposterously, some commentators have taken this to mean that Plato is laying the foundation of theological ethics by claiming that virtue is the product of divine grace. On the contrary, this is a confession of ironic skepticism: it would make a virtuous man no more reliable as a guide to action than a soothsayer.

And so the *Meno* ends in perplexity. Asked whether virtue can be taught, Socrates finally undertakes to settle the matter by use of hypothesis. He assumes that if virtue is knowledge it can be taught, argues that it is knowledge, argues that it cannot be taught because there are no teachers of it, and concludes that it is present in men "by divine apportionment, without intelligence." That is, Socrates assumes an implication, affirms its antecedent, denies its consequent, and ends in skepticism. This structure would be pointless if Plato meant his readers to choose among these premises: the nub lies elsewhere. Socrates and Meno have tried to settle the question of whether virtue can be taught without first finding out what virtue is. They end in bewilderment, and the new method of hypothesis borrowed from the geometers cannot save them. The lesson of their failure is the familiar Socratic lesson that definition is necessary,

that in order to talk, it is good to know what one is talking about (71a–
b, 86d–e, 99e; *Protagoras* 360e–361c). The *Meno*, then, is a piece of dialectical irony, its dramatic structure meant not to proclaim but to exhibit
the need to answer the "What is it?" question. It is not concerned to
recommend moral conclusions, but to indicate the conditions necessary
for such conclusions to be reached. Those conditions imply the doctrine
of recollection, an invitation to belief in the immortality of the soul and
in the reality and necessary connection of the objects of its knowledge,
which are or include Ideas. The search for essence thus issues in a new
theory of mind: not a theory of mind as tabula rasa, on which experience
writes its darkling messages with the images of the senses, but of mind
as containing within its depths the essential nature of all that is.

TRANSLATION

MENO / SOCRATES / BOY / ANYTUS

Introduction (70a–71d)

70a MEN. Can you tell me, Socrates, whether virtue is taught?[1] Or is it not taught but acquired by practice? Or is it neither acquired by practice nor learnt, but present in men by nature or some other way?

SOC. Meno, it used to be that Thessalians were famous among the
b Greeks for their wealth and skill with horses, but it seems now that they are admired for their wisdom, and not least among them the Larisians, fellow citizens of your comrade Aristippus. Gorgias is the reason. He came to Larisa and made the first men of the city eager for his wisdom—your friend Aristippus among them, and the foremost among the other Thessalians too. Specifically, he gave you your habit of answering any question fear-
c lessly, in the style of men who know; for he offers himself for questioning to any Greek who wishes, on any subject he pleases, and there is no one he does not answer. But Meno, my friend, things are just the opposite here in Athens. There is, as it were,
71a a drought of wisdom; very likely she has left our borders for yours. At any rate, if you mean to ask that kind of question of anyone here, he will laugh and say, "Stranger, you must think me

---

1. The word here translated "taught" is *didakton*, a first verbal adjective which may also mean "teachable." In what follows, it will be translated "taught."

151

fortunate indeed, if you suppose I know whether virtue is taught, or how it comes to be present. So far am I from knowing whether or not it is taught, I don't even know what it is at all."

b   Now, I'm that way too, Meno. I share this poverty of my fellow citizens, and reproach myself for knowing nothing at all about virtue. And if I don't know what something is, how am I to know what pertains to it? Or do you think someone could determine, for instance, whether Meno is handsome or wealthy or wellborn, or the opposite of these things, without knowing at all who Meno is? Does that seem possible to you?

MEN. Not to me. But Socrates, is it really true that you don't know

c   what virtue is? Is this the report I am to carry home about you?

soc. Not only that, my friend, but also that I never met anyone else I thought did know.

MEN. Really? Didn't you meet Gorgias when he was here?

soc. I did.

MEN. Well, didn't you think he knew?

soc. I have a poor memory, Meno. I can't say at present what I thought then. Perhaps he did know, and you know what he used

d   to say. Remind me of it. Or if you will, tell me yourself, for no doubt you are in agreement with him.

MEN. Yes, I am.

soc. Then we may as well dismiss him, since he isn't here anyway.

The Request for a Definition (71d–73c)

(*Socrates continues*) What do you say virtue is, Meno? Don't begrudge telling me, so that I may find, should it turn out that you and Gorgias know, that I was in most fortunate error when I said that I had never met anyone who knew.

e   MEN. No difficulty, Socrates. First of all, if it is the virtue of a man you want, that is easy: the virtue of a man is to be capable of managing the affairs of his city, and in this management benefiting his friends and harming his enemies, taking care to suffer no such harm himself. And if it is the virtue of a woman you want, that is not difficult to explain either: she should manage her house well, preserving what is in it, and obey her husband.

72a   There is another virtue for children, male and female; and for an old man, free or slave as you please. And there are a great many other virtues, so that there is no perplexity in saying what virtue is. For each of us, there is a virtue with respect to each

particular activity and time of life, and in relation to each particular function. The same is also true of vice, Socrates.

soc. This is quite a stroke of luck, Meno. I was looking for one
virtue, and here I've found a whole swarm of them settled at
your side. But still, Meno, please keep to this image of a swarm.
b Suppose I were to ask you what it is to be a bee, about its nature
and reality, and you replied that there are many different kinds
of bees. What would your answer be if I then asked you, "Do
you mean that there are many different kinds, and that they
differ from each other in respect to being bees? Do they differ
in that way, or in some other way—in beauty or size, for example,
or something else like that." Tell me, how would you answer such
a question?

MEN. Why, that *as* bees, one is not different from another.

c soc. All right, suppose I went on and said, "Now that's the very
thing I want you to tell me about, Meno: Just what do you say it
is, in respect to which they do not differ but are the same?" You
could surely tell me?

MEN. Of course.

soc. So too then with virtues. Even if there are many different
kinds, they surely all have a certain single characteristic which is
the same, through which they are virtues; it is on this that he
d who would make clear what virtue is should fix his gaze. Do you
understand what I mean?

MEN. I think I do. But I still don't quite grasp the point of your
question.

soc. Well Meno, do you think it is only true of virtue that it is one
thing for a man, another for a woman, and so on? Or is this also
true of health and size and strength? Do you think health is one
thing for a man, and another for a woman? Or is health, if it is
to be health, the same character everywhere, whether in man or
e anything else?

MEN. I would say that health is the same for both man and woman.

soc. What about size and strength then? If a woman is strong, will
she not be strong by reason of the same character, the same
strength? By "the same" I mean this: strength does not differ, in
respect of being strength, whether it be in a man or a woman.
Or do you think there is some difference?

MEN. No.

73a soc. Then will virtue differ, in respect of being virtue, whether it
be in a woman or man, old man or child?

MEN. Somehow, Socrates, I don't think this is like those others any more.

SOC. Really? Didn't you say that a man's virtue is to manage a city well, and a woman's a house?

MEN. Yes, I did.

SOC. Well, is it possible to manage city, house, or anything else well, without managing it temperately and justly?

MEN. Surely not.

b SOC. Now, if people manage justly and temperately, they do so by reason of justice and temperance?

MEN. Necessarily.

SOC. So both men and women alike have need of the same things, namely justice and temperance, if they are to be good.

MEN. It appears they do.

SOC. What about a child or an old man. Could they be good if they were intemperate or unjust?

MEN. Surely not.

SOC. Only if temperate and just?

MEN. Yes.

c SOC. Then all human beings are good in the same way: for they become good by obtaining the same things.

MEN. So it seems.

SOC. But surely they would not be good in the same way unless they possessed the same virtue.[2]

MEN. Of course not.

SOC. Since they all possess the same virtue, try to recollect and tell me what Gorgias, and you with him, say it is.

Virtue as Ability to Rule (73c–74b)

MEN. Virtue is nothing else but ability to rule mankind, if you are
d after some one thing common to all cases.

SOC. I am indeed. But does a child possess the same virtue, Meno, or a slave the ability to rule his master? Does it seem true to you that one who rules would still be a slave?

MEN. It surely doesn't, Socrates.

SOC. No, not likely, my friend. And there is a further point to consider: you say "ability to rule." Are we not to add to that "justly, not unjustly"?

2. *Arete*, given its customary translation "virtue," is "goodness," the abstract noun corresponding to the adjective *agathos* "good."

MEN. Yes, I think so. For justice is virtue, Socrates.

e SOC. Virtue, Meno? Or *a* virtue?

MEN. What do you mean by that?

SOC. Something which holds generally. For example, take roundness if you will. I'd say that it is *a* figure, but not figure without
qualification. The reason I'd say so is that there are other figures
too.

MEN. Yes, and you'd be right. I also say there are other virtues
besides justice.

74a SOC. What are they? As I'd cite other figures for you, if you asked,
so please cite other virtues for me.

MEN. Well, I think courage is a virtue, and temperance, and wisdom, and dignity. And there are a great many others.

SOC. And now we're back where we started, Meno. Looking for one
virtue, we've found many, though by a different way than a moment ago. But the one virtue which runs through them all we
can't find.

b MEN. No, for I can't yet do as you ask, Socrates, and grasp a single
virtue common to all, as in the other cases.

Requirements for Definition (74b–77b)

SOC. Naturally enough. But I'll try if I can to help us on. You
understand, I suppose, that this holds generally: if someone
asked you the question I put just now, "What is figure, Meno?"
and you replied, "Roundness," and he then asked, as I did, "Is
roundness figure or *a* figure?" you'd surely reply that it is *a* figure.

MEN. Of course.

c SOC. And for this reason, that there are other figures too?

MEN. Yes.

SOC. And if he went on and asked you what they were, you'd tell
him?

MEN. I would.

SOC. And again, if he asked in the same way what color is, and you
said "white," and he went on to ask whether white is color or *a*
color, you would say that it is *a* color, because there are other
colors too.

MEN. I would.

SOC. And if he asked you to mention other colors, you'd mention

d others which are no less colors than white?

MEN. Yes.

SOC. Suppose he pursued the argument as I did. Suppose he said, "We keep arriving at a plurality, and that's not what I want. Since you call that plurality by a single name and say that all of its members are figures even though they are opposite to each other, just what is this thing which encompasses the round no less than

e   the straight and which you name figure, saying that the round is no more figure than the straight?" You do make that claim, don't you?

MEN. I do.

SOC. When you do, do you mean that the round is no more round than straight, the straight no more straight than round?

MEN. Of course not, Socrates.

SOC. Rather, you mean that the round is no more *figure* than the straight, and the straight no more than the round.

MEN. True.

SOC. Well then, what is this thing of which "figure" is the name? Try and say. Suppose when asked this question about figure or

75a   color you said, "I don't understand what you want, Sir, nor do I know what you mean." Your questioner might well be surprised and say, "Don't you understand that I'm after what is the same over all these cases?" Would you have no reply, Meno, if someone asked, "What is it that is over the round and the straight and the rest, and which you call figure, as the same over all?" Try and answer, in order to get practice for your reply about virtue.

b MEN. No, please, Socrates, you answer.

SOC. You want me to gratify you?

MEN. Yes, indeed.

SOC. And then you'll tell me about virtue?

MEN. I will.

SOC. Then I must do my best, for it's worth it.

MEN. Yes, certainly.

SOC. Come then, let us try to say what figure is. See if this will do: let figure alone among things which are be that which ever follows color. Is that sufficient, or are you after something else? For my

c   part, I'd be delighted to have you tell me about virtue even that way.

MEN. Yes, but surely this is foolish, Socrates.

SOC. How do you mean?

MEN. According to your account, figure is what ever follows color. All right, suppose someone said he didn't know color, that he

was as much at a loss there as he was about figure. What would
you think of your answer then?

SOC. That is the truth. And if my questioner were one of your
d contentious and eristical wise men, I'd tell him, "I've answered.
If my answer is not good, it is your job to refute me." But with
friends who wish to converse with each other, as in our case, a
gentler answer is indicated, one more suited to dialectic. It is
more dialectical not only to answer what is true, but to do so in
terms which the respondent further agrees that he knows. So
that's how I'll try to answer you. Tell me then, is there something
e you call an end? I mean something like a limit or a boundary—
they are all about the same, though Prodicus[3] perhaps would
disagree. But you surely call something limited and ended, and
that is the kind of thing I mean—nothing fancy.

MEN. To be sure I do, and I think I understand what you mean.

76a SOC. Well then, is there something you call a surface, and still another you call a solid, as in geometry?

MEN. Certainly.

SOC. Then at this point you can understand what I say figure is.
In respect of every figure, I say figure is that in which a solid
terminates. More briefly, figure is the limit of a solid.

MEN. And what do you say color is, Socrates?

SOC. You are outrageous, Meno. You put an old man to the trouble
b of answering, when you won't yourself recollect and say what
Gorgias said virtue is.

MEN. You tell me this, Socrates, and I'll tell you that.

SOC. A man could realize blindfolded, Meno, just from the way you
converse, that you are handsome and still have admirers.

MEN. Why?

SOC. Because you speak only to command, as spoiled favorites do,
who play tyrant as long as the bloom of their beauty lasts. And
c at the same time you've probably noticed my weakness for the
fair, so I'll gratify you and answer.

MEN. By all means do.

SOC. Will you have me answer in the manner of Gorgias, which
would be easiest for you to follow?

MEN. Why, of course.

SOC. Well then, don't you and Gorgias talk about certain effluences
among the things which are, in the same way as Empedocles?

3. A sophist noted for distinguishing between the meaning of words.

MEN. Yes, emphatically.

SOC. And about pores or passages, into which and through which the effluences pass?

MEN. Certainly.

d SOC. And that some of the effluences fit certain of the pores, while some are too large or too small?

MEN. That is so.

SOC. Again, there is something you call sight?

MEN. There is.

SOC. Then "grasp what I tell you," as Pindar says. Color is an effluence of figures, commensurable with sight, therefore perceptible.

MEN. Socrates, I think you've found an answer which is simply superb!

SOC. No doubt because it is put in a way you're accustomed to. At the same time you realize, I suppose, that in a similar way you

e could say what sound is, and smell, and many other things of the sort.

MEN. Of course.

SOC. It is a stately style of answer, Meno, and so you like it better than my answer about figure.

MEN. Yes, I do.

SOC. And yet, son of Alexidemus, I myself am convinced the other answer was better, and I think you would come to agree too, if it weren't necessary for you, as you were saying yesterday, to leave before the mysteries are celebrated, and if you were able to stay to be initiated.

77a MEN. Socrates, I would make it a point to stay if you gave me many such answers as that.

SOC. Then I must spare no effort to do so, both for your sake and my own—though I'm afraid I may not be able to keep to a level like that for very long. But come, it's your turn to pay your promised debt and say what virtue as a whole is. And "stop making one into many," as the joke goes when somebody breaks something. Leave virtue whole and healthy and say what it is. Exam-

b ples you have got from me.

Virtue as Desire for Good Things and Ability to Attain Them (77b–78c)

MEN. Well, I think, Socrates, that as the poet says, virtue is "to rejoice in things beautiful and be capable of them."[4] And that, I claim, is virtue: desire for beautiful things and ability to attain them.

SOC. Do you say that to desire beautiful things is to desire good things?

MEN. Yes, of course.

SOC. Then do some men desire evils, and others goods? Does it not

c seem to you, my friend, that *all* men desire goods?

MEN. No, it doesn't.

SOC. Some desire evils?

MEN. Yes.

SOC. Supposing the evils to be goods, you mean, or recognizing that they are evils and still desiring them?

MEN. Both, I think.

SOC. You think, Meno, that anyone recognizes evils to be evils and still desires them?

MEN. Certainly.

SOC. What do you mean by "desire"? Desire to possess?

d MEN. Why yes, of course.

SOC. Believing that evils benefit, or recognizing that evils harm, those who possess them?

MEN. Some believe evils benefit, others recognize that they harm.

SOC. Does it seem to you that those who believe that evils benefit recognize evils to be evils?

MEN. No, I certainly don't think that.

SOC. Then it is clear that these people, who do not recognize evils for what they are, do not desire evils; rather, they desire things

e they suppose to be good, though in fact those things are evil. Hence, these people, not recognizing evils to be evils, and supposing them to be goods, really desire goods. Not so?

MEN. Yes, very likely it is.

SOC. Now what about those who, as you claim, desire evils believing that evils harm their possessor. Surely they recognize they will be harmed by them?

MEN. They must.

78a SOC. Don't they suppose that people who are harmed are made wretched to the degree they are harmed?

MEN. Again, they must.

SOC. And aren't the wretched unhappy?

4. Perhaps Simonides.

MEN. I should think so.

SOC. Now, does anyone wish to be wretched and unhappy?

MEN. I think not, Socrates.

SOC. Then nobody wishes for evils, Meno, unless he wishes to be in that condition. For what else is it to be wretched, than to desire evils and get them?

b MEN. You are very likely right, Socrates; nobody wishes for evils.

SOC. Now, you were just saying that virtue is to wish for good things and to be able to get them?

MEN. Yes, I did.

SOC. Well, of this claim, the wishing part applies to everybody, so in that respect, one person is no better than another.

MEN. So it appears.

SOC. But it is clear that if one person is better than another, it must be in respect to ability.

MEN. Certainly.

SOC. So it seems that, according to your account, virtue is the ability
c   to attain good things.

MEN. You have now expressed my opinion precisely.

Virtue as Ability to Attain Good Things (78c–80d)

SOC. Then let us consider this and see if you are right, as you very likely are. You say that being able to attain goods is virtue?

MEN. I do.

SOC. And you call such things as health and wealth goods, do you not?

MEN. Yes, I count possession of gold and silver good, as well as civic honors and offices.

SOC. And you don't count other things good besides those sorts of things?

MEN. No, only things such as those.

d SOC. Very well. Then to attain gold and silver is virtue—so says Meno, ancestral guest-friend of the Great King of Persia. Do you add "justly and piously" to that attainment, Meno, or does it make no difference? If someone attains them unjustly, do you call it virtue all the same?

MEN. Surely not, Socrates.

SOC. Vice, rather?

MEN. Of course.

SOC. So it seems that justice or temperance or holiness, or some

other part of virtue, must be present in the attainment. Other-
e   wise, it will not be virtue even if it provides goods.

MEN. No, for how could it be virtue without them?

SOC. And failure to provide gold and silver for oneself or for another when it would not be just to do so—that is virtue too, that
very failure and perplexity of provision?

MEN. So it seems.

SOC. So the provision of such goods is no more virtue than the
failure to provide them. Rather, it seems what is accompanied by
79a   justice is virtue, and what is without anything of the sort will be
vice.

MEN. I think it must be as you say.

SOC. Now we were saying a moment ago that justice and temperance and everything of the sort each are a part of virtue?

MEN. Yes.

SOC. Then, Meno, you're making fun of me.

MEN. But why, Socrates?

SOC. Because I just now begged you not to break virtue up into
bits and pieces, and gave you examples of how you should answer,
and here you are paying no attention to that, but telling me that
b   virtue is the ability to attain good things with justice. And justice,
you say, is a part of virtue?

MEN. Yes.

SOC. So it follows from your own admissions that virtue is doing
whatever one may do with a part of virtue, since you say that
justice and the rest are parts of virtue. What do I mean by that?
Just this: I begged you to say what virtue is as a whole, but you,
so far from saying what it is, claim that every action is virtue if
it is done with a part of virtue—as though you already had said
c   what virtue as a whole is, and I am at this point to understand
even if you break it into parts. So it seems to me that you must
start from the beginning with the same question, my dear Meno:
What is virtue? For that is what is being said when someone says
that every action done with justice is virtue. Don't you think you
need to go back to the original question? Or do you think someone knows what a part of virtue is, without knowing what virtue
is?

MEN. I do not.

d SOC. No, for if you remember when I was answering you just now
about figure, we discarded the sort of answer which is given in
terms of what is still under investigation and not yet agreed upon.

MEN. Yes, and we were right to do so, Socrates.

SOC. Then my friend, as long as what virtue is as a whole is still under investigation, don't suppose that you will clarify virtue for anyone by answering in terms of its parts, or in any other terms
e which contain a similar obscurity. The original question needs to be answered. You talk about virtue—but what is it? Do I seem to be talking nonsense?

MEN. Most certainly not.

SOC. Then answer again from the beginning: what do you and your comrade Gorgias say virtue is?

MEN. Socrates, I kept hearing before I ever met you that you are
80a yourself in perplexity, and cause perplexity in others. And now I think you've cast a spell on me; I am utterly subdued by enchantment, so that I too have become full of perplexity. Am I allowed a small joke? You are both in appearance and other ways very like the stingray in the sea, which benumbs whatever it touches. I think you've now done something of the sort to me.
b My tongue, my soul, are numb—truly—and I cannot answer you. And yet, I've said many things about virtue a thousand times, and to a host of people—and, as I thought, spoken well. But now I'm utterly at a loss to say even what it is. You do well, I think, not to journey abroad from here; for if you worked things like this as a stranger in another city, you might well be arrested as a sorcerer.

SOC. Meno, you are quite unscrupulous. You very nearly fooled me.

MEN. How could I, Socrates!

c SOC. I see the motive in your comparison.

MEN. What do you think it is?

SOC. You want a comparison in return. This I know of all you handsome types—you delight in being compared, because you make a profit on it; your beauty leads to beautiful comparisons. But I won't give you a comparison. As for myself, if the stingray numbs itself as it numbs others, I am like it; otherwise not. For I don't cause perplexity in others while free of perplexities myself; the truth is rather that I cause perplexity in others because
d I am myself perplexed. And so it is now with virtue. I don't know what it is, while you, who may have known before I touched you, are now in like way ignorant. Nevertheless, I wish to join with you in inquiring what it is.

Inquiry and Recollection (80d–81e)

MEN. And how will you inquire into a thing, Socrates, when you are wholly ignorant of what it is? What sort of thing among those you don't know will you set up as the object of your inquiry? Even if you happen to bump right into it, how will you know that it is the thing you didn't know?

SOC. I understand what you want to say, Meno. Do you see what
e an eristical argument you're spinning? It is thus impossible for a man to inquire either into what he knows, or into what he does not know. He cannot inquire into what he knows; for he knows it, and there is no need for inquiry into a thing like that. Nor would he inquire into what he does not know; for he does not know what it is he is to inquire into.

81a MEN. Well, don't you think that's a good argument, Socrates?

SOC. I do not.

MEN. Can you say why?

SOC. Yes. For I have heard from men and women who are wise in things divine—

MEN. What was it they told?

SOC. A noble truth, I think.

MEN. What was it? And who were they who told it?

SOC. Some were priests and priestesses who wanted to explain their
b observances. But Pindar and as many other poets who are inspired have told it too. Here is their tale. See if you think it true. They say that the soul of man is immortal, sometimes reaching an end which men call dying, sometimes born again, but never perishing. Because this is so, one must live his whole life in utmost holiness; for from whomsoever

Persephone shall accept requital for her ancient grief,
Returning their souls in the ninth year to the upper light,
Their term of banishment to darkness done:
c   From them illustrious kings shall spring,
    Lords of rushing wisdom, and strength unsurpassed.
In all remaining time they shall be known
As heroes, and be sanctified by men.[5]

Seeing then that the soul is immortal, and has been born many times, and has beheld all things in this world and the world be-

5. The poet cited by Meno is Pindar.

yond, there is nothing it has not learnt: so it is not surprising that it can be reminded of virtue and other things which it knew before. For since the whole of nature is akin, and the soul has
d   learned all things, there is nothing to prevent someone, upon being reminded of one single thing—which men call learning— from rediscovering all the rest, if he is courageous and faints not in the search. For learning and inquiry are then wholly recollection. Therefore we need not be persuaded by the eristical argument, which would cause us to be idle; it is sweet only to the ear of the soft and weak, whereas this account induces industry and
e   inquiry. I put my trust in its truth, and ask you to join me in inquiring what virtue is.

A Proof of Recollection (81e–86c)

MEN. Yes, Socrates, but what do you mean by saying that we do not learn, that what we call learning is recollection? Can you teach me that this is so?

SOC. Why Meno, I just said you were unscrupulous, and now you are asking me to teach you, when I claim there is no teaching but
82a   recollection, just so I can straightway prove myself inconsistent.

MEN. No, no, Socrates, that was surely not my aim. I just spoke from habit. If you can somehow prove it is as you say, please do so.

SOC. Well, it is not easy, but still, for you I will make the effort. You have many of your attendants here. Summon for me which-
b   ever one you please for the demonstration.

MEN. Certainly. (*Beckoning to a slave boy.*) You there, come here.

SOC. He's a Greek, I assume, and speaks Greek?

MEN. Oh yes, he was born and raised in our house.

SOC. Then pay close attention. See whether it appears to you that he recollects, or learns from me.

MEN. I certainly shall.

SOC. (*Turning to the boy.*) Tell me, my boy. Do you recognize that this sort of figure is a square? (*Socrates traces square ABCD in the sand at his feet.*)

BOY. I do.

c SOC. Now, a square figure is one having all four of these sides equal? (*Indicating the sides.*)

BOY. Of course.

soc. And so is one having these lines drawn through the middle equal too? (*Socrates draws in transversals bisecting each side.*)

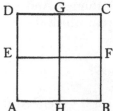

BOY. Yes.

soc. Now, a figure of this sort could be larger or smaller?

BOY. Of course.

soc. Now suppose that this side (AB) were two feet, and this one (AD) two feet. How many feet[6] would the whole be? Look at it this way: if it were two feet this way (AB) and only one foot that way (AE), wouldn't the figure be two feet taken once?

BOY. (*Inspecting ABFE*) Yes.

d soc. But since it is also two feet that way (AD), doesn't it become twice two?

BOY. It does.

soc. Therefore it becomes twice two feet?

BOY. Yes.

soc. Now, how many is twice two feet? Count and tell me. (*The boy looks at ABCD and counts the squares it contains.*)

BOY. Four, Socrates.

soc. Now could there be another figure twice the size of this one, but similar to it—that is, having four sides equal to each other?

BOY. Yes.

soc. How many feet will it be?

BOY. Eight.

soc. Come then. Try and tell me how long each side of it will be.

e   Each side of this one (ABCD) is two feet. What about the side of a figure double this?

6. It is customary here and in what follows to translate "feet" in appropriate contexts as "square feet," a concept for which Greek mathematics had no special term. This lack, however, is no accident, for the Greek mathematicians used geometry to perform both arithmetical and algebraic operations. Thus for example, a side of three and a side of seven expressed as a rectangle yields the equation $3 \times 7 = 21$, and when the operation is viewed in this way, the distinction between feet and square feet obscures its point. I have therefore kept to Greek usage because of the geometrical algebra which explains the use. For further discussion, see T. L. Heath, *The Thirteen Books of Euclid's Elements*, vol. I, New York, 1960, pp. 372–74.

BOY. Clearly it will be double, Socrates.

SOC. Do you see, Meno, that I am teaching him nothing but am asking him all these things? And now he thinks he knows the length of the side from which the eight-foot figure will be generated. Do you agree?

MEN. I do.

SOC. Well, does he know?

MEN. Of course not.

SOC. He merely thinks it is generated from the doubled side?

MEN. Yes.

SOC. Now watch him recollect serially and in order, as is necessary for recollection. (*Turning to the boy*) Tell me: are you saying that 83a the doubled figure is generated from the doubled side? The figure I mean is not to be long one way and short the other; it is to be equal on all sides, as this one (ABCD) is, but double it, eight feet. See if you still think it will result from double the side.

BOY. I do.

SOC. Now, this line (AB) becomes double (AX) if we add another of the same length here?

BOY. Of course.

SOC. So there will be an eight-foot figure from it, you say, if four such sides are generated?

BOY. Yes.

b SOC. Then let us inscribe four equal sides from it. (*Socrates, beginning with base AX, inscribes AXYZ.*)

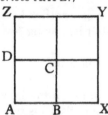

You say this would be eight feet?

BOY. Of course.

SOC. Now, there are four squares in it, each of which is equal to this four-foot figure (ABCD)? (*Socrates completes the transversals begun by DC and BC above.*)

BOY. Yes.

SOC. Then how big has it become? Four times as big?

BOY. Certainly.

SOC. Now, is four times the same as double?

BOY. Surely not.

SOC. How many?

BOY. Fourfold.

c SOC. Then from double the line, my boy, not a double but a four-fold figure is generated.

BOY. True.

SOC. Since four times four is sixteen. Right?

BOY. Yes.

SOC. Well, then, an eight-foot figure will be generated from what line? That one (AX) gave us a four-fold figure, didn't it? (i.e., AXYZ)

BOY. Yes.

SOC. But half of it (AB) gave us four feet? (i.e., ABCD)

BOY. I agree.

SOC. Very well. But an eight-foot figure is double this (ABCD), and half that (AXYZ)?

BOY. Yes.

SOC. Then it will be from a side greater than this (AB) but smaller
d   than that one there (AX), won't it?

BOY. Yes, I think so.

SOC. Excellent. Always answer what you think. Now tell me: wasn't this line (AB) two feet, and that one (AX) four?

BOY. Yes.

SOC. So the side of an eight-foot figure must be greater than this two-foot side here, but smaller than the four-foot side?

BOY. It must.

e SOC. Try and tell me how long you'd say it is.

BOY. Three feet.

SOC. Now, if it is to be three feet, we'll add (to AB) half of this (BX), and it will be three feet; for this (AB) is two, and that (BM) is one. And in the same way over here, this (AD) is two and that (DN) is one; and the figure you speak of is generated. (*Socrates as he speaks marks M and N on BX and DZ, and then completes the square.*)

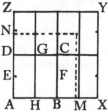

BOY. Yes.

SOC. Now if this (AM) is three and that (AN) is three, the whole figure generated is thrice three feet?

BOY. That follows.

SOC. And how many is thrice three?

BOY. Nine.

SOC. But the double (of the original square) had to be how many feet?

BOY. Eight.

SOC. So somehow the eight foot figure is not generated from the three-foot side either.

BOY. It certainly isn't.

SOC. But from what, then? Try and tell us exactly. If you don't want
84a   to count it out, just point to it.

BOY. Socrates, I really don't know.

SOC. (*Turning to Meno.*) Here again, Meno, do you see the progress in recollection he's made so far? At first he didn't know the side required for an eight-foot figure—and he still doesn't. But earlier he supposed he knew and answered confidently, and did not
b   believe he was in perplexity. But now he *does* believe it, and as he doesn't know, neither does he suppose he knows.

MEN. You are right.

SOC. So he is now better off with respect to the thing which he did not know?

MEN. I agree.

SOC. Well, did we harm him any by numbing him like a stingray and making him aware of his perplexity?

MEN. I think not.

SOC. We have at any rate done something, it seems, to help him discover how things are, for in his present condition of ignorance, he will gladly inquire into the matter, whereas before he might easily have supposed he could speak well, and frequently, and
c   before large audiences, about doubling the square and how the side must be double in length.

MEN. So it seems.

SOC. Well, do you think he would undertake to inquire into or learn what he thought he knew and did not, before he fell into perplexity and became convinced of his ignorance and longed to know?

MEN. I think not, Socrates.

SOC. So numbing benefited him?

MEN. Yes.

SOC. Then please observe what he will discover from this perplexity as he inquires with me—even though I will only ask questions

d and will not teach. Be on guard lest you find that I teach and explain to him, instead of questioning him about his own opinions. (*Socrates at this point rubs out the figures in the sand at his feet, leaving only rectangle ABCD, and turns to the boy.*) Now back to you. We've got this figure of four feet, don't we? Do you follow?

BOY. I do.

SOC. And we can add here another equal to it? (*Inscribes it*)

BOY. Yes.

SOC. And a third here, equal to each of those? (*Inscribes it*)

BOY. Yes.

SOC. Now, we can fill in the one here in the corner? (*Inscribes it*)

BOY. Of course.

SOC. So these four equal figures would be generated?

e BOY. Yes.

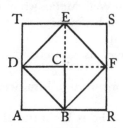

SOC. Now then. How many times larger than this (ABCD) does this whole (ARST) become?

BOY. Four times.

SOC. But we had to generate double. Do you recall?

BOY. Of course.

SOC. Now take this line from corner to corner. (*Socrates inscribes*

85a *BFED.*) Does it cut each of these figures in two?

BOY. Yes.

SOC. Now, have we generated four equal lines here (BD, DE, EF, FB), enclosing this figure (BFED)?

BOY. We have.

SOC. Then consider: how large is this figure?

BOY. I don't understand.

SOC. Hasn't each of these lines cut off the inner half of these four squares?

BOY. Yes.

SOC. Then how many (halves) of that size are in this (BFED)?

BOY. Four.

SOC. And how many in this one (ABCD)?

BOY. Two.

SOC. What is four to two?

BOY. Double.

b SOC. So this becomes how many feet?

BOY. Eight feet.

SOC. From what line?

BOY. That one (BD).

SOC. That is, from the line stretching from corner to corner of the four-foot figure?

BOY. Yes.

SOC. Students of the subject call that the diagonal. So if that is the name for it, then you, Meno's slave, are stating as your view that the double figure would be generated from the diagonal.

BOY. Yes, certainly, Socrates.

SOC. (*Turning to Meno*) Well, Meno, what do you think? Did he reply with any opinion not his own?

c MEN. No, they were his.

SOC. Yet he didn't *know*, as we were saying a little earlier.

MEN. True.

SOC. Yet these opinions were *in* him, weren't they?

MEN. Yes.

SOC. Therefore, while he is ignorant of these things he does not know, there are true opinions in him about these very things?

MEN. That follows.

SOC. For the moment, these opinions have been stirred up in him as in a dream; but if he were repeatedly asked these same questions in different ways, you may rest assured that eventually he

d would know about these things as accurately as anyone.

MEN. It seems so.

SOC. Then he will know without being taught but only questioned, recovering knowledge out of himself?

MEN. Yes.

SOC. And his recovering knowledge which is in him is recollection?

MEN. Yes.

SOC. The knowledge he now has he either gained at some time or always had?

MEN. Yes.

SOC. Well, if he always had it, he always knew. And if he gained it at some time, he surely didn't do so in his present life. Or did e someone teach him geometry? For he will do the very same thing all through geometry, and every other study. Is there anyone who has taught him all this? You ought to know, especially since he was born in your house and raised there.

MEN. I do know: no one ever taught him.

SOC. But he has these opinions, does he not?

MEN. It appears he must, Socrates.

SOC. Well, if he did not get them in his present life, is it not at this
86a point clear he got and learned them at some other time?

MEN. It appears so.

SOC. A time when he was not in human form?

MEN. Yes.

SOC. So if we are to say that there are true opinions present in him both during the time when he is and is not a man, and that those opinions become knowledge when roused by questioning, then his soul will ever be in a state of having learned. For it is clear that through all time he either is or is not a man.

MEN. That follows.

SOC. Now, if the truth of things is always in our soul, the soul is
b immortal. So it is right to try boldly to inquire into and recollect what you do not happen to know at present—that is, what you do not remember.

MEN. I think you are right, Socrates—how, I don't know.

SOC. I think so too, Meno. There are other things about the argument I would not confidently affirm, but that we shall be better men, more courageous and less idle, if we think we ought to inquire into what we do not know, instead of thinking that be-
c cause we cannot find what we do not know we ought not seek it—that I would do battle for, so far as possible, in word and deed.

MEN. Here again, I think you are right, Socrates.

SOC. Then since we are agreed that there must be inquiry about what one does not know, shall we together undertake to investigate what virtue is?

The Method of Hypothesis (86c–87c)

MEN. By all means. But Socrates, what would please me most would be to take up the question I began with and hear you on it: whether virtue is something that is taught, or present by nature,
d or in what way it comes to be present in men.

soc. If I not only ruled myself, Meno, but also ruled you, we'd not consider whether virtue is or is not taught before first considering what it is. But since you do not even attempt to rule yourself—being a free man, after all—and yet still try to rule me, and do,

e   I must perforce go along. What else can I do? It seems then that we must inquire of what sort virtue is, when we don't yet know what it is. But please relax your rule over me a little, and consent to inquire by means of a hypothesis whether it is taught. I mean the sort of thing geometers often use in their inquiries. When someone asks them, say, about an area, whether it is possible for a given area to be stretched as a triangle into a given circle, a

87a geometer might say, "I don't know yet if it is possible, but I think there is, as it were, a hypothesis at hand to deal with the matter. It is this: if this area is such that, when applied along a line given for it, it falls short by an area of the same sort as the area which has already been applied. I think one thing follows: and a different thing follows in turn if it is impossible for the area to be so affected.[7] So I wish to tell you what follows about the stretching

b   out of it into the circle, whether it is possible or not, by using hypothesis."

So too then for us about virtue. Since we know neither what it is nor what is true of it, let us use hypothesis in inquiring whether it is taught. As follows: among things of the soul, of what sort must virtue be if it is taught or if it is not taught? To begin with, if it is the same sort or a different sort than knowledge, is it or is it not taught?—or as we were just now saying, remembered?

c   The name we use makes no difference here: is it taught? Or isn't it quite clear that a man is taught nothing but knowledge?

MEN. I think so.

soc. So if virtue is a kind of knowledge, it clearly would be taught.

MEN. Certainly.

soc. Then we have disposed of this point quickly: it is taught if it is of one sort, but not if of another.

MEN. Of course.

7. The reader may be forgiven if he finds the foregoing translation mildly opaque. For a summary of conjectures on the nature of the hypothesis, see R. S. Bluck, *Plato's Meno*, Cambridge, 1962, Appendix. It is well to point out that the word here translated "figure" may also mean "area," as well as "rectangle" or "square," and that the geometrical technique involved uses application of areas, for which see Euclid, *Elements* I, Prop. 44, and Heath, *Euclid's Elements*, pp. 342–45.

That Virtue Is Knowledge (87c–89a)

soc. The next step, it seems, is to inquire whether virtue is knowledge or of a sort other than knowledge.

d MEN. I agree: that must be examined next.

soc. Well, then, do we say that virtue is good? Does that hypothesis stand fast for us, that it is good?

MEN. Certainly.

soc. Now, if something is good, but other than and separate from knowledge, virtue perhaps would not be a kind of knowledge. But if there is nothing good which knowledge does not encompass, we may rightly suspect that virtue is a kind of knowledge.

MEN. True.

soc. Again, it is by virtue that we are good?

MEN. Yes.

e soc. And if good, beneficial. For all good things are beneficial, are they not?

MEN. Yes.

soc. So virtue is beneficial, then?

MEN. Necessarily, from what has been agreed.

soc. Then let us examine what sort of thing benefits us, taking particular examples. Health, we say, and strength, beauty, and no doubt wealth too—we hold that they and things like them are beneficial, do we not?

MEN. Yes.

88a soc. But we say that those same things sometimes also do harm. Do you dispute that?

MEN. No, it is true.

soc. Then let us consider what guides each of these things when they benefit us, and what guides them when they do harm. Don't they benefit us when there is right use, and harm us when there is not?

MEN. Certainly.

soc. Next, consider things having to do with the soul. Is there something you call temperance, and justice and courage and quick wits, and memory and nobility of character and so on?

b MEN. There is.

soc. Then consider: do those among them which you think are not knowledge, but other than knowledge, sometimes benefit and sometimes harm? Take courage, for example. Suppose that courage is not wisdom but, as it were, a kind of boldness. When a man is bold without intelligence, he is harmed; with intelligence, he is benefited. Isn't that so?

MEN. Yes.

SOC. And so similarly with temperance and quick wits. Things learned or acquired by training are beneficial when accompanied by intelligence, but harmful without it.

c MEN. Very true indeed.

SOC. To sum up then, everything that the soul undertakes or endures, when guided by wisdom, ends in happiness, and in the opposite when guided by folly?

MEN. It seems so.

SOC. Therefore, if virtue is something among things in the soul, and is necessarily beneficial, it must be wisdom, since everything which has to do with the soul is in itself neither beneficial nor harmful, but becomes one or the other by the addition of wisdom d or folly. According to this account, then, virtue, being beneficial, must be a kind of wisdom.

MEN. I agree.

SOC. Returning then to the other things we just mentioned as sometimes good and sometimes harmful—I mean wealth, and so on—isn't the same true there? Just as wisdom, guiding the rest of the soul, makes things of the soul beneficial, while folly makes them e harmful, so too with these: the soul, guiding and using them rightly, makes them beneficial; if not rightly, harmful.

MEN. Of course.

SOC. But it is the wise soul which guides rightly, and the foolish soul which guides with error?

MEN. True.

SOC. So this then is to be asserted generally: in man, all other things depend upon the soul; but things of the soul depend upon wis-89a dom, if they are to be good. And by this account, the beneficial would be wisdom, while virtue, we say, is beneficial.

MEN. Quite so.

SOC. Therefore, we say that virtue is wisdom, either all or some part?

MEN. I think these statements excellent, Socrates.

That Virtue Is Not Taught (89a–e)

SOC. Now if this is true, good men are not good by nature.

MEN. No.

b SOC. Otherwise, this would surely follow: if good men are good by nature, we would no doubt have among us people who could discern among our youth those whose natures are good; and we would take them, once revealed to us, and guard them in a lofty citadel, setting our seal upon them more surely than on our gold, so that no one might corrupt them. For when they reach maturity, they will be of service to their cities.

MEN. Very likely, Socrates.

SOC. Then since good men are not good by nature, are they so by
c learning?

MEN. At this point, it seems necessary. And, Socrates, it is clear from the hypothesis, if virtue is knowledge, it is taught.

SOC. To be sure. But perhaps it was improper to agree to that.

MEN. It surely seemed proper a moment ago.

SOC. Yes, but if there is to be any soundness to it, shouldn't it seem proper not only "a moment ago," but now and in the future as well?

d MEN. No doubt. But what do you see to make you uneasy? Why do you doubt that virtue is knowledge?

SOC. I'll tell you, Meno. I'm not taking back as improper the claim that it is taught if it is knowledge. But consider whether you don't think it reasonable to doubt that it is knowledge. Just tell me this: if anything at all—not just virtue—is taught, must there not be teachers and students of it?

e MEN. I think so.

SOC. Then might we not reasonably conjecture that the opposite also holds—that should there be neither teachers nor students of it, it is not taught?

MEN. Yes. But don't you think there are teachers of virtue?

SOC. Well at any rate I've often inquired if there are, and try as I might, I couldn't find them. And yet I inquired among many people, especially those I thought most experienced in the matter.

The Interview with Anytus (89e–96d)

SOC. But look now, Meno. Here is Anytus sitting down beside us,
90a and just at the right time. Let us make him a partner in our inquiry. It is reasonable that we should, for in the first place, he is the son of a wise and wealthy father, Anthemion, who became rich not by gift or accident, like Ismenias the Theban who has

just recently come into the fortune of Polycrates,[8] but by his own
diligence and skill. Then too, he seems to be a citizen who is not
insolent, or pompous and offensive, but a man of good conduct
b   and well-ordered life. Finally, he raised and educated his son here
well, as the majority of Athenians think; at any rate, they choose
him for their highest offices. It is right, then, to inquire with such
a man whether or not there are teachers of virtue, and who they
are. So Anytus, please join us—your guest-friend Meno here, and
me—and inquire into this matter of who the teachers of virtue
may be. Consider this: if we wished Meno here to become a good
c   physician, to what teachers would we send him? To the physicians,
I assume?

ANY. Of course.

SOC. What if we wished him to become a good cobbler. To the
cobblers?

ANY. Yes.

SOC. And so in other cases?

ANY. Of course.

SOC. Then look again to the same examples and tell me this: We
say we properly send him to the physicians if we wish him to
d   become a physician. When we make that statement, do we mean
that we'd be well advised to send him to people who lay claim to
the art, rather than those who do not, and charge a fee precisely
on that basis, declaring themselves teachers for anyone wishing
to come and learn? Wouldn't this be our proper consideration in
sending him?

ANY. Yes.

SOC. And isn't it just the same with flute playing and so on? It is
the height of unreason, if we wish to make somebody a flute
e   player, not to be willing to send him to people who promise to
teach the art and charge for it, and instead to trouble others to
teach him when they don't claim to be teachers and haven't got
a single pupil in the subject. Don't you think that would be highly
unreasonable?

ANY. I do, and stupid to boot.

SOC. Well said. Accordingly, you and I can now consult together
91a   about your guest-friend Meno here. He has been saying to me
for some time, Anytus, that he desires the wisdom and virtue by

8. The money in question was probably a bribe. Cf. *Republic* 336a. For more on
Ismenias and Polycrates, see Bluck, *Plato's Meno*, 345–47.

which men properly order households and cities, and take care of their parents, and know how to welcome and take leave of fellow citizens and guest-friends in a manner worthy of a good

b man. To whom should we send him for this? Or is it clear from our account just now that we should send him to people who undertake to be teachers of virtue, declaring themselves available to any Greek who wishes to learn, and charging a set fee for it.

ANY. And just who do you mean, Socrates?

SOC. Why, you know as well as I do. The men people call sophists.

c ANY. Good Lord, don't blaspheme, Socrates. May none of my own, not family, not friends, no citizen, no guest, be seized with such madness as to go to these men and be ruined. For they clearly ruin and corrupt anyone who associates with them.

SOC. Why Anytus, what do you mean? Do they therefore differ so much from others who claim to know how to work some good, that they alone not only provide no benefit, as the rest do, to what

d is placed in their hands, but on the contrary corrupt it? They openly demand a fee for doing *that*? I can scarcely believe you. Why, I know one man, Protagoras, who made more money from that wisdom of his than did Phidias, who produced such conspicuously beautiful work, and any ten other sculptors you please. People who mend old shoes and patch cloaks, if they were to hand back articles in worse condition than they got them, would

e not escape detection for thirty days and would quickly starve to death if they tried. You surely utter a portent, then, if Protagoras for more than forty years corrupted those who associated with him, sent them back in worse condition than he got them, and escaped detection by the whole of Greece. He was nearly seventy when he died, I think; he had been forty years in his art; and in all that time, and to the present day, esteem for him has been

92a unceasing. And not just for Protagoras, either. There have been a host of others, some born before him and some still alive now. Are we to say according to your account that they led astray and ruined the youth knowingly, or that they were not even aware of it themselves? Shall we then deem them mad, whom some say are the wisest men of all?

ANY. They are far from mad, Socrates. It is the youths who pay

b them money who are mad, still more the relatives who allow it, and most of all the cities which allow such men to enter and don't drive them out—whether they are foreigners or citizens.

soc. But Anytus, why are you so hard on them? Has one of the sophists wronged you?

any. No indeed, I've never associated with any of them, nor permitted anyone of mine to do so.

soc. So you have no experience of the fellows?

c any. That's right. May it continue so.

soc. Then, my friend, how do you know whether this affair has good or mischief in it, when you have no experience of it?

any. Easily. At any rate, I know who they are and what they are, whether I've had experience with them or not.

soc. You must have second sight, Anytus! I can't see how else you'd know about them, from what you've said. Still, we weren't asking

d where Meno can go to be corrupted. Let it be to the sophists, if you wish. Tell us instead about the others. Benefit this friend of your father's house and inform him to whom he should go in this great city to become distinguished in respect to the virtue I just described.

any. Why don't you tell him yourself?

soc. Why, I did mention whom I thought were teachers of it,

e though it happens I was talking nonsense. So you say, at least, and perhaps you are right. But now it's your turn. Tell him to whom he should go among the Athenians. Mention any name you please.

any. Why should he hear just one name? Any Athenian gentlemen he meets will make him better than would the sophists, provided he is willing to listen.

soc. But did they become fine gentlemen spontaneously? Without having learned from anyone, can they nonetheless teach others

93a what they themselves did not learn?

any. Why, I expect they learned from their elders, who were gentlemen too. Do you deny that there have been many good men in this city?

soc. No, Anytus, I think there are good men in political life here, and that their predecessors were not inferior to them. But have they been good teachers of their own virtue? Our discussion is about that; not whether there are good men here now, or for-

b merly, but whether virtue is taught. We've been asking for some time, and to ask that is to ask this: Do good men, whether of our time or earlier, actually know how to hand down to someone else the virtue in which their goodness consists, or is it impossible for a man to hand it on or receive it from another? That's what Meno

and I have been after for some time. On the basis of your own
c   account, consider: would you say Themistocles was a good man?

ANY. Of course. Eminently good.

SOC. So if anyone else could teach his own virtue, you'd say he'd
be a good teacher?

ANY. I suppose so, at least if he wanted to.

SOC. But don't you suppose he'd have wished others to become
good men, especially his own son? Do you think he'd treat a son
with grudging jealousy, and purposefully not hand on the virtue
d   in which his own goodness consisted? Surely you must have heard
how Themistocles had his son Cleophantus taught to be a good
horseman. Why, he could ride a horse standing bolt upright, and
aim a javelin doing it, and he could do many other amazing
things, because Themistocles educated him and made him skillful in everything which can be got from good teachers. Surely
you've heard all this from your elders?

ANY. I have.

SOC. So no one could claim his son's nature was bad.

e   ANY. Perhaps not.

SOC. But what about this: Did you ever hear anybody, young or
old, say that Cleophantus son of Themistocles was good and wise,
as his father was?

ANY. Certainly not.

SOC. Well, are we to suppose that he wished to educate his son in
other things, but not to make him any better than his neighbors
in respect to the wisdom he himself possessed—that is, assuming
virtue is taught?

ANY. Hardly.

SOC. So there's your teacher of virtue; yet even you agree he was
94a   one of the best men of past generations. But let's examine someone else then, Aristides son of Lysimachus. Or don't you agree
he was good?

ANY. Of course I do.

SOC. Well, he too gave his son Lysimachus the best education in
Athens, so far as it could be got from teachers. Do you think it
made him better than anybody at all? You've associated with him;
b   you see what he's like. Or if you will, take Pericles—so splendidly
wise a man. You know he raised two sons, Paralus and Xanthippus?

ANY. Yes.

SOC. Then you also know he taught them to be horsemen inferior

to none in Athens; he educated them in music and gymnastics
and everything that could be got by art, and they excelled. Didn't
he then wish to make them good men? I think he did, but perhaps this is not taught. But lest you think this has been impossible

c   only for a few Athenians of a quite insignificant sort, think about
Thucydides.[9] He also raised two sons, Melesius and Stephanus,
educated them well in other things, and made them the best
wrestlers in Athens. He had one of them trained by Xanthias and
the other by Eudorus, who were reputed to be the best wrestlers
of their time. You recall?

MEN. Yes, I've heard that.

SOC. Well he clearly would never have gone to the expense needed

d   to teach his children wrestling, and yet fail to teach them at no
cost to himself the thing needed to make them good men—if it
is taught. Was Thucydides perhaps insignificant, without a host
of friends in Athens and among the Allies? To the contrary: he
was great in house and great in power, in this city and in the rest
of Greece. If the thing is taught, he'd certainly have found out
who it was, fellow countryman or foreigner, who would make his

e   sons good, if he himself lacked leisure due to cares of state.
Anytus, my friend, it may well be that virtue is not taught.

ANY. Socrates, it seems to me you slander men lightly. If you will
be persuaded by me, I would advise you to beware. It may be
that in other cities too it is easier to do evil to men than good.

95a   Certainly it is in this one. But then, I think you know that.

SOC. Anytus seems angry, Meno. I'm not surprised. To begin with,
he thinks I am disparaging these men; then too, he thinks he is
one of them. If someday he should understand what slander
really is, he will cease to be angry.[10] At present, he does not know.

But Meno, you tell me: there are gentlemen in your country
too, are there not?

MEN. Of course.

b   SOC. Well then, are they willing to offer themselves as teachers to
the young? Would they agree they are teachers and that virtue
is taught?

MEN. Emphatically not, Socrates; rather, sometimes you hear them
say it is taught, and sometimes not.

---

9. Not the historian, but a political rival of Pericles.
10. The translation could also read, "If someday he should understand what
speaking falsely is, he will cease to be angry."

soc. Well, are we to say they are teachers of it, when they disagree on that very point?

MEN. I think not, Socrates.

c soc. Then what about the sophists? They are the only ones who claim to be teachers of virtue. Do you think they are?

MEN. Socrates, that is why I especially admire Gorgias. You'd never hear him promise that: in fact, he laughs at those who do. He thinks it his business to make men clever speakers.

soc. Then you don't think the sophists are teachers?

MEN. Socrates, I can't say. Actually, I'm just like everybody else: sometimes I think so, sometimes not.

soc. But did you know that it's not just you and other people in public life who sometimes think it is taught and sometimes not?

d Even the poet Theognis said the same thing.

MEN. Really? Where?

soc. In his Elegaics, where he says,

> Sit with them, eat with them, drink with them;
> Be pleasing unto those whose power is great,
> For the good will teach you to be good.
e > Mix with evil and your mind will be lost.

You see that in those lines he says virtue is taught?

MEN. Yes, apparently so.

soc. But in others he shifts his ground a bit. I think it goes

> If thought were something to be made and put into a man,
> They would bear and carry many a fee and large.

Meaning by "they" the people who were able to do it. And again,

96a
> Never is a bad son born of a good father,
> For he is persuaded by precepts of wisdom.
> But never by teaching will you make the bad man good.

You notice how he contradicts himself?

MEN. Apparently.

soc. Well, can you mention any other subject where those who claim to be teachers are not acknowledged as teachers, or even acknowledged to understand their own subject matter, but are

b thought to be bad at the very thing they claim to teach; whereas those acknowledged as accomplished in this subject matter sometimes claim it is taught and sometimes not. Can you in any proper sense say that people so confused are teachers?

MEN. Emphatically not.

soc. Now, if neither sophists nor gentlemen are teachers of the thing, then clearly no one else is.

MEN. I agree.

c soc. And if no teachers, no students?

MEN. I think that's so.

soc. And we agreed that if there are neither teachers nor students of a thing, then it is not taught.

MEN. We did.

soc. Now, it turns out there are no teachers of virtue?

MEN. It does.

soc. And if no teachers, no students?

MEN. That follows.

soc. Therefore, virtue is not taught?

d MEN. It seems not, provided that we've examined it correctly. But the result is that I really wonder, Socrates, whether there even are any good men, or how those who become good can do so.

Knowledge and Right Opinion (96d–98b)

soc. Very likely you and I are pretty poor types, Meno. Gorgias hasn't sufficiently educated you, nor Prodicus me. Beyond all else, we must pay close attention to ourselves and seek someone
e   who will in some way make us better men. I say this with a view to the inquiry just concluded where we wittingly make ourselves ridiculous by neglecting the fact that it is not true that human affairs are carried on rightly and well only through the guidance of knowledge. That is perhaps why recognition of the way good men become good escapes us.

MEN. What do you mean, Socrates?

soc. This: we have agreed—and rightly, since it could hardly be
97a   otherwise—that good men must be beneficial.

MEN. Yes.

soc. And also that they will be beneficial if they guide matters rightly for us?

MEN. Yes.

soc. But that there cannot be right guidance unless there is understanding—to that, it seems, we agreed wrongly.

MEN. Really? Why do you say that?

soc. I'll tell you. Suppose someone who knew the road to Larisa, or any place you please, were to walk there and guide others. He would guide them rightly and well, wouldn't he?

MEN. Of course.

b SOC. But what if someone had right opinion as to the road, but had never taken it and did not know it. Wouldn't he guide rightly too?

MEN. Of course.

SOC. And presumably as long as he has right opinion about matters of which the other has knowledge, he will be no worse a guide than the man who understands it, even though he only believes truly without understanding.

MEN. Quite so.

SOC. Therefore true opinion, concerning rightness of action, is a guide not inferior to understanding; that is what we left out just c now in our inquiry about what sort of thing virtue is. We said that understanding is the only guide to right action, whereas it seems there is also true opinion.

MEN. Yes, it seems so.

SOC. So right opinion is no less beneficial than knowledge.

MEN. Except in this way, Socrates, that a man with knowledge will always hit upon the right answer, whereas a man with right opinion sometimes will and sometimes won't.

SOC. How do you mean? Won't the man who always has right opinion always be right as long as his opinion is right?

MEN. It would appear he must. But Socrates, assuming this is true, d I have to wonder that knowledge is much more highly valued than right opinion, and in what respect one is different from the other.

SOC. Do you know why you're surprised, or should I tell you?

MEN. Tell me, please.

SOC. It's because you haven't paid attention to the statues of Daedalus. Maybe there aren't any in your country.

MEN. What are you getting at?

SOC. Those statues, if they aren't bound, actually get up and run away; but if bound, they stay.

e MEN. Well, so?

SOC. It isn't worth a great deal to own one of his creations if it's loose; like a runaway slave, it will not stay. But it is worth quite a great deal when bound, for his works are very beautiful. What am I getting at? This bears on true opinions. For in fact, true opinions, as long as they stay, are beautiful possessions and ac98a complish all that is good, but they are unwilling to stay very long. They run away from the soul of a man, so that they are not worth much until someone binds them by reflection on the reason for them. And that, my friend Meno, is recollection, as we agreed before.[11] When bound, they in the first place become knowledge; and secondly, they abide. That is why knowledge is more to be valued than right opinion: Knowledge differs from right opinion by its bond.

MEN. Yes, Socrates, it certainly seems that way.

b SOC. Still, I speak as one who conjectures, not as one who knows. But that right opinion is other than knowledge I think is surely not conjecture: if I were to say I knew anything—and I would say it of very little—this one thing I would surely place among things I know.

MEN. Yes, and correctly, Socrates.

Conclusion (98b–100c)

SOC. Well, then, isn't it correct that in each action the guidance of true opinion accomplishes results in no way inferior to those accomplished by knowledge?

MEN. There again, what you say seems true.

c SOC. So right opinion is not worse or less beneficial than knowledge in respect to action; nor is the man who has right opinion inferior to the man who knows.

MEN. True.

SOC. Moreover, we've agreed that good men are beneficial.

MEN. Yes.

SOC. Then since good men would benefit their cities, if they do, not only through knowledge but right opinion, and since neither

d of the two belongs to men by nature, but is acquired—or do you think either knowledge or right opinion is present by nature?

MEN. No, I don't.

SOC. Then since they are not present by nature, good men are not good by nature.

MEN. Of course not.

SOC. Since good men are not good by nature, we next considered if virtue is taught.

MEN. Yes.

SOC. If virtue is wisdom, it seemed it would be taught.

MEN. Yes.

11. See 85c.

soc. And if taught, it would be wisdom?

men. Of course.

e soc. And if there were teachers, it would be taught. If none, it would not be taught.

men. Yes.

soc. We have further agreed that there are no teachers of it?

men. That is so.

soc. Therefore, we have agreed that it is neither taught nor wisdom?

men. Of course.

soc. However, we surely agree that it is good.

men. Yes.

soc. And that which guides rightly is useful and good?

men. Of course.

99a soc. But only these two things, true opinion and knowledge, guide rightly, and a man guides rightly only if he has them. Things which occur rightly by chance occur through no human guidance, but wherever a man guides rightly, one of these two, true opinion or knowledge, is found.

men. I agree.

soc. Now, virtue no longer is knowledge, since it is not taught.

men. It appears not.

b soc. Therefore, of two good and beneficial things, one has been ruled out: knowledge would not be a guide in political affairs.

men. I think not.

soc. So it is not by a kind of wisdom or because they are wise that men such as Themistocles, and those like him whom Anytus here just mentioned, guide their cities. For they cannot make others like themselves, since they are not what they are because of knowledge.

men. That seems to be true, Socrates, as you say.

soc. Then if not by knowledge, only true opinion is left. That is

c what men in political life use to direct their cities rightly, differing in no way from soothsayers and seers in respect to understanding. For the latter also say many things which are true, and understand nothing of what they are saying.

men. Very likely.

soc. Now, Meno, isn't it proper to call men divine, when without possessing intelligence they bring a multitude of important things to successful issue in what they do and say?

men. Of course.

soc. And therefore we rightly call those men divine whom we just
d   mentioned—soothsayers and seers, and the whole race of poets.
And surely we must say that our statesmen, by no means least
among them, are divine and inspired. For when, by speaking,
they bring a multitude of important things to successful issue
without understanding what they are talking about, it is because
they have been breathed upon and laid hold of by the god.

MEN. Of course.

soc. And surely that is the tale the women tell: they call good men
divine. And the Spartans, when they sing the praises of a good
man, say, "He is a man divine."

e MEN. Yes, Socrates, it appears you are right. But Anytus here may
be angry at you for saying it.

soc. That does not concern me. We shall doubtless talk with him
another time, Meno. For the present, if this whole account of
ours has been correctly examined and stated, virtue is neither
present by nature nor taught: it comes to be present, in those to
whom it comes, by divine apportionment, without intelligence—
100a   unless there is among statesmen a man who can make another
man a statesman. If there is, that man might be said to be of the
same sort among the living as Homer claimed Teiresias was
among the dead:

Alone among those below he kept his wits.
The rest are darting, fleeting shadows.

In the same way in this world with regard to virtue, such a man
would be, as among shadows, a thing of reality and truth.

b MEN. I think you put it most excellently, Socrates.

soc. Then from this it appears, Meno, that virtue comes to be
present by divine apportionment in those to whom it comes. But
we shall only know that with clear certainty when, before inquiring how virtue comes to be present in men, we first undertake to
inquire what virtue is.

The hour is come for me to go. Please persuade your host
Anytus here of the things of which you yourself are now per-
c   suaded, so that his anger may be allayed. If you persuade him,
you may also do some benefit to the Athenians.

V: THE GORGIAS

COMMENT

Introduction (447a–449c)

The scene takes place in Athens and opens out of doors; the location is not otherwise specified. Callicles, Socrates, Chaerephon, Polus, and Gorgias, all of the characters who are to speak in the *Gorgias*, are present. They move indoors for the conversation, which perhaps takes place before the audience Gorgias has just been addressing. Yet this too is not specified.

Vagueness of dramatic scene is matched by indeterminacy of dramatic date. Pericles is recently dead (503c), so the date is in or shortly after 429 B.C.; Archelaus, King of Macedon, came to power only the other day (470d), so the date is in or shortly after 413; Callicles quotes one of Euripides' last plays, the *Antiope* (485e), so the date is in or after 411, and more probably 408; the trial of the generals after Arginusae took place last year (473e), so the date is 405.

The *Gorgias* is so riddled with anachronism that no dramatic date can be assigned to it; that this is intentional is shown, not only by the fact that many of the anachronisms are blatant, but also by 521d, where Socrates is made to claim, uncharacteristically, that he is the only true statesman in Athens, and by the repeated prophesies of his trial and death (486a–b, 522b). Given the intentional and repeated conflict of dates, a matter in which Plato is usually very careful, it can scarcely be that Plato did not care how his readers situated his fictions in time, as Dodds infers (*Gorgias*, p. 18). It is rather that tense distinctions lose their relevance in the argument. The *Gorgias* is a meditation on the meaning of Socrates' trial and death, and thereby on the moral foundations of

189

law, politics, and human life. It is the capstone of the *Apology* and the *Crito,* and Plato means to highlight that fact. When the reader reaches the concluding myth or account of the fate of souls in the afterlife, his perspective on the dialogue is meant to be from a time after the trial and death of Socrates, who tells the myth: the reader is looking back upon the completed pattern of a life.

Chaerephon is the impulsive and devoted follower who asked the Oracle at Delphi whether anyone was wiser than Socrates (*Apology* 21a). Polus is a professional teacher of rhetoric, author of a handbook on the subject (448c, 462b, *Phaedrus* 267b) which Aristotle knew (*Meta.*i.981a.4); he is still young and (it is a pun on his name) "coltish." Gorgias is an older man of considerable distinction and is treated by Plato as such: he is the leading teacher of rhetoric in an age of great rhetoricians, and his elliptical, jingling prose influenced the styles of Thucydides and Antiphon, as well as that of his pupil Isocrates (Denniston, *Greek Prose Style,* pp. 10*ff.*). Gorgias, like sophists such as Protagoras with whom he is naturally compared, journeyed from city to city, put on *epideixeis,* exhibitions or performances, and taught for pay. But Gorgias ridiculed the typical sophist's claim to teach virtue or human excellence; he claimed only that as a clever speaker he was able to make others clever speakers too (*Meno* 95c). Callicles of Acharnae is no wandering sophist or rhetorician, but a young Athenian aristocrat ambitious for political power. We know nothing of him beyond what Plato tells us, but there is no adequate reason to think he is fictional: his deme is mentioned, and as Dodds remarks, a man at once so ambitious and so frank may well have died in a troubled time too young to be remembered by anyone but Plato, who described him as willing to say what many men believe but are ashamed to say. His fate, along with that of Alcibiades, is probably foretold at 519a.

According to Themistius, a Hellenistic commentator, Aristotle told the tale of a Corinthian farmer who read the *Gorgias* and forthwith gave up his farm and came to Athens to put his soul under Plato's care (Fr. 64 Rose³, p. 24 Ross). The *Gorgias* examines rhetoric and is itself rhetorical, meant to move the human soul by means of words; it is concerned, that is, with what the *Phaedrus* calls *psychagogia,* leading of souls. The rhetoric of the *Gorgias* is directed not merely at persuasion but at truth founded on an analysis of justice and thereby of moral psychology and at the moral foundations of law and politics. On its deepest level, the *Gorgias* is a protreptic to philosophy, meant to turn the soul toward that happiness which Socrates identified with virtue and wisdom, the realized meaning of human life.

The roots of the analysis of justice in the *Gorgias* lie in the Socratic Proportion, which is enunciated in the *Crito* and here assumed: that virtue is to the soul as health is to the body. This is a medical analogy. It carries the corollary that as we seek the advice of the physician or trainer in matters which pertain to the health of the body, so we ought to seek the advice of one who knows and understands in matters pertaining to virtue and the health of the soul. In the *Gorgias*, this person is identified with the statesman; in the *Crito*, he is identified with the truth itself.

If proportionality is a tool of analysis in dialogues earlier than the *Gorgias*, such as the *Crito*, it is used more explicitly and fully in the *Gorgias* than ever before: it is essential not only to the analysis of justice but to the structure of many arguments. Callicles is said to recommend the practice of excess, *pleonexia*, because he has neglected the study of geometry. It has escaped his notice that geometrical equality or proportion has great power among gods and men, that it is the source of community, friendship, and good order, and of temperance and justice; that it is the very reason why this world is properly called a world-order, a *cosmos*, rather than undisciplined disorder (508a). Geometric as distinct from arithmetic proportion involves identity of ratio rather than identity of number, and identity of ratio, construed as analogy, is a structural feature of arguments throughout the *Gorgias*. The *Gorgias* stands as part of a tradition reaching from Archytas of Tarentum (*DK* B3), whom Plato met on his first journey to Italy and Syracuse in 387–86, through the *Laws* (VI.757b–758a, cf. 744b–c, 848b–c), the last of Plato's works, to Book Five of the *Nicomachean Ethics* (1131b27*ff*; 1158b30*ff*., cf. *Pol.* 1301b29*ff*.): that tradition analyzes justice in terms of proportion theory. If an adequate analysis of justice implies analysis of the human soul and of the social order, and if it implies analysis in terms of geometric proportion, then one may suppose that geometric proportion is an important tool of analysis in moral psychology and politics. Mathematics joins morals and political theory as part of primary inquiry into foundations.

The *Gorgias* begins with the question "What is rhetoric?" and it contrasts that question with the question of what sort of thing rhetoric is, or what it is like, or what happens to be true of it. The *Gorgias*, then, begins by dealing with rhetoric as the *Euthyphro* dealt with holiness and the *Meno* with virtue.

Yet there are differences. Socrates, asking in the *Euthyphro*, "What is holiness?" assumes that there is a Form or Idea of holiness, and that this Form is universal, the same in all holy things; that it may be used as a standard by which to determine what things are holy and what are not; that it is an essence, by which or in virtue of which holy things are holy; and that it is capable of real or essential definition. These assumptions constitute a theory of Forms or Ideas, definable essences and universals which serve as regulative principles of dialectic, principles which determine the range of acceptable answers to the "What is it?" question. But these assumptions do not regulate the dialectic of the *Gorgias*.

The *Meno* connects the search for essence with the doctrine of Recollection, which claims that the truth and reality of things is always in the soul, and that the soul is always in a state of having learned. Once again, this doctrine does not figure in the *Gorgias*, though the *Gorgias* exhibits its affinity with the *Meno* in its concluding eschatological myth, which affirms the immortality of the soul.

Dodds remarked of the *Gorgias* that "here Plato's case is not yet encumbered with all the metaphysical baggage of the *Republic*" (*Gorgias*, p. v). This is a surprising description of the *Republic*, a document which has sustained and nourished the philosophy and theology of the West, and the statement is also muddled in respect to the *Gorgias*. The *Gorgias* clearly refers to Forms at 503e; the *Euthyphro*, written before the *Gorgias*, also assumes a theory of Forms; and the *Meno*, a companion dialogue of the *Gorgias*, is unintelligible without that assumption.

It is nevertheless true that the *Gorgias* attends little to Forms. The "What is it?" question is a request for real definition, not of a word but of an essence. The question therefore implies an ontological commitment to the existence of an Idea of "it" as a regulative principle of dialectic. If, then, it is possible that inquiry should show that there is no such Idea or Form, it must follow that the "What is it?" question can be misapplied, that it may on occasion in some sense be a false question, resting on a false assumption. Put otherwise, the "What is it?" question cannot in principle be answered if it asks for a real definition of what has no essence. Yet this is specifically true of rhetoric: for rhetoric in the *Gorgias* is held to be merely an insubstantial *eidolon,* an image, of something real: it is an imitation of statesmanship. The claim of deficient reality, associated in middle dialogues such as the *Phaedo* and *Republic* with participation in Ideas, is in the *Gorgias*, by means of proportion theory, associated with the meaning of terms: semantics here anticipates ontology.

Socrates and Gorgias: What Is Rhetoric? (449c–461b)

If the *Gorgias* is treated as a play, the first and briefest act is the discussion between Socrates and Gorgias of the nature of rhetoric. It is a pretty piece of dialectic. It begins with a request for a definition of rhetoric, which is assumed to be an art, a *techne*, whose definition will be sought in terms of its subject matter, what the art is about. Gorgias's "short-answer" but rhetorical responses are gradually tamed by precision, and rhetoric is found to be about *logoi*—speeches, discourses, accounts, arguments. But in some sense all arts are about logoi, distinguished only by the fact that the logoi are about a determinate subject matter. If medicine is about speeches, it is about speeches concerning diseases and sick people. Gorgias is not clever enough to suggest at this point that rhetoric is about speeches about speeches, a suggestion which would have raised the problem of the *Charmides* (169a) as to whether anything can have its power relative to itself. Instead, he woolly-mindedly picks up a different point: rhetoric belongs among those arts which are mainly or solely concerned with speeches and not with manual labor. Socrates quickly points out that this is also true of the distinction between number theory and calculation, and yet we can distinguish them from each other, and from astronomy too, by their subject matter.

Socrates thus brings up a question which will prove important: if Gorgias has difficulty in identifying the subject matter of rhetoric, is it in fact true that rhetoric has a subject matter? If not, are Gorgias and Polus correct in claiming that rhetoric is an art?

Socrates leads Gorgias to make three main claims about rhetoric. First, it is a thing of power and therefore a great good, since it gives to its possessor freedom for himself and rule over others (452d). So in the *Meno* (73c–d), we are told that Gorgias defined virtue as the ability to rule men. Young Athenian aristocrats like Callicles did not study rhetoric as a genteel accomplishment but because it offered the keys to the kingdom or, more accurately, the democracy: for in a direct democracy of the sort that Athens was, rhetoric gave the power to bind or loose. Callicles later predicts that it will bind Socrates unto death.

Gorgias claims that rhetoric contains the power of all other arts and produces the greatest good. Powerful as it is, good as it is, Gorgias also wants to claim that rhetoric is morally neutral. The teacher of rhetoric is no more to be blamed if his pupil does injustice by the power of his art than a boxing coach is to be blamed if his pupil beats his father. There is an echo here of Aristophanes' *Clouds*, mentioned in the *Apology* as a source of reproach against Socrates, and it is a point to which Gorgias, as a professional teacher of rhetoric in a city which distrusted as sophists those who made the weaker argument stronger, is sensitive. The teacher imparts his skill to be used justly (457b–c). Rhetoric is merely an artisan or manufacturer (*demiourgos*) of persuasion, producing belief rather than instruction about right and wrong.

The claims that rhetoric is powerful and therefore good, that it is persuasion without instruction about right and wrong, and that it is morally neutral are not by themselves formally incompatible, and they probably match the views of the historical Gorgias with some precision. But to anyone experienced in Socratic dialectic, this collection of views has a suggestion of strain or tension: it is a set of assertions which do not follow and accord (457e, 461a).

With utmost politeness and customary self-deprecation, Socrates elicits Gorgias's agreement that the discussion ought to aim at truth, not victory in argument, and that in such matters as these it is better to be refuted than to refute, in that one is thereby relieved of the greatest of evils: for there is no evil so great as to hold false views concerning the subject with which the discussion deals (458a–b). In the end it will appear that the discussion concerns nothing more nor less than happiness (472c) and how one ought to live (487e, 501c, 527c). The *Gorgias* amplifies a main theme of the *Apology,* that the unexamined life is not worth living.

Socrates' examination of Gorgias ends (460e–461a), not with a logical contradiction, but with a perplexity, a set of statements which are out of tune with each other. How is it possible to harmonize the claim that rhetoric can never be unjust, since it ever makes speeches about justice, with the claim that the orator may use his rhetoric unjustly? That this is not a contradiction might have been shown by the familiar medical analogy. The doctor cannot *as* a doctor cause illness since the aim of his art is to heal, but, because his art involves knowledge of opposites, he can skillfully cause illness not as an artist but as a man. Socrates has offered, not a demonstration of falsity or inconsistency, but a problem for further inquiry, as he states in conclusion (461b).

It is not merely a verbal problem. If rhetoric is an art, and if it includes in its subject matter issues of justice and injustice, right and wrong, then a teacher of the art of rhetoric can scarcely disclaim responsibility for the quality of his pupils' moral understanding, for that understanding is necessary to understanding of the art to be taught. Gorgias customarily denied that he taught virtue and even scoffed at the claim: his business was only to produce clever speakers (456c, *Meno* 95c). It now appears that this denial is incompatible with his claim to teach rhetoric, given that justice is a virtue and that rhetoric involves justice as part of its subject matter. This, of course, is something Gorgias has been driven to by the dialectic, not something he wishes to maintain. The claims that rhetoric is an art which involves issues of right and wrong, and yet an art which is also morally neutral, are not in tune. It remains to ask whether, and in what sense, rhetoric is a source of power.

   The immediate refutation of the claim that rhetoric is morally neutral
depends on the analogy Socrates offers between justice and arts such as
building and music and medicine. It is significant that Gorgias accepts
that analogy without demur, as does Protagoras (*Protagoras* 352c): the
analogy of the arts and the virtues is not specifically Socratic but part of
the sophistic culture of the time, and it is an important reason why
Protagoras could claim that virtue, like other arts, can be taught. The
analogy in Socratic hands, however, proves fertile. If the man who knows
building is a builder, the man who knows music a musician, the man who
knows medicine a doctor, then analogy suggests that the man who knows
justice is just. If rhetoric is an art, and if art implies knowledge of its
subject matter, then it would seem to follow that the rhetorician must be
a man who knows justice and is therefore just.
   As an argument, this does not strike very deep. If knowledge of an
art implies knowledge of its opposite, and the opposite of justice is injustice, then the rhetorician must know injustice and is therefore unjust.
But Gorgias is a respectable sort, and such a reply—which would have
exhibited, not the moral indifference, but the moral ambiguity of his
position—does not occur to him.
   The fundamental problem with Gorgias's position lies deeper, and it
is later uncovered in the conversations with Polus and Callicles. Power is
a relational term, and it takes its value from its objects: in itself it is
neither good nor bad, but good when directed toward good objects and
bad when directed toward evils. So rhetoric apart from knowledge of
good and evil is a blind thing, a thing which acts at random and which
cannot be good except by accident. Given that the rhetorician is blind,
it may then prove that his power to persuade others to do what seems
best to him is in fact an evil and a curse. So far is Gorgias from being
correct in thinking that rhetoric without knowledge is a great good:
rhetoric is not a source of any power to be valued unless it is directed to
the good.

Socrates and Polus (461b–481b)

Polus now breaks in, almost sputtering with indignation, to insist that
mere shame led Gorgias to agree that he would teach the difference
between right and wrong to pupils who came to him ignorant of it.
Callicles later concurs (482c–d). But Polus and Callicles have missed the
point. No doubt Gorgias had no wish to incur the opprobrium attached
to sophistry and clever speaking which stirred Anytus's anger in the *Meno*
and led Socrates to his death. But Gorgias in fact tripped over the joint

claims that rhetoric is an art dealing with issues of right and wrong and yet morally neutral. Polus himself will trip in a different place: if rhetoric is morally neutral, it is not an art, as he had claimed in his treatise, and it is not powerful.

Socrates denies that rhetoric is an art because art implies knowledge of its subject matter, and rhetoric lacks knowledge, specifically knowledge of good and evil. He had already suggested to Gorgias that rhetoric is a trick of persuasion without knowledge (459a–b). He now dismisses it as a mere knack of producing gratification and pleasure (462c).

The contrast between art and knack, *techne* and *empeiria*, is infelicitous in English and yet scarcely avoidable as a translation. It is helpful to gloss the distinction with Aristotle's account in the *Metaphysics* (I.980b28–981a30), which in fact quotes Polus's book. *Empeiria*, knack or experience, is particular and accidental, a practical capacity to produce certain results. *Techne*, art, for Aristotle as for Plato and Socrates, implies knowledge, which is both universal and necessary. Art knows not only the fact (*hoti*) but the reason for the fact (*dioti*); and because it involves knowledge of the universal, it can be taught. In Platonic terms, knowledge is marked by its ability to render an account, *logon didonai*.

Polus rushes to praise rhetoric as fine and beautiful, much as he did earlier (448c–e), without first asking what sort of knack rhetoric is. Socrates' response is to compare it to pastry-cooking and to locate the two as different parts of the same business, namely *kolakeia*, flattery. One cannot say whether rhetoric is beautiful or ugly until he has first determined what it is: and to this, Socrates' answer is that rhetoric is a part of flattery, but also an *eidolon*, an insubstantial image, of politics. Far from being beautiful, it is ugly, for all evil things are ugly (462c–463d). Socrates, at Gorgias's request, next turns to defend these claims.

Distinguish between body and soul. Admit that there is a certain healthy condition for each, and further, a certain condition which seems healthy without being so. In short, assume the medical analogy which underlies Socratic moral philosophy and generates the Socratic Proportion: that virtue is to the soul as health is to the body.

Two arts, medicine and gymnastic, serve the body, as law-giving and judicial justice serve the soul. Law-giving corresponds to gymnastic, judicial justice to medicine: the basis of this correspondence is that gymnastic and law-giving have to do with preserving and enhancing the equilibrium of soul or body, while medicine and judicial justice have to do with restoring equilibrium when it has been disturbed; one may compare Aristotle's account of corrective justice in *Nicomachean Ethics* (5.4).

The distinguishing feature of these four arts is that they determine and provide what is best for body and soul respectively (464c).

Flattery, kolakeia, which aims solely at pleasure and gratification and not at what is best, also divides into four, pretending to be each of the arts it imitates by putting on a mask, like an actor in a play. Pastry-cooking pretends to be medicine, pretends to know what foods are good and bad as doctors do; it is not an art but a knack, for it can offer no account of the nature of the thing to which it administers. It cannot state the cause (*aitia*), and is not an art because it is irrational (465a).

Socrates sums up his account like a geometer. Cosmetics is to gymnastic as pastry-cooking is to medicine. Again, cosmetics is to gymnastic as sophistry is to law-giving. And pastry-cooking is to medicine as rhetoric is to judicial justice. These proportions rest on the Socratic claims that body and soul are distinct, and that soul rules body. For if soul did not rule body and body ruled itself, if the distinction between pastry-cooking and medicine was not recognized by the soul but the body by itself was left to judge, then the saying of Anaxagoras, "Everything alike," would be true: all things would be mixed together, and what pertains to pastry-cooking would be indistinguishable from what pertains to medicine and health (465c–d). This is an important argument for the Socratic thesis that not only are body and soul distinct, but soul—that is, mind—must govern body even with respect to the excellence proper to the body, which is health.

This is an early and very beautiful application of the method of division, *diairesis*, which is later brought to great prominence in the *Phaedrus, Sophist,* and *Statesman.* The method is here directly connected with proportion theory: division is used to show identity of relation between diverse terms, as geometrical proportion shows identity of ratio in diverse multitudes or magnitudes. The result is not a mere Linnaean taxonomy, still less the Tree of Porphyry, but a supple method of inquiry which has much in common with poetry as a source of intellectual insight: for like metaphor and simile in poetry, it is analogical, bringing to intellectual awareness identity of relationship in diverse contexts.

If the use of *diairesis* here relates to and gains much of its intellectual beauty from proportion theory, it is also directly related to the search for definition in the early Socratic dialogues. In the *Euthyphro* (11e–12e), Socrates asks that holiness be defined in terms of a broader whole of which it is a part, as even number is that part of number divisible by two: the process of definition here moves from species to genus. In the *Gorgias,* the movement is more complex: rhetoric is treated as a part of flattery, and flattery is then divided in such a way as to exhibit rhetoric's place within the whole, as by a map. Rhetoric is part of flattery, but flattery is only a quasi-genus, composed of insubstantial images, eidola, of genuine arts. Rhetoric is an image of judicial justice as pastry-cooking is an image of medicine. The analysis once more suggests that the question "What is rhetoric?" though it must take precedence over questions about the worth or value of rhetoric, cannot be answered by a real definition, that is, an account of essence. There can scarcely be real definition of the essence of an imitation of an essence: an eidolon can be defined only in terms of that of which it is an image or spurious imitation.

Arts are distinguished from their corresponding knacks, their imitations, on two grounds. First, arts aim at what is best for body and soul, whereas their counterfeits aim only at gratification and pleasure. Second, arts can render an account of their subject matter and state reasons for their practice, whereas the corresponding knacks are irrational, unable to give reasons: they are the product of guesswork. The relation of a knack to its corresponding art, then, of image to original, is distinct from the principle by which the division of art proceeds. It requires, as it were, a further dimension for its representation: knack stands to art as in the *Phaedo* (74–77) sensibles stand to Ideas, as deficient imitations. It is also worth observing that the *Gorgias* here anticipates the double division in the *Sophist* (265b–266d) between images and originals, made by men and by god.

Socrates has claimed that rhetoric is not beautiful, but ugly and shameful, because it is a species of flattery, which is evil. Polus replies, in effect, that rhetoric is good because it is powerful and power is good. Rhetoric is powerful because orators are like tyrants: they can kill whom they wish and exile whom they think fit.

Socrates proceeds to stand this on its head. If power is good, then orators and tyrants are not powerful. The argument may be compared to that of Thrasymachus in the *Republic*: if you define justice as the interest of the stronger, you cannot claim that those who rule are stronger insofar as they mistake their own interest. In a similar way, Socrates here distinguishes between what orators and tyrants wish and what seems best to them, or what they think it fit to do. Socrates' proof that to do what seems good to one is not thereby to do what one wishes is elegant in its simplicity and weight of implication; it is a beautiful and fertile piece of philosophical analysis.

Assume that men wish for what is beneficial to them. Introduce next the capacity to err, to act unintelligently. It must follow that we can do what seems good to us without doing what we wish, since we can be mistaken about where our own good or advantage lies. In that case, we act without intelligence or wisdom, and to act so is not good; and if power is good, as Polus claims, we cannot when we so act describe ourselves as powerful. So it is possible for a man to do what seems good to him and yet, contrary to Polus's claim, not to have great power or to do what he wishes, on the simple ground that what seems good to a man is not thereby in fact good for him. Since we are speaking of men, and not of Leviathan or Behemoth, those who lack wisdom to understand what is good for them are to that extent not powerful. If ever man was laid by the heels in argument, it was Polus.

The words translated "wish" and "to wish," *boulesis* and *boulesthai*, have no precise English equivalents. Their use here in Greek is, if not quasi-technical, then at least unusual, as witness Polus's surprise at the result they are used to produce, a result which is genuinely paradoxical, as contrary to common opinion. The *Definitions* (413c), which are not Plato's, but which reflect the tradition of the early Academy, define boulesis as "intention with right reason; well reasoned intention; desire with reason according to nature." These elements emphasize that boulesis is purposive, that its object is the true good, and that this object is determined by right reason. Thus the association of the word with other words meaning counsel, design, and deliberation.

It is tempting to translate boulesis as "intention," which catches an important part of its meaning; but it is not correct English to say that if someone does something for a purpose, he does not intend the thing he does, but rather intends that for the sake of which he does it (467d). If a man takes medicine for the sake of health, he intends to take the medicine, and his motive, that is, his reason for forming that intention, is health. Nor should one translate boulesis as "will," a word which obscures much and clarifies nothing—there is no issue of freedom of the boulesis. On the other hand, it is a flat mistranslation to render boulesis, associated with intelligence and directed to the true good, as "desire," for desire is neutral with respect to the real worth of its object and implies no distinction between what seems good and what is good. And to substitute "want" for "desire" is substitution *salva falsitate*. All in all, it is best to translate boulesis as "wish," recognizing with Aristotle that we wish for ends rather than means but choose means to our ends and deliberate about them; and that among ends there are some which we neither choose nor deliberate about because they are ultimate, and yet we wish for them. Such an end is happiness.

A central part of Socrates' account is summed up in the remark that "if a man does something for a purpose, he does not wish the thing he does, but that for the sake of which he does it" (467c). We take medicine, not for the medicine, but for health, as we endure the dangers of the sea for the sake of wealth. In general, actions such as sitting, walking, running, sailing, objects such as sticks and stones, insofar as they are means to ends, are in themselves neither good nor evil, but sometimes good and sometimes evil, depending on their purpose (467e–468a). They are thus intermediate, to be distinguished from such goods as wisdom, health, and wealth, and from evils, the opposites of goods.

Intermediate things are done for the sake of what is good. We walk, when we walk, for the sake of the good, and stand, when we stand, for the same reason. In the same way, we kill or exile or confiscate property, exercise the powers Polus had assigned to the rhetorician and the tyrant, in the belief that it is better to do these things than not. That is, they are done for the sake of the good. Put otherwise, we wish these things because they are beneficial, for we have at this point agreed that we wish for good things, not for intermediate things, and still less for evils (468 a–c). Therefore, if anyone kills or exiles or confiscates believing it better for himself when in fact it is worse, he does what seems good to him but not what he wishes. If great power is good, such a man does not have great power, and since he does not do what he wishes, he is least of all men free.

This is a remarkable essay in value theory, analyzing value in terms of the ultimate purposes of action. It is unfortunately perhaps not apt to describe this theory as teleological. In terms of present-day philosophical usage, or misusage, teleological ethics determines issues of good and evil, right and wrong, in terms of the consequences of action, as does utilitarianism. The theory Socrates defends, on the contrary, evaluates action not in terms of its consequences, but in terms of that for the sake of which it is done. Nor is Socrates' position deontological, implying a distinction between goodness and duty or an ultimate evaluation of action in terms of moral rules. On the contrary, the principles of evaluation are purposes, and the passage leaves open the main question of how purposes or ends such as health, wealth, and wisdom are to be ordered or ranked relative to one another. Given the Socratic Proportion, that issue is not in great doubt.

The *Lysis* (219e–220a) carries the analysis further: if we value *x* for the sake of *y*, we value *y* more than *x*. Health is more valuable than medicine, the means of securing health. Aristotle puts the point in a nutshell: "The cause of our loving anything is dearer to us than the object of our love" (*Post.Anal.*I.72a30). The *Lysis* maintains that the process of desiring one thing for the sake of another cannot go on indefinitely but must terminate in something primary, *to proton philon,* for the sake of which all other things are desired. One may compare Aristotle's analysis in *Nicomachean Ethics* I.i.

It is typical of the *Gorgias* that in this exchange between a man whose death at the hands of men who are not free will be foretold, and a young rhetorician who values rhetoric because it confers the powers of tyranny, there should suddenly loom up a vision of human life established in the nature of things more unchangeably than the mountains. From the bare fact that human beings have purposes and often mistake them, the distinction between what we wish and what seems good to us follows as of course. It is a simple enough distinction in itself, but in Socrates' hands it quickly gains richness. What is it that we wish? What we wish does not consist in action, since any action may be good or bad depending on its purpose, and in itself is neither; actions take their value from the purposes they serve, and the same is true of physical possessions. If then we do not wish the things we do, but that for the sake of which we do them, this brief interchange between Socrates and Polus, the colt, suggests a principle beyond all action, in terms of which action is judged. This principle recollects the Primary Valuable of the *Lysis,* the Beauty of the *Symposium,* the Good of the *Republic.* In this gritty little interchange with Polus, we are suddenly seized of a principle which elicits reverence and awe.

That It Is Better to Suffer Injustice than to Do It (468e–476a)

Socrates has now shown that a man may do what seems best to him, and yet not have great power or do what he wishes. Polus replies with an *argumentum ad hominem:* Socrates would himself surely accept power to do what seemed good to him, and he would envy anyone who, like rhetorician or tyrant, could kill or imprison whom he saw fit. This is a variant of the argument which in the *Republic* will be transformed into the brilliant myth of the Ring of Gyges.

Socrates replies with a question: Does Polus mean these things are to be done justly or unjustly? It is the same question Socrates had asked of Meno when he defined virtue as the power to govern men. Polus, unlike Meno, replies that these things are enviable if done either way, to which Socrates replies that in matters of punishment, those who do these things justly are unenviable, but those who do them unjustly are not only unenviable but wretched and pitiable. The man killed unjustly is less wretched than his killer, or than a man killed justly. Once again, the trial of Socrates is prefigured.

Behind all this lies the most profound of all Socratic paradoxes: that the doing of injustice is the greatest of evils, and that it is better to suffer injustice than to do it (469b). This claim coheres precisely with Socrates' earlier claim that the tyrant, while he does what seems good to him, does not thereby do what he wishes, and is least of all men free.

Polus replies, in effect, by counter-example. Men who do injustice are happy, for Archelaus, King of Macedonia, gained the throne by crime, and any Athenian including Socrates would be glad to change places with him or with the Great King of Persia (470d–471d). Socrates replies that Polus is merely trying to refute him rhetorically, as people do in the lawcourts, summoning a cloud of witnesses in order to refute by persuasion, instead of submitting to the compulsion of argument. By Socrates' own standards, as distinct from those of the lawcourts, if Polus is to refute Socrates he must compel Socrates to agree with him, as Socrates must compel Polus if he is to refute him. The subject on which they now disagree concerns things most excellent to know and shameful not to know: Polus believes that a man can do wrong and prosper, and that an unjust man is wretched if he is punished and happy if he is not; whereas Socrates believes that an unjust man is wretched and unhappy, but more wretched if he is not punished for his wrong and less wretched if he is punished. The paradox that it is better to suffer injustice than to do it implies that the doing of injustice is the worst of evils. That paradox, in turn, has issued in a further paradox of punishment: that punishment is a good for the person justly punished.

The key to the argument is Socrates' claim (470a–c) that what is good is beneficial, and that justice is good: the boundary which divides the better from the worse is justice and injustice. Dodds remarks on 470c 2:

> This criterion, stated also at *Crito* 48c–d, underlies all the apparent paradoxes which Socrates enunciates at 472d ff. The relativism of late fifth-century thought called in question the traditional moral claims of society on the citizen: henceforth the individual, not the *polis,* is the norm. Socrates' reply was that the individual should do what is right, not for the sake of his fellow men or out of deference to current moral standards *but for his own sake*—a position which he maintains throughout the dialogue.

This is well said, and yet imperfectly said. Socrates does indeed suppose that individual men and women, in doing what is just and right, act in their own interest, and that, in doing what is wrong, they harm themselves by harming their own souls. But it by no means follows that in doing what is right they do not act for the sake of their fellows, and even, on occasion, act in deference to current moral standards, as Socrates arguably did in the *Crito* in obeying the Laws of Athens. Dodds suggests a contrast between egoism and altruism which is false to the argument of the *Gorgias,* which on the contrary assumes that men act for their own sake when they act for the common good. Socrates is not arguing a moral theory which rests only on enlightened self-interest, or on self-concern tempered by rational concern for the other fellow. He is arguing that each of us has an interest in right and justice, and that in this respect our interests are identical. Put otherwise, if we are to speak of self-interest, then the interest of the self cannot be clearly distinguished from, and indeed is in fundamental respects identical with, the common good of our fellows, taken both collectively and distributively. Only so can one explain Socrates' decision to go to his death in the *Crito* at the behest of law, or his willingness to risk his life as a soldier as a matter of duty.

Consider the stretch of the *Crito* from 46b to 50a. Socrates begins by rejecting Crito's plea to escape, which is based on the opinions of the Many; the person to attend to, Socrates says, is the one man who knows and understands, at one point identified with the truth itself. An athlete must pay attention to his physician and trainer; if he disobeys the man who knows, if he listens to the Many who do not understand, he will suffer an evil: he will harm his body, and life is not worth living with a wretched body. Neither is it worth living when what is benefited by justice and harmed by injustice has been corrupted. This possession of ours—the soul, though Socrates does not in the *Crito* give it this name—is not of less worth than the body, but more. This then is the context of the conclusion that it is not living, but living well, which is important, and that to live well is to live honorably and justly.

This passage implies, first, that there is such a thing as bodily good, and that it really is good, because life is not worth living without it. In terms of the Socratic Proportion, we can describe health as the virtue of the body, as, *alternando,* we can describe virtue as the health of the soul.

The passage implies, second, that since the good of the soul is more important than the good of the body, the wise man, the man who knows and understands—whom Socrates in the *Gorgias* identifies with the Statesman—if he is forced to choose between doing injustice and doing something very unhealthy, like drinking hemlock, will drink the hemlock. This is the answer to Polus's terrible description of the man burned in a coat of pitch.

This passage at least suggests, third, that the failing of the Many is not that they choose what is instead of what ought to be, or nonmoral goods instead of moral goods, but that they choose what *seems* good instead of what *is* good. Questions about virtue are matters of fact in the same sense that questions about health are matters of fact, and the Many, as badly advised about what is good as the rhetoricians who lead them, though they do what seems best to them—what they desire, what they want—do not do what they wish. They are powerless, indeed, even to do harm in the fundamental sense: for to harm something is to make it worse with respect to its proper excellence, and given that justice is the specific virtue or excellence of a man, it must follow that to harm a man is to make him more unjust.

This claim is quite clearly paradoxical, whether in Greek culture or our own. Gregory Vlastos once remarked that to hold that when men are not made more unjust they are not harmed "flies in the face of the fact that human beings can be harmed in a thousand ways by actions which do not make them more unjust." This is certainly true of the *bodies* of human beings. Does it then follow that it is true of human beings as well? The man who in the *Phaedo* said, "Bury me if you can catch me" did not think so. The central issue of Socratic ethics is the Socratic doctrine of the soul, and that analysis of benefit and self-interest does not imply the contrast between egoism and altruism, but implies that justice is a measure of both individual and common good.

This then is the foundation of Socrates' claim that the doing of injustice is worse than the suffering of it, reaffirmed with uttermost seriousness at 508c–509d. But Polus is here treated to a different and purely dialectical refutation of his views. The argument is an informal *reductio ad absurdum*. Assume, as Polus does, that it is more evil (*kakion*) to suffer injustice than to do it. Assume also, as Polus does, that it is more shameful (*aischion*) to do injustice than to suffer it. It follows that since the evil and the shameful or ugly are not the same, their opposites, the good and the noble or beautiful, are not the same.

Socrates next offers an induction. Under what circumstances will we call a thing beautiful? Bodies, shapes, and colors, sounds and music, laws, practices and institutions, instruction and studies are said to be beautiful if and only if they are beneficial and useful (*ophelimon*) or pleasant (*hedu*). Polus agrees, summing up with a characteristic jingle which also involves a substitution fatal to his cause: "You beautifully mark off the beautiful, defining it by pleasure and good" (475a). The substitution of goodness for what is beneficial and useful allows Socrates, proceeding according to his respondent's own admissions, to infer that the ugly and shameful is defined by what is painful and evil. So, if *a* is more beautiful than *b*, *a* surpasses *b* in pleasure of benefit of both; and if *a* is more ugly or shameful than *b*, *a* surpasses *b* either in pain or in evil. Refutation follows from this lemma as of course. Polus thinks that doing injustice is more ugly than suffering it. If so, it must surpass it in evil or pain or both. The doing of injustice does not surpass the suffering of it in pain, for Polus himself has argued that those who do injustice, such as Archelaus, are not in greater distress than those who have it done to them. But if not in pain, then not both in pain and in evil; therefore, only in evil. But if doing injustice surpasses suffering injustice in evil, then doing injustice is more evil than suffering it. So Polus has been compelled by his own admissions to agree that doing injustice is more evil than suffering it. As Socrates had earlier said, in contrasting the methods of rhetoric and dialectic, "I know how to provide one witness to the truth of what I say, and that is the man to whom the argument is directed" (474a). Polus has now testified.

Callicles will later claim that Polus "conceded to you that doing injustice is uglier than suffering it and afterwards got tied up and had his mouth stopped with that agreement, because he was ashamed to say what he thought" (482e). But Socrates in the *Republic* (I.348e) suggests to Thrasymachus a different explanation:

> If you count injustice as part of virtue and wisdom, and justice among their opposites, I said, this is then a much more difficult position, my friend, and it is no longer easy to know what to say. For if you counted injustice as profitable, but agreed that it is either evil or ugly and shameful, as certain others do, we might argue according to what is customarily acknowledged. But as things stand, you clearly will say that injustice actually is beautiful and strong, and you will add to it all the other things which we attach to justice, since you actually dare count it part of virtue and wisdom.

Thrasymachus, unlike Polus, is too wary to separate the evil from the ugly and shameful, and thereby expose himself to refutation based on the conventional usage of words (cf. *Laws* 627d, 662a, *Politicus* 306a). Polus's mouth is stopped, not by shame, as Callicles maintains, but by the constraints of ordinary moral discourse.

That It Is Worse Not to Be Punished for Injustice than to Be Punished (476a–481b)

The paradox that it is better to suffer injustice than to do it issues in a further paradox of punishment: not to be punished for injustice is worse than to be punished for it. For a person justly punished suffers what is good. Therefore, he is benefited. Since he is not benefited in body, he must be benefited in soul (477a). The judge stands to the soul as the doctor stands to the body: corrective justice takes away intemperance and vice, as medicine cures disease. Like medical treatment, punishment is not pleasant, but it is beneficial, since it gives relief from the greatest of evils, which is vice.

It follows that happiest is the man who has no evil in his soul, and second happiest the man relieved of evil by punishment. The third and worst life belongs to the man who has injustice in his soul and is not relieved of it by punishment. Archelaus and other tyrants are far from being happy; they are in fact the most miserable of men, because they have committed the greatest wrongs and escaped punishment (478e–479c). Where then is the great usefulness Polus had claimed for rhetoric? It is not useful, surely, to escape just punishment. So the usefulness of rhetoric must consist in obtaining punishment for ourselves, our family, or our country when they have done wrong. But *if* it is ever right to do evil to any man, we should contrive that our enemies not be punished when they do wrong, but live on in their evil (480c–481a).

This argument, proceeding as it does from Polus's own admissions, may be regarded as a dialectical triumph issuing in an ingenious paradox. But it is much more, for Socrates will maintain in all seriousness that punishment is needed for vice of soul (505b–c, 508c–509d).

Many commentators have found in this argument no more than a superficial and uninteresting fallacy, that of inferring that since it is good to punish A, punishment is good *for* A, of benefit to him. But fallacy is often in the eye of the beholder. What is at issue is not formal validity, but the meaning of terms, specifically of relational terms, which may be symmetrical, transitive, and reflexive. Socrates assumes that the goodness of just punishment is symmetrical. The main tradition in English moral and political philosophy since Hobbes has assumed that it is, if not asymmetrical, at least nonsymmetrical; that there is an inherent contrast, which may on occasion become a conflict, between what is good for the community and what is good for its individual members. Socrates here supposes that what is good for the individual and good for the community are coimplicant. The good for A implies justice; justice implies what is in the common good; given that just punishment is in the common good, it is good for A. One might indeed suggest that a person justly punished is the inverse of the tyrant. Both have bad souls; but whereas the tyrant does what seems best to him but does not thereby do what he wishes, the person justly punished suffers what he wishes but not thereby what seems best to him.

The force of this may perhaps be brought out by contrast. John Austin in the *Province* provided a utilitarian account of punishment:[1] "A punishment, as a solitary fact, is an evil: the pain inflicted on the criminal being added to the mischief of the crime. But, considered as part of a system, a punishment is useful or beneficent. By a dozen or score of punishments, thousands of crimes are prevented. With the suffering of the guilty few, the security of many is purchased. By the lopping of a peccant member, the body is saved from decay." That is, punishment is bad for the person punished, but good for the social order: there is here a conflict between individual interest and the general good. Punishment is justified by deterrence, and deterrence by utilitarianism, the greatest good for the greatest number, benefits as remainder when discounted by costs. Punishment is not good for the person punished, perhaps even on the utilitarian ground that the pain suffered in any given case outweighs any gain in imposing it; but the greater good must be estimated, not distributively by the consequences of this or that act, but collectively by the consequences of upholding a system of rules. For the offender, justice, the infliction of punishment according to rule, will in general have a higher discount rate than mercy, the diminishment of avoidable suffering. But the offender's perspective in this differs from that of the judge, whose office is to uphold a system of rules. This is another example of the continuing conflict, latent or actual, between individual and social good in a utilitarian universe.

Now, the *Gorgias* certainly supposes that punishment may deter by example and is to be valued for that fact (525a–c). But the primary aim of punishment is not exemplary, but remedial. The aim of just punishment is to make bad men better, to increase the measure of their human excellence and thereby their happiness or well-being (476b–477a, 478 d–e). To suppose that punishment is bad because it is painful is like supposing that medical treatment is bad because it is painful. Bodily pain is less important than benefit to the soul, and punishment, when it is imposed justly, is for the good of the person punished.

If the *Gorgias* rejects deterrence as a primary aim of punishment, so does it also reject retribution, which resembles deterrence in that it involves returning harm for wrong.

The retributionist would claim as heartily as Socrates that one ought

1. *The Province of Jurisprudence Determined* (ed. Hart), London, 1965, p. 40.

never do wrong, and therefore one ought not return wrong for wrong. He would argue, however, that when wrong has in fact been done, there is a duty (the strong form of the theory) or a right (the weak form) to inflict harm on the wrongdoer. Because that infliction is either a duty or a right, it does not involve returning wrong for wrong; on the contrary, it involves (strong theory) returning right for wrong, or (weak theory) what is not wrong for wrong. In the strong form of the theory, to abstain from retribution is to abstain from a duty and is itself wrong; the weak version does not thus make mercy immoral.

Both Socrates and the retributionist, then, accept the proposition that one ought never do injustice. The difference between them lies in their conception of justice.

For the retributive theory, justice is not a matter of consequences: it is connected with debt. It is no accident that "ought" is in origin a past tense of "owe," or that "duty" derives through Norman French from *debere*. *Retributio* is a recompense, a repayment, specifically of desert whether good or ill. If I borrow, I owe; for the retributionist, if I wrong, I also owe. The debt incurred by wrongful harm is discharged by returning harm to the wrongdoer.

The debt analogy also introduces a second main theme of retribution, that of proportionality: repayment is reckoned by the amount of debt incurred. It is often said that retribution is revenge. This is false, since retribution functions both as a measure of and limitation on the amount of harm returned. Right, not wrong, is to be returned for wrong, and as early as the Code of Hammurabi it is insisted, "This much shalt thou take, *and no more*." Proportionality coupled with the strong form of retribution produces the Talian Law. In settled and civilized conditions of life, it will seem savage that eye should go for eye, tooth for tooth, life for life; but there are circumstances in which this has been a law of mercy, providing limits where vengeance knows none.

The account Socrates offers in the *Crito* and the *Gorgias* does not refute the rightfulness of retribution, but makes the constellation of concepts on which it depends irrelevant to the primary moral issue which it is meant to address. Retribution is backward-looking: the justice of inflicting present harm is conditioned by the fact and extent of past wrongdoing. Harm is weighed against harm, punishment against crime, in a proportion which is broadly arithmetical: measure for measure. But if justice has to do with the good of the soul, punishment, when it is imposed justly, is imposed not simply because of past wrongdoing, but for the sake of the soul of the wrongdoer—or if he is beyond cure, for his own sake and that of his fellows (525a–c). This theory is distinct from the retributive theory, and resembles the deterrent theory in that it does not place positive, as distinct from instrumental, value on human suffering, and it does not measure the wickedness of the agent solely by the wickedness of his act. It differs from the deterrent theory in that its primary aim is not exemplary but curative. Just punishment is good, not only for society, but for the soul of the person punished. Because just punishment is measured by the needs of the soul of the person punished, rather than by the harm done by his acts, the proportionality proper to it is geometrical rather than arithmetical. One may remark in passing that the deterrent theory is governed by no proportion at all.

This account may be contrasted with that of Book Five of the *Nicomachean Ethics,* in which Aristotle distinguishes general justice, which is equivalent to virtue (or at least virtue as exhibited in the dealings of man and man), and particular justice, by which each man gets what he deserves, and, unlike general justice, may be treated as a mean between excess and defect, as with other virtues. Particular justice, in turn, divides into distributive justice and corrective justice. Of these, distributive justice is concerned with the distribution of honor, money, or other benefits among men who deserve sometimes equal and sometimes unequal shares. Its common measure is merit. It is in fact an example of geometrical proportion, in that the size of the share alloted is in ratio to the desert of the person to whom it is alloted, and equality is attained when those who deserve more get more, and those less, less. Corrective justice involves correcting inequality arising in transactions between at least two people, one who has received more than his share, the other less. It involves, that is to say, restitution, taking from this party who has too much the excess and giving it to the party which has received too little. It is an example of arithmetical equality, resting on equality of measure rather than of ratio. Aristotle conceives of criminal punishment in these terms: and since punishment often does not benefit the innocent party injured, his treatment of corrective justice should be conceived not only as including restitution, but in some sense as the prevention of unjust enrichment. It is as if the criminal has come out ahead, and punishment deprives him of his gain.

Aristotle bases his treatment of corrective justice on membership in the political community: the arithmetical proportion expresses, in effect, equality before the law. His account of corrective justice is therefore ambiguous: perhaps it is a function of the application of legal rules; perhaps it is an account of moral or legal principles closely akin to retribution—restitution, unjust enrichment—as the foundation on which legal rules rest. To the latter question Plato in the *Gorgias* offers a geo-

metrical rather than an arithmetical account. The measure of punishment is not to be determined by harm done, but by the character of the
wrongdoer and his curative needs—though of course the harm done
may well be an important indication of the nature and extent of those
needs. Nevertheless, the shift from arithmetical to geometrical proportion in the analysis of punishment implies a shift from the wrongful
character of the act to the flawed character of the agent. If distributive
justice is concerned with merit, it is also concerned with demerit: what
is at issue is not the geometrical equality of measure between act and
punishment, but the geometrical equality implied by identity of ratio
between amount of punishment and the needs of the soul of the wrongdoer. In the *Laws* (VI 756e–758a), geometrical equality is treated as
characteristic of justice, and described as the Judgment of Zeus.

The claim that the primary aim of punishment is curative is not the
humanitarian doctrine some critics have seen in it. The *Gorgias* counte-
nances simple extermination of incurables (512a), and though Socrates
attaches only instrumental value to the infliction of suffering, he treats
suffering as an intrinsic means of cure. There is nothing in this of what
has come to be called the "rehabilitative ideal," in which offenders are
not to be punished but treated. Punishment is not inflicted as a means
of obtaining opportunity for treatment: it is treatment, meant by itself
to effect cure.

In what sense can punishment cure vice of soul? In what sense does
it contribute to the happiness of the offender?

The word "happiness" in English tends to suggest an emotional state
which differs from pleasure only in that it is less intense and more prolonged. It is the beginning of wisdom to realize that happiness in the
Gorgias does not imply a state of feeling but a state of being: the state of
living well, living justly and virtuously. The just man can be happy on
the rack; that is, his soul can be in good condition; but he does not feel
any better than the rest of us would.

The claim that just punishment cures the vice of the soul, then, reduces to the claim that just punishment promotes just and virtuous living
in the offender. Punishment does not, at least by itself, conduce to the
highest kind of virtue, which rests on wisdom. But it does lead to that
popular or demotic kind of virtue described in the *Phaedo* (68d–69c) by
which men are brave through a kind of cowardice and temperate by a
kind of self-indulgence, refraining from some pleasures because they
fear to be deprived of others. The wise legislator, the Statesman, working
with this inferior pattern of life, may yet, with due attention to the requirements of proportionality in the souls of those he rules, achieve a

harmonic structure which is good not only for the social order but for the offender. Punishment implies that fear is a moral emotion, in that men may be intimidated into behaving not only as they desire but as they wish.

It would take a loftier view of human nature than Plato espoused to suppose that the breaking of bad habits through fear is not remedial. It would take a lower view to suppose that wrongdoing, left unpunished, benefits the offender. Ultimately the wrongdoer wishes for his own punishment, if it is just, for it is in his own interest, and in the interest of his society, and further, in the interest of each because in the interest of the other. There is nothing mysterious in this claim, which is a claim in moral and political philosophy and supposes that the primary good of the individuals who compose the social order and the good of the social order are identical. This good is not identified with bodily benefit. Only so can one explain the rightness of punishment, or Socrates' willingness to defend his country in war, at the risk of wounds and death, or to abide by the decisions of the courts of his country.

The conversation with Polus began with Socrates dismissing rhetoric as a mere knack of persuasion, a branch of flattery, aimed only at pleasure and gratification and indifferent to truth, irrational because it is unable to give an account of itself or its object. The conversation proceeds to offer the moral aimlessness of rhetoric as primary evidence of its irrationality; rhetoricians are indeed like tyrants in their inability to attain what they wish, although they can attain what seems best to them, that is, the satisfaction of their unreasoned and unreasonable desires. What is at issue between Socrates and Polus is reduced to two paradoxical propositions: that it is better to suffer injustice than to do it, and that it is better to suffer punishment for injustice than to escape it. What is ultimately at issue is who is happy and who is not, exemplified by the contrasting images of the rhetorician as tyrant and the emerging figure of the rhetorician as philosopher and statesman. By the end, the concept of rhetoric has modulated into a new key and has become a kind of rhetoric which would aim at one's own conviction if one had done injustice. Here is rhetoric which is no longer part of flattery, no longer aimed at gratification and pleasure and indifferent to truth.

Was Polus really refuted? The question is asked, and yet its sense is obscure. In dialectic, playing by the rules of the game, he had his mouth stopped in argument: Socrates compels him to testify in behalf of propositions Polus cannot and will not believe. This is dialectical checkmate, and Polus has lost, and there is a certain intellectual interest in replaying the game, analyzing it to see what other moves he might have made. Yet although dialectic may seem a game, the game analogy is inadequate to it, for the purpose is not to win within the rules, but to obtain truth, a truth which has to do with the most fundamental of all human issues, namely, how to live well, that is, with justice and virtue.

How does the interview with Polus relate to that with Gorgias? Dodds remarks (p. 10, abbreviated):

> It is desirable to be clear about the grounds of Plato's quarrel with Gorgias. Plato never doubted that the spoken word could "change the souls of men." ... Nor did Plato think this skill unimportant: he knew that the *rhetores* in the Assembly exercised the power of life and death, and he held that the salvation of Athens depended on the emergence of a new kind of *rhetor*. But he thought the kind of education offered by Gorgias both inadequate and dangerous, for the two reasons indicated at 465a. (*a*) The skill which Gorgias taught was unscientific: it relied solely on an appeal to men's irrational desires, and there can be no true science of the irrational. And (*b*) it was morally neutral; but in Plato's view no society can afford to be content with a morally neutral education which puts the instruments of domination into the hands of the morally ignorant. Men like Callicles did not pay high fees to Gorgias because they enjoyed playing tricks with words, but because they were hungry for power. Gorgias set men's feet on the road to tyranny without warning them that the tyrant is of all men the most unhappy.

If the interview with Gorgias represents the surface of the rhetorical tradition, the interview with Polus represents the beginning of inquiry into its depths. It has brought into clearer view the assumptions about human life and political power implied by rhetoric, and it has held out the vision of another kind of life, which rests on knowledge and abstains from wrong.

Note: The Prisoner's Dilemma

Socratic ethics is often described as a form of egoism; and certainly it is true that Socrates believed that justice and virtue are in the interest of the agent. But it is a strange egoism which cannot be contrasted to altruism, and which extends self-interest to the good of one's neighbor and the community of which one is a part, and which suggests that the primary aim of rational human action is service to a principle of good on which all other good depends.

The concept of rationality here involved contrasts with rational egoism as usually conceived. As an example, consider the game-theoretical problem of the Prisoner's Dilemma, perhaps more accurately called the Plea-bargaining Paradox.

Mark and Luke are arrested for barratry and held in different cells. The District Attorney, who wants a confession, goes to Mark and offers him the following deal: if Mark confesses and Luke does not, the prosecution will recommend to the court that Mark be released on his own recognizance, and that Luke be sentenced to ten years in prison; if Luke confesses and Mark does not, the sentence recommendation will be just the reverse; if they both confess, the recommendation for each will be five years; if neither confesses, they will be tried on the lesser charge of double parking and the sentence recommendation for each will be one year. The matrix looks like this:

		Luke	
		Confess	Not Confess
Mark	Confess	5, 5	0, 10
	Not Confess	10, 0	1, 1

Mark, being seized of this offer, reasons narrowly: either Luke will confess or he will not. If Luke confesses and Mark does not, Mark gets ten years; if Luke confesses and Mark confesses, Mark gets five years; if Mark does not confess and Luke does not confess, Mark gets one year; if Mark confesses and Luke does not confess, Mark will serve no time at all. Thus, whether or not Luke confesses, it is reasonable for Mark to confess. Mark will gain more by choosing this strategy than any other, and Luke, realizing this, will choose his own strategy on the assumption that Mark will make that choice. So Luke will confess too. That is, both will serve five years. They have successfully calculated the path of reason and prudence in a two-person, non-zero-sum, finite game.

The paradox, of course, is that if they had both kept their mouths shut, they would have each served one year instead of five. An individual rationally pursuing his own self-interest, that is, seeking to maximize his own good, may so act that he diminishes both the common good and his own good as well. And the paradox can be generalized. Instead of years in prison, we can mutatis mutandis put allotments of scarce water resources in relation to waste, or restriction on crop production in relation to price, or taxpaying, or other issues involving what has come to be called "the tragedy of the commons." The paradox is perhaps best construed simply in terms of additive units of value—utiles, positive or negative. Game-theoretical Man, pursuing his own self-interest, turns out to be remarkably like Economic Man, and perhaps, given his origins, that is no accident.

The Prisoner's Dilemma suggests a conflict between reasonableness and utility. Perhaps then it should be rephrased as a conflict between two kinds of reasonableness, the reasonableness of self-interest and the reasonableness of concern for the common good:[2] "A *moral* decision is a problem of how different members of society can best promote the *common* good, i.e., can best promote the common interests of society as a whole. In contrast, a *game-theoretical* decision problem is a problem of how two or more rational individuals, with possibly very dissimilar interests, can best promote their *own* interests *against,* or possibly in cooperation *with,* one another." The decision procedure for deciding between these two kinds of decision procedure is, so far as I am aware, undecided. But the dialectical tension between self-interest and the common good has strained the egoistic assumptions of the English tradition in moral theory from Hobbes forward, and "decision theory" merely carries on a long conceptual tradition. It is not, of course, a Platonic tradition. The paradox of the Prisoner's Dilemma arises from the incompatibility of self-interest and best outcome. The paradox will be sterilized if it can be shown that there is no such incompatibility, either by reason of mistaken conception of self-interest, or mistaken conception of best outcome, or both.

Begin with self-interest. Socrates, in argument with Polus and in the *Crito,* a dialogue on which the *Gorgias* stands as comment, argues that it can never be in our interest to do wrong or harm and that it is better—more in our interest—to suffer wrong than to do it. This, then, is a fundamental principle of rationality construed as self-interest. Suppose then that Mark by confessing is harming Luke by making him liable to a ten year sentence and preventing him from obtaining release. Then Mark's calculation turns out to be irrational, for there is an evil incurred which does not appear in the sentencing matrix and outweighs any which does appear, namely, harm to Mark's own soul by reason of the doing of injustice. Mark's difficulty is not that he is self-interested, but that he is not self-interested enough: he has acted against his own interest.

Put otherwise, the notion of self-interest is not self-explanatory. We do not know whether the Prisoner's Dilemma implies a paradox because we

2. John Harsanyi, "Bayesian Probability in Game Theory," in *Science, Belief and Behavior* (ed. D. H. Mellor), Cambridge, 1980, p. 190.

do not know, first, whether it is unjust for Mark to confess, or, second, whether it is in Mark's interest to confess if it is unjust. If the *Gorgias* is right, and if it is unjust for Mark to confess, it is not in Mark's interest to confess. But if this is so, then game theory, which had promised to provide the most prudent and rational strategy, turns out to yield an imprudent and irrational strategy. At best, it is not useful by reason of lack of conceptual clarity in respect of "self-interest."

Then there is best outcome. Generalization of the Prisoner's Dilemma implies a flattened account of goodness: to reduce analysis to utility is to suppose that the difference between one good and another is purely additive and quantitative. As Jeremy Bentham put it, "quantity of pleasure being equal, pushpin is as good as poetry," and on this point there is no need to rehearse Bentham's clarity and Mill's confusion, prettily anticipated by Callicles in the *Gorgias*. It is a corollary that in the computation of aggregate goodness each unit counts for one and none for more than one: goodness becomes collective and egalitarian.[3] But contrast this with the *Gorgias*. If Mark confesses and Luke does not, Mark will go free and Luke will get ten years. This is a reason to suppose that in this case Mark will be worse off, not better off, than Luke, since if confession is wrong or unjust, then Mark has harmed his soul in confessing, and Luke has not. Perhaps, however, Mark and Luke are actually guilty of the crime to which Mark confesses. In that case, the souls of both may benefit from condign punishment, and therefore Mark, because he goes free by reason of confession, is deprived of a benefit, while Luke receives a punishment which is a condition for the cure of his soul, and therefore a good.

In a Socratic context, the calculus of utilities is a veil which must be pierced if moral reasoning is so much as to begin: for we cannot determine what is useful until we determine what is good, nor what is good until we determine what is just and right. Once again, game theory turns out to be unhelpful by reason of lack of clarity in its concepts. The matrices of game theory are relatively unimportant until we have determined the sense of the terms which will be plugged into them. Terms such as "self-interest," "utility," "best outcome" are abstract in such a way as to be unusefully vague. The Prisoner's Dilemma in ethics suggests a conclusion which Whitehead reached in respect to the application of symbolic logic to metaphysics: the exactness is a fake.

3. See also P. S. Atiyah, *The Rise and Fall of Freedom of Contract*, Oxford, 1979, pp. 340–41.

Socrates and Callicles: Pleasure and Persuasion (481b–505d)

Callicles now intervenes to ask whether Socrates is jesting or in earnest: "For if you are in earnest and what you say is really true, our human life would be turned upside down. We are doing exactly the opposite, it seems, of what we should" (481c). This is a fair inference from the claims that it is better to suffer injustice than to do it and better to suffer punishment for injustice than to escape it.

Socrates' response to Callicles is not only an argument but an invitation and a protreptic: "Follow me then, as one persuaded, to where when you arrive you will be happy both in living and dying" (527c). Socrates had maintained against Polus that real good consists in the practice of justice at whatever cost. Polus's mouth having been stopped, Callicles now attempts to controvert this claim.

If a primary theme of the *Gorgias* is rhetoric, Callicles' speech is a leading example of it. It is base rhetoric, random in order, confused in thought. Those critics who have seen it as a piece of philosophical profundity tacitly testify that base rhetoric does indeed work.

Dodds (p. 14) speaks of the "powerful and disturbing eloquence that Plato has bestowed on Callicles—an eloquence destined to convince the young Nietzsche, while Socrates' reasoning left him cold. One is tempted to believe Callicles stands for something which Plato had it in him to become (and would perhaps have become, but for Socrates), an unrealized Plato who, as Jaeger said, lies deeply buried beneath the foundations of the *Republic*." It is difficult to know how to verify or falsify this claim. It offers an account of the author of the *Gorgias* in and through an account of one of the characters he created, as one might construe Shakespeare from the character of Lady Macbeth (and Falstaff too?). Genius does not fit in common molds, and inference from the mask the author has created to the character of the author himself would be worthless even if Dodds' account of the mask were true. Yet the "powerful and disturbing eloquence" of which Dodds speaks is that of a mind without the audacity or subtleness of Thrasymachus, who in *Republic* I formulates a clear version of legal positivism, and Callicles' speech surely lacks the conceptual fertility and power of Glaucon's account of the Social Contract in *Republic* II. The mind of Callicles is in fact of no greater power or subtlety than that of Polus. Polus, indeed, is merely a wandering teacher of rhetoric from Acragas in Sicily, whereas Callicles is a wellborn Athenian. But what most particularly distinguishes Callicles from Polus is not intelligence, but brutality.

Polus had accused Gorgias of faltering in argument out of mere shame; Callicles begins by accusing Polus of the same failing. And Callicles offers a diagnosis of why this occurred. Polus conceded to Socrates that doing injustice is more ugly and shameful than suffering it. But this, Callicles holds, is so only according to *nomos*, law, custom, or convention, whereas the opposite is true according to *phusis*, nature: "By nature everything is more ugly and shameful which is also more evil, and it is more evil to suffer wrong; but by law, doing wrong is more evil" (483a). So the argument between Polus and Socrates confused evil by nature with evil by law. Law proclaims the goodness of equal shares; nature proclaims that the better man should have more than the worse, the powerful more than the weak. This is natural justice, and it is a very law of nature, a *nomos tēs phuseōs*, though it is not perhaps just according to the laws which we lay down.

This is the first use of the expression "law of nature" in literature, and it has a chilling antecedent. The Athenian emissaries announce to the Melian elders (Thucydides V.105): "For of gods we believe, and of men we know, that by a necessity of nature [*phusis*], they rule where they have power. We neither made this law [*nomos*], nor, once made, were we first to use it; finding it in existence, we shall leave it in existence for all time, and use it, knowing that you and others, if you had our power, would do the same thing." This before Melos was sacked, all men over the age of fourteen killed, and the women and children sold into slavery. Plato knew his Thucydides, as the *Menexenus* shows, and the audience to whom the *Gorgias* was directed would have been reminded by Callicles' appeal to the "law of nature" of a haunting chorus in Euripides' *Trojan Women* line 95): "How are ye blind, ye who lay waste to cities, and cast down temples, and defile graves—yourselves so soon to die." The *Trojan Women* was produced only a few months after the sack of Melos in the winter of 416–15, the same winter in which the Athenians decided to conquer Sicily, an act of blind folly in which Athens lost a fleet and an army and from which she never recovered. Callicles was a real person, an example of a real class of people whom, as we know from the *Gorgias*, Plato despised. The audience to whom the *Gorgias* is directed is told that Callicles is just beginning his political career (515a); perhaps they also knew that he died young and violently (cf. 519a–b).

Conceptually, Callicles has failed to diagnose the difficulty Polus had because he stands on exactly the same ground. The nomos/phusis distinction has the ring of gorgeous intellectual daring. It is in fact a response to the same linguistic conventions which undid Polus (cf. *Republic* I.348e). The conventions of our language imply that justice is good. But if then we are to adapt what is perceived as the realities of human affairs, as exhibited, say, at Melos, to the conventions of speech, we must distinguish real justice from what people merely think is justice. The distinction between just by nature and just by convention is a tool for accomplishing this; the distinction purports to clarify an ambiguity, but actually proves to be a source of conceptual confusion. Thrasymachus in the *Republic* (348e, cf. *Laws* 859d–860b) cuts deeper: he will say what few men, including Callicles and Polus, are willing to say: that justice is not good, and that injustice is good.

The law of nature is that the few strong should rule the many weak and commit *pleonexia*, taking more than their share; but the many weak enact laws to control the few strong and enforce equality. Callicles' position collapses at a touch. If nomos is the product of the strength of the Many, who are stronger by nature than any individual, then nomos defines what is just by nature. Nomos claims that it is worse to do wrong than to suffer it, and that equal sharing is just. So this must be true according to nature too, and Callicles is mistaken in claiming that law and nature are opposites (489a–b).

Callicles tries to distinguish. By "stronger" he meant "better": the better should rule their inferiors. They must be wise in the affairs of their city and its government, and not only wise but courageous, adequate for what they set out to achieve without faltering through softness of soul (491a–b).

Socrates asks whether these rulers must not rule themselves, that is, be temperate and self-controlled in respect to their own desires and pleasures. Callicles denies this. A man cannot be happy if he is enslaved by anyone at all, even himself; what is just and good according to nature is to allow desires to grow as great as possible and not restrain them, and when they have waxed great, to be adequate to minister to them with courage and wisdom. Happiness consists in excess and lack of restraint (491e–492c). Here then is Callicles' answer to the questions of how to live and in what happiness consists. He has said what many men believe but are not willing to say (492d).

Socrates answers, not directly with an argument, but with stories, myths. He has heard a wise man say that we are now dead, and our bodies are our tombs. And some clever fellow, perhaps a Sicilian or an Italian, compared that part of the soul in which desires exist to a leaky jug which can never be filled, but which we dead men try to fill with a leaky sieve. The sieve is the foolish soul which cannot hold water by reason of forgetfulness and unbelief. Socrates suggests in place of unrestraint and intemperance a life which is well-ordered and content with what it has (493c). When Callicles refuses, Socrates tells a second myth.

Suppose there are two men, and one has sound jars which he keeps full of all good things, while the other has leaky jars which he must keep refilling with labor and difficulty. Suppose that each of the two lives is of that sort: is not then the temperate and well-ordered life superior to intemperate profligacy?

Callicles rejects the conclusion. The fellow with the full jars no longer has pleasure, and this is to live like a stone. The good life is the life of pleasure, and that consists in maximum flow. To which Socrates replies that if this is so, a life of constant itching and scratching, culminating in the life of a catamite, is as good as any other. It is to this that Callicles' good by nature has been reduced. It is the result of claiming that those who attain pleasure, whatever the pleasure, are happy.

The myths offer a somber account of pleasure. Hunger, thirst, and in general all lack and desire are unpleasant and painful, whereas eating, drinking, and satisfaction are pleasant. So these pleasures, at least, seem to have pains as their conditions. Furthermore, pleasure is directly, not inversely, related to pain: pleasure diminishes and stops with pain, when desire is satisfied. It is pleasures such as these, immediately yoked with pains, which in the *Republic* (583b–585a) are described as unreal. Against this criterion, not only popular rhetoric, but popular leaders such as Themistocles and Pericles, Miltiades and Cimon, fail.

This leads to the deeper theme of the *Gorgias*, the theme of order and proportionality as the basis of moral and political purpose. The good man, who speaks for what is best, will not speak at random, but with a view toward something, as other artists do, combining the elements of their art in due order and proper arrangement (503e–504a). Due order and proper arrangement of the soul are lawfulness and law, and justice and temperance. It is to this that good and skillful orators will look (504d–e). Since it is not all desires but only beneficial desires whose gratification is good, the statesman, like the doctor, will restrain gratification. Correction or chastisement is therefore better for the soul than lack of restraint, contrary to what Callicles had first supposed. And Callicles is at this point himself reduced to silence, his mouth stopped.

Note: Callicles and Nietzsche

E. R. Dodds, in an appendix to his commentary on the *Gorgias*, remarks a resemblance between Callicles and Nietzsche. He had earlier suggested (p. 291) that men of the caliber of Nietzsche and Pareto had made respectable the Calliclean proposition that "power belongs of right, not to casual majorities, and not to some specialized class of technicians, but to the man who is shrewd enough and bold enough to grasp it." Dodds does not pause to explain what the phrase "power belongs of right" means in this context, if it means anything, or, given that the putative proposition is respectable, to whom it is respectable other than tyrants. But Dodds catalogues a series of themes Nietzsche may have taken from the speech of Callicles: the lion unleashed and its power (483e–484a); the nomos/phusis distinction in which nomos, convention or law, is conceived as a kind of social contract by which the many weak band together to get safety from the few strong (483b); the rejection of nomos as a slave morality (483b, 492a); the emphasis on hardness as an attribute of a master class (491b); the goodness of pleonexia, giving the desires free rein (491e). These resemblances are of course too striking to be accidental: Nietzsche is an extraordinarily derivative thinker. Yet it may perhaps be some small service to point out that Nietzsche differs radically from Callicles in his basic assumptions, and that Callicles is the better philosopher.

Begin with Nietzsche's claim that God is dead. It is a claim which has endeared itself to those who share something of Nietzsche's deep and abiding hatred and fear of Christianity, and yet it is doubtful that it is not sound without sense. Death implies ceasing to exist, and God is a necessary being; therefore, if God exists, God cannot cease to exist; and if God does not exist, God cannot cease to exist. So the claim that God is dead is in a strict sense absurd; nor is it less absurd for confusing what has life with what is life. Confused metaphysics leads to demonic ethics: "I give you this new law: 'Make yourselves hard.'" It is the law of those who are either at your throat or at your feet. So much for charity.

Nietzsche's central concept, the will to power, is a product of nineteenth century post-Kantian irrationalism. Kant, in the *Critique of Pure Reason,* undertook to deny knowledge in order to make room for faith. Assuming without argument the nonexistence of intellectual intuition, on which the classical tradition in metaphysics is based, he undertook to prove that what he called theoretical reason is powerless in metaphysics and ethics, whose characteristic themes he took to be God, freedom, and immortality. But ethics gave means of recovering the central themes of metaphysics, which are also the central concerns of the human heart and of religion. Practical as opposed to theoretical reason, reason exhibited in moral action as distinct from speculation, is the key. As moral agents, we are led to recognize that nothing is good in itself but a good will, and that a good will is not defined by any principle of goodness extrinsic to itself—Kant here had in mind utilitarianism—but by the pure form of the will itself, when it wills so to act that the maxim of its action can become a universal law. This is the first formulation of the so-called "categorical imperative." The second formulation issues in autonomy, the will as its own legislator, giving laws to itself. The Kantian enterprise consists in attempting to derive moral content from the mere form of a rule, and many of his later critics assumed that in this he failed. If so, the good will is deprived of the universalization principle, and if it cannot be defined in terms extrinsic to it, it may be conceived as Nietzsche conceived it: the good will is the self-determined will, and what is essential to will is the will to power. This then is Nietzsche's gloss on the first formulation of the categorical imperative. Nietzsche's superman, who is a law unto himself, is the mere pictorial or literary representation of Kant's concept of autonomy in the second formulation, when autonomy is defined in terms of power and deprived of any reference to self-government. The third formulation of the categorical imperative, which involves treating (all) human beings as members of a kingdom of ends, was also transformed by Nietzsche's imagination: the kingdom of ends became a master class.

The roots of these notions, so fundamental to Nietzsche, are far more obviously in Kant than in Callicles or in Greek sources generally. His three central concepts—the will to power, the superman, and the supremacy of a master class—are degenerate versions of the categorical imperative. The *Birth of Tragedy* has very little to do with the origins of Attic drama; and his account of Socrates and Plato is, at the very least, not scholarship. He even errs in making Callicles a spokesman for "the Sophists." Dodds supposes:

> Nietzsche was a man of subtler analytic intelligence and more sensitive moral fibre than the Platonic Callicles, and he wrestled with the moral problems of his time at a far deeper level. Callicles would have relished the purely destructive side of his teaching; but he would certainly not have understood concepts like "sublimation" and "self-transcendence", while Nietzsche would have rejected with contempt the crude hedonism on which Callicles falls back at 494a.

Callicles had not read Kant, but his philosophical abilities are surely superior to those of Nietzsche, and this precisely because of his hedonism, as distinct from Nietzsche's will to power. Crude as Callicles' hedonism may be, it at least provides an object toward which power may be directed. For power is a relational term and takes its value from its object. Nietzsche, in making the will to power supreme, offers sound without sense—appropriately enough, when what is at issue is not a philosophical theory but a perverted religion, whose twisted emblem was ultimately to become the swastika.

Socrates Alone: The Meaning of Human Life (505e–522e)

The meaning of life is the purpose of life, and the purpose of life is not something extrinsic, to which life itself is only a means. In Socratic terms, the meaning of life is to live and, specifically, to live well. The purpose of life is the good life, and the good life is defined by the possession of virtue. With Callicles silenced, Socrates turns to this theme, and the result is a protreptic to philosophy.

Socrates begins (506c–507a) by summarizing the leading points of the previous discussion. The pleasant and the good are not the same; what is pleasant ought to be done for the sake of the good, not the good for the sake of the pleasant. Things are good if they possess some virtue. The virtue of each thing consists in proper arrangement and good order. There is thus a certain order for each thing which provides it with a good naturally suited to it. Now the orderly soul is temperate, and the temperate soul is good.

There follows (507a–c) a brief proof that the virtues are one and the good man happy. The temperate man does what is fitting in respect to men and gods; but this is to do what is just and holy, and he who does just and holy things is himself just and holy. Furthermore, he is courageous, pursuing and fleeing what he ought. Therefore, the temperate man is just, courageous, and holy, and thus completely good. The unity of the virtues is their coimplication. The fact that the virtues all depend upon proper order of soul implies that the presence of temperance, or any virtue, requires the presence of the rest. This anticipates the account of justice in *Republic* IV.

Again in anticipation of the *Republic*, virtue implies happiness. The good man, the wise and temperate man, does what he does well and nobly, and by doing and faring well (*eu prattein*), he is blessed and happy. The play on words involved in *eu prattein*, between doing and faring well, right action, good character, and good fortune, is of course characteristically Platonic. These are the last words of the *Republic*.

If goodness and happiness consist in right order of soul, in what does that order consist? The answer is given by implication. Callicles recommends a life of aimless, endless evil, the life of a robber. But the principle of order embraces not only the human soul but the whole universe: heaven and earth and gods and men are bound together by community and friendship, orderliness, temperance and justice, and this is why the world is called a *cosmos*, a word which signifies both beauty and order (507e–508a). Callicles has forgotten that geometrical equality has great power among both gods and men; he recommends excess because he has forgotten geometry (508a). The moral argument of the *Gorgias* rests ultimately on proportion theory, and proportion theory is the structural principle of the world. This is also seen in the *Timaeus* (31b–32c), where the body of the cosmos is brought into existence through proportion and in this way begets friendship, *philia*. Both nomos and phusis are governed by the same mathematical structure, and the claim of a fundamental conflict between them is absurd.

In the *Laws* (VI 757a–c, cf. V 744c), it is said that equality produces friendship (philia), but that there are two kinds of equality: equality in respect to measure, multitude, or magnitude, and equality in respect to ratio. The latter, which is best, is the judgment of Zeus, and it produces all good things, distributing more to the greater and less to the smaller, giving due measure to each relative to its nature. And assigning what is fit to each according to ratio is political justice. Plato here draws on a tradition at least as old as Archytas of Tarentum, and one which permeates the *Gorgias*.

Aristotle later remarked (*Pol.*1301b29–35, trans. Jowett): "Equality is of two kinds, numerical and proportional; by the first I mean sameness or equality in number or size; by the second, equality of ratios. For example, the excess of three over two is numerically equal to the excess of two over one; whereas four exceeds two in the same ratio in which two exceeds one, for two is the same part of four that one is of two, namely, the half. . . . Men agree that justice in the abstract is proportion." As a purely mathematical matter, Aristotle's meaning is perhaps best expressed, not in terms of progression, but in terms of ratios of difference. In arithmetical proportion, difference is constant in number or quantity:

$$\frac{a - b}{b - c} = \frac{a}{a} = \frac{b}{b} = \frac{c}{c} \qquad \text{least solution: } a = 3, b = 2, c = 1.$$

In geometric proportion, "the judgment of Zeus," there is identity of ratio:

$$\frac{a - b}{b - c} = \frac{a}{b} = \frac{b}{c} \qquad \text{least solution: } a = 4, b = 2, c = 1.$$

Geometric proportion is here presented as continuous; but as a tool of moral analysis, it cannot be continuous. Aristotle presents the central point of the analysis in brief (*Nicomachean Ethics* 5.1131a17–20): "The just, therefore, involves at least four terms: for the persons to whom it is in fact just are two, and things in which it is manifested, the objects distributed, are two." Whence Aristotle infers (*Nicomachean Ethics* 5.1131b15–16): "Distributive justice is not a continuous proportion, for its second and third terms, a recipient and a share, do not constitute a single term."

The force of *Gorgias* 507e–508a is that the principles of morality admit of mathematical analysis, specifically in terms of proportion theory and, more specifically still, in terms of geometric proportion. The diagnosis of Callicles' attempt to provide a moral basis for excess, pleonexia, is that it is ultimately immoralism, the denial of all proportion in the boundlessness of ceaseless flow. To the Socratic Proportion that soul is to body as virtue is to health, there is now added the principle that virtue, like health, is itself a matter of good order, an order intrinsically proportional and expressed in temperance and self-restraint.

In the context of the *Gorgias,* which is directly concerned not with political justice but with moral psychology, the terms in geometric proportion must be taken as desires and satisfactions. If geometric proportion is superior to arithmetic proportion, as is here assumed, this must mean that the gratification of some desires instead of others, as opposed to the arithmetic principle of the claim of all desires for gratification, is proportionally proper. This in turn implies a natural order of desires within the soul, some superior to others, some perhaps needing to be extirpated. One way of stating the criticism of Callicles, then, is that he has defended arithmetic instead of geometric proportion. But matters are really worse than that. Callicles, in his defense of excess, pleonexia, has argued not only that all desires should be satisfied—the catamite— but that they should be constantly increased beyond the measure of their satisfaction—the curlew. The aim is not tranquillity, but constant flow, constant increase in desire along with increase in ability to satisfy desire, and constant dissatisfaction. Arithmetical equality is a democratic principle. Callicles represents what in the *Republic* will be called the tyrannical, not the democratic, man.

The connection of this analysis with rhetoric is direct. The man who rightly intends to be an orator must be just and know what things are just, which Polus thought Gorgias admitted out of sheer embarrassment; and Polus's own agreement that doing injustice is more ugly and shameful than suffering it is also true (508b–c). So the kind of rhetoric Callicles has recommended reduces to no more than lifesaving.

It is best, of course, neither to suffer injustice nor to do it. But how can this be achieved? The mere wish not to suffer injustice does not suffice; what is needed is a kind of power or art. But the means which most easily secure us from suffering injustice, namely, identifying ourselves with the existing constitution, are precisely those which require us to do injustice (509e–511a). Callicles' defense of rhetoric reduces the aims of living to the saving of life, as though the power and art required were like swimming, or being a pilot or an engineer. But the true aim is not living, but living nobly and well, and tried by this test, Callicles is ill advised to undertake to become like the existing constitution of his city (511a–513c). Callicles means to embark on a political career without understanding the true aim of politics, which is to make his fellow citizens better men; wealth and power do no good to people who do not know how to use them (513c–515b). Men like Pericles and Themistocles, Cimon and Miltiades made the city great; but its greatness is that of a tumor, which in the end will destroy Athens. The results of false statesmanship do not show themselves immediately, and if Callicles does not take care, he will be made to suffer, as will Alcibiades, for the mistakes of the older generation of statesmen. Callicles warns Socrates that it is he who is in danger. Socrates then describes himself as the only true statesman in Athens, and, foreseeing his own trial and its result, repeats the analogy with which his discussion with Polus began: he will be as helpless in an Athenian court of law as a doctor tried before a jury of children on charges brought by a pastry-cook. But the result is of relatively small importance if he has kept himself clear of wickedness (521c–522e); in confirmation whereof, he offers to tell Callicles a story, a vision of judgment.

Note: Friendship, Justice, and Proportion Theory

The theme of friendship, in the *Gorgias,* has not only a personal and social but an ontological dimension, and this by way of proportion theory. Heaven and earth and gods and men are bound together by it. Put otherwise, proportion—geometrical equality—is a structural principle of the common good.

The theme of the common good is fundamental to Socratic and Platonic moral and political theory. It is the theme that virtue, human excellence, implies pursuit of one's own good, and that pursuit of one's own good implies pursuit of the good of one's fellows and of the social order of which one is a part. In the *Gorgias,* these aims imply a congruence between action and character and proportionality.

Socratic ethics is commonly regarded as purposive, and the purpose is identified with happiness. This is not false, but it is neither the whole nor the most illuminating part of the truth. For if we ask in what happiness consists, the Socratic answer is that it consists in living well; and if we in turn ask in what living well consists, the Socratic answer is that it consists in living justly and virtuously. In the *Crito,* the periphrasis used for soul is "that in us which is benefited by justice and harmed by injustice." Socrates and Plato are "naturalists" in ethics only if we conceive nature to be suffused with moral principle.

How does proportionality bear on justice? How do morals become mathematized? The *Gorgias* presents not one but three theories of justice. There is Socrates' theory that justice is to be analyzed in terms of geometrical equality. There is Callicles' claim that justice, as ordinarily understood, is a matter of convention or law, nomos, which implicitly treats justice as a matter of arithmetical equality, based on a social contract: ordinary men delight in equality because of their inferiority (483c). Finally, there is Callicles' own theory of natural justice, which denies that justice is to be analyzed in terms of any sort of proportion at all and recommends excess, over-reaching, pleonexia.

Justice according to nomos, which Callicles condemns as a morality fit for slaves, consists in doing right for fear of the consequences of doing wrong. Implicitly, it is a morality which consists in trading pleasures for pleasures, and pains for pains, so that men are courageous through a kind of cowardice, temperate through a kind of licentiousness. This is the justice of arithmetical equality, and its negative afterimage is the Talian Law; it includes, if it is not equivalent to, the state of soul of an adequately deterred criminal. In the *Protagoras* (356a–e), arithmetical equality, as it relates to the art of measurement, leads to a concept of good and evil which issues in (to borrow Bentham's phrase) the "Nautical Almanac" of hedonism; some critics, astonishingly, have taken it to be Plato's own view. Hedonism is a natural correlate of arithmetical proportion, in that hedonism purports to offer a set of comparable units of measurement which may be treated as summative, to be added or subtracted, balanced against each other. For arithmetical equality is equality in number or magnitude. This is the proportion associated with the kind of justice Callicles describes as conventional or legal and denounces as fit only for slaves. It is the kind of justice which, according to Glaucon in the *Republic*, is believed in by not only Thrasymachus but the majority of men. It is not good in itself, but only in its consequences. In the *Protagoras* (361c), Socrates is led finally to remark that he and Protagoras do not know what virtue is.

Callicles proposes to substitute natural for conventional justice, and natural justice, in his hands, is denial of any proportion at all. It is a life of unbridled self-aggrandizement, the pursuit of pleasure of any kind and in all amounts, a life of ceaseless and constant flow. No social contract here, but brigandage: not trading, but taking.

Does Callicles have a moral philosophy? In one sense, he surely does, for his distinction between what is just by nature and what is just by convention is an implicit recommendation about how to live a human life, and as Socrates examines his view, his praise of power transposes into hedonism. Put otherwise, Callicles offers a moral theory because he contradicts a moral theory, that of Socrates—he contradicts the doctrines that it is better to suffer injustice than to do it, better to suffer punishment for injustice than to escape it, and better to pursue temperance and wisdom than unbridled pleasure. But of course what Callicles recommends is only for those whom he believes to be the strong, that is, those who can protect themselves against the penalties of over-reaching; his morality therefore issues in a profoundly self-destructive immoralism. His is a principle of disorder, of enmity rather than friendship. *Homo homini lupus*—man is a wolf to man. Plato, indeed, regarded this as implicit in the claim that it is better to do injustice than to suffer it: Callicles is saying what many men believe but are ashamed to say. The remark suggests that Callicles' vision of natural justice is the dirty underside of conventional justice.

To this, Socrates opposes his own vision of justice, associated with temperance and good order of soul and analyzed in terms of geometrical proportion. Geometrical proportion expresses equality of ratio, not equality of measure or share, and, in a moral context, equality of ratio of merit or worth. Since this is so, geometrical proportion, taken as a mathematical analysis of justice, does not define justice, since it presupposes justice. Rather, it expresses a structural relation present in souls or societies when they are properly said to be just. That relation implies an identity between the good of individuals and their fellows. To satisfy our own needs we must rely on our fellows not only to help us but also not to harm us; and if we are to rely on our fellows, we must aim at their good as well as, and as part of, our own—including especially their goodness of character. Put otherwise, if friendship aims at another person's good, the structural relation which justice implies also implies friendship. In the *Republic*, this will lead to a political theory which treats the state as properly concerned with the human goodness of each of its citizens, taken distributively, as well as with the collective good of the society at large.

A Vision of Judgment (523a–527e)

Socrates in the *Gorgias*, having said that life is a kind of death and the body a tomb, suggests at the conclusion of the *Gorgias* that after death there is a kind of life, and that the fate of the soul depends on a judgment of its character and deeds. The Vision of Judgment lends dramatic content to Socrates' claim in the *Apology* that there is no evil for a man in living or dying, and the gods do not neglect his affairs. Death is represented as governed by the same moral order which governs life, and that moral order is ratified by the judgment of Zeus.

There is a meadow where three ways meet. One way runs from this world to the meadow; a second from the meadow to the Isles of the Blessed; a third from the meadow to Tartarus, the dungeon of Hell. In that meadow, Rhadamanthus, Aeacus, and Minos, sons of Zeus, sit as judges of the souls of the dead, which appear naked before them. These are the true judges Socrates mentions in the *Apology* (41a). Death, in anticipation of the *Phaedo*, is defined as the separation of soul and body; the judge contemplates each soul alone by itself with his own soul alone by itself, not veiled or muffled by eyes and ears and the rest of the body (cf. *Phaedo* 64e). Virtuous souls, after judgment, are sent to the Isles of the Blessed, where they are forever happy. Bad souls are sent to Tartarus, the place of punishment. They are marked as curable or incurable; curable souls are subjected to suffering in order to effect their cure, that is, chasten or eradicate their wrongful desires; the incurable, who are of no use to themselves, are made useful to others by being gibbeted, made perpetual examples so that their sufferings will teach others to fear wrongdoing. The primary aim of punishment is remedial, but the remedy is suffering, and deterrence may also teach.

The elements of Socrates' tale derive from various sources. The meadow is Homeric. Hesiod has the Isles of the Blessed. There is a judgment of the dead in Aeschylus and Pindar. The notion that the soul is judged naked, and that the marks of its injustice appear on it like the scars of whippings on the back of a beaten slave, is Platonic—or perhaps it is Orphic or Pythagorean. It may be an old woman's tale, or perhaps there is some connection to the Eleusinian Mysteries (527e, cf. 497c, 512e). No doubt such questions have their own interest, but they do not settle the primary issue of interpretation: given that the elements of the story have antecedents, why did Plato choose to combine those elements in this way at the conclusion of the *Gorgias*?

The Vision of Judgment is not a mere postscript to the *Gorgias*, but part of its argument. Throughout the dialogue, that argument has been analogical, in structure an extension of geometrical proportion: the reader, shown relations which hold in one domain, is asked to recognize those same relations obtaining in another. This is why a story, a piece of fiction, can be described as not a myth but a true account, a logos which is *alethes* (523a). One may compare the myth of the water-carriers (493 a–d), with its introductory suggestion that the body is the tomb and that our life is actually death, or the story of the two men with jars (493d– 494c). These too are fictions; yet they are meant to persuade Callicles that the well-ordered soul is happier than the intemperate, and they come very close to succeeding. These stories are in fact rhetorical arguments, aimed at persuasion; they are rhetoric which has learned to understand its own purpose. Their themes are taken from the moral theory Socrates has already advanced; they are clarifying metaphors for that theory; and they are brought back to discourse and dialectic in order to make it more perspicuous. Fiction, which can persuade, also has power not only to entertain and provide pleasure, but to exhibit truth or falsehood. It is surely no accident that the *Gorgias* (502a–b) suggests that poetry and drama are species of popular rhetoric. Plato, who knew the power of words, did not believe that the stories men hear and tell are irrelevant to what they do, or what they are, or what they may become.

Did Plato himself believe the elements of the story of the Vision of Judgment, as distinct from the truth of the story itself? Surely not. He did not, that is to say, believe that souls detached from bodies inhabit meadows, or that discarnate souls can be gibbeted, or seen by other discarnate souls. The truth of the logos lies not in its concrete elements, but in what it represents or shows. Neither did Plato believe, one may suppose, in the doctrine of the eternal torment of incurables, later to have so fateful an influence on Christian eschatology. The moral truth represented by this doctrine is not savage but simple: a soul which is vicious and incurable cannot, by definition, be relieved of its own wretchedness, and it must therefore suffer the extremity of unhappiness as long as it exists.

The Vision of Judgment aims at convincing Callicles that he ought to fear injustice rather than death (522e); that it is better to suffer injustice than to do it; better to be good than to seem good; better to be punished for injustice than to escape punishment; that all flattery should be shunned; that rhetoric and every practice should be used for what is just (527b–c). The life of justice and temperance, in short, is the best life, and the life recommended by Callicles is worthless. The Vision of Judgment, with extraordinarily rhetorical power, enlists the emotions of hope and fear and pity in order to transform these claims from abstract propositions, maintained through dialectic, to principles of living. The primary application is not to an afterlife but to this life: for the unjust man, as for Marlowe's Faustus, Hell is not bounded nor circumscribed in one place, for where we are is Hell. If the subject of the Vision of Judgment is death, its purpose is more abundant life. It offers a vision of the soul as possessed of a heavenly destiny which may be achieved no less in the here and now than in the hereafter, in the life of justice and temperance.

The Vision of Judgment is often described as an eschatological myth, a story of last things, and so inherently religious. This may be true, though one may perhaps wonder what is meant by religion. By itself, the story provides no call to prayer or worship. Yet it is directed to the inner lives of men, and by way of the proportionality inherent in the concept of virtue, it provides a foundation for communion and friendship with divinity. Put in this way, the happiness which is virtue is in some sense experience of the life of God in the lives of men. But if the Vision of Judgment is in this sense religious, it is not less a protreptic to philosophy. Stories about last things prompt inquiry into the nature of first things.

TRANSLATION

CALLICLES / SOCRATES / CHAEREPHON / GORGIAS / POLUS

Introduction (447a–449c)

447a CAL. "Too late for a share in the fight," as the saying goes, Socrates.

SOC. Really? Don't you rather mean too late for the feast?[1]

CAL. Yes, and an elegant feast it was. Gorgias gave us a fine and varied exhibition just a while ago.

SOC. Chaerephon here is to blame, Callicles. He made us waste time in the Agora.

b CHR. No matter, Socrates, I'll cure what caused it. Gorgias is a friend of mine, so he'll give us a performance—now if you like, later if you wish it.

CAL. Really, Chaerephon? Does Socrates want to hear Gorgias?

CHR. That's just why we came.

CAL. Then please come to my house whenever you wish. Gorgias is staying with me, and he'll give you a performance.

SOC. That's good of you, Callicles. But would he be willing to dis-
c cuss with us instead? I wish to ask the man what the power of his art is, and what it is he professes and teaches. As for the other thing, the exhibition you mention, let him give it later.

CAL. Nothing like asking him, Socrates. In fact, that's part of his performance; at any rate he was just now soliciting questions from any of the people inside on whatever they pleased, and said he would answer whatever anyone asked.

1. Dodds quotes Falstaff: "The latter end of a fray and the beginning of a feast fits a dull fighter and a keen guest." (*Henry IV*, act 4, sc. 3)

231

soc. Well that's just fine. Chaerephon, ask him.

CHR. Ask him what?

d soc. Who he is.

CHR. What do you mean?

soc. Well, if he made shoes, for example, he would doubtless tell you he was a cobbler. Do you see what I mean?

CHR. Yes, and I'll ask him. Tell me, Gorgias, is Callicles here telling the truth? Do you profess to answer any question asked?

448a GOR. Yes, Chaerephon. In fact, I just now promised that very thing, and I say no one has asked me anything new for many years.

CHR. Ah, then answering will surely be easy, Gorgias.

GOR. Feel free to test the matter, Chaerephon.

POL. Yes, by all means. But kindly put your questions to me, Chaerephon. I think Gorgias is quite tired after the lengthy discourse he just gave.

CHR. Why Polus, do you think your answers are finer than his?

b POL. What difference does it make, as long as they do for you?

CHR. Why, none whatever. Since you wish it, answer.

POL. You have only to ask.

CHR. Very well, then, suppose Gorgias had knowledge of the art which belongs to his brother Herodicus. What sort of man would we properly call him? The sort we call his brother?

POL. Of course.

CHR. So we'd correctly say he's a doctor?

POL. Yes.

CHR. But suppose he was skilled in the art of Aristophon son of Aglaophon or his brother Polygnotus. What would we correctly call him then?

c POL. A painter, clearly.

CHR. Now since Gorgias has knowledge of some art, what would we correctly call him?

POL. Many are the arts among men, Chaerephon, skillfully discovered from skills, for skill makes our human life proceed according to art, but lack of skill according to chance. Different men get a share of these different arts differently, but the best men of the best arts, among whom in fact is Gorgias here, who partakes of the most noble of arts.

d soc. Polus surely seems nobly equipped for speech, Gorgias, but he is not keeping his promise to Chaerephon.

GOR. In just what way, Socrates?

soc. He hardly appears to me to be answering the question he was asked.

gor. Well, if you wish, ask him yourself.

soc. No, I'd much rather ask you, if you're willing to answer. It is clear to me that Polus, from what he said, has had more practice in what they call rhetoric than in discussion.

e pol. How so, Socrates?

soc. Because, Polus, when Chaerephon asked you what art Gorgias knew, you eulogized his art as though it were being disparaged, but you didn't answer what it is.

pol. Why, didn't I say it was most noble?

soc. You certainly did. But nobody asked of what sort Gorgias's 449a art is, but what it is, and what one should call Gorgias. Just as Chaerephon gave the previous examples to you and you answered him well and briefly, so in the same way now, tell us what Gorgias's art is and what we are to call him. Better yet, Gorgias, tell us yourself: What shall we call you? That is, what is your art?

gor. Rhetoric, Socrates.

soc. We are therefore to call you a rhetorician?

gor. Yes, and a good one, Socrates, if you wish, as Homer puts it, to call me what "I boast myself to be."

soc. But of course I do.

gor. Then pray do.

b soc. Are we then also to say that you can make others rhetoricians?

gor. That is just what I profess, not only here but elsewhere.

soc. Then would you be willing to put aside for later that lengthy kind of discourse Polus began, and keep on discussing by alternate question and answer as we are doing now? Don't go back on your promise; be willing to give short answers to what I ask.

gor. Some answers require length, Socrates. Nevertheless, I shall c certainly try to be as brief as possible. In point of fact, that's also one of my claims: no one can say the same things more briefly than I can.

soc. Just what I want, Gorgias. Give me an exhibition of your short-answer method, and leave the long-answer style for later.

gor. I will, and you will agree that you never heard anyone speak more briefly.

Socrates and Gorgias:
What Is Rhetoric? (449c–461b)

soc. Come then. You say you know the art of rhetoric, and how to

d   make other people rhetoricians. Well just what is rhetoric about?
     Weaving, for example, is about making clothes, isn't it?

GOR. Yes.

SOC. And the art of music about making melodies?

GOR. Yes.

SOC. I certainly do admire your answers, Gorgias. They couldn't
     be shorter.

GOR. Yes, I think I do this nicely, Socrates.

SOC. And you're right. So give me the same kind of answer about
     rhetoric. What is it knowledge about?

GOR. Speeches.

e SOC. What sort of speeches, Gorgias? The sort that explain to sick
     people the regimen they should follow to get well?

GOR. No.

SOC. So rhetoric isn't about all speeches.

GOR. Of course not.

SOC. Yet it does produce ability to speak.

GOR. Yes.

SOC. And also to understand what is spoken of?

GOR. Of course.

450a SOC. Now, we just mentioned medicine. Does medicine, then, pro-
     duce ability to understand and speak about sick people?

GOR. Necessarily.

SOC. So medicine too, it seems, is about speeches.

GOR. Yes.

SOC. Speeches about diseases?

GOR. Especially.

SOC. And isn't the art of the trainer about speeches, speeches about
     good and bad conditions of the body?

GOR. Certainly.

SOC. Furthermore, the same is true of the other arts, Gorgias. Each
b   of them is about the speeches which have to do with the subject
     matter of each art.

GOR. It appears so.

SOC. Then if you say rhetoric is speeches, why don't you call the
     other arts, since they are about speeches, rhetoric?

GOR. Because, Socrates, the knowledge involved in other arts is
     almost completely about manual labor and such activities,
c   whereas rhetoric is nothing of the sort; its whole action and au-
     thority is through speeches. That is why I deem it proper to say

that the art of rhetoric is about speeches—and this puts it correctly, as I claim.

soc. I still don't understand what sort of thing you wish to call it,
but perhaps we'll get clearer. Do please answer; we have arts, do
we not?

gor. Yes.

soc. Now among those various arts, I believe, some require mostly
labor and little speech, while some require no speech at all and
could even achieve their aim in silence—painting, for example,
and sculpture, and a good many others. Those are the kinds of
d   arts, I take it, you deny that rhetoric is about.

gor. Certainly, Socrates. You understand very well.

soc. But there are other arts which achieve their entire aim
through speech, and which require practically no work beyond
it or very little. There is number theory, for example, and computation and geometry, yes, and backgammon and many others.
With some of them, speech and action are about equal, but many
have more speech than action, or even completely have all their
e   work and authority through speech. I take it you mean rhetoric
is an art of that sort.

gor. You are right.

soc. But surely you don't wish to call any of them rhetoric, I suppose, notwithstanding the fact that, as you express it, rhetoric
has its authority through speech. If a person wished to be captious he might retort, "Then you mean number theory is rhetoric,
Gorgias?" But I don't think you mean number theory or geometry is rhetoric.

451a gor. You think correctly, Socrates, and your retort is justified.

soc. Then come finish your answer to my question. For since rhetoric is one of those arts which mostly use speech, while it happens
there are also other arts of the same sort, try to state what rhetoric, given that it has its authority in speeches, is about. For
example, if someone asked me about some one of the arts I just
mentioned—"Socrates, what art is number theory?"—I'd tell
b   him, as you just told me, that it is an art which has its authority
through speech. And if he then asked me, "What is it about?"
I'd reply that it is one of the arts concerned with the odd and
even, however many each may happen to be. And if he were
again to ask, "But what is the art you call computation?" I'd reply
that it too is one of the arts which has its whole authority through
speech, and if he continued, "What is it about?" I'd reply as

c   though I were drafting a law in the Assembly, that whereas num-
      ber theory and computation are mutatis mutandis otherwise
      alike, for they are about the same thing, to wit and viz. the odd
      and even, nevertheless they differ inasmuch as computation con-
      siders the odd and even relative to themselves and to each other
      in respect of multitude. And if somebody were to ask about as-
      tronomy, I'd also say its whole authority consists in speech, and
      if he were then to say, "But what are the speeches of astronomy
      about, Socrates?" I'd reply that they are about the motion of the
      stars and sun moon, how they have speeds relative to each other.

      GOR. Yes, and you'd be correct, Socrates.

d   SOC. Well then, it's your turn, Gorgias. Rhetoric is one of the arts
      whose whole action and authority consists in speech. Not so?

      GOR. It is.

      SOC. Then please state what it is about. Rhetoric uses speeches.
      What are those speeches about?

      GOR. The greatest of human affairs, Socrates, and the best.

e   SOC. But Gorgias, that again is both debatable and unclear. I sup-
      pose you've heard the old drinking song where people chant and
      count, "Health is best, and beauty second, and third. . . ," so the
      author of the catch has it, "wealth got without fraud."

      GOR. Yes, I've heard it, but what's your point?

452a SOC. Just this. Suppose the artisans who produce the things the
      author of that song praises—the doctor, the trainer, the busi-
      nessman—were standing in front of you right now, and the doc-
      tor spoke first and said, "Gorgias is deceiving you, Socrates. It's
      not his art that's about the greatest good for men, but mine."
      And if I asked, "Who are you to say that?" he'd perhaps reply,
      "A doctor." "Then what are you saying? That the product of your
b   art is the greatest good?" He'd perhaps reply, "Why of course,
      Socrates. What good is greater for men than health?" Next comes
      the trainer. He says, "I too would be very much surprised, Soc-
      rates, if Gorgias can show you a greater good from his art than
      I can from mine." So again I say to him too, "Who are you, fellow,
      and what is your product?" "A trainer," he'd reply, "and my prod-
      uct is making the bodies of men beautiful and strong." Next after
      the trainer comes the businessman, who I expect rather looks
c   down a bit on everybody else: "You must surely consider, Soc-
      rates, whether wealth does not appear to you to be a good greater
      than any that Gorgias or the rest can show." We'd say to him,
      "Really? Do you produce it?" He'd say yes. "Who are you?" "A

businessman." We'll say, "Really? Do you then judge wealth to be the greatest good for men?" He'll reply, "Of course." "Yes, but Gorgias here contends that the art he possesses is cause of a greater good than yours," we'll say. It is clear what his next ques-

d   tion will be: "And just what is this good? Let Gorgias answer." So, come, Gorgias. Consider yourself questioned both by them and by me, and answer: What is this thing you claim is the greatest good for men, and that you are an artisan of?

GOR. That which in very truth is the greatest good, Socrates, is at once cause of freedom for men themselves and of rule over others in their city.

SOC. Then what do you say this is?

e   GOR. I say it is ability to persuade by speeches judges in a lawcourt, Senators in the Council chamber, Assemblymen in the Assembly, or in political gatherings of any other kind whatever. Indeed by virtue of this power you will have the doctor as your slave, and the trainer too, and this businessman of yours will make his next appearance earning money not for himself but someone else— for you—because of your ability to speak and persuade the multitude.

SOC. I think you now are much closer to making clear what art you

453a believe rhetoric to be, Gorgias; if I follow, you are saying that rhetoric is a manufacturer of persuasion: its whole business comes to that, and that sums up its aim. Or can you say that rhetoric has any power beyond producing persuasion in the soul of the hearers?

GOR. Not at all, Socrates. I think you've sufficiently marked it off. That sums it up.

SOC. Then hear me, Gorgias. Be well assured that if ever a man

b   discussed with another through a wish to know the very thing the discussion concerned, I—or so I am convinced—am such a man. And I trust you are another.

GOR. What about it, Socrates?

SOC. Just this. Understand that I don't know clearly just what persuasion it is which you say derives from rhetoric, or what sorts of things the persuasion is about. Oh, not that I couldn't hazard a guess as to what I suspect you mean, and what it's about. Never-

c   theless, I'll ask you to tell me what persuasion it is you say derives from rhetoric and what it is about. Why do I ask you when I already suspect the answer, instead of giving it myself? Not for your sake but for the sake of the argument, in order that in this way it may progress as far as possible in clarity about its subject matter. Consider: don't you think it would be a fair question if, for example, I asked you what kind of painter Zeuxis is and you told me a picture painter, to ask what sort of pictures he paints, and where?

GOR. Certainly.

d SOC. And this for the reason that there are many other painters, painting many other kinds of pictures?

GOR. Yes.

SOC. But if nobody besides Zeuxis painted, your answer would have been fine.

GOR. Of course.

SOC. Then apply this to rhetoric. Do you think that rhetoric alone produces persuasion, or do other arts too? I mean this: Does everybody who teaches anything persuade?

GOR. Most certainly, Socrates.

e SOC. Now let's return to the very arts we just mentioned. Doesn't number theory or a person who knows number theory teach us as much as pertains to number?

GOR. Certainly.

SOC. And persuades also?

GOR. Yes.

SOC. Therefore number theory too is a manufacturer of persuasion.

GOR. It appears so.

SOC. Now, if someone asked me what sort of persuasion, and about what, we would reply, I suppose, that it is persuasion derived
454a   from instruction about how many the odd and the even are. And we can further show all the other arts we just mentioned are manufacturers of persuasion, and show the kind of persuasion, and what it is about. Agreed?

GOR. Yes.

SOC. Rhetoric therefore is not the only manufacturer of persuasion.

GOR. True.

SOC. Then since it is not alone in producing this product, but there are also others, we may justly ask next, as we did about the
b   painter, what sort of persuasion the art of rhetoric produces, and what the persuasion is about. Don't you think it just to ask?

GOR. I do.

CAL. Then since you do, Gorgias, please answer.

GOR. Well, Socrates, I mean the sort of persuasion used in lawcourts and other gatherings, as I now said. And it is about what things are just and unjust.

soc. That's about what I guessed you meant, Gorgias. Please don't be surprised if I presently ask you something a little further along
c these same lines. What I ask may seem obvious, and yet I'll ask it anyway, for as I say, my questioning is not for your sake, but for the sake of carrying the argument through consecutively and in good order, so that we may not fall into the habit of guessing at what is meant and snatching at each other's words, but you may carry through in accordance with the hypothesis in whatever way you wish.

GOR. Yes, you seem to me quite right to do this, Socrates.

soc. Come, then, let us also consider the next point: Is there something you call "having learned"?

GOR. Yes.

soc. What about "having believed"?

GOR. Yes.

d soc. Now, do you think "having learned" and "having believed," and likewise learning and belief, are the same or different?

GOR. Why, I suppose they're different, Socrates.

soc. And you suppose well, as you can tell from this: if someone asked you, "Is there false and true belief, Gorgias?" you'd doubtless agree that there is.

GOR. Yes.

soc. Now, is there false and true knowledge?

GOR. Certainly not.

soc. It is therefore clear that the two are not the same.

GOR. True.

e soc. Moreover, those who have learned have been persuaded, as also have those who believe.

GOR. That is so.

soc. Then do you wish us to assume two forms of persuasion, the one providing belief without knowledge, the other providing knowledge?

GOR. Yes, certainly.

soc. Now, rhetoric produces persuasion in lawcourts and other public assemblies about things which are just and unjust. What kind of persuasion? The kind from which arises belief without knowledge, or the kind from which arises knowledge?

GOR. Clearly, Socrates, the kind from which arises belief.

455a SOC. So rhetoric is, it seems, a manufacturer of persuasion producing belief but not instruction about the just and unjust.

GOR. Yes.

SOC. Therefore, the rhetorician does not provide instruction to courts and other assemblies about things which are just and unjust. He only creates belief. For after all, it would be impossible to instruct so large a crowd in a short time about matters of such importance.

GOR. Indeed.

SOC. Come, then, let's see what it is we are really saying about
b rhetoric, for even I cannot yet grasp what I mean. When a meeting is held in the city to appoint public physicians or shipbuilders, or any other kind of artisan, surely at that time the rhetorician will not give his advice. For, clearly, it is in each case necessary to choose the most skillful: architects when the subject is building walls or constructing harbors or dockyards; or again, when it is a question of choosing a general, or some disposition of troops
c against the enemy, or seizing territory, advice is given not by rhetoricians but by generals. What do you say, Gorgias? For since you claim to be a rhetorician yourself and to make others rhetoricians, it is proper to learn about your art from you. And regard me now as furthering your own interests, for it may well be that there is someone within these walls who wishes to become your pupil—I note quite a few, in fact—and they perhaps would
d be ashamed to question you. So please consider yourself questioned by them when you are questioned by me. "What will we get, Gorgias, if we join your company? What subjects will we be able to advise the city about? Only about the just and unjust, or also about the other things Socrates just now mentioned?" Try to answer them.

GOR. Socrates, I will try to reveal clearly to you the entire power
e of rhetoric. You gave an excellent lead yourself, for you surely know that these dockyards and walls of Athens, and its harbors too, rose through the advice of Themistocles and in part of Pericles, but not of the artisans.

SOC. They do say that about Themistocles, Gorgias. And I myself heard Pericles advise us about the Middle Wall.[2]

2. "The original Long Walls, built between 461 and 456, linked Athens with Piraeus and Phaleron respectively, thus enclosing the city and its two ports within a triangular fortification whose third side was the sea. Later, perhaps because the use of Phaleron as a harbor had been given up, a third wall was built, within and parallel to the north or Piraeus wall, so as to enclose the military road from Athens to Piraeus. This is usually thought to be the 'middle wall' referred to here." Dodds, *Gorgias.*

456a GOR. So you see, when there is a choice of the kind you mention, Socrates, it is the orators who advise and whose resolutions are carried.

SOC. Yes, Gorgias, and that's just what surprises me. I've been asking for some time what power rhetoric has; for its greatness appears almost preternatural to me.

GOR. Ah, Socrates, if only you knew the whole of it. You see, rhetoric virtually encompasses and contains within itself all powers.

b I'll give you a striking example. I often go with my brother and other doctors to visit patients who are unwilling to take medicine or submit to surgery or cautery, and when the doctor cannot persuade them, I do, by no other art but rhetoric. In fact, I say that if a doctor and a rhetorician were to enter any city you please, and had there to contend through speeches in the assembly or some other public gathering about which of them should be ap-

c pointed physician, the doctor would be left at the post. The man who can speak would be chosen if he wished it. And if he were to contend with any other artisan whatever, the rhetorician would persuade people to choose himself over anyone else; for there is no subject on which a rhetorician cannot speak more persuasively before a multitude than any artisan whatever. Such and so great is the power of the art. But of course, Socrates, rhetoric must be

d used like any other competitive skill, for such skills are not to be used against people indiscriminately. Just because a man has learned to box or wrestle or fight in armor, so that he is stronger than friend and foe alike, does not mean that he is to beat his friends or stab them to death. Why for heaven's sake, if a man goes to wrestling school and gets in shape and learns to box, and then proceeds to beat his mother and father or any of his friends

e and relations, that is no reason to hate trainers or the people who teach fighting in armor and banish them from the city. They imparted their skills to be used justly, against enemies and wrong-

457a doers, in self-defense, not aggression; but the others perverted their strength and their art to improper use. Thus the teachers are not bad, nor is the art bad or guilty, but rather, I think, those who misuse it. The same is true of rhetoric. The orator has power to speak to everyone about everything, so that he is more persuasive in a short time in a public gathering about whatever he

b wishes. But simply because he is able to diminish the reputation of doctors and other artisans, that is no reason why he should do it; rather, he should use his rhetoric justly, as with other competitive skills. But I think that if a man becomes a rhetorician and then commits injustice through this power and this art, that is no reason for hating his teacher and banishing him from the city. For the teacher imparted his skill to be used justly, and his pupil acted oppositely. So it is the man who misused it, and not his teacher, who is justly hated and banished and killed.

soc. I suppose, Gorgias, that you also have had much experience in discussions, and have observed the following fact: it is not easy for the parties to be able to define for one another the subject they are attempting to discuss, and thus, by mutual learning and teaching, to bring their conversation to a conclusion. On the contrary, if they disagree about something, and if one claims that the other is not speaking correctly or clearly, they grow angry and think the other speaks only out of grudgingness, being contentious instead of inquiring into the matter put forward in argument. Why, sometimes they finish and take leave of each other disgracefully, being reviled, and speaking and hearing such abuse about themselves that even the bystanders become angry at themselves for thinking it worth listening to such men. Why do I mention this? Because what you are saying now seems to me not really to follow or accord with the first account of rhetoric you gave. And I am afraid to refute you, lest you suspect me of contentiousness, of not speaking toward the issue and its clarification, but toward you. Now, if you're the kind of man I am, I'll gladly keep on questioning you. Otherwise, I'll let it go. What kind am I? Glad to be refuted if I say anything untrue, but not more displeased to be refuted than to refute; for I believe it greater good to be refuted, inasmuch as it is greater good to be oneself delivered from the greatest of evils than to deliver another. For I think there is no evil so great for a man as false opinion about the subject of our present discussion. Now if you say you are of this sort too, let us carry through the conversation. But if it seems better to let it go, let us dismiss it forthwith and bring the discussion to an end.

gor. Why, I certainly say I am the sort of man you indicate, Socrates. Perhaps, however, the others present should be kept in mind too. For I gave them quite a lengthy performance before you came, and if we continue our discussion now, we'll perhaps unduly prolong the session. So we should consider their interests too. We don't want to detain anybody who wishes to do something else.

chr. Gorgias, Socrates, you hear their applause. If you have something to say, these people wish to hear it. For my own part, surely, I hope never to be so busy that I'd leave such arguments, so conducted, because it had become more important to do something else.

d CAL. Yes indeed, Chaerephon. At this point I've been present at many a discussion myself, and I don't know that I was ever so delighted as right now. As far as I'm concerned, you will only oblige me if you will go on with the discussion, even if it takes all day.

SOC. To be sure, Callicles, nothing prevents it on my part, if Gorgias is willing.

GOR. But it would be disgraceful for me not to be willing, Socrates, after all this, especially when I profess to answer whatever anyone

e wishes to ask. And if it seems good to the company, continue the discussion and ask what you will.

SOC. Then hear what surprises me in what you've said, Gorgias; though perhaps you spoke correctly and I do not correctly understand you. You say you are able to make a rhetorician of anyone who wishes to learn from you?

GOR. Yes.

SOC. With the result that he will be convincing to the public about everything, not through instruction but persuasion?

459a GOR. Quite so.

SOC. And you said just now that the orator will be more persuasive even than the doctor on the subject of health.

GOR. Yes, at least to the public.

SOC. Now, "to the public" means "to the ignorant"? For surely he will not be more persuasive than the doctor to those who know.

GOR. True.

SOC. So if the orator is more persuasive than the doctor, he is more persuasive than someone who knows?

GOR. Indeed.

b SOC. And he is not a doctor—correct?

GOR. Yes.

SOC. And if he is not a doctor, I presume he lacks knowledge of what the doctor knows.

GOR. Clearly.

SOC. Therefore, when the orator is more persuasive than the doctor, someone who does not know is more persuasive to the unknowing than someone who knows. Does that follow, or not?

GOR. Yes, in this case, it does.

soc. But the same is true of all the other arts too. Rhetoric and the orator have no need to know how things really stand with things themselves; they need only to discover some trick of per-

c suasion, so as to appear to the unknowing to know more than those who know.

GOR. Well, but doesn't that make it a great deal easier, Socrates? You don't have to learn any other arts but this single one, and you're in no way inferior to the artisan.

soc. Whether or not the orator is inferior to others because of this we shall shortly examine, if it matters to the argument. But right now let us first consider whether what is true of the rhetorician

d about health and the subject matter of the other arts is also true about the just and the unjust, the ugly and the beautiful, and good and evil. Does the orator then not know the very things themselves—what is good and what evil, beautiful and shameful, just or unjust? Has he instead devised a trick of persuasion about them, so as to seem among the unknowing to know, although not

e knowing, better than one who knows? Or must the orator know these things, and must the person who is to learn rhetoric from you come knowing these things beforehand? If he does not, will you as a teacher of rhetoric give such a pupil no instruction in these things—that not being your job—but only make him seem among the multitude to know such things without really knowing them, and seem a good man without really being one? Or will you be quite unable to teach him rhetoric if he does not know the truth about these things beforehand? How do things stand here, Gorgias? I beg you in the name of Zeus, please draw aside

460a the veil of rhetoric, as you just promised, and state what its power and function really is.

GOR. Well, I suppose, Socrates, that if he doesn't know these things, he'll learn them from me also.

soc. Hold it right there. That's just fine. If you make somebody a rhetorician, he must either know what things are just and unjust to begin with, or learn it later from you.

GOR. Of course.

b soc. Well now. A person who has learned building is a builder?

GOR. Yes.

soc. And a person who has learned music is a musician?

GOR. Yes.

soc. And medicine a doctor? And so, by the same account generally, he who has learned each of these things is of the same sort as the knowledge which accomplishes each?

GOR. Certainly.

SOC. Then by this account, a person who has learned what things are just is just?

GOR. Why, certainly.

SOC. And the just man, I take it, does just things?

GOR. Yes.

c SOC. Then the rhetorician is necessarily just, and the just man wishes to do just things?

GOR. It seems so.

SOC. So the just man will never wish to do injustice.

GOR. Necessarily.

SOC. And the rhetorician is by this account necessarily just.

GOR. Yes.

SOC. Therefore, the rhetorician will never wish to do injustice.

GOR. It appears not.

SOC. Remember then what you said a little while ago; that we are
d not to complain about trainers or banish them from our cities if the boxer uses his skill wrongfully and does injustice, and so similarly, if an orator makes unjust use of his rhetoric, we are not to complain against his teacher nor expel him from the city, but only the man who did the wrong and abused his skill in rhetoric. That was the claim, wasn't it?

GOR. It was.

e SOC. Whereas now it appears that this very man, the rhetorician, would never do wrong?

GOR. It does.

SOC. And at the beginning of the discussion, Gorgias, it was said that rhetoric is about speeches—not speeches about the odd and even, but about the just and unjust.

GOR. Yes.

SOC. Well, I thought, when you said this, that rhetoric could never be unjust, since it is always making speeches about justice. But then a little later I was quite surprised to hear you say that the
461a orator could also use his rhetoric unjustly, and I believed these statements were not in accord. That's why I said what I did: that if you counted it gain to be refuted, as I do, it would be worth continuing the discussion, and otherwise not. And since we have come at last to examine it, you surely see for yourself that it is now agreed that the rhetorician cannot use his rhetoric unjustly,

and cannot be willing to do injustice. So to determine satisfac-
b   torily how matters actually stand, Gorgias, will require, and emphatically, no slight conversation.

Socrates and Polus: Real and
Apparent Good (461b–481b)

POL. What is this, Socrates! Do you really believe what you've been
saying about rhetoric? Do you think that Gorgias was too
ashamed not to admit that a rhetorician is not ignorant of what
things are just and beautiful and good, and that if he didn't know
when he came he'd teach him, and then from this admission a
c   certain inconsistency perhaps crept into his statements—which is
just what delights you, of course, when the results of your questioning lead to it—for do you think anyone would deny that he
knew what is just and could teach it to others? It is just plain
boorish of you to lead arguments into things like that.

SOC. Ah, pretty Polus, why else do we purposely possess friends
and children, unless it be that when, as we grow older and we
stumble, you young folk will be there to straighten out our lives
d   in words and in deeds. Just so now, if Gorgias and I have somehow stumbled in discussion, do come and set us straight. It is but
your duty. For my part, I am willing to take back any agreement
you think was reached improperly, whichever you please—but on
one condition.

POL. What is that?

SOC. That you bridle that long-answer method you tried using at
first.

POL. Why? Can't I talk any way I wish?

e   SOC. You would be treated terribly indeed, my friend, if having
come to Athens, where there is more freedom to talk than anywhere else in Greece, you were the only person here denied it.
But there is another side. If you speak at length and won't answer
462a   what is asked, wouldn't I in turn be terribly treated if I couldn't
leave and not listen to you? Now if you're concerned for the
argument we've carried on and wish to set it straight, then as I
just said, take back whatever you think you should, asking and
answering questions in turn just as Gorgias and I did, refuting
and being refuted. For you doubtless claim to know just what
Gorgias does, don't you?

POL. I do.

soc. Then do you also bid us on each occasion to ask whatever we wish of you, as a man who knows how to answer?

POL. Certainly.

b soc. Then do now whichever you wish: ask or answer.

POL. Very well, I will. Answer me, Socrates: since you think Gorgias is in perplexity about rhetoric, what do you say it is?

soc. Are you asking what art I say it is?

POL. Yes.

soc. It's no art at all, Polus, in my opinion, to answer you truthfully.

POL. Then what do you think it is?

c soc. A thing you claim to have made an art out of in that treatise of yours I read lately.

POL. What do you mean?

soc. I mean a certain knack.

POL. Then you think rhetoric is a knack?

soc. I do—subject, of course, to your correction.

POL. A knack for what?

soc. For producing a kind of gratification and pleasure.

POL. Then don't you think rhetoric is beautiful, if it can gratify people?

soc. What, Polus? Have you already learned what I claim it is, so
d that you can go on to ask whether I think it is beautiful?

POL. But haven't I learned that you say it is a knack?

soc. Please, since you value gratification, gratify me in one small thing.

POL. Very well.

soc. Ask me now what art I think pastry-cooking is.

POL. Then I ask, what art is pastry-cooking?

soc. None at all, Polus. Now say, "What is it, then?"

POL. I say it.

soc. A knack. Now say, "A knack for what?"

POL. I say it.

e soc. Then I say, a knack of producing gratification and pleasure, Polus.

POL. So pastry-cooking and rhetoric are the same?

soc. Not at all, but certainly part of the same practice.

POL. What practice do you mean?

soc. I'm afraid it may be rather boorish to state the truth; I hesitate because of Gorgias—I don't want him to think I am ridiculing
463a his pursuit. Actually, I don't really know whether what I call rhetoric is the rhetoric Gorgias pursues, for the argument just now didn't make clear to me what he believes it is. But what I call

rhetoric is a part of something which has nothing beautiful about it.

GOR. Please tell us what it is, Socrates. Don't be embarrassed on my account.

SOC. Very well, then, Gorgias, I think it is not the result of pursuing an art, but belongs to a soul given to boldness, shrewd at guess-
b   work, naturally clever in intercourse with people. I call its sum and substance flattery. This practice has many other parts also, one of which is pastry-cooking, which seems to be an art, but by my account is no art at all but merely a knack and a trick. I also call rhetoric part of this, along with cosmetics and sophistry— four parts dealing with four objects. If then Polus wishes to in-quire, let him do so, for he has not yet learned what part of
c   flattery I say rhetoric is. It escaped his notice that I hadn't an-swered yet, and he asked instead whether I didn't believe it beau-tiful. I will not answer whether I believe rhetoric beautiful or shameful before I first answer what it is. It would not be right, Polus. So if you wish to find out, ask me what part of flattery I say rhetoric is.

POL. Then I do ask: What part is it?

d   SOC. Will you understand when I answer? Rhetoric, according to my account, is an insubstantial image of a part of politics.

POL. What! Do you say it is beautiful, or shameful?

SOC. Shameful, say I, for I call evil things shameful, since I must answer you as though you already know what I mean.

GOR. By Zeus, Socrates, even I don't follow what you're saying.

e   SOC. Yes, and no wonder, Gorgias, for as yet I've said nothing clear. But Polus here is young and keen.

GOR. Then let him go, but please tell me why you say rhetoric is an insubstantial image of a part of politics.

SOC. Well, I will try to state what rhetoric appears to me to be, and if I miss the mark, Polus here will refute me. I assume you call something body, and something soul?

464a GOR. Of course.

SOC. And you also think there is a certain healthy condition for each?

GOR. I do.

SOC. And further a condition which seems healthy without really being so? I mean something like this: many people seem to have healthy bodies, and it would not be easy for anyone but a doctor or some trainer to recognize that they don't.

GOR. True.

SOC. Well, I say that such a thing exists both for body and soul, which makes the body and the soul seem to be in healthy condition while none the more so in fact.

b GOR. That is so.

SOC. Come then. If I can, I'll show you more clearly what I mean. I say that two arts correspond to these two objects. One art, dealing with the soul, I call politics. The other art deals with the body; I can't give you a single name for it, but I say that gymnastic and medicine are two parts of a single art of serving the body. In politics put law-giving for gymnastic and let corrective justice be the counterpart of medicine. Each of them has something in
c common with the other, medicine with gymnastic, justice with law-giving, because they are concerned with the same object; nevertheless, they also differ in some respect. Now there are these four things, and they ever serve what is best for the body and the soul respectively. Flattery perceives this. I don't mean she knows, but she shrewdly guesses, and she divides herself in four,
d puts on the mask of each part, and pretends to be the character she puts on,[3] caring nothing for what is best. She ever hunts after folly and deceives with what is most pleasant, so that she seems to be of highest worth. Pastry-cooking puts on the mask of medicine and pretends to know what foods are best for the body, so that if cook and doctor had to dispute before children, or before
e adults as foolish as children, about which of them, the doctor or the cook, understands what foods are good and bad, the doctor would starve to death. I call it flattery, and I say the thing is ugly
465a and shameful—this I direct to you, Polus—because it shrewdly guesses at what is pleasant, omitting what is best. And it is no art, I claim, but only a knack, for it has no reasoned account of the nature of what it administers or of those to whom it administers, with the result that it cannot state the cause of each treatment. I do not give the name of art to a thing which is irrational; if you dispute this, I'm willing to provide a reasoned account.

b   So I repeat: pastry-cooking is flattery disguised as medicine. In the same way, cosmetics is disguised gymnastic. Cosmetics is actually a fraudulent, baseborn, slavish knave; it tricks us with padding and makeup and polish and clothes, so that people carry around beauty not their own to the neglect of the beauty properly

3. The metaphor is that of actors wearing masks in a play.

theirs through gymnastic. To avoid a lengthy speech, I will put
it to you like a geometer, for at this point perhaps you may follow.

c Cosmetics is to gymnastic as pastry-cooking is to medicine. Furthermore, cosmetics is to gymnastic as sophistry is to law-giving;
and pastry-cooking is to medicine as rhetoric is to corrective justice. But I say that though sophist and rhetorician are in this way
distinct in nature, yet, because they are close, they get mixed up
in the same places and about the same things; they don't know
what to do with themselves, and neither does anyone else. In fact,

d if the soul didn't rule the body, but rather the body ruled itself,
if pastry-cooking and medicine were not recognized and distinguished by the soul, but the body by itself was left to judge,
measuring its interests by the gratification given it, the saying of
Anaxagoras would be only too true—you're familiar with it, my
dear Polus—"All things alike," mixed up together in the same
place. What belongs to pastry-cooking would be indistinguishable
from what belongs to medicine and health.

So you've heard what I say rhetoric is. It is the counterpart in

e the soul of pastry-cooking, as pastry-cooking is bodily rhetoric.
Maybe it's absurd for me to have spoken at such length myself
when I didn't allow you long speeches. Still, I have a good excuse.
You didn't understand when I spoke briefly, and you couldn't
make any use of the answers I gave you. You needed a thorough

466a explanation. So, too, if I can't make use of your answers either,
then you may speak at length, but if I can, then you ought to let
me do so. And if you can now make some use of this answer,
pray do.

POL. What are you saying then? You think rhetoric is flattery?

SOC. Why, I said part of flattery. You're too young to be forgetful,
Polus. What will you do later on?

POL. Then you think that, as flatterers, our good orators are regarded as worthless in their cities?

b SOC. Are you asking a question or beginning a speech?

POL. Asking a question.

SOC. Then I don't think they're regarded at all.

POL. Not regarded! Don't they have greatest power in their cities?

SOC. No, if by "power" you mean something good for him who has
it.

POL. Certainly I mean that.

SOC. Then orators have less power in their cities than anyone, it
seems to me.

c POL. What? Aren't they like tyrants? Don't they put to death whomever they wish, confiscate property, and send into exile whomever
they think fit?

SOC. I swear, Polus, I'm undecided each time you speak whether
you're asserting these things yourself and presenting your own
judgment, or questioning me.

POL. Why, I'm questioning you.

SOC. Very well, my friend. In that case you're asking me two questions at once.

POL. Why two?

d SOC. I think you just said something to this effect, that orators, like
tyrants, put to death whomever they wish, and confiscate property and drive into exile whomever they think fit.

POL. Yes.

SOC. Then I say these are two questions, and I'll answer them both
for you. I claim, Polus, that orators and tyrants have the least

e power in their cities, as I just said; for they virtually never do
what they wish, even though they do whatever may seem best to
them.

POL. Isn't that great power?

SOC. No—so Polus says, at least.

POL. I say no? No, I say yes!

SOC. No, by God, you don't, since you said that great power is good
for him who has it.

POL. Yes, I say that.

SOC. Then do you think it good if a man does what he thinks best,
but lacks intelligence? Do you call that great power too?

POL. No, I don't.

SOC. Then will you show that orators possess intelligence, that rhet-
467a oric is art and not flattery, and so refute me? If you leave me
unrefuted, the orators who do what seems good to them in their
cities, and the tyrants, will have got nothing good from it. But
power is good, you claim, and doing what seems good without
intelligence you also agree is evil, don't you?

POL. I do.

SOC. Then how could orators and tyrants have great power in their
cities, unless Socrates is refuted by Polus and convinced that they
do what they wish?

b POL. Listen to the fellow!

SOC. I deny that they do what they wish. Refute me.

POL. Didn't you just agree that they do what seems best to them?

soc. Yes, and I agree to it now.

pol. Then don't they do what they wish?

soc. I say no.

pol. Even though they do what seems best to them?

soc. I say yes.

pol. This is shocking, Socrates, monstrously so.

c soc. Cease censure, peerless Polus—to address you in your own style. If you can question me, then show that I'm wrong; if not, then answer yourself.

pol. But I am willing to answer just to see what you mean.

soc. Do people seem to you to wish the things they on each occasion do, or rather that for the sake of which they do them? For example: do patients who drink medicine by doctor's orders seem to you to wish what they do, to drink medicine and suffer, or do they wish rather to be healthy, and drink for the sake of that?

pol. Clearly, they wish to be healthy.

d soc. So too with seafarers and other businessmen engaged in trade. They do not wish the thing they on each occasion do, for who wishes to sail and run risks and have trouble? But they do, I think, wish that for the sake of which they sail, namely, to be wealthy. They sail for the sake of wealth.

pol. Of course.

soc. Then isn't this so with everything? If someone does something for the sake of something, he does not wish the thing he does, but that for the sake of which he does it?

e pol. Yes.

soc. Now, is there anything at all that is not either good, or evil, or intermediate between these and neither good nor evil?

pol. Necessarily not, Socrates.

soc. Then do you say that wisdom and health and wealth and other such things are good, and their opposites bad?

pol. I do.

soc. But by things neither good nor evil, do you mean things which
468a sometimes partake of good but sometimes of evil and sometimes of neither—sitting, for example, and walking and running and sailing, or for example again, sticks and stones and things of that sort. Do you mean these? Or is there something else you call neither good nor evil?

pol. No, these.

soc. Now, when people do these intermediate things, do they do them for the sake of good things, or good things for the sake of intermediate things?

POL. Intermediate things for good things, surely.

b SOC. Therefore it is in pursuit of the good that we in fact walk when we walk, believing it to be better, and oppositely, we stand when we stand for the sake of the same thing, namely the good. Not so?

POL. Yes.

SOC. And so also we kill, if we kill someone, and exile and confiscate property, in the belief that it is better for us to do these things than not?

POL. Certainly.

SOC. Therefore, it is for the sake of the good that those who do all these things do them.

POL. I agree.

SOC. And we agreed that what we do for the sake of something else is not itself wished, but rather that for the sake of which we do it?

c POL. Yes, certainly.

SOC. So we do not wish simply to kill or exile or confiscate. If these are beneficial we wish to do them, but if harmful we do not. For we wish for good things, as you say, but we do not wish for things neither good nor evil, nor for evils. Do you think I speak truth, Polus, or not? Why don't you answer?

POL. Yes, truth.

d SOC. If we do agree on this, then if anyone, tyrant or orator, kills someone or exiles him or confiscates property, believing it better for himself when it is in fact worse, he surely does what seems good to him. Not so?

POL. Yes.

SOC. Does he then also do what he wishes, if these things are in fact evils? Why don't you answer?

POL. All right. I don't think he does what he wishes.

e SOC. Then if according to your agreement great power is something good, how is it possible for a man such as this to have great power in that city?

POL. It is not.

SOC. So I spoke the truth when I said that it is possible for a man to do in a city what seems good to him, and yet not to have great power, and not to do what he wishes.

POL. Oh, of course, Socrates. As though you wouldn't accept the

ability to do what seemed good to you in the city rather than not,
nor be envious when you saw somebody killing whom he saw fit,
or seizing property or imprisoning him!

soc. Justly, you mean, or unjustly?

469a POL. Whichever. Isn't it enviable either way?

soc. Hold your tongue, Polus!

POL. Why?

soc. Because one must not envy the unenviable or wretched, but
pity them.

POL. Really! You think that's how it is with the men I mentioned?

soc. Of course.

POL. You think a man who can kill whomever he thinks fit, and kill
justly, is wretched and pitiable?

soc. No I don't, but neither do I think him enviable.

POL. But didn't you just say he was wretched?

b soc. Yes, my friend, if he kills unjustly, and he is pitiable in addition. If justly, he is merely unenviable.

POL. Well, at least the man unjustly killed is pitiable and wretched.

soc. Less than his killer, Polus, and less than a man killed justly.

POL. How can that be, Socrates?

soc. Because the greatest of evils is the doing of injustice.

POL. The greatest? Isn't suffering injustice greater?

soc. By no means.

POL. You therefore would wish to suffer injustice rather than do
it?

c soc. I would wish neither. But if it were necessary either to do
injustice or suffer it, I would choose to suffer it rather than to
do it.

POL. Then you wouldn't accept being a tyrant?

soc. No, not if you mean by tyranny what I do.

POL. Why, I mean what I was just saying: a man with power in the
city to do what he thinks fit—kill, exile, do anything as suits his
own judgment.

soc. Dear friend, let me state a case, and then please take up the

d   argument. Suppose I had a knife under my arm in a crowded
marketplace and I said to you, "Polus, I've just now acquired a
kind of power which is tyrannical and astonishing; for if it seems
to me that one of these people you see here ought to die this very
moment, die he will, whomever I think fit; and if it seems to me
he ought to have his head split open, split at once it will be; and

e   if his cloak needs slitting, slit it will be—so great is my power in this our city!" And if you didn't believe me, I'd show you the knife. When you saw it you might say, "Why Socrates, everybody then has great power, since in this way you could burn down a house, whichever one you thought fit, yes, and even the dock-yards of Athens and the fleet and the rest of the shipping too, public and private." But surely, that's not great power, merely doing what seems good to one. Or do you think so?

POL. Of course not, in those cases.

470a SOC. Then can you state why you might complain against that sort of power?

POL. I can.

SOC. Why? Please tell me.

POL. Because necessarily, anyone who acts that way will be pun-ished.

SOC. Being punished isn't bad?

POL. Of course it is.

SOC. Then, my friend, it appears once again for you that if doing what *seems* good is followed by doing what is beneficial, it *is* good; and this, as it seems, is great power. Otherwise, it is bad and
b   amounts to weakness. Let us also consider this: should we agree that sometimes it is better to do the things we just mentioned, killing and exiling and confiscating property, and sometimes not?

POL. Of course.

SOC. Then this too, as it seems, is agreed by you and by me.

POL. Yes.

SOC. Now, when do you say it is better to do these things? State by what mark you distinguish.

POL. Socrates, why don't you answer that yourself?

c SOC. Well, I say, Polus, if you'd rather hear it from me, that it is better when someone does these things justly, but when unjustly, worse.

POL. You're really hard to refute, Socrates! Even a child could show you're wrong.

SOC. Then I shall be exceedingly grateful to the child, and equally so to you, if you refute me and relieve me of nonsense. So please don't grow weary in doing good to a friend, but refute me.

d POL. Well, Socrates, there's no need to refute you with events from the distant past. Only the other day things happened sufficient to refute you and prove that many men who do injustice are happy.

SOC. What sort of things?

POL. No doubt you observe this fellow Archelaus son of Perdiccas, ruler of Macedonia?

SOC. If not, at least I hear of him.

POL. Well, does he seem to you wretched or happy?

SOC. I don't know, Polus, for I've never met the man.

e POL. Really? You could tell if you met him, but you otherwise don't know right off that he's happy?

SOC. I most emphatically do not.

POL. Clearly, then, Socrates, you'll even say you don't know whether the Great King is happy.

SOC. Yes, and I'll be telling the truth, for I don't know how he is in respect to education and justice.

POL. Really? One's whole happiness consists in that?

SOC. So at least I claim, Polus. For I say that the beautiful and good man and woman are happy, but the unjust and wicked are wretched.

471a POL. So according to your account, this fellow Archelaus is wretched?

SOC. Provided, my friend, that he is unjust.

POL. But how could he not be unjust! The kingdom he now holds did not belong to him, because his mother was slave to Alcetas, Perdiccas's brother, and so by rights he himself was Alcetas's slave, and if he wished to do the just thing he'd be a slave to Alcetas, and, by your account, be happy. But as it is, he has become most remarkably wretched, since he has done the great-
b est wrongs. First he summoned his master and uncle Alcetas under the pretext of restoring the kingdom Perdiccas took from him, entertained him as a guest, got him drunk, along with his son Alexander, his own cousin and just about his own age, threw them both into a wagon, took them out by night, cut their throats and did away with them. Furthermore, after he did these wrongs, he failed to see that he had now become wretched, nor did he
c repent, but a little later took his brother, a lad about seven years old, the legitimate son of Perdiccas to whom the kingdom rightly belonged, and having no wish to make himself happy by justly raising him and handing the kingdom over to him, he instead threw him into a well and drowned him and told his mother Cleopatra that he fell into a well and died while chasing a goose. So now, accordingly, since he is the greatest wrongdoer in Macedonia, he is also the most wretched man in all Macedonia, rather than the happiest, and perhaps there is any Athenian, beginning

d   with yourself, who would prefer to be some other Macedonian
     than Archelaus.
    SOC. At the beginning of our talk, Polus, I commended you because
     you seemed to me well educated in rhetoric, though neglectful
     of dialectic. Is this now the argument by which even a child might
     refute me? By which, as you think, you have now refuted my
     claim that he who does injustice is not happy? How so, my friend?
     On the contrary, I don't agree to a thing you've said.
e   POL. You don't want to agree, because what I say seems as true to
     you as it does to me.
    SOC. No, my dear friend. You keep trying to refute me rhetorically,
     as people in the lawcourts believe they refute. One party there
     actually thinks he refutes the other when he provides a multitude
     of well-esteemed witnesses for the things he says, while the op-
     posing party produces only one or none. But that kind of refu-
472a tation is worth nothing in regard to truth; sometimes a man may
     in fact be overwhelmed by the multitude of false but respectable
     witnesses against him. And so it is now with your claims. Nearly
     everybody, Athenians and foreigners, will say the same thing,
     should you wish to provide witnesses to testify that I am not
     telling the truth. You may have for your witnesses, if you wish,
     Nicias son of Niceratus, and his brothers along with him, whose
     tripods stand lined in a row in the precinct of Dionysius. Or if
b   you wish, there is Aristocrates son of Scellias, whose beautiful
     votive offering is set up at Delphi; or the whole house of Pericles;
     or any other family you may wish to pick out from among the
     people here. While I being but one, do not agree with you; for
     you do not compel me, but instead provide a cloud of false wit-
     nesses against me, attempting to oust me from my patrimony,
     which is the truth. But if I do not provide you yourself as a
     witness, being but one man, to testify to the truth of what I say,
c   then I think I have accomplished nothing important concerning
     the issues of our argument. Nor have you, unless I, but one man,
     testify in your behalf, and you dismiss all the others. Thus you
     and many others mean one thing by refutation, I on the contrary
     mean another. Let us then lay them alongside each other and
     investigate how they differ. After all, the subject about which we
     disagree is hardly trivial, but in effect concerns things about
     which it is most excellent to know and most shameful not to know,
     for the sum and substance of it is knowledge or ignorance of who
     is happy and who is not. Take first the immediate question which

d   the argument now concerns. You believe it possible for a man to
prosper and yet do wrong and be unjust, since you believe
Archelaus is unjust but happy. Isn't this what we are to consider
as your view?

POL. Yes, certainly.

SOC. And I say it's impossible. So here is one point in dispute. Very
well, take the next. Being unjust, will he be happy if he pays the
penalty and is punished?

POL. By no means, since in that case he would be most miserable.

e   SOC. Then if the unjust man is not punished, according to your
account he will be happy?

POL. Yes.

SOC. But according to my opinion, Polus, he who does injustice,
the unjust man, is utterly wretched; more wretched, however, if
he is not punished and does not pay the penalty, and less
wretched if he does pay and meets with justice at the hands of
gods and men.

473a POL. Surely you try to state absurdities, Socrates!

SOC. And I shall also try to make you, Polus, state the same thing,
for I consider you a friend. Now these are the points on which
we differ. Examine them for yourself. I said earlier, I think, that
doing injustice is more evil than suffering injustice.

POL. Quite so.

SOC. But you, that suffering injustice is worse.

POL. Yes.

SOC. And I asserted that those who do injustice are wretched, and
I was refuted by you.

POL. You most certainly were.

b   SOC. So you think at least, Polus.

POL. Yes, and think truly.

SOC. Perhaps. But those who do injustice are in turn happy, you
think, if they go unpunished.

POL. Certainly.

SOC. While I claim that those are the most wretched who are punished least. Do you wish to refute this too?

POL. It's no harder to refute this than the other, Socrates.

SOC. No, not harder, Polus, but impossible. For the truth is never
refuted.

POL. What do you mean? Suppose a man is caught wrongfully plot-
c   ting to make himself a tyrant. He is caught, racked, castrated,
has his eyes burnt out. Horribly mutilated in all sorts of ways, he

is made to watch his wife and children subjected to every kind
of torment, and at the end he is crucified or burnt in a coat of
pitch. That man will be happier than if he had escaped, established himself as tyrant, lived out his life ruling his city and doing
whatever he wished, envied and felicitated by citizens and for-

d eigners alike? You mean it is impossible to refute *that*?

soc. This time you make my flesh creep, noble Polus, and yet you
do not refute. And just now you were summoning witnesses.
Nevertheless, please do refresh my memory a little: wrongfully
plotting to become tyrant, you said?

pol. I did.

soc. Then neither of them will ever be happier, neither the man
who unjustly makes himself a tyrant nor the man who is pun-

e ished, for of two wretched people, neither is happier. However,
the man who escapes punishment and becomes tyrant is more
wretched.

What is this, Polus? You laugh? Is this yet another form of
refutation, to laugh at someone when he says something but not
refute him?

pol. Don't you think you have been refuted, Socrates, when you
say such things as no man would assent to? Just ask anybody here.

soc. Why Polus, I'm not one of your politicians. Only last year
when I was chosen by lot for the Council and my deme had the

474a Prytany and I had to put a question to the vote, I was laughed
at for not knowing how to do it. So don't now bid me take a vote
among our company. As I was just saying, if you do not have a
better refutation than this, then let me take a turn and try the
sort of refutation I think is required. For I know how to provide
one witness to what I say, namely, the man to whom my argument
is directed; I dismiss a multitude of witnesses because I can't
carry on a discussion with a crowd, but I know how to put the

b vote to one. See then if you are willing to answer my questions
and so give me a turn at refuting you. I really do suppose that
you and I and everyone else believe the doing of injustice to be
more evil than the suffering of it, and not being punished more
evil than being punished.

pol. And I say, not I, nor anyone else. Would you accept suffering
injustice rather than doing it?

soc. Yes, and so would you and everybody else.

pol. Far from it. Not I, not you, not anyone.

c soc. Very well, answer my questions.

POL. Certainly. In fact, I want to know what you'll say.

soc. Then in order to know, please reply as though I were questioning you from the very beginning: Which seems to you more evil, Polus, doing injustice or suffering it?

POL. Suffering it.

soc. Really? Which of the two, doing injustice or suffering it, is more ugly? Please answer.

POL. Doing it.

soc. If more ugly, then also more evil?

POL. Not at all.

soc. I see. You believe, it seems, that beautiful and good, ugly and
d   evil, are not the same.

POL. Indeed.

soc. But what about this: Is there nothing you look to on each occasion in calling all beautiful things such as bodies and colors, shapes and sounds and practices, beautiful? For example, first take beautiful bodies. Don't you either call them beautiful according to the use relative to which each may be useful, or according to a kind of pleasure, if they cause delight to the beholder in viewing them? Can you mention any beauty of body outside these?

e POL. No, I can't.

soc. And so too for everything else. Take shapes and colors; it is either through some pleasure or some benefit, or both, that you call them beautiful?

POL. I do.

soc. And so similarly with sounds and all that has to do with music?

POL. Yes.

soc. Moreover, what is beautiful respecting laws and practices is surely not outside these, namely, being either beneficial or pleasant or both.

475a POL. It does not seem so to me.

soc. And so similarly with the beauty of studies?

POL. Certainly. You now beautifully mark off the beautiful, Socrates, defining it by pleasure and good.

soc. Then the ugly is defined by the opposite, by pain and evil?

POL. Necessarily.

soc. When therefore of two beautiful things, one is more beautiful, it will be more beautiful because it surpasses the other in one or both of two things, either in pleasure or in benefit, or both.

POL. Certainly.

b SOC. When of two ugly things, one is more ugly, it will be more ugly because it surpasses either in pain or in evil. Or is this not necessary?

POL. Yes, it is.

SOC. Come, then, what did you mean just now about the doing and suffering of injustice? Weren't you claiming that suffering it is more evil, doing it more ugly?

POL. I was.

SOC. Now if doing injustice is more ugly and shameful than suffering it, it is more ugly and shameful either because it surpasses it in pain, or in evil, or in both. Or is this not also necessary?

POL. Of course it is.

c SOC. First then let us consider whether doing injustice surpasses suffering it in pain. Are those who do injustice in greater distress than those who suffer injustice?

POL. By no means, Socrates.

SOC. So therefore it does not exceed in pain.

POL. No indeed.

SOC. If not in pain, then not in both.

POL. It appears not.

SOC. Only the other is left.

POL. Yes.

SOC. In evil.

POL. It seems so.

SOC. So doing injustice is more evil than suffering injustice because it surpasses it in evil.

POL. Clearly.

d SOC. Now, wasn't it agreed by most of mankind, and formerly by you, that doing injustice is more ugly than suffering it?

POL. Yes.

SOC. But now it appeared more evil.

POL. It seems so.

SOC. Then would you rather accept what is more evil and more ugly in place of what is less so? Don't shrink from answering, Polus, it won't hurt you. Nobly submit to the argument, as to a doctor, and answer Yea or Nay.

e POL. Well, I would not accept it, Socrates.

SOC. Would any other man?

POL. It seems to me not, at least according to this argument.

SOC. I spoke the truth, therefore, in saying that neither I nor you nor any other man would choose doing injustice over suffering it, for it is more evil.

POL. It appears so.

SOC. Do you see, Polus, that when this kind of refutation is laid alongside that one, they are not at all alike? Even though everyone else agrees with you except me, you, being but one man alone, suffice for me as the supporting witness, and I put the vote to you alone and dismiss the rest. Let then this stand as true for us.

476a

Next, let us examine the second point over which we disagreed: whether being punished for injustice is the greatest of evils, as you believed, or whether not being punished is greater, as I, on the contrary, believe. Let us consider it in this way: do you call being punished[4] and being justly chastised for doing injustice the same?

POL. I do.

b SOC. Then can you say that all just things are not beautiful insofar as they are just? Please consider carefully and answer.

POL. Why, it seems to me they are, Socrates.

SOC. Then consider this too: if someone does something, isn't there necessarily also something affected by what he does?

POL. Yes, I think so.

SOC. Does the thing affected suffer what the doer does in the way the doer does it? I mean this: if someone strikes, something necessarily is struck?

POL. Necessarily.

SOC. And if the striker strikes hard or quickly, the thing struck is so struck?

c POL. Yes.

SOC. Therefore, the effect on the thing struck is of the same sort as the action of the striker?

POL. Certainly.

SOC. Again, if someone burns, something necessarily is burned?

POL. Of course.

SOC. And if he burns severely or painfully, what is burned is so burned as the burner burns?

POL. Certainly.

SOC. The same account too if someone cuts? For something is cut.

POL. Yes.

---

4. *to didonai diken,* literally, "to give right."

soc. And if the cut is large or deep or painful, what is cut is cut
d the same way the cutter cuts.

pol. It appears so.

soc. Now see whether you agree that what I've just been saying
can be summed up in a general way: as the doer does, in that
same way does the sufferer suffer.

pol. Yes, I agree.

soc. Then since this is agreed, is being punished suffering something or doing it?

pol. Necessarily, Socrates, it is suffering something.

soc. At the hands of someone doing something?

pol. Of course, the person who chastises.

soc. And when he chastises correctly, he chastises justly?

e pol. Yes.

soc. Doing what is just, or not?

pol. What is just.

soc. So the person chastised, in being punished, suffers what is
just?

pol. It appears so.

soc. And it was agreed, I think, that just things are beautiful?

pol. Indeed.

soc. Therefore, one of them does beautiful things, and the other,
the person punished, suffers them?

pol. Yes.

477a soc. Then if beautiful things, good things? For either pleasant or
beneficial?

pol. Necessarily.

soc. Therefore, he who is punished suffers good things?

pol. It seems so.

soc. He is therefore benefited?

pol. Yes.

soc. Is it the benefit I understand? Does his soul become better, if
he is chastised justly?

pol. Yes, probably.

soc. The person punished, therefore, is relieved of evil of soul?

pol. Yes.

b soc. And so relieved of the greatest evil? Consider as follows: in
the constitution of one's fortune, do you observe any other evil
than poverty?

pol. No, it is poverty.

SOC. What about the constitution of the body? Would you say evil is weakness and disease and deformity and things like that?

POL. I would.

SOC. Now, you believe that there is such a thing as vice in a soul?

POL. Of course.

SOC. Now, don't you call this injustice and folly and cowardice and such things as that?

POL. Certainly.

SOC. So in respect of money, body, and soul, three things, you have c named three vices, namely, poverty, disease, and injustice.

POL. Yes.

SOC. Now, which of these vices is most ugly? Is it not injustice, and in sum, vice of soul?

POL. Certainly.

SOC. If then most ugly, also most evil?

POL. What do you mean, Socrates?

SOC. This. It was agreed before that what is most ugly is ever so either because it produces greatest pain, or harm, or both.

POL. Certainly.

SOC. And we just now agreed that injustice and all vice of soul is most ugly?

d POL. We did.

SOC. So either it is most painful, and most ugly because it surpasses in pain, or because it surpasses in harm, or both.

POL. Necessarily.

SOC. Well, is it more painful to be unjust, cowardly, foolish, and intemperate than to be poor and sick?

POL. I don't think so, Socrates, at least from these admissions.

SOC. Yet vice of soul is of all things most ugly. How monstrously e great then must be its harm, how extraordinarily it must therefore surpass other things in evil, since according to your account it does not in fact surpass in pain.

POL. So it appears.

SOC. Moreover, surely what surpasses in greatest harm would be surpassing great in evil.

POL. Yes.

SOC. Injustice, therefore, and intemperance and the other vices of the soul, are the greatest of all evils.

POL. It appears so.

SOC. What art, then, relieves poverty? Money-making?

POL. Yes.

soc. And what relieves disease? Medicine?

478a POL. Necessarily.

soc. But what relieves vice and injustice? If you do not find such easy passage here, consider this: whither and to whom do we take those ill of body?

POL. To the doctors, Socrates.

soc. And whither those unjust and intemperate?

POL. You mean to the judge?

soc. Yes, and in order to be punished?

POL. Yes.

soc. Now, don't those who chasten correctly use a kind of justice in chastening?

POL. Plainly they do.

b soc. Money-making therefore takes away poverty, medicine takes away disease, and corrective justice takes away intemperance and injustice.

POL. It appears so.

soc. Which of them is most beautiful?

POL. How do you mean?

soc. Among money-making, medicine and corrective justice.

POL. Why, justice far excels, Socrates.

soc. Then once again, it produces either the greatest pleasure or benefit or both, if most beautiful.

POL. Yes.

soc. Now, is medical treatment pleasant? Do those who are doctored rejoice?

POL. I think not.

soc. Yet it is beneficial, isn't it?

c POL. Yes.

soc. Because it takes away great evil, so that it is of advantage to endure the pain and be well.

POL. Of course.

soc. Now so far as the body is concerned, would a man be happier being doctored, or not being sick to begin with?

POL. Clearly, not being sick.

soc. Yes, for happiness does not consist in relief from evil, it seems, but in not possessing evil to begin with.

POL. That is true.

d soc. Really? Of two people who have an evil in body or soul, which of the two is more wretched, the man who is doctored and relieved of the evil, or the man who is not doctored and keeps it?

POL. The man not doctored, it appears to me.

SOC. Now, being punished was relief from the greatest evil, namely vice?

POL. It was.

SOC. Because corrective justice causes temperance and makes men more just, and is medicine for vice.

POL. Yes.

SOC. Happiest therefore is the man who has no evil in his soul, since that appeared greatest among evils.

e POL. Clearly so.

SOC. Second, I suppose, the man relieved of it.

POL. It seems so.

SOC. That is, the man who has been admonished, rebuked, and punished.

POL. Yes.

SOC. The worst life, therefore, is his who has injustice and is not relieved of it.

POL. It appears so.

SOC. Now, that is the man who does the greatest wrongs and com-
479a mits the greatest injustice but contrives not to be admonished nor chastened nor punished, as you say is the condition of Archelaus and those other tyrants and orators and potentates.

POL. It seems so.

SOC. Yet surely, my friend, these men have contrived virtually the same thing as someone afflicted with the greatest diseases who contrives not to pay penalty to the doctors nor suffer treatment for faults of the body, frightened like a little child at the cutting
b and burning, because it hurts. Doesn't it seem so to you too?

POL. It does.

SOC. Yes, and it is due, it seems, to ignorance of the nature of bodily health and virtue. For from what we have now agreed, those who flee justice very likely do something of this sort, Polus: They look at the pain of it but are blind to its benefits, ignorant of how much more wretched it is to dwell with an unhealthy soul than an unhealthy body, a soul rotted by injustice and unholiness.
c Whence it is they do everything so as not to be punished and relieved of the greatest evil, and contrive to acquire money and friends and ability to speak as persuasively as possible. But if what we have agreed to is true, Polus, do you perceive the consequences of the argument? Or do you wish us to reckon them up?

POL. If it seems good to you.

SOC. Very well: does it follow that injustice and the doing of it are the greatest evil?

d POL. It appears so.

SOC. Moreover, punishment, paying the penalty, appeared to take away this evil?

POL. Very probably.

SOC. And not paying the penalty keeping the evil?

POL. Yes.

SOC. The doing of injustice, therefore, is second in magnitude among evils; but to do injustice and not be punished is greatest of all and by nature first among evils.

POL. It seems so.

SOC. Now, didn't we disagree about just this, my friend? You, on the one hand, counted Archelaus happy, even though he did the

e greatest injustice and paid no penalty, while I, on the contrary, believed that Archelaus or any other man who is not punished for doing injustice is wretched beyond the rest of men, and that he who does injustice is even more wretched than he who suffers it, and that he who does not pay the penalty is more wretched than he who does. Weren't those the things I said?

POL. Yes.

SOC. It has, then, been shown that they were said truly?

POL. It appears so.

480a SOC. Very well. Then if these things are true, Polus, what is the great usefulness of rhetoric? It follows from what has now been agreed that a man must especially be on guard not to do injustice, and thus get sufficiency of evil. Not so?

POL. Of course.

SOC. But if he does do injustice, either himself or anyone he cares about, he should voluntarily go to where he will be punished as quickly as possible; he should go to the judge as to the doctor,

b eagerly, lest the disease of injustice become chronic and cause a hidden festering in his soul, incurable. What is our view, Polus, if the former agreements stand for us? Is it not necessary that these in this way accord with those, but not otherwise?

POL. What else can we say, Socrates?

SOC. In offering a defense for injustice, therefore, whether it is ourselves, our parents, our friends, our children, or our country which has done wrong, rhetoric is of no use at all to us, Polus—

c unless one puts it to the opposite use. A man must especially accuse himself, and next his family, and any of his friends who happen to do injustice. He must not conceal it, but must drag the injustice to light in order to be punished and become healthy. He must force himself and others not to flinch, but close his eyes and submit well and bravely to the cutting and burning, as though it were by the doctor, for he is in pursuit of what is beautiful and good, and does not take pain into consideration. If the injustice he has done deserves a flogging, he must submit to blows; if

d prison, to bondage; if a fine, to payment; if exile, to exile; if death, then to death. He is to be the first accuser of himself and his relatives, and should use his rhetoric for that purpose, so that when their injustices have been brought to light they may be relieved of the greatest evil, which is injustice. Do we assert this or not, Polus?

e POL. It seems crazy to me, Socrates. And yet, perhaps it agrees with what was said earlier.

SOC. Then either those agreements must be overturned, or these necessarily follow?

POL. Yes, that is surely so.

SOC. Turn it around again the opposite way. If ever it were necessary to do evil to someone, enemy or anyone else, provided only that it is not oneself who is wronged by the enemy—for this must be guarded against—but if the enemy does injustice to someone else, then one must contrive in every way, by word and deed, that

481a he not be punished nor brought before the judge; but if he is brought, one should ensure that he, the enemy, get off and not be punished. If he has stolen much gold, he is not to restore it but keep it and squander it unjustly and godlessly on himself and his companions. If in turn he has done injustice worthy of death, he must not die, not ever, if possible, but be immortal in his

b wickedness, or if not, then live as long as possible being such as he is. It is for this kind of thing, it seems to me, Polus, that rhetoric is useful. I doubt that someone who does not intend to do injustice has any great use for it—assuming, of course, that there is any use for it at all, a thing which has nowhere appeared in our previous arguments.

Socrates and Callicles: Two Visions of Life (481b–505d)

CAL. Tell me, Chaerephon, is Socrates jesting or in earnest?

CHR. Why Callicles, he seems to me immensely in earnest. Still, nothing like asking him.

CAL. I want to, most emphatically. Tell me, Socrates, should we take
c   you now as in earnest or jesting? For if you are in earnest and what you say is really true, our human life would be turned upside down. We would be doing exactly the opposite, it seems, of what we should.

SOC. Why Callicles, if men had no common feelings, some feeling one thing, some another, if instead each of us was affected in a way peculiar to himself and unshared by others, it would be no
d   easy thing to indicate what we feel to one another. I say this because I recognize that you and I are at the moment affected in somewhat the same way. Each of has two loves: I love philosophy and Alcibiades son of Cleinias, and you love the Athenian demos, the popular majority, and also Demos son of Pyrilampes. Now I perceive that, for all your cleverness, you can't contradict
e   what your beloved says however he says it: you shift back and forth. In the Assembly, if the demos of Athens denies something you say is true, you change and say what they wish, and you're affected that way too by this beautiful youth, the son of Pyrilampes here. You can't contradict the counsel and arguments of those you love, so that if someone were surprised at what you sometimes say because it's so absurd, you might perhaps tell him,
482a if you wished to tell the truth, that unless somebody stops those you love from saying those things, you won't stop saying them either.

Well, consider yourself then also obliged to hear something different but of the same sort from me. Don't be surprised at what I say, but make philosophy, my own beloved, stop saying them; for she says what you just heard me say, my friend, and she is far less fickle than other loves. The son of Cleinias here has different arguments on different occasions, but philosophy
b   ever the same ones, and though what she says now surprises you, you were present when she spoke. So either refute what she just said, and prove that doing wrong and being punished for it are not ultimate among evils, or if you leave this unrefuted, then by the Egyptian dog-god, Callicles will not agree with Callicles, and you will be at discord with yourself throughout your life. For my own part, my friend, I would think it better that my lyre be out
c   of tune and discordant or a chorus I might direct, better that a

whole multitude of people disagree and contradict me, than that
I, but one man, should contradict and be at discord with myself.

CAL. Socrates, I think you speak with a kind of childish extrava-
gance, like a real demagogue. You play the orator now because
Polus got himself in the same fix he accused Gorgias of. He said,
I think, that when you asked Gorgias whether, if someone came
to him wishing to learn rhetoric without knowing what things are
d   just, he would teach him, Gorgias was ashamed and said he'd
teach him, because by common custom people would be angered
if anyone should refuse. Because of that agreement, Gorgias was
compelled to contradict himself, which is just what you like. And
at that point Polus laughed at you, and rightly, I think, but now
he in turn has suffered the same thing himself. That's just why
I don't admire Polus: he conceded to you that doing injustice is
more ugly than suffering it, and he in turn got tied up and had
e   his mouth stopped with that agreement, because he was ashamed
to say what he thought. Really, Socrates, you keep leading matters
around to such vulgar demagoguery as this—to what is not beautiful by nature but by custom and law—while claiming to pursue
the truth. But nature and law are for the most part opposite to
483a   each other, so that if a man is ashamed and doesn't dare say what
he thinks, he is compelled to contradict himself, which is the basis
for the clever trick you've invented for spoiling arguments; you
reply by a question according to nature if someone means law,
and according to law if he means nature. Right here, the question
about doing and suffering wrong is a clear example. Polus meant
that doing wrong is more ugly according to law, and you pursued
the argument according to nature, for by nature everything is
more ugly which is also more evil, and it is more evil to suffer
wrong, but by law, doing wrong is more evil. It is not the part of
b   a man to suffer wrong, but of some slave better off dead than
alive, or anyone else who, wronged and abused, cannot protect
himself or someone he cares for.

But I think that those who lay down laws are weak and numerous, so they lay down laws and assign their praise and blame
relative to themselves and to their own advantage. They frighten
c   the stronger among their fellows, who are able to get a greater
share, so that they may not have a larger share than themselves,
claiming that overreaching is ugly and unjust and that to seek to
have more than others is to do wrong. I think they delight in
equality because they are inferior. That is why by law it is said to

be ugly and unjust to seek a share greater than the multitude, and why they call it wrongdoing.

d   But nature herself reveals, I think, that it is just for the better to have a greater share than the worse, right for the more powerful to have more than the weak. For this is clearly true everywhere, among other animals, and in every city and every race of men, it has been counted just that the stronger should rule the weaker and have a greater share. By what other justice did Xerxes

e   invade Greece, or his father Scythia?—one could mention a thousand examples of the sort. I think they acted according to what is just by nature, and yes, by Zeus, according to a very law of nature—though not, perhaps, according to that law which we lay down.

We shape and mold the best and strongest among us, catching them in youth like young lions, and we enslave them with magic

484a and incantations, telling them that equality is necessary, that this is what is beautiful and just. But when a man is born of sufficient nature he will I think shake off all these fetters, break through his bonds and run free, trampling under foot our writings and charms and spells and laws, which are all contrary to nature. Then is our slave, risen up, revealed to be our master. There and

b   at that point does the justice of nature flash forth.

I think Pindar indicates what I mean in the ode where he says,

> Law king of all,
> Of mortals and immortals

and then says that law,

> Takes greatest violence
> with the high hand, making it just.
> In witness I call the deeds of Heracles,
> Since, with price unpaid

Something like that, I don't know the ode exactly, but he tells

c   how Heracles drove off the cattle of Geryones neither given nor purchased, because it was just by nature and the chattels and other possessions of worse and inferior men all belong to the better and stronger.

That is the real truth of the matter, and you will understand it when you at last dismiss philosophy and go on to more important things. Philosophy is no doubt pleasant enough, Socrates, taken moderately and in youth, but it is the ruination of a man if he stays in it too long. However well endowed his nature, if he dwells in philosophy much past youth he necessarily becomes a

d   stranger to affairs in which he ought to be experienced, if he is to be well regarded and a gentleman, noble and good. Philosophers in fact are inexperienced in the laws of their city, inexperienced in the language to be used in business contracts, public and private, inexperienced in human pleasures and desires, utterly inexperienced, in a word, in human character. So when they come to action, public or private, they make fools of themselves,

e   just as, I think, politicians do when they turn to your discussions and disputes. Euripides drew the proper consequence: "Each man is drawn to the thing in which he shines, Allotting the greatest part of his day where he is at his best." He avoids and decries

485a what he is weak at, and praises the other out of kind regard for his own, thinking that in that way he praises himself.

But the most proper way I think is to get a share of both. It is a fine thing to partake of philosophy for the sake of education, and it is not shameful to pursue philosophy while young. But

b   when a man is old and still at it, the thing becomes ridiculous, Socrates, and I feel very much the same toward people who engage in philosophy as I do toward grown men who act childishly and lisp. When I see a little child doing that at an age when it is still proper, playing and lisping, I rejoice; it appears pleasing and freeborn and befitting his childish years, and when I hear a little child speaking distinctly, it seems distasteful and hurts my ears, and seems like something slavish. But when one sees a grown

c   man act childishly and hears him lisp, he appears ridiculous and effeminate and worthy of a whipping. That's just how I feel about philosophers. I like to see philosophy in a lad; it seems fitting, and I believe there is even a certain freeborn liberality in the young man, and that if he doesn't engage in philosophy he is

d   unfree, someone who will never think himself worthy of any noble or beautiful thing. But when I see an older man still engaged in philosophy and not turning from it, I think the fellow at that point deserves a whipping, Socrates. For as I just said, a fellow like that, even if well-endowed by nature, is bound to become unmanly, fleeing the center of the city and its marketplace where, as the poet said, "Men grow distinguished";[5] he is sunk and hid-

e   den from sight, spending the rest of his life whispering with three

5. Homer, *Iliad* xi.441.

or four kids in a corner, never uttering anything free, important or sufficient.

Now, Socrates, I feel somewhat friendly to you. I feel very much as Zethus, whom I just recalled, felt toward Amphion in Euripides. It occurred to me in fact to say that same sort of thing to you that he said to his brother: "Socrates, you neglect what you ought to care for. The nature of your soul is noble, and yet you bend it out of shape into something very like that of a schoolboy. You add no proper word to the counsels of justice, you accept none as fair and convincing, and you advise no vigorous plan in behalf of others." And yet, my dear Socrates—and please don't be angry at me, for I speak with kind regard—don't you think it's shameful to be as, I think, you are, you and others who keep driving ever farther into philosophy?

486a

For as it is, if someone were to take you or anyone like you and drag you off to jail, accusing you of guilt when you had done no wrong, you know perfectly well you wouldn't know what to do. You'd gape with dizziness and wouldn't have a word to say. And once brought to court, even though your accuser was ever so contemptible a knave, if he chose to exact the death penalty you would die. Yet how is this wise, Socrates? What sort of art is it which "takes folk well endowed and makes them worse," unable to help or save themselves or anyone else from the greatest dangers, but stripped of their whole estate by their enemies, they live on in their own city utterly without rights. To put it perhaps crudely, one can punch a man like that on the chin and pay no penalty.

b

c

Dear friend, be persuaded by me. Cease from refutation and practice the music of affairs. Practice that which will make you seem wise. Leave these bits of cleverness to others, whether they should be called nonsense or folly, "from which you'll dwell in empty houses." Do not emulate men who practice refutation in these petty matters, but rather those who possess life and glory and many other goods.

d

soc. If my soul were gold, Callicles, don't you think I'd delight in finding a touchstone to put that gold to the test?[6] The best touchstone available, one which if I applied it and the stone agreed

6. "The touchstone, a kind of black quartz or jasper, was used for assaying samples of gold by rubbing them against the touchstone and comparing the streaks which they left on it." Dodds, *Gorgias*.

with me that my soul had been well cared for, I might be assured at last that I sufficed, and needed no other test?

e CAL. Why ask that question, Socrates?

SOC. I'll tell you. I think I've been lucky to meet with a real godsend in you.

CAL. Why so?

SOC. Because I well know that should you agree with me in the
487a things my soul believes, they are then the very truth. For I think that whoever is to test a soul sufficiently about correctness of life or the lack of it needs three things, all of which you have: knowledge, kind regard, and frankness. I meet many people who can't test me because they're not wise, as you are; still others are wise and yet unwilling to tell me the truth because they don't care for
b me, as you do. Again, both our two guests here, Gorgias and Polus, are wise and friendly to me, but deficient in frankness and rather more ashamed than they need be. It must be so, for they both have reached such a pitch of modesty that each of them, being ashamed, dares to contradict himself before a large group of people, and this in matters of the utmost importance. You have everything the others don't; for you have been sufficiently educated, so many Athenians would say, and you have kind re-
c gard for me. What is my evidence? I'll tell you. I know, Callicles, that you belong to a group of four wise companions: you, and Tisander of Aphidnae, and Adron son of Androtion, and Nausicydes of Cholarges. I once overheard you consulting about how far wisdom should be cultivated, and I know that a judgment something like this prevailed: not to be eager for philosophy to
d the point of narrow precision, but rather to beware, so you bid each other, lest you unwittingly be corrupted by becoming wise beyond the bounds of what is needful. I hear you now giving me the same advice you gave your friends, and that is sufficient indication to me that you truly hold me in kind regard. Furthermore, you are one of the kind to speak frankly and not be ashamed, as you yourself admit, and the argument you just put confirms it.

So it is clear how matters now stand. If you agree with me on
e something in our argument, it will then have been sufficiently tested, and need no longer be referred to another touchstone. For you would never agree for lack of wisdom, or presence of shame, nor again would you agree in order to deceive me; for you are my friend, as indeed you say yourself. Really then, your

agreement and mine will at last end in truth. And surely, Callicles, inquiry into the subjects about which you rebuked me is of
all inquiry most beautiful: about what sort of man one should
488a be, and what he should practice, and up to what point, when old
or young. For my part, if I have been doing something incorrect
in my life, be assured that I do not err willingly and wittingly but
by reason of my ignorance. So as you began to correct me, please
do not stop, but show me sufficiently what it is I must pursue and
how I may attain it, and if you catch me agreeing with you now,
but later not doing the things I agreed to, count me a worthless
b sluggard and never again correct me. So please return to the
beginning for me. What is it you and Pindar claim is the just
according to nature? That the stronger should take by force what
belongs to the weaker, the better rule the worse, and the superior
have more than the inferior? Is that not what you say the just is,
or do I remember correctly?

CAL. I said it then, and I say it now.

SOC. Do you call the same man better and stronger? I wasn't quite
c able to understand just what you meant then. Do you call those
with more physical strength stronger, and should the physically
weaker acknowledge the authority of the physically stronger, as
you seemed to indicate just now in saying that big cities proceed
against little ones according to what is just by nature because they
are stronger and physically stronger, as though it is the same to
be stronger, physically stronger, and better. Or is it possible to be
d better, but smaller and physically weaker, and to be stronger but
inferior? Is the definition of better and stronger the same? Please
mark this off for me plainly: Are the stronger and the better and
the physically stronger the same or different?

CAL. Why, I tell you plainly, they are the same.

SOC. Then the multitude is stronger than any one person according
to nature? After all, they lay down laws constraining that one
person, as indeed you just now were saying.

CAL. Certainly.

SOC. So the conventional legal rules of the multitude are rules of
the stronger?

CAL. Of course.

e SOC. And therefore of the better? For the stronger are better, I
suppose, by your account.

CAL. Yes.

SOC. Then since stronger, their conventional legal rules are beautiful according to nature.

CAL. I agree.

SOC. Now doesn't the multitude believe, as again you were saying 489a just now, that to have the equal is just, and that it is more ugly to do injustice than to suffer it? Is that so, or not? You must take care that you in your turn aren't caught being ashamed here: do or do not the multitude think that it is just to have the equal instead of the more, and that it is more shameful to do wrong than to suffer it? Please don't begrudge me an answer to this, Callicles, so that if you agree I may at this point be confirmed by you, for you are a man sufficient to decide.

CAL. Well, the multitude does believe that.

SOC. So it is not only by conventional law that it is more shameful to do wrong than to suffer it, or that having the equal is just, but b also by nature. The result is that you very likely didn't tell the truth or correctly accuse me earlier, when you said that law and nature are opposite and that I, realizing it, used this to spoil arguments, taking law if somebody means nature, and nature if they mean law.

CAL. The man won't stop babbling! Tell me, Socrates, aren't you c ashamed at your age to catch at words, and treat it as a godsend if somebody mistakes a phrase? Do you think I meant by the stronger anything else but the better? Haven't I been telling you for some time that I claim the better and the stronger are the same? Or did you think I meant that if a rabble of slaves and all sorts of low fellows worth nothing except maybe in the strength of their bodies should assemble together and speak, whatever they utter would be legal rules?

SOC. Very well, my wise Callicles, is this then what you mean?

CAL. Of course.

d SOC. Well, I've been guessing for some time that by the stronger you meant something like that, my fortunate friend, and I repeated my question out of greedy desire to know plainly just what you do mean. You surely don't mean you believe two men are better than one, or that your slaves are better than you because they're physically stronger than you. But tell me again from the beginning: Just who do you mean are better, if not the physically stronger? And do please teach me my lessons more gently, dear friend, lest I stop attending your class.

e CAL. You're playing sly fox, Socrates.

SOC. No, by Zethus, whom you just now made so much use of, Callicles, it is you who are being sly with me. Come and tell me: Whom do you mean by the better?

CAL. I mean the superior.

SOC. Do you then see that you're merely uttering words and clarifying nothing? Won't you say whether by the better and stronger you mean the wiser, or somebody else?

CAL. Why of course I mean them. Emphatically so.

490a SOC. So by your account, one wise man is often stronger than thousands of fools, and he should rule and they be ruled, and the ruler should have a greater share than the ruled. This is what you seem to wish to say, and surely I am not catching at phrases, if one man is to be stronger than thousands.

CAL. No, that's just what I mean. I think that the just by nature consists in the better and wiser ruling and having a greater share than their inferiors.

b SOC. Hold it right there. What do you mean this time? Suppose many of us were gathered in the same place, as we are now, with plenty to eat and drink in common; and suppose we were people of all sorts, some physically stronger, some weaker, and suppose one of us was wiser than the rest in such matters because he was a doctor, though possibly physically stronger than some, weaker than others. Being wiser than we, won't he also be better and stronger in respect to these matters?

CAL. Of course.

c SOC. Then is he to have more food than we because he is better? Or should he distribute it all by virtue of his authority as a doctor, but not go to excess by squandering food or using most of it for his own body, if he does not intend to be harmed, but take more than some and less than others? And if he happens to be physically weakest of all, should he take the least even though he is best, Callicles? Isn't that so, dear friend?

d CAL. You talk foods and drinks and doctors and nonsense—that's not what I mean.

SOC. But didn't you say the wiser are better? Yes or no.

CAL. Yes.

SOC. Shouldn't the better have more?

CAL. No, not of food and drink.

SOC. I see. Well, maybe cloaks. The best weaver should have the biggest cloak, and the most cloaks, and go around in the prettiest cloaks.

CAL. Cloaks? What is this?

SOC. Well, clearly shoes then. He who is wisest and best about shoes
e should have an excess of them. Maybe the cobbler should have
the biggest shoes, and walk around wearing the most shoes.

CAL. Shoes? Why shoes? You talk nonsense.

SOC. Well, if not that, maybe you mean this: a farmer, for example,
is wise and beautiful and good about land. So maybe he should
take an excess of seeds, and use the largest possible amount of
them on his land.

CAL. Socrates, you keep saying the same things.

SOC. Not only that, Callicles, but also about the same things.

491a CAL. Yes indeed. You simply never stop talking about cobblers and
clothes-cleaners and doctors and cooks, as though our argument
was about them.

SOC. Then please say what things the stronger and wiser has more
of, when he justly overreaches and gets more than his share? Or
do you intend to reject my suggestions while offering none of
your own?

CAL. But I've been saying it for some time. First, by the stronger I
b don't mean cobblers and cooks, but those who are wise in the
affairs of the city and how it may be well governed, and not only
wise but courageous, adequate for what they intend to achieve
without faltering through softness of soul.

SOC. Do you see, good Callicles? You're surely not accusing me of
what I accuse you of. You blame me for always saying the same
thing, but I say it's just the opposite with you: you never say the
same things about the same subjects. One time you define the
c better and stronger as physically stronger, another time as wiser,
and now you come bringing something different still: certain
courageous folk are said by you to be the stronger and better.
Dear friend, speak and get rid of it; just who do you say are the
better and stronger, and in respect to what?

CAL. Surely, I've told you: people who are wise in the affairs of the
d city, and courageous. Those are the persons who should rule
their cities, and the just lies here, that they should have more
than the others, the rulers more than the ruled.

SOC. Really? More than themselves, my friend? Ruling and ruled
in what way?

CAL. How do you mean?

SOC. I mean that each of us is his own ruler. Or is there no need
to rule oneself, but only others?

CAL. What do you mean by ruling oneself?

SOC. Nothing fancy, just what most people mean: being temperate and controlling oneself, ruling the pleasures and desires in one-
c   self.

CAL. How sweet you are. You mean by the temperate the stupid.

SOC. Surely not. There's nobody who wouldn't recognize that's not what I mean.

CAL. Why of course you do, Socrates. How can a man be happy if he's enslaved by anyone at all? I tell you now quite frankly that the beautiful and just according to nature is this, that he who would live rightly should allow his desires to become as great as possible and not restrain them, and when they have waxed great,
492a he must be adequate to minister to them with courage and wis-dom, satisfying whatever desire he may chance to have. But this I think is impossible for most men, whence it is that out of shame they find fault with such people, hiding their own powerlessness and claiming that lack of restraint is shameful. This is why men of better nature are enslaved, as I said before, and those who
b   cannot provide for their pleasures to the full praise temperance and justice due to their own unmanliness. If they started out as sons of kings, or were adequate in nature to achieve some kind of absolute rule, sole or oligarchic, what could in truth be more shameful and evil than temperance and justice for these men to whom it is given to enjoy good things without impediment? Would they then introduce a master over themselves, namely the law, the speech and the censure of the multitude? How would
c   they not become wretched through the beauty of justice and tem-perance, distributing no greater shares to their friends than to their enemies, even though they rule in their own cities? The truth, Socrates, which you claim to pursue, is this: excess, lack of restraint and freedom, if adequately abetted, are virtue and hap-piness, and these other embellishments, these agreements of men contrary to nature, are worthless nonsense.

d SOC. You prosecute your case with a not ignoble frankness, Calli-cles; you now say plainly what other men believe but are unwilling to say. I beg you not to draw back from it in any way, in order that it may really become clear how one ought to live. Now tell me: you say that the desires are not to be restrained, if one is to become the sort of person he should; he is to let them wax as great as possible, prepare to satisfy them in any way, and this is
e   virtue?

CAL. I say exactly that.

SOC. It is therefore mistaken to say that those who need nothing are happy?

CAL. Otherwise, stones and corpses would be happiest of all.

SOC. But then again, the life you describe is a rather strange one too. I wouldn't be surprised if Euripides told the truth when he
493a said, "Who knows whether to live is to be dead, and being dead to live?" Perhaps we are really dead. I once heard a wise man say that we are now dead and our body [*sōma*] is our tomb [*sēma*], but this part of the soul in which desires exist is, as it were, seduced, and wanders up and down; and therefore some storyteller, a clever fellow, perhaps a Sicilian or an Italian, compared this part of the soul to a jug [*pithos*], playing on the name because it juggles belief [*pithanon*] and is so easily persuaded, and called
b the unintelligent [*anoetous*] the uninitiated [*amyetous*]; and for the unintelligent, that part of the soul in which desires exist is unrestrained and porous, like a jug full of holes, so represented because it cannot be filled.

So this man, Callicles, indicates just the opposite of you: that in the Place of the Dead [*Hades*]—meaning of course the Invisible [*aides*]—it is the uninitiated who will be most wretched, carrying water to the leaky jar with something else of the same sort, a leaky sieve. The person who told me the story said that by the
c sieve he meant the soul, and he likened the soul of the unintelligent to a sieve, because it leaks; it can't hold water by reason of forgetfulness and unbelief.

No doubt this is all a bit absurd, and yet it makes clear what I wish to show you, if I somehow can, in order to convince you to change, and in place of a life of unchastened intemperance, to
d choose a life which is well-ordered, sufficient and content with what it has. Do I in any way then persuade you to change, to believe that the well-ordered are happier than the intemperate? Or will you not change any the more, even if I tell many other stories like this?

CAL. The latter is more true, Socrates.

SOC. Come, then, I put to you another comparison from the same school. Consider whether you are not saying something of this sort about the life of temperate and intemperate men. Picture
e two men, each with many jars. One has sound jars, some full of wine, some of milk and some of honey, and many more full of many other things, the sources of each scarce and hard to come

by, procured only with much labor and difficulty. Well, the one man, when his jars are full, gives no thought to piping more into them; his mind is at rest about it. But the other man, though he can provide sources like the first, though with difficulty, has

494a leaky, rotten vessels, and so he is ever compelled to keep filling them day and night or else suffer the extremities of pain. Suppose then that each life is of this sort. Do you still say the life of the intemperate man is happier than that of the well-ordered? Do I at all persuade you in saying this to agree that the well-ordered life is better than the intemperate? Or do I fail?

CAL. You fail, Socrates. That fellow with the full jars no longer has any pleasure, and as I just said, that is to live like a stone. Once

b he is satisfied, he neither rejoices nor feels pain. The life of pleasure consists in just this: maximum flow.

SOC. Then necessarily if the inflow is large, won't the outflow be large too, with big holes to flow out of?

CAL. Of course.

SOC. Well, no corpse, no stone. This time you're describing the life of a curlew.[7] But tell me, do you agree that there is such a thing as hunger, and eating when hungry?

CAL. I do.

c SOC. And thirst and drinking when thirsty?

CAL. Yes, and having all the other desires and being able to satisfy them, and enjoying a happy life.

SOC. Fine, my friend. Please go on as you've begun, but take care lest you become ashamed. It seems I must not be ashamed either. So first, tell us about itching and scratching, with ungrudging plenty of scratching. Is it possible to live life happily constantly scratching an itch?

d CAL. You're absurd, Socrates, an outright demagogue.

SOC. Why, that's just how I surprised Polus and Gorgias, Callicles, and made them ashamed. But you must not be surprised or ashamed, for you're manly and courageous. So please just answer the question.

CAL. Well I say he'd live pleasantly scratching himself.

SOC. If pleasantly, happily?

CAL. Of course.

e SOC. What if he only wants to scratch his head—or need I inquire

---

7. The reference is to a bird which constantly strains water through its beak and ejects it.

further? Consider what you will answer, Callicles, if you are questioned about it all serially and in order. And when such things are summed up in the life of a catamite, isn't that awful, shameful, wretched? Or will you dare claim that even they are happy, as long as they have ungrudging plenty of what they need?

CAL. Aren't you ashamed, Socrates, to lead the argument into a topic like this?

SOC. Is it I who lead it there, noble friend? Or is it rather the person who claims without reservation that those thus delighted, however they are delighted, are happy, and does not distinguish what kinds of pleasures are good and bad? But tell me further: do you claim that the pleasant and good are the same, or are there some pleasures which are not good?

CAL. In order that the argument may not disagree with me if I say they are different, I say they are the same.

SOC. You're wrecking your first arguments, Callicles. You're no longer sufficiently examining with me things which are, if you speak contrary to what seems true to you.

b CAL. You do it too, Socrates.

SOC. Well if I do, I don't do it rightly, and neither do you. But consider, my happy friend, surely the good does not consist in pleasure at any price. If this were so, these disgusting and shameful consequences I just mentioned would appear to follow, along with many others.

CAL. So you think, Socrates.

SOC. You really do persist in this, Callicles?

CAL. I do.

c SOC. We are therefore to undertake the argument assuming you to be in earnest?

CAL. I am quite in earnest.

SOC. Then since it seems so, come and distinguish the following for me. There is, I suppose, something you call knowledge?

CAL. I do.

SOC. And didn't you just now say that courage exists along with knowledge?

CAL. Yes.

SOC. Do you claim they are two, on the ground that courage is different from knowledge?

CAL. Certainly.

SOC. Really? Then are knowledge and pleasure the same or different?

d CAL. Different of course, thou wisest of men.

SOC. And courage different from pleasure?

CAL. Of course.

SOC. Come then, so that we'll well remember: Callicles of Acharnia deposes and states that pleasure and good are the same, but knowledge and courage are different from each other and from the good.

CAL. And Socrates of Alopece dissents. Or does he join us?

e SOC. He does not. Nor will Callicles, I think, when he sees himself correctly. For tell me: do you believe that those who do and fare well undergo an affection opposite to those who do and fare ill?

CAL. I do.

SOC. Then if opposite to each other, it must be with them as it is with health and disease, for doubtless a man is not both well and ill at the same time, nor gets and gets rid of both health and disease at the same time.

CAL. How do you mean?

496a SOC. Take any part of the body you wish and consider it. A man no doubt can have a disease of the eyes named ophthalmia?

CAL. Of course.

SOC. The eyes are not surely at the same time healthy?

CAL. By no means.

SOC. What happens when he gets rid of ophthalmia? Does he also then get rid of the health of his eyes and finish by being rid of both at once?

CAL. Hardly.

SOC. No, for I suppose that is strange and unreasonable, isn't it?

b CAL. Certainly.

SOC. I suppose he rather gets and gets rid of each alternately.

CAL. I agree.

SOC. And so in like manner with strength and weakness?

CAL. Yes.

SOC. And swiftness and slowness?

CAL. Of course.

SOC. So too with good things and happiness and their opposites, evils and wretchedness: he gets and gets rid of each alternately?

CAL. Absolutely.

c SOC. Then if we should find certain things a man both has and gets rid of at the same time, it is clear these things would not be the good and the evil. Do we agree on this? Consider very carefully before you answer.

CAL. I emphatically agree.

SOC. Then go back to our former admissions. Did you say that being hungry was pleasant or distressing? Hunger by itself, I mean.

CAL. Why, distressing. But I also say eating when hungry is pleasant.

d SOC. I understand. But hunger by itself is unpleasant. Not so?

CAL. I agree.

SOC. So too for thirst?

CAL. Yes, certainly.

SOC. Now, shall I inquire further, or do you agree that all lack and desire is distressing?

CAL. I agree. You needn't ask.

SOC. Very well. But do you then say that to drink when thirsty is anything other than pleasant?

CAL. I do.

SOC. Now, the thirst you speak of is doubtless painful?

e CAL. Yes.

SOC. But drinking is fulfillment of the lack, and pleasure?

CAL. Yes.

SOC. So you count drinking as enjoyable?

CAL. Certainly.

SOC. At least when thirsty.

CAL. Yes.

SOC. Being in pain.

CAL. Yes.

SOC. Do you perceive the consequence? When you say a man drinks when thirsty, you are saying he is at the same time both pleased and in pain. Isn't that what happens, at the same time, and in the same place, and in respect either of body and soul as you wish—for I think it makes no difference. Is this so or not?

CAL. It is.

SOC. And yet, you claim it is impossible to do and fare well and to do and fare ill at the same time?

497a CAL. I do.

SOC. But you've agreed that it's possible to be pleased while in distress.

CAL. It appears so.

SOC. Therefore to be pleased is not the same as to do and fare well, nor to be distressed to do and fare ill; with the result that the pleasant becomes different from the good.

CAL. I don't know what kind of clever tricks you're up to, Socrates.

SOC. Oh, you know all right, Callicles. You're just being coy. Keep on a little further, so you can know how wise you are in correcting

b me. Doesn't each of us at the same time stop being thirsty and stop being pleased through drinking?

CAL. I don't know what you mean.

GOR. (*interrupting*) No, no, Callicles. Answer at least for our sake, so that the argument can be carried through.

CAL. But Socrates is always like this, Gorgias. He keeps on asking worthless little questions and then refutes you.

GOR. What difference does it make to you? Their value isn't yours to estimate, Callicles; you submitted to Socrates to be examined as he might wish.

c CAL. (*turning to Socrates*) Then go ahead and ask those narrow little questions of yours, since it seems fit to Gorgias.

SOC. You're a happy man, Callicles; you've been initiated into the Greater Mysteries before the Lesser. I didn't think that was religiously permitted. Now answer from where you left off: does each of us stop being thirsty and being pleased at the same time?

CAL. Yes.

SOC. Again, hunger and the other desires and pleasures also stop together?

CAL. True.

SOC. Then both pain and pleasure stop together?

d CAL. Yes.

SOC. Furthermore, goods and evils do not stop together, as you agree—you do still agree?

CAL. I do. What about it?

SOC. Just this, my friend, that the goods are not the same as the pleasures, nor the evils the same as the pains. For these stop together and the others do not, because they are different kinds of things. How then can the pleasant things be the same as the good things, or painful things the same as evils? If you wish, look

e at it this way—I don't suppose you'll agree, but consider it: don't you call good men good by reason of the presence of good things, just as the beautiful are those to whom beauty is present?

CAL. Yes.

SOC. Well then. Do you call ignorant and cowardly men good? You didn't just now, at least, but mentioned the wise and courageous. Or don't you call them good?

CAL. Certainly I do.

soc. Really? Then did you ever see a foolish child being pleased?

cal. Yes.

soc. And have you never seen a foolish man being pleased?

cal. I suppose I have. Why?

498a soc. Nothing. Just answer.

cal. Yes, I've seen it.

soc. Really? And also a wise man both pleased and in pain?

cal. Yes.

soc. Are wise men more pleased and pained than the ignorant?

cal. I don't suppose there's much difference.

soc. There, that's enough. Did you ever see a coward in battle?

cal. Of course.

soc. Then who seemed to you to be more pleased when the enemy withdrew, the cowardly or the courageous?

cal. Both equally, or very nearly so.

b soc. It makes no difference. The cowards at any rate were pleased?

cal. Very much so.

soc. As were the foolish, it seems.

cal. Yes.

soc. Were only cowards pained when the enemy advanced, or brave men too?

cal. Both.

soc. Equally?

cal. The cowards perhaps more.

soc. But not more pleased when the enemy retreated?

cal. Perhaps.

soc. So the foolish and the wise, the cowards and the courageous,
c   feel pleasure and pain about equally, you claim, but the cowards more than the brave.

cal. I agree.

soc. Furthermore, the wise and courageous are good, but cowards and the foolish are bad?

cal. Yes.

soc. Good and bad men, therefore, feel pleasure and pain about equally?

cal. I agree.

soc. Now, are good and bad men good and bad about equally, or are the bad actually better?

d cal. I don't know what in Heaven's name you mean!

soc. You don't know you said that good men are good by the pres-

ence of good things, and bad men by the presence of evils? And
that pleasures are good things, and pains bad?

CAL. Yes, I said that.

SOC. And goods, namely pleasures, are present to those who are
pleased, when they are pleased.

CAL. Of course.

SOC. Now, when good things are present, those pleased are good?

CAL. Yes.

SOC. Really? Are not evils, that is, pains, present to those in distress?

CAL. They are.

e SOC. But you claim bad men are bad by presence of evils. Or do
you claim it no longer?

CAL. Of course I do.

SOC. Therefore whoever is pleased is good, and whoever is in distress bad?

CAL. Quite so.

SOC. And whoever feels more so is more, whoever feels less less,
whoever about equally about equally?

CAL. Yes.

SOC. Now, you say the wise and the foolish, the courageous and the
cowardly, are pleased and distressed about equally, or maybe the
cowards somewhat more?

CAL. Yes.

SOC. Then, together with me, reckon up what follows for us from
499a these agreements. For they say it is "twice and thrice beautiful to
say beautiful things and examine them." Now we say, do we not,
that the wise and courageous are good?

CAL. Yes.

SOC. And the foolish and cowardly bad?

CAL. Of course.

SOC. Again, he who is pleased is good?

CAL. Yes.

SOC. And he who is in distress is bad?

CAL. Necessarily.

SOC. But the good and the bad man are equally pleased and distressed, the bad man perhaps even more?

CAL. Yes.

SOC. Then does the bad man become bad and good in like manner
b   to the good man, or does he actually become more good? Doesn't
this result follow with the previous ones, if someone claims that

pleasant things and good things are the same? Isn't this necessary, Callicles?

CAL. Socrates, I've been listening to you for some time and agreeing, while thinking that if anybody grants you something even as
a joke, you delight in it like a boy. Do you suppose that I and
every other man don't believe some pleasures better and others
worse?

SOC. Alas, alas, Callicles, you're a scoundrel, and you treat me like
a child. One time you say the same things are one way and the
c   next time another, just to deceive me. And yet in the beginning
I didn't think you'd willingly do that, because you are my friend.
But since I've now been deceived, it seems, as the old saying goes,
that I must make the best of what I've got and accept what you
give. What you're now claiming, it seems, is that some pleasures
are good and some bad. Not so?

d CAL. Yes.

SOC. Now, the beneficial pleasures are good and the harmful pleasures bad?

CAL. Of course.

SOC. Those pleasures are beneficial which do some good, and those
pleasures are bad which do some evil? Not so?

CAL. Yes.

SOC. Then is this what you mean: for example, in respect to the
body, which we were just mentioning in the pleasures of eating
and drinking, are the pleasures which produce bodily health or
strength or any other virtue good, and their opposites evil?

e CAL. Of course.

SOC. And similarly some pains are beneficial and some harmful?

CAL. To be sure.

SOC. Now, it is beneficial pleasures and pains which are to be chosen and made use of?

CAL. Of course.

SOC. But not harmful pleasures?

CAL. Clearly not.

SOC. No, for it surely seemed to Polus and me, if you recall, that
everything is to be done for the sake of the good. And do you
also thus concur that the good is the end of all our actions, and
500a   that all other things must be done for the sake of that, and not
that for the sake of other things? Do you cast your vote with us
as a third?

CAL. I do.

soc. It is therefore necessary to do pleasant things, as well as others, for the sake of good things, not good things for the sake of
pleasures.

cal. Of course.

soc. Is it every man who can pick out which pleasant things are
good and which evil, or is skill needed in each case?

cal. Skill is needed.

soc. Then let us again recollect what I said to Polus and Gorgias.
b   If you recall, I said that there are practices which are concerned
only with pleasure and provide just that alone, but are ignorant
of the better and the worse, while other practices know what is
good and what is bad. I counted among practices concerned with
pleasure the knack, not the art, of pastry-cooking, and among
those concerned with the good the art of medicine. In the name
of Zeus who is the God of Friendship, Callicles, do not think you
c   need to joke with me, or answer contrary to what seems true to
you; and do not accept things from me as though I were joking.
For you see that our argument now concerns what even a man
of scant intelligence must needs be in utmost earnest about,
namely, the way one ought to live: whether it is the life to which
you summon me, doing such manly things as speaking in public,
practicing rhetoric, engaging in politics as you do now; or
d   whether it is this life of mine in philosophy; and how this life
differs from that. Perhaps then it is best to distinguish them as
I just now tried to do; and when in agreement with each other
we have drawn that distinction, then, if these are really two lives,
to examine the difference between them, and which of them is
to be lived. But perhaps you don't yet understand what I mean.

cal. I certainly don't.

soc. I'll say it for you more clearly. Since you and I have agreed
that there is something good, and something pleasant, and that
the pleasant is different from the good, and that there is a certain
preparation and practice for possessing each of the two, one existing for the pursuit of pleasure, the other for pursuit of the
e   good—but first of all, please agree or disagree with me on this
point. Do you agree?

cal. Yes.

soc. Then come and agree also to what I was saying to these others
here, if I seemed to you at the time to speak the truth. I said, I
think, that pastry-cooking did not seem to me to be an art but a
501a   knack, but that medicine is an art, meaning that it considers the

nature of the person it serves and the cause of what it does and is able to render an account of each. This is medicine. But the other is directed wholly to the service of pleasure and goes after it quite without art, considering neither the nature of pleasure or its cause, irrational in that it proceeds making virtually no distinctions, preserving only memory through knack and expe-
b   rience of what usually happens; by this it provides pleasures.

First of all, then, consider whether this seems to you adequately stated, and whether there are other such occupations of the same sort concerning the soul; some of them skills with a certain fore-thought for what is best for the soul, and others unconcerned for this and considering on the contrary, as in the other case, only the pleasure of the soul and how it may be obtained, not inquiring which pleasures are better or worse for the soul, and concerned
c   only with gratification whether for better or worse. It seems to me such practices exist, Callicles, and I say it is flattery whenever someone serves pleasure without considering the better and the worse, be it for body, soul, or anything else. Do you support me in the same opinion, or gainsay it?

CAL. No, I concur, in order that you may carry through your argument, and I may gratify Gorgias here.

d SOC. Does this result hold for one soul, but not for two or many?

CAL. No, also for two or many.

SOC. Then is it also possible to please many at once, together, in a group, without considering at all what is best?

CAL. I would think so.

SOC. Can you state just what pursuits do this? Or if you prefer, let me do the asking, and say Yes to what seems good to you and
e   No to what does not. First, let's consider flute playing. Doesn't it seem to you, Callicles, to be the sort of thing which seeks only our pleasure and thinks of nothing else?

CAL. It does.

SOC. So also then for everything else of the sort? For example, lyre playing at contests?

CAL. Yes.

SOC. What about directing a chorus or composing dithyrambs? Don't they appear to be the same sort of thing too? Do you believe Cinesias son of Meles thinks at all about how to say something to
502a   make his hearers better, or do you rather believe his concern is to please the audience?

CAL. Clearly that, Socrates, at least in the case of Cinesias.

soc. What about his father, Meles. Do you think he looked to what is best in his lyre playing? Why, he didn't even look to what is most pleasant, since his singing gave his audience such pain. Consider then: does it seem to you that all lyre playing and dithyramb-making were invented for the sake of pleasure?

cal. It does.

b soc. Then just what is it on which our stately and wonderful tragic poetry is so intent? Is its purpose and concern fixed in your opinion only on gratifying the audience? Or does it struggle not to say something, if it is pleasing and gratifying but bad, and to the contrary will it say and sing anything that is displeasing and beneficial, whether the audience likes it or not? Which do you think is the aim of tragic poetry?

cal. Clearly, Socrates, its impulse is rather toward pleasure and
c the satisfaction of the audience.

soc. And isn't this the sort of thing we just now said was flattery, Callicles?

cal. Of course.

soc. Come then: take away melody, rhythm, and meter from any kind of poetry, and only speech is left?

cal. Necessarily.

soc. Speech directed to a large crowd and in public?

cal. Yes.

soc. So poetry is a kind of demagoguery.

d cal. It appears so.

soc. Now demagoguery is rhetoric? Or don't you think the poets orate in the theaters?

cal. They do.

soc. We have therefore now found a kind of rhetoric addressed to a public composed of women, men, and children, slave and free. But we do not quite approve of it, for we say it is flattery.

cal. Of course.

soc. Very well. What about the rhetoric addressed to the Athenian
e demos, or to other assemblies of free men in other cities? Just what have we there? Does it seem to you that orators always speak to what is best, aiming at making their citizens as good as possible due to their speeches? Or is their impulse in fact rather toward pleasing the citizens, slighting the common good for the sake of their private interests, treating the demos like children and trying only to please? But as to whether the public will be better or
503a worse because of it—to that they give no thought.

CAL. This is not still a simple question you're asking. There are some who say what they say out of concern for their citizens, whereas others are of the sort you describe.

SOC. It suffices. For if this really is a double question, then surely one part of it involves flattery and public oratory which is shameful, while the other part is noble, securing that the souls of the citizens shall be as good as possible and struggling to say what is

b best, be it more pleasant or painful to the hearers. But you never yet have seen this kind of rhetoric. Or, if you can mention an orator of this sort, tell me who he is.

CAL. I most certainly couldn't mention to you any of our present-day orators.

SOC. Really? Then can you mention any orators of old who caused the Athenians to become better after he began making speeches to them, they having been worse before? I don't know who he would be.

c CAL. Really? You haven't heard what a good man Themistocles was, and Cimon and Miltiades, and Pericles who so recently died,[8] and whom you heard yourself?

SOC. Yes, Callicles, if true virtue is what you just said it was, the fulfilling of desires, one's own and those of others, then yes, they were good men. But if this is not true virtue, if virtue is what we were later compelled to agree it was, namely, satisfying only those desires whose fulfillment makes men better and not satisfying those that make them worse, and if we agree that this involves a

d kind of art—then I cannot claim there was any man of that sort among them.

CAL. But if you seek well, you shall find.

SOC. Then let us quietly consider whether any of them was a man of that sort. Come: the good man who in fact speaks for what is best will not speak at random, but speaks with a view toward

e something, just as all other craftsmen each look to their own work and apply the means they apply not by choosing at random, but in order that the work may have a given character. Consider for example, if you wish, painters, builders, shipfitters, any other public craftsmen you please: you see each arranging each thing

504a he arranges in a given order, compelling one thing to suit and fit another until all is combined and established in good order and

8. Pericles died in 429 B.C., so the allusion places this conversation in the 420s. But at 473e, Socrates referred to the sea battle at Arginusae as happening "last year"; it occurred in 406 B.C.

proper arrangement. The other craftsmen we just mentioned who deal with the body, namely trainers and doctors, surely put the body in good order and proper arrangement. Do we agree this is so, or not?

CAL. Let it be so.

SOC. So a well-ordered and properly arranged house would be good, but bad if disordered?

CAL. I agree.

SOC. So similarly too for a boat.

b CAL. Yes.

SOC. And we also assert this of our bodies?

CAL. Of course.

SOC. What about the soul? Will the soul be good if disordered, or does it require a certain arrangement and order?

CAL. From what has been said, it is necessary to agree to this too.

SOC. What name then belongs to the body which has gained order and proper arrangement?

CAL. Health and strength, perhaps you mean.

c SOC. I do. Again, what name belongs to the soul which has gained order and proper arrangement? Try to find the name and state it as you did the other.

CAL. Why not say it yourself, Socrates?

SOC. If it's more pleasing to you, I will. But you in your turn will please say Yes if I seem to you to speak well, but if not, refute it and do not let it be. I think "healthy" is the name for proper arrangement of the body from which health and other bodily virtue come to exist in it. Is this so or not?

CAL. It is.

d SOC. But proper arrangement and good order of the soul have the name of lawfulness and law, whence souls become law-abiding and orderly; and this is justice and temperance. Do you agree or not?

CAL. Let it be so.

SOC. Now, the good and skillful orator looks to this, and in applying all his speech and all his action to our souls, in giving any gift, in taking anything away, he will do so with this thought ever

e before his mind: how justice may be produced in the souls of his citizens and injustice removed, temperance instilled and lack of restraint removed, how the rest of virtue may come to exist there and vice be removed. Do you agree or not?

CAL. I agree.

soc. Yes, Callicles. For what does it benefit a sick and wretched body to be given many sweet foods or drinks or anything else, when by any just account the body cannot any the more profit by that than by the opposite, and perhaps less? Not so?

505a CAL. Let it be so.

soc. For I suppose it is no gain for a man to live with a wretched body. For necessarily, in that case, he too lives wretchedly. True?

CAL. Yes.

soc. So too with fulfillment of the desires—eating as much as one wishes when hungry, for example, or drinking when thirsty. The doctors generally permit a healthy man, but scarcely ever a sick one, to fulfill his desires. Do you again agree?

CAL. I do.

b soc. Isn't it just the same way with the soul, my friend? So long as it is bad, so long as it is unwise and intemperate and unjust and unholy, it should be held back from its desires and not permitted to do anything except what will make it better. Do you agree or not?

CAL. I agree.

soc. For it is surely in this way better for the soul.

CAL. Certainly.

soc. Now, to hold it back is to restrain it from those things which it desires?

CAL. Yes.

soc. Correction is therefore better for the soul than lack of restraint, contrary to what you just thought.

c CAL. I don't know what you mean, Socrates. Please ask your questions of someone else.

soc. Why, the man can't stand being benefited and suffering the very thing the argument concerns, namely, being corrected.

CAL. It doesn't matter at all to me what you say. I was only answering you for Gorgias's sake.

soc. Very well then, what shall we do? Break off the argument in the middle?

CAL. Decide for yourself.

soc. Why, they say it isn't even right to break off stories in the d middle—"add a head, so it won't go around headless." So please answer what remains, so that our argument may get its head.

CAL. You are violent, Socrates. If you take my advice, you'll dismiss this argument, or carry it on with someone else.

soc. Then who else is willing? For surely we can't leave the argument incomplete.

CAL. Why not go through the argument yourself. You can talk to yourself and answer by yourself.

Socrates Alone: The Meaning of
Human Life (505e–522e)

e soc. So as Epicharmus has it, whereas "previously two men spoke," I am now to suffice as one. Well, very likely it's most necessary. However, if we are to do this, I think we all ought to be contentious in respect to knowing what is true and false concerning the matters of which we speak. For it is of common good to all that the thing itself become manifest. Now, I am going through the 506a argument in the way I think best; but if I seem to any of you to agree with myself in something that is not the case, you must lay hold on it and refute me. For I do not speak as one who knows, but join with you in common inquiry, so that if someone disagrees with me and what he says appears to amount to something, I'll be the first to agree with him. I say this, however, only if you think my argument should be carried through. If not, let us dismiss it and take our leave.

GOR. I certainly don't think we should leave just yet, Socrates, but b that you should go through with the argument. It appears the others think so too. Certainly I myself very much wish to hear you go through what remains by yourself.

soc. Why, I'd happily go on discussing with Callicles here, Gorgias, up until I'd given him the speech of Amphion to put in place of that of Zethus. But Callicles, if you aren't willing to see the argument through with me, at any rate listen, and please interrupt c me if I seem to you not to speak well in something. And if you refute me, I will not be angry with you, as you are with me, but record you as my greatest benefactor.

CAL. Speak on, friend, and finish by yourself.

soc. Hear me then as I take up the argument again from the beginning. Are the pleasant and the good the same? Not the same, as Callicles and I agreed. Is the pleasant then to be done for the sake of the good or the good for the sake of the pleasant? d The pleasant for the sake of the good. Is it pleasure by whose presence we are pleased and good by whose presence we are good? Of course. Still further, are we and all other things, insofar

as they are good, good by the presence of some virtue? That seems quite necessary to me, Callicles. But then the virtue of each thing, whether of artifacts, body, soul, and every living thing, is most beautifully produced, not at random, but by proper arrangement and correctness and art, whichever given art is as-
e   signed as appropriate; is that so? I agree. Does the virtue of each thing consist in its arrangement, in being arranged in good or-der? I say yes. So there is a certain order properly present in each thing, and akin to it, which provides a good naturally suited to it? I think so. Then a soul having good order is better than it is if disordered? Necessarily. Furthermore the soul which has
507a good order is orderly? How could it not be? But surely to be orderly is to be temperate? Quite necessary. Therefore the tem-perate soul is good.

I can't say anything but that, my dear Callicles. If you can, teach.

CAL. Say on, friend.

SOC. Then I say that, if the temperate soul is good, then the soul affected by the opposite of temperance is evil, and that soul is both foolish and intemperate. Of course. Moreover he who is temperate does what is fitting concerning both gods and men,
b   for not to do what is fitting would not be temperate. Necessarily so. Furthermore in doing what is fitting concerning men he does what is just, and concerning gods, what is holy; and he who does just and holy things necessarily is just and holy? True. Further-more, he is necessarily courageous, for it is surely not the part of a temperate man either to pursue or flee when he should not; rather, it is his part to pursue and flee what he ought, whether things or people, pleasures or pains, and with stout heart to stand
c   fast where he ought. So it is quite necessary, Callicles, that the temperate man, because he is also, as we've explained, just and courageous and holy, should be completely a good man; and the good man does what he does well and nobly, and by doing and faring well is blessed and happy, while the bad man does and fares ill and is wretched. This man, who is opposite to the tem-perate man, is the intemperate man whom you praised.

Now, I hold these things so and I say that they are true. But
d   if true, then he who wishes to be happy must, it seems, pursue and practice temperance, and each of us must flee licentiousness as fast as our feet will carry us, and so far as possible see to it that we need no chastisement. But if someone does need it, he

or any kin of his, private person or city, then justice must be exacted and correction done if he is to be happy. This seems to me to be the mark at which we ought to look and aim in living; so to act as to draw everything of our own and of the city toward
e   this, that justice and temperance shall be present to him who is to be happy. He must not permit unchastened desires to exist or undertake to fulfill them, for then an endless, aimless evil will be his, and he will live the life of a robber. Such a one is dear neither to god nor to any man, for it is impossible to live in association with him, and where there is not association, there is no friendship. Wise men say, Callicles, that heaven and earth and gods
508a and men are bound together by communion and friendship, orderliness, temperance, and justice, and it is for that reason they call this Whole a Cosmos, my friend, and not intemperate disorder. But you, I think, have not attended to this, wise as you are; you have forgotten that geometrical equality has great power among both gods and men, and you recommend excess because you neglect geometry.

Very well. Either this account of mine is to be refuted, namely,
b   that the happy are happy by possession of justice and temperance and the wretched are wretched by possession of evils, or, if the account is true, the consequences of it must be examined. The former results surely all follow, Callicles. You asked whether I was in earnest in saying a man is to accuse even himself or his son or his friend if they've done something wrong, and that this is the use of rhetoric. What you thought Polus agreed to out of mere shame is true: doing injustice is more ugly and shameful
c   than suffering injustice, insofar as it is worse. He who rightly intends to be an orator must therefore be just and know what things are just, which Polus in turn claimed Gorgias admitted through mere shame.

If all this be so, let us examine what it is you reproach me for. Is it well said or not that I am unable to help myself or any of my friends or those akin to me, or to save them from the greatest dangers, but that I am subject, like people without civil rights, to
d   the will of any man, whether he wishes to punch me on the chin— the fresh young expression is yours—or confiscate my goods, or exile me from my city, or ultimately slay me. Your account has it that to be so situated is most ugly and shameful of all things. But my own account—I have at this point stated it often, but nothing
e   prevents me stating it again—is this: I deny, Callicles, that getting

unjustly punched on the chin is most ugly and shameful, or being cut in my person or purse; to punch me or mine unjustly, to cut my person or purse wrongfully, is more ugly and shameful, and more evil; it belongs with theft and slave-trading and burglary. In sum, the doing of any injustice whatever to me and mine is more evil and more ugly and shameful for him who does the injustice than for me to whom the wrong is done. This appeared true in our former discussion, as I say, and it is secured and

509a bound fast, if it is not too rude to say so, with arguments of adamant and iron. So, at any rate, it would seem, and unless you, or someone younger and more daring than you, shall unbind and loose those arguments, it is impossible to speak well and yet say other than what I am saying now. The same account is ever mine, namely, that while I do not know how things stand in these matters, I have never met anyone able to speak otherwise without

b being ridiculous, as now. So again, I take these things to be so. If they are so, if injustice is the greatest of evils for him who does it, and if to do injustice and not pay the penalty is an evil still greater than that, if such is possible, then what sort of help is it that would make a man who cannot help himself ridiculous in very truth? Is it not that help which will turn us from the greatest harm? Quite necessarily, this is the kind of help it is most ugly and shameful not to be able to give one's self or family or friends; and the second kind of help is against the second kind of evil,

c third against third, and so on. For in proportion to the natural enormity of each evil is the beauty of being able to help and the ugliness and shame of not being able to help. Do things stand otherwise, or thus, Callicles?

CAL. Not otherwise.

SOC. Then of two things, doing injustice and suffering injustice, we say the greater evil is to do injustice and the lesser to suffer it.

d What then should a man provide in order to help himself so that he has both the benefits of not doing wrong and of not suffering wrong? Is it power, or wish? I mean this: if a man does not wish to suffer injustice, will he therefore not suffer it, or will he rather not suffer it if he procures the power not to suffer it?

CAL. Why clearly, Socrates, it is power.

SOC. Then what about doing injustice? Is it sufficient that if a man

e should not wish to do injustice—for he will not then do it—or must he in this too provide a kind of power and art, because, unless he learns and practices it, he will do injustice? Why not answer that for me, Callicles? Do Polus and I seem to you to have been rightly compelled to agree in the former arguments that no one wishes to do injustice, but that all wrongdoers do wrong unwittingly and unwillingly?

510a CAL. Let it be so, Socrates, so that you can finish the argument.

SOC. Then it seems that a certain power and art must be procured in addition, in order that we may not do injustice.

CAL. Of course.

SOC. Then just what art is it which provides that one suffer no wrong, or as little as possible? Consider whether this seems to you as it does to me: that a man needs to rule in his city, or even be a tyrant, or be a friend to the existing constitution.

CAL. You see how ready I am to praise you, Socrates, when you
b   speak well? This seems excellently said.

SOC. Well, consider whether you think I speak well in this too: it seems to me that, as the ancient and wise say, each is friend to each in the highest degree possible who is "as like to like." Doesn't that seem true to you too?

CAL. It does.

SOC. Then wherever a savage and uneducated tyrant rules, if some-one in the city should be far better than he, the tyrant would surely fear him, and he would never wholeheartedly be able to
c   become his friend.

CAL. That is true.

SOC. Nor would he be a friend to someone far inferior to himself; for the tyrant would despise him and never be in earnest toward him, as one would toward a friend.

CAL. That also is true.

SOC. The only friend left worth mentioning for a man of this sort is someone like him, someone who praises and blames the same
d   things, and is willing to be ruled and to submit to the ruler. That man will have great power in his city. No one will wrong him and enjoy it. Isn't that so?

CAL. Yes.

SOC. Suppose one of the young men in that city should reflect, "How can I get great power and have no one wrong me?" This it seems is the road for him. Straight from youth he must accus-tom himself to rejoice in and be angered at the same things as his master, and so constitute himself as to be as like him as pos-sible. Not so?

CAL. Yes.

soc. He will then have attained to not suffering wrong, and to great
e   power in his city—as your account has it.

CAL. Of course.

soc. Has he also then attained to not doing injustice? Or is he far
from it indeed, if he is like the man who rules him in being
unjust, and if he is to have great power at his side. I suppose he
will be constituted in exactly the opposite way; he will be able to
do as much injustice as possible and not pay penalty for his
wrong. Not so?

CAL. It appears so.

511a soc. Then the greatest evil shall belong to him, that of having a
wicked, mutilated soul, because of his imitation of his master,
and because of power.

CAL. I don't know how you do it, Socrates. You turn arguments
upside down every time. Don't you know that this imitator of
yours will kill the fellow who refuses to imitate that man, if he
wishes, and confiscate his property?

b soc. I do know, good Callicles, unless I'm deaf. I hear it often
enough, from you and Polus now, and from just about everybody
else in the city. But do you therefore now also hear me: he may
kill him if he wishes, but it is a wicked man killing a good and
noble one.

CAL. Isn't that exactly what's so hard to bear?

soc. Not for a man of intelligence, so the argument signifies. Or
do you think that a man ought to contrive to live as long as
possible and be concerned for those arts which always save us
c   from danger, as you bid me be concerned for rhetoric, which
preserves us in lawcourts.

CAL. Yes, and surely I advised you correctly.

soc. Really, dear friend? Tell me, does knowing how to swim seem
to you to be something august and stately?

CAL. Surely not.

soc. Yet it certainly saves men from death, when they fall into the
d   sort of thing where this knowledge is needed. If that seems a
little matter, I offer you a bigger one, the art of the pilot, which
saves not only lives and souls but also bodies and possessions from
the most extreme dangers, just as rhetoric does. And yet, the
pilot is unassuming and orderly, and does not solemnly pose as
working a thing surpassing marvelous. No. For doing the same
sort of thing as forensic rhetoric—safe passage from Aegina,

say—I think the charge is two obols, and at the most a couple of
drachmas from Egypt or the Pontus—this for working the great

e   benefits I just mentioned, saving one's self, one's women and
children, one's possessions, conducting them to safe harbor, all
for two drachmas! And the man who has the art to do this then
disembarks and modestly strolls along the sea by his ship. For he
knows enough to calculate, I suppose, that it is not clear which
among his passengers he has benefited by not allowing them to
drown, and which he has harmed. He knows he has put them
ashore no better in body or soul than they were when they

512a boarded. He calculates that if someone with great and incurable
bodily diseases did not drown, then that person is wretched because he did not die, and got no benefit from him; and therefore,
if someone has many and incurable diseases in what is more
valuable than the body, namely, the soul, that person should not
live and he will not benefit him by saving him, whether from sea,

b   lawcourt or anywhere else. He knows that it is not better for a
wicked man to live; for, necessarily, he lives ill.

This is why the pilot is not accustomed to puff with solemn
pride, even though he saves us. Nor the mechanic either, who
can sometimes save as many lives as a general, let alone a pilot
or someone else. For there are times when he can save whole
cities. You surely don't think him the equal of a forensic advocate,

c   and yet if he wished to speak as you people do, Callicles, puffed
with pride in his business, he could bury you with arguments
stating and proclaiming how one ought to become a mechanic,
since other things are nothing—he could make an ample case.
But you nonetheless look down on him and his art, you call him
"mechanic" as if it were an insult, and you'd refuse to give your
daughter to his son or yourself take his daughter. And yet, given
what you praise of your own, by what just argument do you look
down on the mechanic and the others I mentioned? I know you

d   would say you are a better man derived from better stock. But if
the better is not what I claim it to be, if virtue is just this, saving
yourself and what is yours no matter what sort of man you happen to be, then disapproval of the mechanic and the doctor and
as many other arts as are practiced for the sake of safety becomes
ridiculous. Consider, my fortunate friend, whether the beautiful
and the good consist in something other than saving and being

e   saved. As for living any given length of time, it is truly not something a man should be concerned about, but dismiss. He should in these affairs put his trust in the god, and be persuaded by the women[9] that not one of us can escape his destiny.

It is necessary to inquire in addition how one should pass his life so that he may live best. Is he to become like the constitution of the city in which he dwells? Must you now therefore become most like the Athenian demos, if you are to be loved by it and have great power in the city? Consider then whether this is to your advantage and mine, dear friend, so that we will not suffer what they say happens to the witches of Thessaly, who draw down the moon and cause an eclipse; the choice of such power in the city would then be at the cost of what we hold most dear.[10] If you think any man whatever can give you an art that will make you have great power in this city while yet being unlike its constitution, for better or worse, Callicles, I think you ill advised. You need to be, not merely an imitator, but naturally like them, if you are to achieve any genuine friendship with the Athenian demos, yes, and by Heaven, even with Demos son of Pyrilampes here. Whoever will make you most like them will also make you, as you desire to be a statesman, a statesman and a rhetorician: for each man rejoices in arguments which suit his character, but is irked by those alien to it—unless you mean to say something else, noble friend? Do we have anything to add, Callicles?

CAL. I don't know why, but you seem to me to make sense, Socrates. Yet I suffer the affection of the multitude: I don't quite believe you.

SOC. It is your love of Demos, Callicles. It is in your soul, and it opposes me. But if we should consider these same issues better and more often, you will be persuaded. Anyway, please recall that we said there are two kinds of practices for serving each thing, whether body or soul: one kind aims at pleasure, the other at what is best, not gratifying but struggling with it. Wasn't this the distinction we drew?

CAL. Of course.

SOC. Now, the kind that aims at pleasure is ugly and shameful, nothing more than flattery. Not so?

9. A reference to the Eleusinian Mysteries.

10. Dodds remarks, "The reference is to the widespread belief that a witch must pay for her powers either by a mutilation (often blindness) or by the sacrifice of a member of her family. The blindness of legendary seers and poets has sometimes been understood in the same way, as the price they had to pay for their powers" (Dodds, *Gorgias*).

e CAL. Let it be so for you if you wish.

SOC. But the aim of the other is that what we serve, whether body
or soul, shall be as good as possible?

CAL. Of course.

SOC. So we are to undertake to serve the city and its citizens by
making the citizens themselves as good as possible? For without
that, as we discovered in our former arguments, it is useless to
514a offer any other benefit at all, unless the mind of those who intend
to receive great wealth or authority over people or any other sort
of power is noble and good. Should we say this is so?

CAL. Certainly, if it pleases you.

SOC. Suppose then we were to consult with each other, Callicles,
for purposes of public action in political affairs on the subject of
architecture, about the construction of walls, dockyards, and tem-
b ples, about its greatest structures. Would we need to inquire and
examine ourselves, first, as to whether we know the art of architecture or not, and from whom we' learned it? Would we need to
do that, or not?

CAL. Of course.

SOC. In the second place again, we'd need to ask ourselves whether
we'd ever built a structure for some private person, one of our
friends, say, or ourselves, and whether the building was beautiful
or ugly. And if on examination we found that we'd had notable
c and good teachers, that we'd erected many fine buildings with
our teachers, and many private buildings by ourselves after we'd
left our teachers—then if we were so situated it would make sense
for us to enter on public works. But if we had no teacher of our
own to point to, no buildings to show or many worthless ones, it
d would surely be foolish to undertake public works or consult with
each other about them. Do we say this is correctly stated or not?

CAL. Certainly.

SOC. Well isn't it so in everything? Suppose we undertook to enter
public life and consulted with each other in the capacity of com-
petent doctors. Surely we'd inquire, I of you, you of me, "Come,
just how does Socrates stand in the matter of bodily health? Has
anyone else up to now, slave or free, ever been relieved of disease
through Socrates?" And suppose I might make similar inquiries
e about you. And if we found no one, citizen or stranger, man or
woman, whose body had become better by reason of our ministrations, Callicles, would it not be ridiculous in very truth for
men to reach such a pitch of unreason that, before being in

private practice and doing many things indifferently but also
many well, and being sufficiently exercised in the art, they undertook to try to learn pottery on the big jar, as the saying goes,
trying their own hand at public practice and consulting with others like themselves. Don't you think it would be absurd to act like
that?

CAL. I do.

515a SOC. But as it is, good friend, since you yourself are just now beginning to engage in the affairs of the city, and you consult with
me and blame me because I do not, shall we not examine each
other? "Come, has Callicles up to now made any of our citizens
better? Is there anyone, stranger or citizen, slave or free, who
was bad before, who was unjust and intemperate and foolish, but
b   through Callicles has become noble and good?" Tell me, Callicles,
if someone should examine you on this, what will you say? What
man will you claim has been made better by your company? Do
you shrink from answering whether there is any work of yours
done in private, before undertaking public life?

CAL. You are contentious, Socrates.

SOC. But I surely do not inquire out of contentiousness, but because
I truly wish to know what you think political life among us requires. Will you then care for anything else in entering on the
c   affairs of our city than how we as citizens may be as good as
possible? Have we not often at this point agreed that this is what
a public man should do? Have we agreed or not? Answer me.
     We have. I'll answer for you. So if the good man should aim
at accomplishing this in his own city, please now recollect and tell
me about those men you spoke of a little while ago. Do Pericles
d   and Cimon and Miltiades and Themistocles still seem to you to
have been good citizens?

CAL. They do.

SOC. Then if good, clearly each made his fellow citizens better instead of worse. Did they do that or not?

CAL. Yes.

SOC. So when Pericles first began to speak to the demos, the Athenians were worse than when he made his last speeches?

CAL. Perhaps.

SOC. No perhaps about it, dear friend, but necessarily from what
we've agreed, if, that is, he was a good citizen.

e CAL. Well, what about it?

SOC. Nothing. But please tell me this in addition: are the Athenians said to have become better due to Pericles, or, quite the contrary, to have been corrupted by him? For I do hear that. I hear that Pericles made the Athenians lazy, avaricious, talkative, and cowardly, by first instituting the system of public pay.

CAL. You hear that from the fellows with the broken ears, Socrates.[11]

SOC. But this much I didn't just hear but know clearly, and so do you: Pericles was well regarded in the beginning, and the Athenians voted no shameful judgment on him when they were worse; 516a but when, due to him, they had become noble and good, at the end of his life they convicted him of fraud and very nearly condemned him to death, and this clearly because they thought he was wicked.

CAL. What about it? Was Pericles for that reason bad?

SOC. Well at any rate, an overseer of jackasses or horses or oxen who was like that would seem bad, if he took animals which didn't kick him or butt or bite and left them doing all those things b through sheer wildness. Or doesn't it seem to you that any overseer of any animal is bad, if he takes them more tame and leaves them wilder than he took them?

CAL. I agree to please you.

SOC. Then please me again by answering this: is man also one of the animals, or not?

CAL. Of course.

SOC. Now, Pericles had oversight of men?

CAL. Yes.

SOC. Really? Then shouldn't they have become more just due to c him, instead of more unjust, as we agreed, if he had care of them and was good in political matters?

CAL. Of course.

SOC. Now, as Homer said, "the just are tame and gentle." What do you say? Isn't that so?

CAL. Yes.

SOC. Well now, Pericles surely left the Athenians wilder than he found them, and wild against himself, whom he would least wish.

CAL. Do you wish me to agree with you?

SOC. Yes, if it seems true to you.

---

11. "'The lads with the cauliflower ears' are the young oligarchs of the late fifth century, who advertised their political sympathies by adopting Spartan tastes—one of which was, or was thought to be, the taste for boxing—and Spartan fashions of dress." Dodds, *Gorgias*.

CAL. Then let it be so.

SOC. Now if wilder, then more unjust and worse?

d CAL. Let it be so.

SOC. So by this account, Pericles was not good in political matters after all.

CAL. You say so, at least.

SOC. Yes, and so do you, from what you've agreed to. But again, tell me about Cimon. Didn't the very people he served ostracize him in order not to hear his voice for ten years? And they did the same thing to Themistocles, with the additional punishment of exile. They voted to throw the hero of Marathon, Miltiades,
e into the pit, and if it hadn't been for the President of the Prytany, in he'd have gone. And yet surely, if they were good men as you claim, they would never have suffered these things. Good chariot drivers, at any rate, do not manage to keep their seats when they begin, and then get thrown after they've taken care of their horses and become better drivers. That's not possible in driving chariots or any other line of work. Or do you think so?

CAL. I don't.

SOC. So it seems the earlier account was true: we know of no one
517a who has been a good man in the political affairs of this city. You agree there are none now, but claimed there used to be, and picked out these men. They turn out to be on a level with those now. The result is that if they were orators they did not practice true and genuine rhetoric, or flattery either, for then they would not have been thrown.

CAL. But surely, Socrates, present-day politicians are far from ac-
b complishing the sort of results the others of the past did, whomever you please.

SOC. Dear friend, I'm not blaming them either, at least as servants of the city. On the contrary, they seem to me to have been more serviceable than those now and better able to provide what the city desired. But as for changing those desires and not giving in to them, as for persuading and compelling to that through which
c the citizens will become better—they were scarcely any different. Yet this is the only work of a good citizen. I grant you they were more clever at providing ships, walls, docks, such stuff as that.

Now, we're doing a ridiculous thing in our discussion, you and I. The whole while we've been talking we've never stopped being carried back to the same place, ignorant of what the other is saying. At any rate, I believe you have many times acknowledged and agreed that there is a twofold treatment respecting body and

d   soul: one a kind of service by which it is possible to provide food
for our bodies when hungry, drink when thirsty, cloaks, bedding,
and shoes when cold, and the other things bodies come to desire.
And I purposely speak to you in terms of these comparisons in
order that you may more easily understand. For if one provides
these things either as tradesman or merchant or manufacturer

e   of any of them, baker or cook, weaver, shoemaker, or tanner, it
is hardly surprising that such a person should seem to himself
and others to serve the body. Seem so, that is, to anyone who
does not know that there is, besides all these, an art of gymnastic
and medicine which is the real servant of the body, and to which
belongs authority over all other arts and the use of the works of
them, because it knows what is useful and bad among food and

518a drink in respect to the virtue and excellence of the body, while
the other practices are ignorant; this is why they are slavish and
unfree servants in their treatment of the body, while the arts of
gymnastic and medicine are justly their natural masters.

These same things are also true of the soul. At one point I
thought you understood what I meant, and that you agreed be-

b   cause you understood; but a little later you came and said there
have been good and noble men as citizens in our city, and when
I asked you who they were, you put forward, I think, exactly the
kind of men—in this case regarding political affairs—as you
would if I asked you about gymnastic, about who are or have
been good servants of the body, and you replied quite earnestly,
"Thearion the baker, Mithaecus who wrote the Sicilian cookbook,
Sarambus the vintner. They have been wonderful servants of the

c   body; one makes marvelous cakes, the other exquisite dishes, the
third fine wine." Perhaps then you'd be angered if I said to you,
"Man, you don't understand a thing about gymnastic. You tell
me about servants who cater to desires, without realizing there is
nothing fine or good about them. They blindly fill and stuff the
bodies of men, and so are praised by them, while taking away

d   the original flesh they once had. But those folk in turn, due to
perplexity, do not blame the hosts of their feast as causes of their
diseases and the ruin of their original flesh; they rather blame
those who happen to be present and giving advice at the time.
Then, when earlier stuffing brings later disease because they have
done without what is healthy, they hold those present responsible
and blame them, and will do them some evil if they can; while

they praise those earlier men who were the actual causes of their ills.

e   What you're doing now is just like that, Callicles. You're praising the men who fed and feasted the citizens on what they desired. People say those men of earlier times made the city great. They are unaware that its greatness, due to them, is that of a
519a   tumor, scabbed over and festering. They have filled the city with harbors and dockyards and walls and tribute and other such nonsense without justice and temperance, and then when the fit of weakness is upon them they blame their present advisers, while praising Themistocles and Cimon and Pericles, the causes of their evils. Perhaps they'll attack you too, if you're not careful, and my
b   companion Alcibiades, when they lose what they originally had in addition to what they've since got, even though you're not the principal causes of their ills, though perhaps accessories. It is an irrational thing I see happening now and hear about the men of the past. For I perceive that when the city takes in hand one of its politicians for wrongdoing, he is angry and bitterly complains that he is suffering terrible things; having done many good things for the city, is he now to be unjustly destroyed by her?—such is the burden of his plaint.

c   But the whole thing is a lie. Not one real leader of a city would ever be unjustly destroyed by the city he leads. It is very much the same with people who pretend to be politicians as it is with sophists. The sophists, in fact, wise as they are in other things, reach this absurd result: they claim to be teachers of virtue and yet often accuse their students of unjustly depriving them of their
d   fee, and not giving any gain for the good they got. And yet, what could be more unreasonable! Men who have become good and just, because their injustice has been taken away by their teacher and justice put in its place, are committing injustice by reason of what they haven't got. Doesn't that seem absurd to you, my friend?

       You are compelling me to be a public speaker in very truth, Callicles, since you're unwilling to answer.

       CAL. Can't you speak unless someone answers you?

e SOC. Yes, apparently. At any rate I tend now toward long speeches, since as things stand, you're not willing to answer me. But in the name of Zeus, God of Friendship, tell me, good fellow: don't you find it unreasonable for a man to claim to have made somebody good and then to blame him because, having been made good and being good still, he's bad?

CAL. Yes, it seems so to me.

SOC. Well, don't you hear things of that sort said by the people who claim to teach men virtue?

520a CAL. I do. But what can you say about such worthless fellows.

SOC. What can you say about people who claim to govern the city and to exercise care that it should be as good as possible, and then when it suits their purpose accuse her of immense evil? Do you think there's any difference between these and those? Sophist and orator are the same, my fortunate friend, or very nearly so and very close, as I was just telling Polus. Through ignorance,

b you think that the one, rhetoric, is utterly beautiful, and you despise the other. But in truth, sophistry is more beautiful than rhetoric in the same ratio that law-giving is more beautiful than judging and gymnastic than medicine. Indeed, I should have thought it is only sophists and orators who are not in a position to blame the business they teach for wickedness to them, or at once, by the same argument, accuse themselves of having rendered no benefit to those they claim to benefit. Isn't that so?

c CAL. Of course.

SOC. And yet, it is only they, surely, or so it is reasonable to think, who are in a position to give their services freely and without pay, if indeed they are telling the truth. A person benefited by another kind of service, for example, becoming a fast runner due to a trainer, would perhaps deprive him of gain if the trainer gave to him freely and did not agree with him on a fee, the money

d to be received as nearly as possible at the same time the speed is imparted. For men do not do wrong by being slow of foot, but by injustice. Not so?

CAL. Yes.

SOC. Then if someone removed that very thing, injustice, he would never have reason to fear being unjustly treated. This benefit is the only one which it is safe to give freely, if in fact one can really make people good. Not so?

CAL. I agree.

SOC. So for that reason, it seems, there is nothing ugly and shameful about taking money for giving advice in other affairs, for example in architecture and the other arts.

e CAL. So it seems.

soc. But in just this one case, dealing with how one may be as good as possible and best manage one's household or city, it is considered ugly and shameful to refuse to give advice unless someone pays for it. Not so?

cal. Yes.

soc. And the cause is clearly this, that it is only this service which makes the man benefited desire to do good in return, so that it seems a noble sign if one returns the benefit in kind; but if not, not. Are these things so?

521a cal. Yes.

soc. Then please distinguish for me the kind of service to the city to which you summon me: is it the kind which struggles with the Athenians so that they will be as good as possible, like a doctor, or is it like a servant who deals with them only for his own gain? Tell me the truth, Callicles. It is right, since you began by speaking so frankly, to finish by saying what you think. Speak out now, nobly and well.

cal. I say, then, it is the kind like a servant.

b soc. So you summon me to be a flatterer, my most noble friend.

cal. Yes, Socrates, if you are pleased to use a derogatory name. Because unless you do this . . .

soc. Please don't say what you've so often said, that whoever wishes will kill me, in order that I may not again reply that it is in that case a wicked man killing a good one. Again, don't say he will take what I own, in order that I may not again reply that when he has taken it he will not know how to use it, but that as he took

c it from me unjustly so in taking it he will also use it unjustly, and if unjustly, shamefully, and if shamefully, badly.

cal. Socrates, you seem to believe you will not suffer any of these things, as though you dwelt out of harm's way, and couldn't be brought to court perhaps even by a very low and paltry fellow.

soc. Then I'm a fool, Callicles, and truly a fool, if I don't think that in this city anything can happen to anybody. But this I will

d know: if I go to court and run any of the risks you mention, my prosecutor will be a wicked man, for no one just and good would prosecute a man who has done no wrong. Nor would it be surprising if I were put to death. Shall I tell you why I expect this?

cal. Of course.

soc. I think that I am one of the few Athenians, and I say few in order that I may not say only, who undertakes to practice the true art of politics, and that I alone among our contemporaries perform the statesman's task. Now, because the arguments I on each occasion put are not put for gain or favor, but for what is

e   best, not for what is most pleasant, and, because I am not willing to do these clevernesses you bid me do, I shall have nothing to say in court. That same story I told to Polus will apply to me: I'll be judged like a doctor before a jury of children on charges brought by a pastry-cook. What defense could such a man make if accused before them? "Children, the defendant here has done many bad things to you. He corrupts the youngest among you

522a by cutting and burning, he reduces them to perplexity by drying them out and stewing them, prescribing the most bitter potions, compelling hunger and thirst; nor does he entertain you, as I do, with all kinds of delicious treats." What do you think a doctor caught up in this evil could say? If he told the truth, if he said, "Children, I did do all these things, and for your health," how great do you think the outcry from such judges would be? A pretty big one?

CAL. Perhaps. One must suppose so.

SOC. Do you then think he'd be reduced to utter perplexity about

b   what he should say?

CAL. Of course.

SOC. I know that if I am brought into court, it will be the same with me. I will not be able to tell them of pleasures I've provided, the things they consider kindnesses and benefits; and I envy neither those who provide them nor those for whom they are provided. If someone accuses me of corrupting the youth by reducing them to perplexity, or of abusing their elders with sharp and pointed speech, in public or private, I won't be able to tell

c   the truth, which is, "I say all these things justly, Gentlemen and Judges, and do so for your benefit." Nor will I be able to say anything else. The result, no doubt, will be that I'll take whatever comes.

CAL. Then you think, Socrates, that a man so situated in his own city, unable to help himself, is well off?

SOC. Yes, Callicles, if he but have one thing to which you have often

d   agreed: if he has helped himself by doing no injustice, in word or deed, to gods or men. For we have often agreed that it is this means of self-help which is strongest. If I am convicted of being unable to render that kind of help to myself or another, I would then indeed be ashamed, whether I am convicted before many, or few, or as one single man convicted by another; and if I were to die for lack of that ability, I would be distressed indeed. But if I should reach my end for lack of flattering rhetoric, be assured

e   that you would then see me bear death lightly. No man not utterly unreasonable and cowardly fears dying in itself; but he fears the doing of injustice. For the ultimate evil is for a soul to arrive at the Place of the Dead teeming with multiple injustices.

But if you wish, I will offer an account of this too.

CAL. Well, since you finished the other arguments, please finish this as well.

A Vision of Judgment (523a–527e)

523a SOC. Hear then, as they say, a very beautiful story, which you will consider a myth, I suppose, but I a true account. For I relate this to you as the truth. Homer tells how Zeus, Poseidon, and Pluto divided authority among themselves when they received it from their father. Now, it was law for men in the time of Cronos, and ever is and is still among gods, that he among men who passes his life justly and in holiness, when he dies, goes hence to the

b   Isles of the Blessed, to dwell in complete happiness, away from evils; but he who passes his life unjustly and godlessly goes hence to the prison of justice and punishment which they call Tartarus. Now, there were judges of such men in the time of Cronos, and early in the time of Zeus, living men having authority over the living, judging them on the day they were to die.

Now, the judgments were badly rendered. So Pluto and the overseers of the Isles of the Blessed went to Zeus and told him that men were passing to each place contrary to desert.

c   Now, Zeus said, "I will put a stop to this. Judgments are now badly rendered because those judged are judged while still alive. Many people," he said, "have wicked souls dressed up in beautiful bodies, with ancestry and wealth, and when they come to judgment they bring many witnesses to appear in their behalf, testi-

d   fying that they lived justly. The judges are confused by this, and at the same time, they are clothed themselves when they render judgment, and their souls veiled by eyes and ears and the whole of the body. All these things are impediments to them, both their own clothing and those of the people they judge. First of all, then," he said, "it is necessary to put a stop to foreknowledge of death: for now people know in advance. And so Prometheus has

e   already been told to put an end to this. Next, let all of them be judged naked, for they must be judged dead; and their judge too must be naked, and dead, contemplating the soul alone by itself by means of the soul alone by itself at the very moment each person dies, bereft of all family and leaving behind on this earth all ornament and dress, in order that the judgment may be just. Now, I realized this before you did, and have appointed my own sons as judges: two from Asia, Minos and Rhadamanthus, and

524a one from Europe, Aeacus. These then, when they die, shall render judgment in the meadow where three ways meet, whence lead two roads, one to the Isles of the Blessed, the other to Tartarus. Rhadamanthus shall judge those from Asia, Aeacus those from Europe, but I shall grant to Minos authority to judge on review, if either of the other two are perplexed, in order that judgment concerning the journey of men may be most just."

b   This I have heard, Callicles, and I believe it true. And I reckon that something of this sort follows: that death, or so it seems to me, is nothing other than the separation of two things, soul and body, from each other. And when they are separate from each other, each of the two has its own disposition very much as when it was man alive. The body has its own nature, and the results

c   of its treatment and what it suffered are all evident upon it. For example, if the body was large by nature or by diet or by both when alive, the corpse will be large when he is dead, if fat alive, then fat dead, and so on. If again he let his hair grow long, he will have a long-haired corpse. Again, if a common criminal had the mark of blows as scars on his body from whips or other wounds when alive, the body at death is seen to have them too. If someone's limbs have been broken or deformed while alive,

d   the same thing will be evident in death. In a word, as the body has been constituted while alive, so these things also are evident at death, either entirely or for the most part, for some time.

        This same thing then also seems true to me of the soul, Callicles. Stripped of the body, everything is evident in the soul, what is in it by nature as well as the effects on it the man got in life by his various pursuits. Now, when they come before their judge,

e   as those from Asia before Rhadamanthus, Rhadamanthus stops them and inspects the soul of each, not knowing whose it is. Many a time he has laid hold of the Great King or some other king or

525a potentate, and seen nothing healthy in their soul, whipped and scarred by perjury and injustice. Each act has left its stain on it, and it is all limping and crooked due to falsity and pretense, and nothing straight because it was brought up without truth. He saw that due to license and luxury, the insolence and intemperance of its deeds, it teemed with ugliness and lack of proportion, and seeing this, he sent it dishonored straight to the Prison where,

b   arriving, it suffers what befits it. Now, it pertains to everyone punished, if rightly punished, either to become better and profit by it, or to be an example to others, in order that they, by seeing what he suffers, may fear and so become better. Those who are benefited by paying penalty at the hands of gods and men are those who have erred with sins which admit of cure. Nevertheless, it is through pain and suffering that their benefit comes, both here and in the Place of the Dead, for it is impossible otherwise

c   to be relieved of injustice. But those who have done the extreme of injustice, and as a result of such wrongs have become incurable, serve as examples; they are no longer any good to themselves, because incurable, but others may profit from seeing them suffer the greatest and most painful and frightful sufferings for all time because of their sins. They therefore are gibbeted in the prison of the Dead simply as examples, spectacles and warnings to those who ever come there for injustice.

d   I say that Archelaus too will be one of them, if Polus tells the truth, as well as any other tyrant of the sort. Indeed, I suppose most of these examples are got from tyrants and kings and potentates, and those who conduct the business of cities, for it is they who commit the greatest and most unholy sins, because of their resources. Homer also testifies to this: for he makes kings

e   and potentates be punished in the Place of the Dead for all time— Tantalus and Sisyphus and Tityus. But no one portrayed Thersites, or any other private person who was wicked, as subjected to great punishments because incurable; I suppose it wasn't possible for him, and he was therefore more happy than those for whom it was possible. In fact, Callicles, it is among the powerful

526a   that especially wicked men arise. Still, nothing prevents men from becoming good even among them, and when that happens it is especially worthy of admiration. For it is a hard thing, Callicles, and worthy of great praise, to pass one's life justly in the midst of great resources for injustice. Such men as this are few. But here and elsewhere there have been, and I think will continue to

b   be, men who are noble and good in that virtue which justly handles what is entrusted to their charge. One such man, famous even in the rest of Greece, is Aristides son of Lysimachus. But many among the powerful, my friend, are bad.

Now, as I was saying, when Rhadamanthus takes hold of someone of this sort, he knows nothing else about him, neither who he is nor of what family, but only that he is someone wicked, and when he sees this, he sends him straight to Tartarus, marking him with a sign indicating whether he thinks him curable or incurable. And when he arrives there he suffers what is fit.

c   But sometimes Rhadamanthus sees another kind of soul, who has lived life in holiness and in the company of truth, whether as private person or someone else, but especially, as I claim, Callicles, as a philosopher who has tended his own affairs and did not during his life officiously intermeddle with others. Rhadamanthus is filled with admiration, and sends him to the Isles of the Blessed. And the same is true of Aeacus. Each of them has
d   a staff of office as he renders judgment, but Minos sits as Odysseus in Homer says he saw him, "holding a golden scepter, laying down ordinances for the dead."

Now, I am convinced by this account, Callicles, and I consider how I shall show my judge that my soul is as healthy as possible. So, bidding farewell to the honors of the majority of men, and practicing the truth, I shall really try to be and live in the truth, so that I may be as good as possible, and, when I die, to die in
e   it. And I summon all other men, so far as I am able, and in answer to your summons, Callicles, I also summon you to this life and this contest, which I claim is superior to all the other contests here. I reproach you because you will be unable to help yourself when you come to the trial and judgment I have just described. When you come before your judge, the son of Aegina,
527a   Aeacus, when he lays hold on you and drags you away, then your jaw will drop with dizziness, yours there no less than mine here, and it will be you, perhaps, who is ignobly punched on the chin and treated with foul insult.

Perhaps these things will seem to you like a tale told by an old woman, and you will despise them. Surely there would be nothing strange in despising them, if somehow by searching we might find a better, truer story. But as it is, you see that you are three men among the wisest of any now in Greece, you and Polus and
b   Gorgias, and you cannot show that a person should live any other life than this, which also appears to be of advantage there, in the

beyond. Among so many arguments, others have been refuted but this alone abides: that the doing of injustice is more to be guarded against than the suffering of injustice, that more than anything else a man must take care not to seem good but to be good, both in public and private; that if someone becomes bad in some respect he must be punished, and this is a second good after actually being just, namely, becoming just by paying the penalty and being punished; furthermore, that all flattery, whether of oneself or others, whether of few or of many, is to be shunned, and that rhetoric, and every other practice, is to be used ever for what is just.

Follow me then, as one persuaded, to where when you arrive you will as this account signifies be happy both in living and dying. Permit anyone to despise you as a fool and treat you with contumely if he wishes, and yes, by Zeus, be of good cheer and let him strike that unworthy blow; for you will suffer nothing terrible, if you practice virtue and are noble and good in reality and truth. Afterwards, as we thus practice virtue together, if then, at that point, it seems right that we should enter politics or do any other thing which seems good to us, we shall then decide as we wish, for then we shall be better able to decide as we wish than now. For being as we now appear to be, it is ugly and shameful to boast of being something, when the same things never seem true to us about the same subjects, and this in matters of uttermost importance. So lacking are we in true education. Let us therefore use as a guide the account now revealed, which signifies to us that this is the best manner of life, to live and die in the practice of justice and the rest of virtue. Let us then follow this, and summon others to follow it, rather than that thing in which you believe and to which you summon me. For it is worthless, Callicles.

VI: MENEXENUS

COMMENT

Plato's *Menexenus* is a stumbling block to students of ancient philosophy, and a scandal to historians. Students of ancient rhetoric, however, tend to like it a lot.

In the *Menexenus*, Socrates narrates an *epitaphios*, a funeral oration over the dead in battle—never mind which battle, or which war—which he claims to have heard from Aspasia, the mistress of Pericles. The speech covers a great deal of ground, offering a history of Athens beginning with the contest of Athena and Poseidon for possession of Attica. This is like beginning a history of the United States with the first chapter of *Genesis*. The story is carried down to the end of the Corinthian War and the King's Peace of 387 B.C. Because Socrates died in 399 B.C., almost fifteen years before, this is an anachronism. Aspasia almost certainly died before Socrates. Pericles, who died in the autumn of 429 B.C., is at one point spoken of as if still alive (235e). The history, in its descent from Olympian legend to remembered fact, is distorted and falsified. But it is a wonderful speech.

Not surprisingly, many scholars would gladly relieve Plato of responsibility for this puzzling piece of work if they could. They can't. Aristotle in the *Rhetoric* (1367b8) ascribes to Socrates the dictum that it is not difficult to praise Athenians among Athenians; the reference is to *Menexenus* 236a. Later on in the *Rhetoric* (1415b30), Aristotle says that Socrates said in the *Epitaphios* that the difficulty is not to praise Athenians in Athens but in Sparta; the reference is to *Menexenus* 235d, and represents Socrates' own view of the speech, which is meant for an Athenian audience: the speech is flattery. Aristotle not only establishes the genuineness of the *Menexenus*, but also, probably following the tradition of the early Academy, provides a key to its interpretation.

319

Rhetorical flattery is the theme of the *Menexenus*, a fact indicated by the introduction alone. Socrates there suggests that it is well worth dying in battle, because you get a fine funeral even if you are poor, and people praise you even if you are worthless. Wise men proclaim your virtue whether you had it or not, and the whole performance has about it a kind of witchery which can make a man forget himself, and make him feel bigger, better-born and better-looking—sometimes for as much as a week afterwards. Menexenus replies that Socrates is always poking fun at the orators.

Flattery is connected with falsehood. If we follow Mark Twain's distinction between lies, damn lies, and statistics, the speech of Aspasia is very nearly a statistic. The defeat of Athens by Sparta in the Peloponnesian War, the most important event in the history of Athens since the Persian invasion nearly a century before it, is glossed over and ignored (243d). The bloody reign of the Thirty Tyrants is barely alluded to, and then palliated (243e–244a). When Imperial Athens is described as ever too prone to pity, and the servant of the weak (244e, cf. 242d), we recall with a shiver the massacre she almost committed at Mytilene and finally did commit at Melos in 416, and we remember the concluding chorus of Euripides's *Trojan Women*, performed the following year: "How are ye blind, ye who lay waste to cities and cast down temples and defile graves—yourselves so soon to die."

That was the year of the Sicilian expedition, of which Aspasia says that those who took part got more praise for their temperance and virtue from their enemies than other men get from their friends (243a). There is no mention of the fact that Athens lost a fleet and an army in this expedition, that the survivors were captured and enslaved, that they were so tightly packed into a stone quarry that they stood in their own waste as they died of wounds and exposure. Nor does Aspasia mention that the Sicilians celebrated their own release from the threat of Athens as joyously as ever Athens celebrated Salamis and her release from the threat of Persia.

We know where we are. Socrates in the *Gorgias* distinguishes two kinds of rhetoric. There is philosophical rhetoric, aimed at truth and the good of the soul, whether it gives pleasure or pain to the hearer, and organized like the work of an artist to attain its aim. Then there is base rhetoric, aimed at gratification and pleasure, organized randomly according to knack and experience, a species of flattery; its effect on the hearer is like witchcraft or enchantment.

Tried by this touchstone, it is clear that the speech of Aspasia is base rhetoric. As Socrates himself suggests, it is witchcraft or enchantment which is eminently gratifying but which produces false beliefs (235a–c); it is flattery, praising the Athenians to their faces (235d, 236a); it does not aim at truth, but consciously says both what is true and what is false (234e, cf. 249d–e); it is organized randomly, "glued together" with left-overs from Pericles's Funeral Oration, some of it composed before, and some made up on the spot (236b). Its falsity is emphasized by the gorgeous anachronism of having both Aspasia and Socrates speak on well after their deaths, and by pretending that Aspasia is its author (cf. 249d–e).

There is a persistent scholarly tradition which, while admitting that the speech of Aspasia is sandwiched between two puzzling pieces of dialogue which seem to deny its seriousness, affirms its excellence as a specimen of Greek oratory. It is said that the speech is in structure a model funeral oration, offering Eulogy for the dead, Exhortation and Consolation to the living; or it is said that it is an appeal to the Athenians of 386 B.C. to prove themselves worthy of the noble and glorious traditions of their city. The speech, it is said, is not random, but well organized; it thus meets the requirements of philosophical rhetoric. The multiple falsehoods it contains can be explained as "noble lies," for lying is good for the soul when it increases civic pride. And even if the eulogy is full of historical falsehoods, the consolation offered to the living is profoundly moving and too serious a subject to admit of parody or satire. The speech was read as a genuine funeral oration in antiquity: by Dionysius of Halicarnassus at the end of the first century B.C. and by Hermogenes in the second century A.D. And if Cicero is right (*Or.* 44.151), the Athenians of his time had revived the oration and recited it publicly once a year as part of the Athenian equivalent of an Independence Day celebration—letting the owl hoot as we might let the eagle scream.

The short answer to this is that it is impossible to reconcile claims of seriousness with the introduction to the *Menexenus* and that such an interpretation therefore neglects the manifest sense of the document it interprets. The speech is no doubt good of its kind, but its kind is not good: it is base rhetoric. Rhetoric which aims at the good of the soul must aim also at truth, or so the *Gorgias* claims, and if the *Menexenus* conforms to the accepted structure of a funeral oration, that structure is itself the product merely of knack and experience in achieving a desired effect. The oration uses a multitude of rhetorical figures, but uses them at random, as Dionysius of Halicarnassus himself complained, and it conceals by the glister of style its hollowness of substance. Thus for example its concept of virtue, *arete*, human excellence, is in Platonic terms clearly debased: Aspasia uses the word to mean valor, excellence as a soldier, a meaning associated with the commonsense view which identified the virtue of a man with helping friends, harming enemies, and managing the affairs of the city. So Meno thought, and so Polemarchus. In the same vein, the consolation offered to the living, so widely admired by students of rhetoric, offers a lovely parody of Socrates' speech in the *Apology* (246a–b), with overtones of the Speech of the Laws in the *Crito* (246d). This is self-parody, a trick only a master of style could play. The Socratic doctrine that virtue is knowledge is again parodied by the claim that knowledge, when separated from justice and other virtues, is unscrupulous (247a): the difference in the two concepts of virtue could hardly be more pronounced (cf. *Gorgias* 502d–503d). That several Hellenistic critics, and the apparently love-starved Athenians of Cicero's time, took the speech seriously is one more indication of the necessity of relying, in matters of interpretation, not on arguments from authority, even ancient authority, but on texts. If the Athenians of Cicero's time read Aspasia's speech as part of a public ceremony in praise of their polity, they were like the Scots and the bagpipe: the Irish gave the Scots the bagpipe as a joke, or so it is told, and the Scots didn't get it.

If finally it is asked how Plato could produce a mock funeral oration which is in some sense a spoof, the answer is that a funeral oration has a very different meaning to an ordinary Athenian than it does to a man who believes in the immortality of the soul, and further believes that in some metaphorical sense, the dead now praised have on the day of their death already faced their judgment stripped of clothes and all other concealment—not to mention armor. Funeral orations take on a different sense when read in light of the eschatology of the *Gorgias*. A bad man praised because he has died in battle is not ahead of the game, if he died a bad man.

The *Menexenus* is clearly related to the *Gorgias*. E. R. Dodds, indeed, thought they were related as example to theory (*Gorgias*, pp. 23–24):

> Both deal with rhetoric and with the use of rhetoric by Athenian politicians; but while the *Gorgias* examines its theoretic basis, the *Menexenus* illustrates its practice by means of an imaginary funeral oration which parodies the stylistic tricks and historical falsifications of patriotic oratory. The two of them are complementary, unequal though they are in length and importance; and both of them convey the same criticisms of Athenian democracy and Athenian foreign policy, though the expression is direct in one case, ironical in the other.

Given that the *Menexenus* is ironical, it is irony with a serious purpose.

The choice of Aspasia as its author, the frequent verbal and structural resemblances, the direct mention of Pericles and his speech, leave no doubt that it is aimed at Thucydides' report (*Hist.*ii.33–46) of Pericles's Funeral Oration. Is the irony then aimed at Pericles, or Thucydides?

Plato entertained no high regard for Pericles as a statesman. In the *Gorgias,* Socrates says that he made Athens great, but the greatness was like that of a tumor. We may perhaps find this unfair to the man who built the Parthenon and Erectheum as public works projects: Plutarch, long after, would say, "There exudes from these monuments a spirit of youth which has not been affected by time, and the images are still imbued with the breath of life, as if endowed with a soul which will never grow old" (*Pericles* 159.3). No one has ever thought to compare the Parthenon with the Post Office architecture of the New Deal, nor the aesthetic imagination of Phidias with that of Postmaster General James Farley, but there is one respect in which Pericles surely lagged. He had not discovered that public debt is wealth, and he financed his army of artists and builders with tribute exacted from Athens's erstwhile allies. It was a policy of coercion which would ultimately lead, after Pericles's death, to the tragedy of Melos. Pericles could boast truly that no Athenian ever put on black because of him; and yet, the monuments for which we reverence his name were bought at the cost of freedom, of avoidable human suffering, and in the long run of the continued vitality of Greek political institutions.

Yet it is clear that the *Menexenus,* considered as satire, is not aimed at any speech of Pericles, unless Thucydides' account of the Funeral Oration by Pericles is essentially accurate to what Pericles said.

This is a matter of considerable debate among students of Thucydides. That is, there is debate whether his account of the Funeral Oration represents what Pericles did say or could have said in 431–30, the first winter of the War, when it was supposed to have been delivered, or whether, on the contrary, it represents Thucydides' own thoughts after 404 B.C., when Athens was beaten and humbled, when Pericles's policy of imperialism, followed by lesser men, had put in doubt the very value of Athenian civilization, when Athens, "the education of Hellas," had ceased to teach. The ever-judicious Gomme is extremely reserved on the point (*Commentary on Thucydides* iii.104), but this much can be surely ascertained. The speeches of the historical Pericles, though lost, were of an oratorical style which Plato himself praised as outstanding (*Phaedrus* 269e) even though he could not have heard them delivered, and distinguished by their simplicity of diction. Their style was very different from that of the Funeral Oration Thucydides presents (Denniston, *Greek Prose Style* 9.12–13), and very different again from the style of Aspasia's oration, with its frequent, elaborate, and random use of figures of speech.

Yet Aspasia's speech constantly recalls Thucydides. It begins with his overworked antithesis between words and deeds (236d–e; cf. Denniston, 13), and concludes by directly quoting the last sentences of Thucydides' account (249c; cf. *Hist*.ii.46.2). And, though there are various factual divergences from the *History*, the wonderful description of the Athenian polity as "aristocracy with the approval of the multitude" (238c) is a direct quotation from Thucydides (ii.37.1).

To this may be added that Thucydides is almost certainly directly referred to in the *Menexenus*. At 236a, Socrates speaks disparagingly of someone who learned his music from Lamprus and his rhetoric from Antiphon of Rhamnusia: even he, though not as well trained as Socrates, who has studied under Aspasia and Connus, might still be well-esteemed if he praised Athenians among Athenians. We know very little of the life of Thucydides son of Olorus. In particular, we do not know with whom he studied music. But his reference to Antiphon of Rhamnusia (*Hist*.viii.68) reads like a tribute to an honored teacher, and a tradition derived from Pseudo-Plutarch (who is, of course, Pseudo only in that he is not Plutarch, but an unknown author of a work ascribed to Plutarch) also claims that Thucydides was Antiphon's pupil.

The circle is complete. Aristotle identifies the speech of Aspasia in the *Menexenus* as flattery. Examination of the *Menexenus* shows it is Thucydides, in his account of Pericles's Funeral Oration, who is the primary flatterer in view. Here is Thucydides' Pericles, in J. B. Bury's admirable translation:

> I would have you day by day fix your eyes on the greatness of Athens, until you become filled with the love of her; and when you are impressed by the spectacle of her glory, reflect that this empire has been acquired by men who knew their duty and had the courage to do it. The whole earth is the sepulchre of famous men; not only are they commemorated by columns and inscriptions in their own country, but in foreign lands there dwells an unwritten memorial to them, graven not in stone but in the hearts of men. Make them your examples.

This is indeed the sort of thing which could make an Athenian feel bigger, better-born and better-looking on the spot. And if we are to trust the *Menexenus*, it is flattery. One might recall by way of contrast Abraham Lincoln's story of the tough who said, "I feel patriotic," and when asked what he meant replied, "I feel like either killing somebody or stealing something." *Dulce et decorum est pro patria mori,* no doubt; but not in abstraction from the justice of the cause, and the worth of the values defended.

The *Menexenus* is primarily a criticism of Thucydides, not Pericles. We miss this point because we fall into a fallacy of referential opacity. We think that Thucydides is a great historian. We think that Plato is a great philosopher. We therefore think that Plato thought that Thucydides is a great historian. The inference does not follow, and it neglects, among other things, the radical, root-and-branch criticism Plato offers of the intellectual life of his time.

Plato's criticism of Thucydides must surely have extended beyond the Funeral Oration. Thucydides offered his history as a *ktema es aiei,* a possession forever (i.22), in the belief that human nature being what it is, past events will be repeated in much the same way in the future. This is the ultimate source of Santayana's remark that those who cannot remember the past are condemned to repeat it. And yet to Plato, this must surely have seemed foolish. History, to borrow from Gibbon in a mood not averse to Thucydides, is little more than the register of the crimes, follies, and misfortunes of mankind. Plato thought that while goodness is one, the forms and kinds of evils are, if not infinite, indefinitely multitudinous. History is fecund, all too fecund: no record of the ways in which our forebears went wrong will prevent us from finding new ways to go wrong if we are bad men. That is, vice always implies a certain originality, and evil is not generally banal. We admire villains by reason of our interest in novelty. If you want knowledge about human nature that you can trust, you had better study not history but moral philosophy.

Plato's skepticism of history must surely have run deep. Ranke, the proponent of "scientific" history, history *wie es denn eigentlich gewesen ist,* saw in Thucydides his most distinguished predecessor. And Thucydides himself stresses repeatedly the care he has taken to find out "how it really was," both in respect to verification of facts and reports of speeches. Yet when Aspasia ironically follows Thucydides' Pericles (cf. Gomme, *Commentary* ii.104, 109, 110) in praising the glorious heritage and traditions of the city in which the dead were born and raised, we recall the *archeology* of the *History,* where Thucydides decides that Attica has always been inhabited by the same race of people, free of political division due to the poverty of its soil (i.2); he accepts Homer as a historical authority, assumes that the Trojan War actually happened, and takes Minos (i.4) and Agamemnon (i.9) as real people; he then solemnly explains the trouble he has been at to achieve accuracy in these matters (i.20). Aspasia goes him one better. She begins Athenian history with the contest of Poseidon and Athena for Attica, and decides that Attica has always been inhabited by the same race of people because of the richness of the land, which first in all the world brought forth, not only men, but wheat and barley and the fruit of the olive. The contradiction with Thucydides is direct—and in the fourth century there was no way of verifying either view.

Thucydides, and Ranke after him, supposed that history could provide knowledge. Plato, on the contrary, would have supposed that the past is not a guide to the future, being indefinitely particular, and that there is no knowledge in history. For knowledge consists in what could not have been otherwise, and Plato inferred that it is therefore of what always is and never changes. History, on the contrary, consists always in what could have been otherwise. It is in some sense inconceivable that snow should be hot; it is not inconceivable that the Athenians should have lost at Marathon.

To carry this one step further, history, res gestae, is a record of events, and events are apprehended by perception. Not only is what is apprehended by perception not knowledge, but a record of events is twice removed from knowledge, because it requires not only perception but remembered perception. History is opinion about past events based on the report of someone who claims to have observed and remembered them. Failure of perception, failure of memory, are sources of error. If this seems unduly stringent, listen to Henry Adams: "Historians undertake to arrange sequences—called stories, or histories—assuming in silence a relation of cause and effect. These assumptions, hidden in the depths of dusty libraries, have been astounding, but uncommonly unconscious and childlike, so much so that if any captious critic were to drag them to light, historians would probably reply, with one voice, that they never supposed themselves required to know what they were talking about." This of course is precisely the Platonic criticism: without knowledge of essence, historians quite literally cannot know what they are talking about. As a result, they are constantly open to the kind of bias, or so the *Menexenus* suggests, associated with rhetoric and flattery. Thucydides, often acclaimed the dean of scientific historians, was in Plato's view in some measure a propagandist. Nor would this estimate have changed if Plato understood Thucydides to be concerned with morality and character rather than value-free inquiry: if there are moral claims in the *History*, they are founded on popular rhetoric and events, rather than dialectical inquiry into the aims of human life and thereby into what virtue is.

As history, res gestae, is not knowledge, so there is no such thing as philosophy of history. In a Platonic universe, history, res actae, has no immanent or transcendent purpose. Nor is there any epistemology suited to history alone. If we seek to understand history, we must first understand knowledge, and we will then understand why history is not knowledge. Aristotle put the point directly in *Poetics* (9): poetry is more philosophical than history, because it pertains more closely to the universal. History at best is annalism, at worst flattery and propaganda, and in either case unimportant in comparison to moral philosophy. And Plato never feels called to so much as mention Thucydides by name.

TRANSLATION

SOCRATES / MENEXENUS

Introduction (234a–236d)

234a SOC. Where from, Menexenus? The Agora?

MEN. Yes, from the Council Chamber, Socrates.

SOC. Why there, especially? But then, you no doubt believe you've finally finished with education and philosophy, and are now ready to turn your attention to more important things. And young as
b you are, do you mean to rule your elders, so that your house may never fail to provide an overseer for us?

MEN. Why Socrates, if you allow it and advise me to rule, I'll do so eagerly, but not otherwise. Actually though, I went because I heard the Council was going to choose the Funeral Orator. They're about to perform the rites, you know.

SOC. Of course. Whom did they choose?

MEN. No one. They put it off till tomorrow. But I think it will be Archinus or Dion.

c SOC. Actually, Menexenus, in many ways it's a fine thing to die in battle. A man gets a magnificent funeral even if he dies poor, and people praise him even if he was worthless. Wise men lavish praise on him, and not at random but in speeches prepared long in advance, and the praise is so beautiful that although they speak
235a things both true and untrue of each man, the extreme beauty and diversity of their words bewitches our souls. For in every way, they eulogize the city and those who died in battle and all

329

our forebears, and even us who are still alive, until finally, Menexenus, I feel myself ennobled by them. I every time stand and
b   listen, charmed, believing I have become bigger, better-born, and better-looking on the spot. And since there are almost always foreigners with me, and they listen too, I feel more distinguished on the spot. In fact, I think they are affected the same toward me and the rest of the city, believing it more marvelous than before because they are seduced by the speaker. This ascendancy
c   stays with me for three days together, and the sound of the speaker's voice rings so fresh in my ear that until four or five days have passed I can hardly recall who it is I am or where in the world I am. I almost suppose I'm dwelling in the Isles of the Blessed. So skillful are our orators.

MEN. You're always poking fun at the orators, Socrates. This time, I think, the one they pick will not be very well prepared, for the election has occurred on the spur of the moment, so the speaker will pretty much have to extemporize.

d   SOC. But why, dear friend? Each of them has speeches already prepared, and besides, it isn't hard to extemporize such things. If one had to speak well of Athenians to Peloponnesians, or of Peloponnesians to Athenians, he would have to be a very good orator indeed to be persuasive. But when one performs before the very people he is praising, it is perhaps no great thing to appear to speak well.

MEN. You don't think so, Socrates?

SOC. I certainly do not.

e   MEN. Then you think you could speak yourself, if you needed to, if the Council elected you?

SOC. Why, I shouldn't be surprised if I could, Menexenus. As it happens, I have no mean teacher in matters rhetorical: she has made many other people good orators, one of whom surpasses all other Greeks, Pericles son of Xanthippus.

MEN. Who is she? Or is it clear you mean Aspasia?

236a   SOC. Of course, and there is Connus son of Metrobius too. These are my teachers, one of music and the other rhetoric. No reason for surprise if a man so reared is a clever speaker: even someone less well instructed than me, someone who learned his music from Lamprus and his rhetoric from Antiphon of Rhamnusia, might nonetheless be held in esteem if he praised Athenians among Athenians.

MEN. Well, what would you say if you had to make a speech?

soc. Of my own, probably nothing. But just yesterday I heard As-
b   pasia go through a funeral oration for these very people, for she
had heard just what you mention, that the Athenians were about
to pick a speaker. She went on to recite to me the kind of thing
which needs to be said. Some came on the spur of the moment
but the rest had been prepared before, because, I think, she
composed the Funeral Oration which Pericles delivered, and she
pieced together leftovers from that.

MEN. Can you remember what Aspasia said?

c   soc. I'd be reprehensible if I didn't. I learned it from her, and
nearly got a whipping for whatever I forgot.

MEN. Then why not recite it?

soc. But I'm afraid lest my teacher be angry if I recite her speech.

MEN. Never mind, Socrates. Deliver it, and you will greatly oblige
me, whether it be Aspasia's as you claim or somebody else's. Just
deliver it.

soc. Perhaps you'll laugh at me, if you find me, an old man, still
playing games.

MEN. I promise I won't, Socrates. By all means deliver it.

d   soc. Well, I must surely oblige. Even if you told me to take off my
clothes and dance for you, I could scarcely refuse, especially since
the two of us are alone. Listen then. For she spoke, I think, first
of the dead themselves, as follows:

The Speech of Aspasia (236d–249c)

soc. As to deeds, those who lie here have received from us what
is their due, for they set forth on their destined journey supported publicly by the city, privately by their kinsmen.

As to words, the law commands that we render to them that
e   honor which still remains due. For those who hear of well-done
deeds well spoken of give honor and renown to those who do
them.

Thus it is necessary that there be a speech which praises the
dead sufficiently, which offers kindly counsel to the living, which
summons children and brothers to imitate the virtue of these
men, which gives comfort to fathers and mothers and other progenitors left behind.

237a   How then may such speech be found? How may we begin
rightly to praise good men who in life gladdened those around
them by their virtue and then accepted death in exchange for
the safety of the living? It seems to me to be in accord with nature

that they be praised in accord with their goodness. They were
good because they sprang from good men. Let us then first praise
their nobility of birth, and second, their nurture and education,
and after that let us proclaim the nobility of their deeds, and
how worthily it befits their background.

First, then, their nobility of birth. Their progenitors were not
foreigners, nor are these their offspring settlers in this land, de-
scended from strangers who came to our country from abroad.
These men were autochthonous, sprung from the land itself,
living and dwelling in their true fatherland, nurtured by no nig-
gardly stepmother, as others are, but by their mother, the land
wherein they dwell. And now in death they lie in the place proper
to them, received back again by the mother who bore and nurtured them.

It is most just, then, first to honor their mother herself: for at
the same time the noble descent of these men shall be honored.

Our fatherland is worthy of praise by all men and not only by
ourselves; of the many reasons for this, the first and foremost is
that she is loved by the gods, as is witnessed to us by the strife
and judgment of those gods [Athena and Poseidon] who once
disputed over her. How then will she, whom the very gods
praised, not rightly be praised by all mankind?

Second, she is rightly to be praised because in that season in
which all the earth gave forth every sort of animal, wild and tame,
our country remained free and pure of all that is wild, but chose
among the animals and gave birth to man, who surpasses all
others in understanding and alone acknowledges justice and the
gods. It is a great proof that this account is true that our land
gave birth to the forefathers of these our dead and of ourselves:
for all that gives birth has the resources to nurture what it has
borne. With these resources a woman is clearly a true mother,
but a false one if she is without fountains of nourishment for
what is born. Likewise does our land, our mother, provide sufficient proof that she has given birth to men. For she alone at
that time first bore human nourishment, fruit of wheat and barley, by which humankind is best nourished, since this was the
animal she bore.

Such proofs as these are more readily to be accepted in behalf
of a land than of a woman, for in conception and birth, land
does not imitate woman, but woman land. And our land was not
grudging of her fruit, but distributed it to others too, and after-

wards produced for her children the olive, whose oil is the succor
b   of toil. Then when she had nourished and raised her children to
their youthful prime, she introduced gods as their rulers and
teachers, whose names we properly pass over in a speech such as
this, for we know them. It was they who fashioned the resources
and regimen of our daily lives, who taught us the primary arts,
and the possession and use of weapons in the defense of our
fatherland.

Thus born, thus educated, the forefathers of those who lie here
c   devised and dwelt under a constitution which it is right to call
briefly to mind. For a constitution is the nurture of men: of good
men when it is noble, of evil men when it is the opposite. It is
therefore necessary to show that those who lived before us were
nurtured by a noble constitution, through which both they and
their descendants to the present day, including these our dead,
were good. For the same constitution existed then as now, Government by the Best, and under this we dwell as citizens now,
and have done so for almost all time since then. One man calls
it democracy, another what he pleases. But in truth it is Govern-
d   ment by the Best, aristocracy, with the approval of the multitude.
We have always had kings, sometimes by birth and sometimes by
election. And while the multitude has control over most things
in the city, they give authority and rule to those they believe are
the best, and no one is excluded by reason of physical weakness
nor poverty nor ignorance of his fathers nor, as in other cities,
esteemed by reason of their opposites. There is but one standard:
he who seems to be wise or good is to rule and govern.

e   The cause of our constitution is equality of birth. Other cities
are compounded of varied and unequal conditions of men, therefore their constitutions are also unequal in their diversity—they
are tyrannies and oligarchies. And therefore they live acknowl-
239a   edging one another either as slaves or as masters. But we and
those who belong to us, all of us brothers sprung from a single
mother, do not think it fit to be either slave or master to each
other: our equal birth according to nature compels us to seek
equal rights according to law. We defer to each other in nothing
except the appearance of virtue and wisdom.

This is why the fathers of these men and of us, and these men
themselves, having been nobly born and nurtured in full free-
b   dom, showed forth a multitude of beautiful deeds to all men in
public and private, considering it necessary to fight in behalf of

freedom: to fight with Greeks in behalf of other Greeks and with Barbarians in behalf of all the Greeks. How they warded off Eumolpus and later the Amazons when they invaded our country, and others too who came earlier, how they defended the Argives against the Cadmeians, and the Heracleidae against the Ar-gives—the time is too brief for a worthy presentment, and poets

c   have already sufficiently hymned their virtue in music heard by all. And thus we would probably take but second place if we tried to adorn the same things in simple prose. Therefore it seems better to me to dismiss these things, since, further, they already have received their due. But of things which no poet ever yet has worthily grasped as gloriously worthy, and still therefore lie for-gotten—these things, it seems to me, I should call to mind both by praising them and wooing others to do the same in song and story befitting the doers of the deeds. Their deeds, then, I shall speak of first.

d   The Persians governed Asia and were enslaving Europe when they were met by the offspring of this land, and it is fit and meet that we first recall and praise the virtue of these our parents. If one is to praise it well, one must mentally place himself in that time when the whole of Asia already was enslaved to the third King. The first King was Cyrus, who by his intelligence and will

e   in one stroke freed his fellow citizens, the Persians, and enslaved the Medes their masters [in 559 B.C.], and ruled the rest of Asia to the borders of Egypt. His son [Cambyses, 529–522 B.C.] ruled Egypt itself and as much of Libya as was accessible. The third King, Darius [522–485 B.C.], bounded his rule as far as the bor-

240a   ders of Scythia by land, and with his ships mastered both the sea and the Islands, so that no one even thought to contend against him: the minds of all men were enslaved. Thus did the rule of the Persians reduce to slavery many great and warlike races.

Now Darius alleged that we and the Eretrians were plotting against Sardis and sent fifty times ten thousand men in transports and war vessels, three hundred ships, with Datis as their com-

b   mander. Darius told Datis to return leading the Eretrians and Athenians captive if he wished to keep his head on. Datis sailed to Eretria [in 490 B.C.] against men, and not a few of them, who were among the most highly esteemed warriors in Greece, and subdued them in three days. So that none might escape, he hunted them down through the whole country in the following way: his soldiers went to the boundaries of Eretria, stationed c   themselves in a line from sea to sea, joined hands and marched through the whole country, so that they could tell the King that no one had escaped. They passed from Eretria to Marathon with the same intention, prepared to yoke the Athenians in the same necessity by which they led the Eretrians captive.

When the former deeds were done, and the latter attempted, no Greeks came to the aid of the Eretrians or the Athenians except the Spartans, and these arrived the day after the battle. The rest were stricken with fear and, delighting in their present

d   safety, kept quiet. Someone born then could recognize of just what sort were the men of Marathon, who in their virtue awaited the power of the Barbarians, chastized the overweening pride of the whole of Asia, and erected the first trophies of defeat over the Barbarians. Thereby they taught others that the power of Persia was not invincible, that every multitude and all wealth

e   yields to virtue. So I say of these men that they are fathers not only of our bodies but of our freedom—our own and that of everyone on this continent. For the rest of Greece looked to the deed and having become students of the men of Marathon, dared to risk the battles that came afterward in defense of their own safety.

Let these men therefore be given the highest awards by our

241a   words. And let the second place of honor be awarded to those who fought and won in the sea battles at Salamis and off Artemesium [during the second Persian invasion under Xerxes in 480 B.C.]. To be sure, one might relate many things of these men, the sorts of attack they withstood by land and by sea, and how they repelled them. But what seems to me their finest achievement, and which I shall therefore call to mind, is that they effected a deed which stands next in rank to the men of Marathon. The men of Marathon showed the Greeks only that, few against

b   many, it was possible to ward off the Barbarians on land. Yet this was still unclear at sea, and the Persians were reported invincible at sea by reason of their numbers, their wealth, their strength, and their skill. This then is why the men who fought those sea battles are worthy of praise: they freed the Greeks from this next fear, putting an end to their fright at a multitude not only of men but of ships. Thus it resulted both from the soldiers of Marathon and the sailors of Salamis that the rest of Greece was

c   educated, taught, and accustomed not to fear the Barbarians by land or by sea.

Third for the safety of Greece both in number and virtue I mention the deeds at Plataea [where the Persians were defeated in 479 B.C.], this time the common effort of Athenians and Spartans. All these men warded off the greatest and most difficult danger, and by reason of that virtue we eulogize them now as they will be eulogized in the future by those who come after us.

d   But after this, many Greek cities were still in league with the Barbarians, and the Great King himself was reported to be considering how he might make another attempt against the Greeks. And it is surely right that we call to mind also those who brought the work of their predecessors to a conclusion of safety by clearing the sea and driving the whole Barbarian power from it. These were the men who fought the sea battle off the Eurymedon

e   [468 B.C.], those who served at Cyprus, those who sailed against Egypt and many other places [461–458 B.C.]—men whom we must remember with gratitude, recognizing that they caused the Great King himself to be afraid and to look to his own safety instead of plotting the destruction of Greece.

This war against Barbarians was fought through to an end by

242a   the whole city, in her own behalf and in behalf of those who spoke our common tongue. But when peace was achieved and our city was honored, there came to her at the hands of men what commonly befalls those who do and fare well: first jealousy, and from jealousy, grudging envy, whereby this city became engaged against her will in war with other Greeks.

After the war had broken out, they met the Spartans in battle

b   at Tanagra [457 B.C.], defending the freedom of Boeotia, and though the outcome of the battle was disputed, the subsequent event decided it, for whereas the other side retired and left, deserting those they were to help, our side won on the third day at Oenophyta, and rightfully restored those wrongfully exiled. After the Persian Wars, they were the ones who first came to the aid of Greeks against Greeks in behalf of freedom. They were

c   good men, and set free those whom they aided. And they were the first to be honored by the city and buried in this tomb.

After this many wars broke out, and the whole of Greece came in arms against us, ravaging our land and paying ill gratitude to our city. But our forefathers defeated them by sea and captured their leaders, who were Spartans, at Sphacteria [425 B.C.], and

d   though they could have destroyed them, they spared them, gave them back, and made peace, believing it right to wage war against their fellow tribesmen only to the point of victory, and not through the private anger of a city to destroy what is common to Greece, whereas against Barbarians war ought to be waged to destruction. It is therefore proper to praise those men too who fought that war and now lie here, for they have proved that if

e any argued that in the earlier war against the Barbarians other cities might have been better than the Athenians, they did not argue truly. For these men proved this, by prevailing when Greece was divided in fraternal strife, by besting those who stood first among the rest of Greece, conquering single-handedly those with whom they once in common cause conquered the Barbarians.

After that peace, there was a third war, unwanted and terrible, in which many good men fell and now lie here. Many of these men raised a good many trophies of victory in Sicily [the Sicilian Expedition in 415 B.C.] in behalf of the freedom of Leontini; they

243a sailed and aided Leontini because of sworn oaths. Because of the length of the voyage, our city was reduced to perplexity and unable to help them, and they met with bad luck and abandoned their plans. The very enemies who fought them had more praise for their temperance and virtue than other men receive from their friends.

Many, too, fought in the sea battles at the Hellespont, where

b every ship of the enemy was captured in a single day. And they were victorious in many other engagements. But I have said that the war was unwanted and terrible, and I meant this: the other Greeks had come to such contentiousness against our city that they actually dared propose a treaty with their bitterest enemy, the Great King, whom they and we had driven out in public, but they now privately invited him back again, Barbarian against Greek, and collected together all Greeks and Barbarians against

c our city. [Sparta allied with Persia against Athens in 412 B.C.]

Then indeed did the strength and virtue of this city shine forth, for when it was supposed that she had already been worn out by war and her ships were detained at Mytilene [407 B.C.], her citizens sent sixty ships to the rescue and embarked on them themselves; and by common consent they were men of the best sort, conquering their enemies and freeing their friends, even though they met an unworthy fate and their bodies were not recovered from the sea, but lie there [Arginusae, 406 B.C.].

d These men also ought to be remembered and praised, for it was by their virtue that we conquered not only in the sea battle but in the whole war. For through them, the city gained the appearance and repute that she could never be worn out by war, not even if all mankind appeared in arms against her. And the appearance was true. We were not beaten by others but by our own differences. We remain undefeated by others: we conquered and defeated ourselves.

e   After this, when we were quiet and at peace with other states, our civil war arose and was fought in such a way that if it were fated for men to stand in party strife, there is no one who would not pray that his own city should suffer such illness in a similar manner. For the citizens of the Piraeus and the city had gladsome and familiar intercourse with each other, and also against all hope with other Greeks. Further, they conducted the war with the men at Eleusis [the Thirty Tyrants] with moderation. There was no

244a   other cause of all this than real kinship, which provides, not in word but in deed, firm friendship and sameness of race. And it is necessary to hold in memory those who died at one another's hands in that war, necessary to reconcile them to each other by prayers and sacrifices so far as we are able, praying to those who govern them there since we have been reconciled here. For they

b   did not lay hold on each other through vice or enmity, but ill fortune. We ourselves are the living witnesses to this, for we are of the same race as they, and we have forgiveness for one another both for what we did and what we suffered.

Afterward, when peace was completely restored, our city was quiet. It forgave the Barbarians for defending themselves so thoroughly against the evils suffered at the city's hands, but was angry

c   at the Greeks, remembering the thanks they gave her for the benefits they received, for making common cause with the Barbarians, for confiscating the very ships that once saved them, for pulling down walls as recompense to us for preventing their own walls from falling. The city decided never again to prevent the enslavement of Greeks by Greeks or by Barbarians, and so she dwelt. Since this was our decision, the Spartans believed that we

d   had fallen as guardians of freedom, and that the way was now open to them to reduce the rest of the Greeks to slavery. And this they did.

But why go on at length? The tale I tell next did not happen long ago, or to men of another time. We know how, struck with fear, the foremost among the Greeks came in their need to our

city—Argives and Boeotians and Corinthians, yes, and most remarkable of all, even the Great King, reduced to such perplexity
that he could secure his own safety only from this city which he
had been eager to destroy. Indeed, if one wished to lodge a just
accusation against the city, it could rightly be accused only of
this, that it is ever too prone to pity and the servant of the weak.
Even at such a time as that, she would not harden her heart or
hold to her resolution to refuse aid to anyone being enslaved
against those wronging them; she was moved by entreaty and
helped them. She helped the Greeks and released them from
slavery, so that they were free until such time as they again enslaved themselves. But she did not dare aid the Great King because the trophies at Marathon and Salamis and Plataea shamed
her; she allowed only exiles and volunteers to aid him, and it is
generally agreed that she saved him. Having rebuilt her walls and
her navy, she accepted war, since she was compelled to it, and
fought the Spartans in behalf of the Parians.

But the King was afraid of our city and wished to desert, since
he saw the Spartans growing weary of the war at sea, and he
demanded rule over the Greek cities on the Continent, which the
Spartans had given over to him, as the price of alliance with us
and our allies, believing that we would refuse and he might then
have a pretext for defection. In this he was mistaken so far as
the other allies were concerned, for the Corinthians, the Argives,
the Boeotians, and the rest consented; they swore an oath that
they would give over the Greeks on the Continent in exchange
for money. We alone did not dare to swear and betray them, so
firm and healthy is the nobility and freedom of this city, hating
Barbarians by nature because we are purely Greek and unmixed
with Barbarian stock. There dwells among us no stock from Pe-
lops, nor Cadmus, nor Egyptus, nor Danaus, nor the many others
who are Greek by law but Barbarian by nature. Greeks ourselves,
we live unmixed with Barbarians, whence arises the pure hatred
in our city of alien natures. Nevertheless, we were once again
deserted for being unwilling to do the shameful and unholy deed
of giving over Greeks to Barbarians. So we were in the same
position in which formerly we had been defeated, but with the
God's help we brought the war to a better conclusion, for we kept
our fleet, our walls, and our own colonies when we ended the
war—so glad were our enemies to end it. [This refers to the terms
of the King's Peace, or the Peace of Antalcidas, in 387–86 B.C.]

Nevertheless, in this war too we lost good men, men who faced
246a   poor field position at Corinth and treachery at Lechaeum. Those
who freed the King and drove the Spartans from the seas were
good men too. I recall them to your mind, and it is fitting that
you should praise and honor such men.

Exhortation (246a–247c)

soc. Many beautiful things have been said of the deeds of those
who lie here, and of many others who died for the city. And
things still more numerous and more beautiful remain to be said:
b   many days and nights would not suffice to recount them all.
Therefore it is necessary that all remembering these men should
exhort their children, as in war, not to desert the station of their
forefathers, nor retreat and give way through vice. Therefore I
also exhort you, children of good men, now and in times to come,
c   wherever I may encounter some one of you, I shall remind you
and continually exhort you to be as good as possible. It is right
for me now to say what your fathers, when they were about to
risk their lives, strictly charged us to announce to those who survived if they should suffer. I shall tell you what I heard from
these men, and what things they would be glad now to say to you
if they had the power, as indicated by what they said then. In
what I now say you must believe you hear the very voices of the
men themselves. Here is what they said:
d   "Children, that you are sprung from good fathers is proved by
the present circumstances: we who might have lived ignobly instead chose nobly to die, before we disgraced you and those who
come after you, and before bringing shame on our own fathers
and all our previous race. For we believe that life is not worth
living for a man who brings shame to what is his own, and those
of that sort are dear neither to man nor to god, on earth or
beneath earth when dead. Therefore it is necessary to bear in
e   mind our words, and even if you actually practice something else,
practice it with virtue, knowing that without this, all pursuits and
possessions are shameful and bad. For wealth accompanied with
cowardice brings no beauty to him who possesses it: such a man
is rich for another and not for himself. Neither do beauty of body
and strength appear fitting, but rather unfitting, when they dwell
in one who is cowardly and bad: they make the man who has
247a   them more conspicuous, and reveal his cowardice. And all knowl-

edge, when separated from justice and the other virtues, appears as unscrupulous, not as wisdom. Because of this, you must try first and last, you must make it your wholehearted desire, to excel both us and those who went before us in renowned glory. If you do not, be well assured that if we conquer you in virtue the victory brings shame, but if we are defeated the defeat brings happiness. Most of all would we be conquered and you victorious if you take

b care not to abuse or squander the reputation of your ancestors, realizing that for a man who thinks anything of himself there is nothing more shameful than to allow himself to be honored for the reputation of his ancestors and not for himself. Children have a beautiful and imposing treasure in the honors given their parents, but it is shameful and unmanly to squander a treasure, whether of wealth or honor, and not to hand it on to one's children through a lack of possessions and good repute of one's own.

c If you practice these precepts, you will come to join us as friends to friends, when your apportionment sends you forth. But if you neglect these precepts and behave basely, no one will receive you kindly.

"Let these things then be said to our children."

Consolation (247c–249c)

"Those among us who have fathers and mothers must not commiserate with them, but must encourage them to bear what has happened, if it has happened to them, as lightly as they can, for

d they need no further lament. The fortune which has come to pass is sufficient to provide it. Rather you must soothe and calm them, and remind them that in the most important of their prayers the gods have heard them. For they prayed not that their children should be immortal, but that they should be good and well-renowned: and these, the greatest goods, have been given them. For mortal man it is not easy for all things to proceed as

e he intends in his own life. But if they bear their misfortune bravely, they will seem as fathers to be of the same sort as their brave children; but if they give way to grief, they will provoke suspicion either that they are not our fathers or that those who have praised us have lied. Neither of these things should be: they especially must be our eulogists by their deeds, making sure to appear as manly fathers of men. 'Nothing too much' was said anciently, and seems to be said beautifully; for it is truly said well.

That man is best prepared to live who makes everything which
248a   concerns his happiness depend upon himself, or nearly so, and
does not hang on other men, compelled to wander with them in
doing and faring well or ill. This man is the temperate man, the
courageous and wise man, the man who, when money or children
are made or destroyed, will especially be persuaded by the prov-
erb: he will appear neither to rejoice nor to grieve too much,
because of his trust in himself. Such men we think fit to honor,
b   and such do we wish and claim our parents to be. And such we
now make it our business to be, neither too much aggrieved, nor
too much afraid if at present we must die. We therefore require
both of our fathers and mothers that they pass the remainder of
their lives in this same mind, knowing that it is not by grief or
lamentation that they will most gratify us but that, on the con-
c   trary, if the dead have any perception of the living, they would
in that way gratify us least, behaving badly toward themselves
and bearing the misfortune with heavy heart, but that they will
most delight us if they bear it lightly and moderately. Our own
affairs have already reached an end which is the fairest given to
man, so that it befits them to honor this end rather than to lament
it. Let them then look to our wives and children, care for them
and nurture them, so that they may forget this misfortune and
thereby live lives more beautiful, more upright, and more pleas-
d   ing to us.

"Let this be sufficient message from us to our families.

"But in addition we bid the city care for our parents and our
sons, fittingly educating the one, worthily tending the other. Yet
we know that this will be sufficiently cared for without our bidding."

This, then, children and parents of the dead, they strictly en-
e   joined us to announce to you, and I do announce it as zealously
as I can. And on their behalf, I beg you, the sons of these men,
that you imitate your fathers; the parents of these, that you be
of good cheer for them, since we will nurture you in old age and
care for you in public and private, wherever each of us happens
to meet any who belongs to them. You surely recognize the concern of the city: she has laid down laws to care for the children
and parents of those who die in war, and highest authority has
249a   commanded that they be watched over beyond all other citizens,
in order that the fathers and mothers of these men not be
wronged. And the city joins in nurturing their children, earnestly

desiring that their orphanhood be as little before their minds as possible; while they are still children she stands to them in the figure of a father, and when they reach manhood, she sends them to their own pursuits arrayed in full armor, indicating and re-
b minding them of the pursuits of their fathers by giving them the tools of their fathers' virtue, while at the same time they auspiciously begin their journey to the hearth of their fathers, there to rule with strength, arrayed in arms. Nor does the city ever omit to honor the dead who have fallen: every year she performs for all in common the customary rites which each family privately performs for its own, and in addition, she has established gymnastic contests and horse races and all sorts of music. In this way
c she stands to the fallen in the apportionment of son and heir, and to their sons as a father, and to their parents as guardian, allowing all aid to all at all times. Realizing this, you should bear the misfortune more gently, for in this way you will be most beloved both to the dead and to the living, and most easily will heal and be healed.

But now you and all the rest, having lamented for the dead in common according to law, depart.

d   This is the speech of Aspasia the Milesian, Menexenus.

Epilogue (249d–e)

MEN. Really, Socrates, the Aspasia you speak of is surely fortunate, if as a woman she could compose a speech like that.

soc. Well if you don't believe it, just follow me and you will hear her recite it herself.

MEN. I've met Aspasia often, Socrates. I know what kind of woman she is.

soc. Really? Then don't you admire her? Aren't you grateful to her for her speech?

MEN. Oh, to be sure, Socrates—that is, grateful to her or whoever
e it was who recited it to you. And of course, I'm grateful to the man who recited it to me.

soc. Well that's just fine. But don't tell on me, so I can declaim for you many other fine speeches of hers on politics later on.

MEN. Don't worry, I won't tell. Declaim away.

soc. It shall be done.

INDEX

References to translator's comments are given according to the pagination of this book. References to Platonic dialogues are given by Stephanus pages in the margin of the translations; these pages are subdivided according to the letters a, b, c, d, e, answering to divisions in the original folio page. Titles of dialogues are abbreviated as follows:

345